English Grammar

English Grammar

Prescriptive
Descriptive
Generative
Performance

Kathryn Riley

University of Minnesota–Duluth

Frank Parker

Louisiana State University

Allyn and Bacon

Boston London Toronto Sydney Tokyo Singapore

Vice President, Humanities: Joseph Opiela
Editorial Assistant: Rebecca Ritchey
Marketing Manager: Lisa Kimball
Editorial Production Service: Chestnut Hill Enterprises, Inc.
Cover Administrator: Jennifer Hart
Interior Designer: Greta D. Sibley & Associates

Allyn and Bacon
A Viacom Company
160 Gould Street
Needham Heights, MA 02194

Internet: www.abacon.com
America Online: keyword: College Online

Library of Congress Cataloging-in-Publication Data

Riley, Kathryn Louise
English grammar: prescriptive, descriptive, generative, performance / Kathryn Riley, Frank Parker.
p. cm.
Includes bibliographical references and index.
ISBN 0-205-20025-7 (pbk.)
1. English language—Grammar. I. Parker, Frank
II. Title.
PE1112.R45 1998
425—dc21 98-12889
CIP

Printed in the United States of America
10 9 8 7 6 5 4 3 2 1 RRD-VA 03 02 01 00 99 98

Contents

Preface

English Grammar: Prescriptive, Descriptive, Generative, Performance is written primarily for advanced undergraduates, graduate students, and others who have a professional interest in language in general and in English grammar in particular. That is, our intended audience consists of students who will make their living by analyzing and evaluating other people's language. This audience includes those preparing for professions in fields such as English, linguistics, education, communication, speech-language pathology, and ESL.

The subtitle of our book reflects the fact that there are four distinct approaches to English grammar, each covered in a different section of the book. Prescriptive grammar emphasizes questions of usage. Descriptive grammar categorizes the parts of speech and sentence types in English. Generative grammar attempts to discover more abstract underlying regularities in syntax. And performance grammar explores the way that sentences and larger texts are actually processed by readers and listeners. *English Grammar* is designed to explain the history, goals, strengths, and weaknesses of each of these approaches, as well as to introduce readers to the major claims and findings of each one. While each of the four major sections of the book can be taught as a self-contained unit, we begin each section by looking at how and why each approach evolved; that is, by looking at the issues and questions that led grammarians to develop each approach.

Most textbooks on English grammar emphasize one, or perhaps two, of these approaches, to the exclusion of the others. However, our experience in preparing students for language-related professions has convinced us that an understanding of all four approaches is essential to a comprehensive view of the English language. For example, a student becoming certified to teach English requires a thorough understanding of prescriptive grammar. On the other hand, concentrating solely on prescriptive grammar would leave the student unaware of important recent advances in understanding the structure of English.

In addition, we firmly believe that students can come to an understanding of English grammar only by "doing" grammar, that is, by answering questions, analyzing data, and solving problems. In keeping with this view, we have included exercises throughout each chapter. These exercises serve two functions: to allow students to check their comprehension of what they have read, and to stimulate further thought and discussion. To help students assess their own work, at the back of the book we have included answers to selected exercises marked with a dagger (†). An Instructor's Manual provides answers to all the other exercises as well. The Supplementary Exercises at the end of each chapter are designed to lead students to discover more about the topic covered in each chapter. Also important is an understanding of how the various approaches to English grammar can be applied in practical situations. To this end, many of the exercises explore problems that arise in applied fields such as teaching, writing, and editing. Also included is a glossary of terms that appear in boldface in the text.

We would like to thank the reviewers for their intelligent comments and suggestions on earlier drafts of this book: John W. Ferstel, University of Southwestern Louisiana; Robert W. Funk, Eastern Illinois University; Anne LeCroy, Eastern Tennessee State University; Charles Meyer, University of Massachusetts, Boston; Ronald Shook, Utah State University; Kim Sydow Campbell, Air Force Institute of Technology; Cindy L. Vitto, Rowan College of New Jersey. Jo Mackiewicz provided invaluable help at various stages of manuscript preparation. We are indebted most of all to the hundreds of students to whom we have taught English grammar over the years, many of whose questions and observations we have attempted to address in this book.

Kathryn Riley

Frank Parker

Knife River, Minnesota

English Grammar

▲▲▲ Introduction

Four Conceptions of Grammar

By the time students get to college, they have had some exposure to what most people call "grammar." However, if you ask a random group of educated people what is meant by this term, they come up with a widely divergent range of explanations and examples. For instance, consider the following student responses to the question, "How would you define 'grammar'?" The responses were given on the first day of an upper-level college course in English grammar.

- "Grammar is a technical description of a language."
- "A standard of word order and punctuation."
- "Unconscious rules that people follow when they speak."
- "A broad terminology used to encompass syntax, usage."
- "Grammar is what you use to decide how to talk to your parents versus how to talk to your friends."
- "Grammar is the rules of writing correctly."
- "I see grammar as sort of the 'government' of words. It contains rules and regulations that help words get along with each other."
- "Grammar is the correct usage of the English language."
- "Grammatical sentences are easier to understand than ungrammatical ones."
- "Grammar is the structure and content of language. It varies according to language (English, Russian . . .), regions, individuals, and environments (workplace, home, bar). Includes sounds, punctuation, word choice, word order, etc."
- "'Grammar' means the system by which we have chosen to write and speak."

The variety in these responses is to be expected. According to one prominent American grammarian,

> when two people talk about grammar, they may actually be discussing two different areas of subject matter entirely; they may be as much at cross-purposes as a Russian and an American discussing democracy, or a fashion-designer and a literary critic discussing style. (Francis, p. 222)

The reason for this divergence is that at least four different conceptions of grammar contribute to our modern understanding of this term. As a result, it is used in a number of different, and often mutually exclusive, senses. Consider, for example, the following passages, each of which uses the term *grammar* differently.

A. "Grammar exists mainly to clarify meaning. . . . There is . . . a morality of language: an obligation to preserve and nurture the niceties, the fine distinctions, that have been handed down to us." (Simon, p. 91)
B. "Since grammar is a science, it must describe and analyze the basic facts of speech, and explain and interpret the laws governing the behavior of language." (House & Harman, p. 11)
C. "Any interesting . . . grammar will be dealing . . . with mental processes that are far beyond the level of actual or even potential consciousness . . . . Thus, . . . grammar attempts to specify what the speaker actually knows. . . . " (Chomsky, 1965, p. 8)
D. "Structural units of clause or sentence are not necessarily the most important units for language study . . . . beyond the tidy and well-pruned bonsai trees of syntax lies the jungle: menus, road signs, advertisements, propaganda . . . and the like . . . . [Grammar and] situation . . . are interrelated." (Stubbs, pp. 5–6)

The term *grammar* in passage (A) refers to a prescriptive and proscriptive system of rules—a catalog of do's and don't's—that one is expected to follow in speaking and writing the most prestigious variety of a language. These rules arbitrate questions such as the acceptability of *It is me* and *between you and I.* This conception of grammar originated in eighteenth-century England and has come to be known as **prescriptive grammar**. It is also known in some circles as "normative" grammar or "school" grammar. Prescriptive grammar is essentially linguistic "etiquette"—the study of elegant or proper language use. The fundamental goal of the prescriptive grammarian is to prescribe usage within a specific language.

The term *grammar* in passage (B) refers to a set of generalizations that describe the building blocks of sentence structure. For example, a **prepositional phrase** consists of a **preposition** (e.g., *in*) followed by a **noun phrase** (e.g., *the car*). This conception of grammar began to take root in nineteenth-century Europe but did not become widespread in the United States until the early twentieth century. It has come to be known as **descriptive grammar**, but is also known as "structural" grammar. This brand of grammar is essentially linguistic "botany"—the classification of phrase and sentence types. The fundamental goal of the descriptive grammarian is to describe the various types of structures found in a specific language.

The term *grammar* in passage (C) refers to the unconscious knowledge of language that humans are born with, regardless of the language they eventually speak. For example, speakers seem to know without reflection or instruction that a **phrase** can be moved rightward *within* a **clause** but not *out of* that clause. For instance, in the following example, the prepositional phrase *about Hillary* can be moved within the clause marked off by brackets, as in (1b), but not out of that clause, as in (1c).

1a. [That a book *about Hillary* has just come out] is exciting.
1b. [That a book has just come out *about Hillary*] is exciting.
1c. *[That a book has just come out] is exciting *about Hillary*.

(An asterisk preceding a form indicates that it is unacceptable for one reason or another.) This conception of grammar began developing around 1950 and is known as **generative grammar.** It is also known as "transformational" grammar and is essentially linguistic "biology"—the study of the representation of language in the mind. The fundamental goal of the generative grammarian is to describe the unconscious linguistic knowledge of the speaker, especially the knowledge common to speakers of all languages.

The term *grammar* in passage (D) refers to the effect of context and/or real-time limitations on the way speakers process language. For example, consider the following discourse consisting of just two sentences: *The haystack was important. The cloth had ripped.* This discourse is easier to understand and remember if you know that it occurs in a passage entitled "Sky Diving." This conception of grammar developed as an alternative to generative grammar and might be termed **performance grammar**. It is also known as "rhetorical" grammar or "discourse analysis" and is essentially linguistic "psychology"—the study of language processing. The fundamental goal of the performance grammarian is to describe the effect of context (linguistic or nonlinguistic) on the way people produce and interpret language.

The point is that "grammar" is not a simple, unified subject. Rather, it is a cover term for at least four different, and sometimes mutually exclusive, conceptions of grammar: prescriptive, descriptive, generative, and performance.

Each of these theories of grammar investigates different questions. Prescriptive grammar is primarily interested in constructing rules of usage for the prestige variety of a language. Descriptive grammar is primarily interested in describing the basic sentence patterns of all varieties of a language. Generative grammar is primarily interested in discovering those principles of sentence formation that are part of the human biological endowment. Performance grammar is primarily interested in the effects of context and real-time limitations on language use. These differences are summarized in the following table.

Grammar	Synonyms	Purpose	Analogy	Domain
Prescriptive	normative; school	prescribe language	etiquette	prestige dialect
Descriptive	structural	describe language	botany	all dialects
Generative	transformational	describe speaker (static)	biology	all languages
Performance	rhetorical; discourse analysis	describe speaker (dynamic)	psychology	language in context

The purpose of this book is to explain how these different conceptions of grammar arose, how they relate to each other today, and how they can best be used to analyze Modern English. Accordingly, this book consists of four parts, each devoted to one of these brands of grammar.

SUPPLEMENTARY EXERCISES

1. Consider the following statements about language. What understanding of grammar does each one represent: prescriptive, descriptive, generative, or performance?

a. "Each language has its own scheme. Everything depends on the formal demarcations which it recognizes."

b. "The language faculty is a component of the mind/brain, part of the human biological endowment. Presented with data, the child . . . forms a language, a computational system of some kind that provides structured representations of linguistic expressions that determine their sound and meaning."

c. "In colloquial speech, *like* is sometimes used as a conjunction . . . , but cultured speakers prefer *as*, *as if*, or *as though*."

d. "Linguists have increasingly realized that the context of an utterance plays an important part in determining its meaning, as do beliefs that are shared by a speaker and a hearer."

e. "The material in the exercises in correcting substandard English comes from . . ." (Preface to grammar book)

f. "Someone who says 'he don't' for 'he doesn't' has a systematic way of relating sound and meaning."

g. "In keeping with all these excellent qualities would you please see that the grammar used in describing your clothing is of equal quality. I am sure you are quite aware that a garment doesn't 'wash easy.' Is this use of adjectives in the place of adverbs an affectation or is it a stylistic quirk?" (Letter to the editor of a mail-order catalog)

2. Consider the following student definitions of grammar (repeated here from earlier in the chapter). For each definition, try to determine if it illustrates a basically prescriptive, descriptive, generative, or performance attitude. (Suggestion: If you can't pin a definition down to a single approach, try to at least *eliminate* one of the four.)

a. "Grammar is a technical description of a language."
b. "A standard of word order and punctuation."
c. "Unconscious rules that people follow when they speak."
d. "A broad terminology used to encompass syntax, usage."
e. "Grammar is what you use to decide how to talk to your parents versus how to talk to your friends."
f. "Grammar is the rules of writing correctly."
g. "I see grammar as sort of the 'government' of words. It contains rules and regulations that help words get along with each other."
h. "Grammar is the correct usage of the English language."
i. "Grammatical sentences are easier to understand than ungrammatical ones."
j. "Grammar is the structure and content of language. It varies according to language (English, Russian . . .), regions, individuals, and environments (workplace, home, bar). Includes sounds, punctuation, word choice, word order, etc."
k. "'Grammar' means the system by which we have chosen to write and speak."

3. Consider the following quotation.

> "You get a picture of this gallant little band of the last literates going down to defeat with 'Warriner's Grade Four Grammar' in one hand and 'Best-Loved Poems of College English Departments' in the other. . . . Though our popularizers of good grammar . . . think they are defending standards and traditions, they keep attacking idioms that are centuries old." (Quinn, p. 9)

a. What theory of grammar is the author talking about? Explain.
b. What theory of grammar does the author most likely adhere to? Explain.

4. In the movie *Running on Empty,* one character says of his mother, "I said: 'I wish it was easier' and she said: 'You wish it *were* easier!' She's correcting my grammar like one of the kids she teaches." What type of grammar does the mother teach: prescriptive, descriptive, generative, or performance?

5. Consider the following three sentences.

A. John hurt himself.
B. John hurt hisself.
C. John hurt heself.

a. What would a prescriptive grammarian say about these sentences, if anything?
b. What would a descriptive grammarian say about these sentences, if anything?
c. What would a generative grammarian say about these sentences, if anything?
d. What would a performance grammarian say about these sentences, if anything?

6. Consider the following quotation.

> "Professor Lasher adduced two sentences—'we was at the ball game last night' and 'Mary had five card'—calling them . . . logical attempts to simplify the language. . . . [This] is a benighted . . . catering to mass ignorance under the supposed aegis of democracy." (Simon, pp. 90–91)

a. What theory of grammar does Professor Lasher adhere to? Explain.
b. What theory of grammar does the author adhere to? Explain.

Part I

Prescriptive Grammar

This section of the book explores the rules of usage established by the prescriptive grammarians of the eighteenth century and traces their continuing influence on present-day conceptions of grammar, especially among nonspecialists.

▲▲▲ CHAPTER 1

Before the Prescriptive Period

Prescriptive grammar is, ultimately, based on grammatical classifications established in antiquity by the Greeks and Romans. Therefore, this chapter begins with an overview of the classical approach to grammar. We move then to grammatical developments in the Middle Ages and the Renaissance.

THE CLASSICAL PERIOD (500 B.C.–500 A.D.)

The Classical period encompasses language study carried out by the Greeks and Romans. Of the ideas presented here, the Greeks were primarily the innovators and the Romans were generally the transmitters. That is, the ideas of this period were originated by the Greeks and spread throughout Europe by the Romans.

The Greeks developed an interest in language for several reasons. First was an awareness of other languages, which grew out of the Greeks' contacts in trade and diplomacy. In fact, the Greeks even had a word for speakers of other languages. They called them *bárbaroi*, which means literally 'people who speak unintelligibly.'

Second was an awareness of distinct dialects within the Greek language. This diversity was due to the influx of invaders and to geographical boundaries such as mountains and islands within Greece itself. Likewise, there was a growing awareness of differences between the earlier classical literary dialect and the *koinē*, the standard vernacular eventually used in trade, education, and government.

Development of the Alphabet

The achievements of Greek linguistic scholarship lie in three distinct areas. First was the development of an alphabetic writing system. This was conceived during the first millennium B.C. and is the parent alphabet of the most widely used systems today. (Both the Cyrillic, or Russian, and the Roman, or English, alphabets were derived independently from the Greek.) It was not the first writing system, but it was the first alphabet in that it assigned a unique symbol to every distinct consonant and vowel.

Conscious Speculation about Language

Second, the Greeks popularized a tradition of conscious speculation about the nature and use of language. The main figures associated with this tradition were Socrates (469?–399 B.C.), Plato (427–347 B.C.), Aristotle (384–322 B.C.), and a group of philosophers termed the Stoics (c. 300 B.C.). One issue that the Greeks debated concerned the roles of **nature** versus **convention** in language: that is, do words imitate nature, or do they have an arbitrary relationship to what they represent? For example, *cock-a-doodle-doo* is presumably imitative of the sound a rooster makes, but the word *rooster* itself is only arbitrarily associated with the animal that makes this sound. Plato believed most words were imitative, while Aristotle held that most were arbitrary.

They also debated the relative contribution of **analogy** versus **anomaly** to language structure. Essentially this was a debate over how much order is found in language: Do words of the same class have the same structure? (Most English nouns, for example, form their plural with *-s* [*boy-boys*], but some don't [*man-men*].) And do words with similar meanings have similar structures? (*Purchase*, for example, has a regular past tense form, represented in spelling by *-ed*; but *buy* has an irregular past tense form: *bought*.) Analogists like Aristotle believed that language was essentially regular, while anomalists like the Stoics believed that it was not.

Parts of Speech

A third major contribution of the Greeks was the investigation and establishment of the concept "parts of speech." Around 400 B.C., in his treatises *Cratylus* and *Sophistes*, Plato mentions the concepts of **noun** (*ónoma*) and **verb** (*rhēma*). Fifty years later, around 350 B.C., in his *Rhetoric* and *Poetics*, Aristotle adds **conjunction** (*sýndesmos* 'linking particle'), including not only conjunctions, but articles, pronouns, and prepositions—items that hold discourse together.

Meanwhile, in the third century B.C., the Greeks had expanded their influence south into Egypt and established the city of Alexandria there. Around 100 B.C., the Alexandrian Dionysius Thrax wrote *Téchnē grammatikē*, or *The Art of Grammar*, which was only 25 paragraphs long but which would serve as the basic model for the traditional grammar books of the later prescriptive period. In this work Dionysius classifies words into eight classes, thereby adding five new categories to Plato's noun and verb and Aristotle's conjunction: **participle**, **article**, **pronoun**, **preposition**, and **adverb**.

Dionysius further identified attributes, or *parapómena*, of nouns and verbs. Nouns could be described according to characteristics such as **gender**, **number**, and **case**. For example, *boy's* is masculine, singular, and possessive. This type of description has come to be known as "declining" a noun. Verbs could be described according to attributes such as **mood**, **voice**, **number**, **person**, and **tense**. For example, *walks* is indicative, active, singular, third-person, and present. This type of description has come to be known as "conjugating" a verb.

While the Greeks laid the basic groundwork for the study of grammar in the Western tradition, the Romans continued to develop and disseminate it. Especially influential on the view of grammar that eventually came to be developed in eighteenth-century England was Priscian's *Institutiones Grammaticae*, an 18-book work of 1000 pages. Priscian classifies words into eight parts of speech. His categories follow those of Dionysius, with one exception: Priscian omits articles (since Latin has no articles), but adds a category for **interjections**. As we will see in the next section, Priscian's work was highly influential during the Middle Ages, where it was used as a model for one of the first grammars written for speakers of English.

It was not until nearly 1700 years later that we were finally to get the eight parts of speech we generally recognize today. In 1761, well into the prescriptive period, Joseph Priestley wrote *The Rudiments of English Grammar*, where he substituted **adjective** for participle. The relative contributions to the parts of speech are summarized in the following table.

	Noun	Verb	Conj.	Prep.	Pronoun	Adv.	Interj.	Adj.
Plato (400 B.C.)	X	X						
Aristotle (350 B.C.)			X					
Dionysius Thrax (100 B.C.)				X	X	X		
Priscian (100 A.D.)							X	
Priestley (1761)								X

As this overview illustrates, the parts of speech are not in any way absolute. That is, the number and description of the parts of speech depend upon the theoretical orientation of the linguist and the language being described. In addition, note that the traditional eight parts of speech in English are based almost entirely on analyses of Greek and Latin.

Exercise A

Answer the following questions based on the preceding table.

a.† What *group* did the most to establish what has come down to us today as the "eight parts of speech"? What *person* did the most?

b. For Aristotle, how many word classes were there and what do you think were their basic functions?

c. What was Priscian's *main* contribution to our modern understanding of "parts of speech"? How significant do you think his contribution is?

Related Ideas

This study of the parts of speech gave rise to three closely related ideas during the classical period. First was the concept of sentence **parsing**; that is, the process of breaking a sentence up into words, identifying the part of speech to which each belongs, and identifying the function (e.g., subject, object, modifier) of each. The word *parse* itself comes from a shortened form of the Latin phrase *pars ōrātiōnis* 'part of speech.'

Second was the idea of organizing verbs according to **conjugation**, that is, by identifying the root of each verb and its **suffixes**. For example, in the present tense, Latin verbs of the first conjugation take the following endings, based on the person (first, second, third) and number (singular, plural) of the subject of the sentence.

	Singular	**Plural**
1st person	-ō	-āmus
2nd person	-ās	-ātis
3rd person	-at	-ant

Thus, if *kiss* were a Latin verb, it would be conjugated as follows.

kissō 'I kiss'	kissāmus 'we kiss'
kissās 'you kiss'	kissātis 'you kiss'
kissat 'he/she/it kisses'	kissant 'they kiss'

Third was the idea of organizing nouns according to **declension**, that is, by identifying the root of each noun and its suffixes. For example, Latin nouns of the second declension take the following endings, based on case (nominative, genitive, etc.) and number.

	Singular	**Plural**
Nominative	-us	-ī
Genitive	-ī	-ōrum
Dative	-ō	-īs
Accusative	-um	-ōs

Thus, if *Biff* were a Latin noun, it would be declined as follows.

Biffus	Biffī
Biffī	Biffōrum
Biffō	Biffīs
Biffum	Biffōs

According to this system, *Biff kisses Gwen* would appear in Latin as *Biffus Gwenam kissat.*

Exercise B

Identify each of the following assertions as an instance of parsing, conjugation, or declension.

a. The possessive of *boy* is *boy's*; the plural is *boys*; and the possessive plural is *boys'*.
b. The verb *give* has four principal parts: *give, gave, giving,* and *given*.
c.† The subject of *Who killed Cock Robin?* is the interrogative pronoun *Who*.

Deficits in Knowledge

Despite the advances made during the classical period of language study, there remained numerous gaps in knowledge. First, there was no understanding of the genetic relation among languages, especially between Latin and Greek. Apparently, Latin was often mistakenly thought to be directly descended from Greek. This misunderstanding may have come from structural similarities, such as the fact that many Latin words have Greek roots (e.g., *electric* comes from Latin *electrum*, which in turn comes from Greek *ēlektron*). Actually, Latin and Greek are sister languages, descended from a common origin, but not one from the other. This, however, was not fully appreciated until very late in the eighteenth century.

Second, there was a fundamental, mistaken belief that any type of language change was a form of language "decay." This idea has its roots in the Alexandrian Greeks of the third century B.C. (As Athens declined, the city of Alexandria in Egypt was established in 332 B.C. and became a Greek power under Alexander the Great.) Alexandrian scholars studied the literary language of the preceding two centuries. Because of the normal process of language change, this literary language was not identical to the vernacular language spoken in Alexandria at the time. This situation would be similar to our reading Shakespeare today. We recognize the language as English, yet it is a different variety from that spoken currently. The Alexandrians mistakenly assumed that the changes in their language represented a degenerate or decayed version of the original.

Third, there arose a mistaken conception that spoken language is secondary to written language: that is, that speech is an imperfect representation of writing. The Greeks were led to this conclusion because of the content of the language they were studying. Recall that they were comparing the *written* literary language of an earlier period to the *spoken* language of their day. Since the language spoken around them was considered a corrupt form of the earlier language, they extended this mistaken notion to conclude that the spoken language is a corruption of the written.

THE MIDDLE AGES (500 – 1500 A.D.)

The Middle Ages encompass roughly that period between the decline of the Roman Empire (500 A.D.) and the emergence of the Renaissance in Europe (1500 A.D.). However, the contribution of the Middle Ages to the study of grammar is not well understood. In fact, many linguistic treatises of this period are not widely available to modern scholarship, since they are still in manuscript form. With regard to the study of grammar, this period seems to be primarily one of maintaining and commenting on previous ideas.

Importance of Latin

One characteristic of the Middle Ages was the elevation of Latin to a position of importance; it was the language of learning, literature, church services, and administration. Thus, Latin was the primary subject of language study during this period. In addition to its status within the church and among learned people, the teaching of Latin was associated with missionary and didactic functions. In England, for example, Aelfric's *Latin Grammar* and *Colloquium* ("Conversations"), composed c. 1000, were written as instructional materials for children. Based on Priscian, Aelfric's grammar is one of the earliest grammars aimed specifically at English speakers. According to linguistic historian R. H. Robins, while Aelfric intended his work as a grammar of Latin, he viewed it as equally suitable for introducing students to English grammar. This is significant because it foreshadows the later prescriptive tendency to base English grammar on Latin models.

Concept of "Grammar"

The second half of the Middle Ages (1100–1500) saw an increased interest in language studies. The major contribution of this period is "speculative grammar," named for the Latin word *speculum* 'mirror' and based upon the idea that language is the "mirror" of reality. That is, one could learn about the nature of the world by studying the way that language was used to refer to things in the world. Speculative grammar was the product of medieval scholars called the *modistae*, who wrote between 1250 and 1350. The *modistae* were so named because of their treatise *De modis significandi tractatus* 'Treatise Concerning the Modes of Signifying.' In this series of works, the *modistae* tried to relate language to the natural world. They were concerned with such questions as "How do words match mental perceptions of things?" Moreover, the *modistae* were the first to view grammar as a separate field of study. Before them, grammar had always been conceived of as part of other fields such as literary criticism or foreign language study.

One representative work from this period is the German scholar Thomas of Erfurt's *Grammatica Speculativa* (c. 1300). In it he recounted principles for constructing acceptable sentences: he theorized that they must have the necessary components, be inflected correctly, and be collocable (i.e., each word must be compatible with adjacent words). For example, these principles would rule out the sentence *Lapis amat filium* 'The stone loves the boy.' Even though the sentence has the necessary components, and they are inflected correctly, they are not collocable: i.e., the subject *stone* cannot co-occur with the verb *love.*

Also, it was during the Middle Ages that the parts of speech, parsing, conjugation, and declension were incorporated into the curriculum as the study of grammar. In fact, the liberal arts were divided into two tiers. The lower tier was called the *trivium* and included the subjects of grammar, logic, and rhetoric, while the higher tier was called the *quadrivium* and included arithmetic, geometry, astronomy, and music. A saying from that time sums up the role of each:

> *"Gram loquitur; dia vēra docet; rhet verba colōrat; mūs canit; ar numerat; ge ponderat; ast colit astra."* ('Grammar speaks; logic teaches the truth; rhetoric adorns our words; music sings; arithmetic counts; geometry measures; astronomy studies the stars.') (Quoted in Robins, p. 69)

In this curriculum, grammar served as the basis for teaching students to read and write Latin, which was the universal language of learning much like English is now the universal language of commerce. It is thus this conception of grammar, rising out of the medieval trivium, that gives rise to the modern term *grammar school.*

Exercise C

Answer the following questions based on the quotation from Robins above.

a. Speculate on the distinction between grammar and rhetoric in the Middle Ages.
b. Speculate on the distinction between the trivium and quadrivium in the Middle Ages. (Hint: What do the subjects within each area have in common?)

THE RENAISSANCE (1500–1650)

Rise of Vernacular Languages

The Renaissance, traditionally viewed as a "rebirth" of culture and scholarship in Europe, saw an increased attention by European scholars to classical languages other than Greek and Latin, notably Hebrew, Arabic, and Chinese. There was also a revival of classical texts being read in the original rather than interpreted by theologians. Just as importantly, the Renaissance saw the first systematic study of the **vernacular** languages of Europe (i.e., ordinary, everyday language, as opposed to literary or learned), as well as the more exotic vernacular languages of Africa, Asia, and the Americas. As we will see, it was the vernacular nationalism of the Renaissance that laid the foundation for the attitudes of the prescriptive period of eighteenth-century England. Vernaculars began to be used for scholarly and scientific publication; the fifteenth and sixteenth centuries saw the first grammars of Spanish, French, Italian, and Polish. In fact, there was a self-conscious attempt to elevate the stature of the vernacular languages, as reflected in this excerpt from Robert Ascham's *Treatise on Archery*, 1545.

> If any man woulde blame me, eyther for takynge such a matter in hande, or els 1
> for writting it in the Englyshe tongue, this answere I maye make him, that what the beste 2
> of the realme thinke it honest for them to vse, I one of the meanest sorte, ought not to 3
> suppose it vile for me to write. . . . And as for ye Latin or Greke tonge, euery thyng is so 4
> excellently done in them, that none can do better. In the Englysh tonge contrary, euery 5
> thinge in a maner so meanly, both for the matter and handelynge, that no man can do 6
> worse. (Quoted in Harris & Taylor, pp. 87–88) 7

Advent of Printing

In addition to an increased interest in vernacular tongues, the Renaissance witnessed the expansion of printing in Europe. This coincided with the gradual spread of literacy and demand for education (including foreign-language education) by means of texts, grammars, and dictionaries. William Caxton, the first English printer, comments on some linguistic trends in the following passage written in 1490.

> And certaynly our langage now vsed varyeth ferre from that whiche was vsed and spoken 1
> whan I was borne. For we Englysshe men ben borne vnder the domynacyon of the mone, 2
> whiche is neuer stedfaste but euer wauerynge, wexynge one season, and waneth and 3
> dyscreaseth another season. And that comyn Englysshe that is spoken in one shyre 4
> varyeth from a nother. In so moche that in my dayes happened that certayn marchauntes 5
> were in a shippe in Tamyse, for to haue sayled ouer the see into Zelande, and for lacke of 6
> wynde thei taryed atte Forlond, and wente to lande for to refreshe them; And one of theym 7
> named Sheffelde, a mercer, cam in-to an hows and axed for mete; and specyally he axyd 8
> after eggys; And the goode wyf answerde, that she coude not speke no Frenshe. And the 9
> marchaunt was angry, for he also coude speke no Frenshe, but wolde haue hadde egges, 10
> and she vnderstode hym not. And thenne at laste a nother sayd that he wold haue eyren: 11
> then the good wyf sayd that she vnderstood him wel. Loo, what sholde a man in thyse 12
> dayes now wryte, egges or eyren. Certainly it is harde to playse eueryman by cause of 13
> dyuersite and chaunge of langage. (Quoted in Harris & Taylor, p. 86) 14

Exercise D

Answer the following questions based on the preceding passage.

a. Translate this passage into idiomatic modern English.

b. What does *varyeth* (l. 1) mean?

c.† What does *mone* (l. 2) mean?

d. What do *wexynge* and *waneth* (l. 3) mean?

e. What does *comyn* (l. 4) mean?

f.† Speculate on the meaning of *Tamyse* and *Zelande* (l. 6).

g. What is the relationship between the words *marchauntes* (l. 5) and *mercer* (l. 8)?

h.† How is the word *hows* (l. 8) pronounced? What is your evidence?

i. What do *axed* and *axyd* (l. 8) mean? Are these words still pronounced this way in any dialects of Modern English?

j. What does *a nother* (l. 11) mean? How would we write this phrase in Modern English?

Universal Grammar

A third trend that developed during the late Renaissance period was the rationalist grammar developed by the Port Royal school (1637–1661). The Solitaires, a group of hermits living in the deserted Port-Royal abbey in France, came to be known as the Port-Royal grammarians and attempted to write a grammar containing all the properties common to languages known at the time—a kind of universal grammar. This goal had not interested the Greeks and Romans, who were concerned with just Greek and Latin. The Port-Royal grammarians analyzed sentences into their underlying propositions. For example, the sentence *Invisible God created the visible world* embodies three propositions: 'God is invisible,' 'God created the world,' and 'The world is visible.'

Propositions, in turn, were analyzed into "concepts" and "judgments"; these, in turn, corresponded roughly, on the syntactic level, to subjects and predicates. This division is discussed by Antoine Arnauld and Claude Lancelot in *General and Rational Grammar* (1660). In this work, Arnauld and Lancelot recognize both language universals and language-specific variations. They attempt to explain features shared by all languages, arguing that if language's function is to communicate thoughts, then speech must reflect the structure of the thoughts being expressed. Their ideas on the relationship between thought and language are laid out in the following passage.

> A judgment that we make about things, as when I say, *The earth is round*, is called a *proposition*, and thus every proposition necessarily embodies two terms: the first is called the *subject* and is that of which one predicates, as *earth* in the above example, and the second is called the *predicate* and is that which is predicated, as *round* in the above example. In addition to the terms, a proposition includes the connection between the two terms, the copula, *is*. . . .
>
> It follows from this that men, . . . also found it necessary to draw a most general distinction among words into those that signify the objects of thoughts and those that signify the form and the manner or mode of our thoughts, . . .
>
> Words of the first kind are those which are called *nouns*, *articles*, *pronouns*, *participles*, *prepositions*, and *adverbs*. Those of the second kind are *verbs*, *conjunctions*, and *interjections*. These are all derived as a necessary consequence from the natural manner in which we express our thoughts. . . . (Quoted in Harris & Taylor, pp. 95–96)

Summary

By 1650 in western Europe, knowledge of vernacular languages was growing; literacy was rising (as a result of the advent of printing); and, in addition to classifying words into parts of speech and parsing sentences, grammarians were investigating deeper properties of grammar: for example, the philosophical basis of concepts such as "subject," "predicate," and "proposition."

However, the study of language was still largely prescientific. First, knowledge of particular languages was limited. Educated individuals might know, at most, their native language, a neighboring language, and Latin. Second, there was little understanding of the genetic relationships among languages. For all anyone knew, English was descended from Latin, and Latin was descended from Greek. Third, there was no understanding of the process of language change. Change, in fact, was equated with corruption and decay. Finally, there was little understanding of the relation between the written language and speech. In fact, speech was considered to be an imperfect representation of writing.

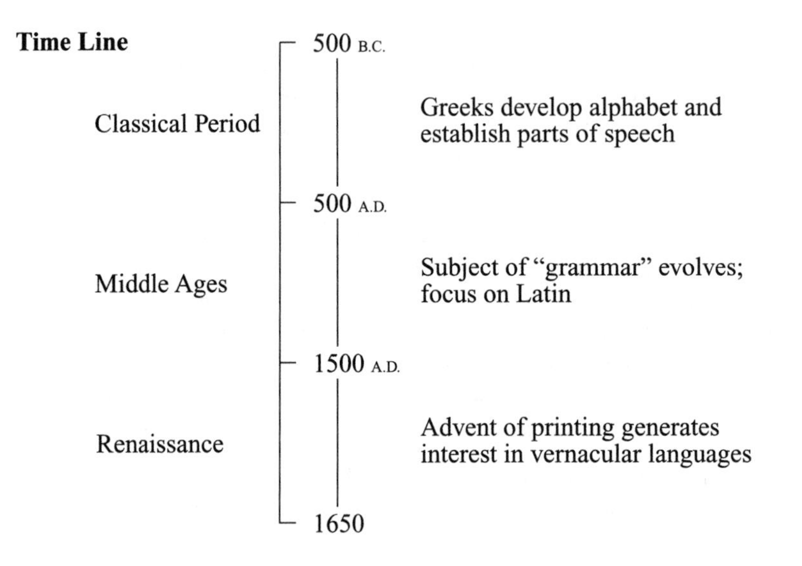

SUPPLEMENTARY EXERCISES

1. Our Modern English word *barbarian* is derived from the same root as the Greek word *bárbaroi*. What does this suggest about our attitude toward speakers of other languages?
2. Consider the Greek alphabet and the corresponding English letters.

A	α	alpha	N	ν	nu
B	β	beta	Ξ	ξ	xi
Γ	γ	gamma	O	o	omicron
Δ	δ	delta	Π	π	pi
E	ϵ	epsilon	P	ρ	rho
Z	ζ	zeta	Σ	σ ς	sigma
H	η	eta	T	τ	tau
Θ	θ	theta	Υ	υ	upsilon
I	ι	iota	Φ	φ	phi
K	κ	kappa	X	χ	chi
Λ	λ	lambda	Ψ	ψ	psi
M	μ	mu	Ω	ω	omega

a. What do you think the term *alpha male* refers to? Explain.
b. Speculate on the origin of the English word *alphabet.*
c. What do you think the movie title *The Omega Man* refers to? Explain.
d. Speculate on the origin of the phrase *It doesn't matter one iota.*
e. What do you think the biblical phrase *the alpha and the omega* refers to?

3. Answer the following questions based on the passage from Ascham's *Treatise on Archery* (p. 15).

a. Translate the passage into idiomatic Modern English.
b. What do the words *meanest* (l. 3) and *meanly* (l. 6) *mean?*
c. What does *matter* (l. 6) mean?
d. What reasons does Ascham give for presenting his work in English rather than in Latin or Greek?

4. Answer the following questions after examining the passage from Caxton (p. 15).

a. List five linguistic changes (i.e., changes in word or sentence structure) that have occurred in English since this passage was written.
b. List five orthographic changes (i.e., changes in spelling) that have occurred in English since this passage was written.

▲▲▲ CHAPTER 2

The Prescriptive Period

This chapter traces the evolution of prescriptive grammar in eighteenth-century England and examines the social atmosphere that allowed this approach to flourish there and, later, in the United States.

IN ENGLAND (1650–1800)

This period gives rise to an attitude toward language developed in England beginning with the second half of the seventeenth century and extending through the eighteenth century. This attitude is important to understand because many of the assumptions that inform it are still with us today. A good illustration is John Simon's comment about "a morality of language," which was cited in the Introduction. In order to comprehend this attitude, it is first necessary to understand the political and social climate of the era. Civil war had raged in England from 1642 to 1649, when King Charles I was beheaded. The Puritan Oliver Cromwell and his son, Richard, then governed the Commonwealth until 1660, when Charles II was restored to the throne. Thus, from 1642 until 1660, England was in a state of turmoil, as summarized in the following table.

1642–49: Civil War under Charles I

1649–60: Commonwealth under Cromwell

1660–85: Restoration under Charles II

After all this, the English were interested in bringing order out of political and social chaos. The bywords of this period were *order*, *regulation*, *conformity*, and *correctness*, and above all, *reason*. (These terms held the same status then as *family values* does today.) In fact, the period from 1700 to 1750 in England is commonly referred to as the Age of Reason.

The social regulation of the late seventeenth and early eighteenth centuries expanded to include language regulation as well. Attitudes toward language had undergone a shift since the Middle Ages. The Renaissance, which had spread throughout western Europe by the seventeenth century, created a climate of "vernacular nationalism," that is, a shift in interest from Latin and Greek as languages of learning to an increased interest and pride in the various national languages of western Europe. At the same time in England, there was a renewed interest in the golden age of Latin literature, especially the poetry of Horace and Virgil, who wrote around the time that Augustus was Emperor of Rome (27 B.C.–14 A.D.). Thus, the first half of the eighteenth century is also referred to as the Augustan Age or the neoclassical period.

In short, there were three major forces affecting the intellectual climate of the prescriptive period. First, there was a desire for regulation and control—not only of society but of language as well. Second, there was an interest in English as opposed to Latin. Third, there was a tendency to look to the past as an era of linguistic "purity."

The intellectual movement to regulate language was led by four great literary figures of the late seventeenth and the eighteenth centuries: John Dryden (1631–1700), Daniel Defoe (1659?–1731), Jonathan Swift (1667–1745), and Samuel Johnson (1709–1784). They had three goals, which have been categorized by Baugh (1935) as follows.

- First, they wanted to "standardize" English. That is, they wanted to reduce English to a system of rules, much like those that existed for Latin.
- Second, they wanted to "refine" English. That is, they wanted to remove its "defects" and return the language to an earlier, "purer" state. (One problem was that the reformers could not agree on when English had reached its perfection. For example, Dryden admired Chaucerian English, whereas Swift preferred the language of Shakespeare. Johnson, on the other hand, was partial to pre-Restoration English.)
- Third, they wanted to "ascertain" English. That is, they wanted to stop English from undergoing further change, to "fix" the language once and for all in time. There is speculation that this goal grew out of the fear that their works would be unintelligible to future generations.

It was felt that these goals could best be met in the form of an authoritative dictionary of English. This is not to say that no dictionaries had ever been written. Dictionaries of English date from 1604, when Robert Cawdrey wrote *A Table Alphabeticall*. And English grammars go back to 1586, when William Bullokar wrote *Brefe Grammar for English*. However, none of these works had become standards by which usage could be judged.

Exercise A

Relate each of the following quotations to the eighteenth-century prescriptivists' desire to "standardize, refine, and ascertain" English.

a. "Maintaining these alleged niceties links our language to that of the giants of the English tongue who preceded us, all those great writers and speakers." (Simon, p. 91)

b.† "Though our popularizers of good grammar . . . think they are defending standards and traditions, they keep attacking idioms that are centuries old." (Quinn, p. 9)

c. "Does it even matter that the apostrophe is going the way of the stop sign and the directional signal in our society? . . . Who cares whether it's *its* or *it's*?" (Larson, p. 31)

d.† "I've seen the dirty three-letter word even punctuated as *its'*. What's next? *I'ts? 'Its?* How complicated can this be?" (Larson, p. 31)

An English Academy

In order to ensure the outcome of an *authoritative* dictionary, the reformers undertook to establish an English Academy, essentially a regulatory agency for the language. The English modeled their idea of an academy on similar efforts by the Italians and the French. In 1582 the Italians established an academy and by 1612, only 30 years later, they had compiled a dictionary. Likewise, in 1635 the French established an academy and by 1694, less than 60 years later, they too had a dictionary. (Similarly, Spain and Sweden established academies in 1713 and 1739, respectively.) Since the establishment of an academy had led to a dictionary for the Italians and the French, it seemed reasonable to assume that the same could work for the English. A number of prominent figures called for an academy during the seventeenth and eighteenth centuries. Following are a few representative quotations:

> **John Dryden (1679):** I am desirous, if it were possible, that we might all arrive with the same certainty of words, and purity of phrase, to which the Italians first arrived, and after them the French; at least that we might advance so far, as our tongue is capable of such a standard.
>
> **Daniel Defoe (1697):** [An Academy is needed] to polish and refine the *English* Tongue, and advance the so much neglected Faculty of Correct Language, to establish Purity and Propriety of Stile, and to purge it from all the Irregular Additions that Ignorance and Affectation have introduc'd.
>
> **Jonathan Swift (1712):** What I have most at Heart is, that some Method should be thought on for *ascertaining* and *fixing* our Language

> for ever, after such Alterations are made in it that shall be thought requisite. For I am of Opinion, that it is better a Language should not be wholly perfect, than that it should be perpetually changing; and we must give over at one Time, or at length infallibly change for the worse. (Quoted in Finegan, pp. 20–21)

Exercise B

Answer the following questions based on the preceding quotations.

a. What do you think Dryden means by the phrase "certainty of words"?

b.† What do you think Defoe means by "the Irregular Additions that Ignorance and Affectation have introduc'd"?

c. Swift states, "it is better a language should not be wholly perfect, than that it should be perpetually changing." What do you think is more important to Swift: to "refine" or to "ascertain" the language?

In 1662, the English had already founded the Royal Society, which was established primarily to further scientific interests. In 1664, the Royal Society established a committee for improving the English language. This committee consisted of 22 members, including Dryden. However, after a few meetings, the committee seems to have dissolved from lack of interest. Over 30 years later, in 1697, Defoe attempted to renew interest in an English academy in his *Essay Upon Projects*. He states,

> The reputation of this society would be enough to make them the allowed judges of style and language; and no author would have the impudence to coin without their authority . . . . *it would be as criminal then to coin words as money.* (Quoted in Baugh, p. 328; emphasis added)

Note the emotion surrounding this issue, illustrated by Defoe's analogy comparing the introduction of new words into English with counterfeiting.

The final and most persuasive attempt to establish an English academy was a letter Swift wrote in 1712 to the Earl of Oxford, the Lord Treasurer of England. The letter was entitled *A Proposal for Correcting, Improving, and Ascertaining the English Tongue*. In it, Swift states,

> . . . our language is extremely imperfect; . . . its daily improvements are by no means in proportion to its daily corruptions; . . . the pretenders to polish and refine it have chiefly multiplied abuses and absurdities; and, . . . in many instances it offends against every part of grammar." (Quoted in Baugh, p. 329)

Again, note the emotion that underlies Swift's urge to reform the language and its users.

Swift's push for an academy had the necessary momentum and would likely have succeeded. A quirk of fate, however, intervened to ensure that the idea was lost forever. In 1714, two years after Swift's letter was published, Queen Anne died, the last of the House of Stuart. In her place, George I of the German House of Hanover came to the throne of England. The new monarch spoke only German, and thus the idea of an English Academy fell by the wayside. The idea was never revived with any force, for two reasons. First, people figured that if someone of Swift's eminence had failed, it was useless for less powerful beings to try. Second, there was a growing notion that linguistic regulation might interfere with the people's individual liberty, a right dear to the English heart, especially at a time when the country was emerging from social and political upheaval.

Despite this setback, however, Samuel Johnson did manage to publish his famous work, *A Dictionary of the English Language*, in 1755. In his *Plan* for the dictionary (1747), addressed to his patron the Earl of Chesterfield, Johnson wrote:

> This, my lord, is my idea of an English dictionary, a dictionary by which the pronunciation of our language may be fixed, and its attainment facilitated; by which its purity may be preserved, its use ascertained, and its duration lengthened. . . . it is natural likewise to hope . . . that it may contribute to the preservation of antient [sic], and the improvement of modern writers; that it may promote the reformation of those translators, who for want of understanding the characteristical difference of tongues, have formed a chaotic dialect of heterogeneous phrases; and awaken to the care of purer diction, some men of genius, whose attention to argument makes them negligent of stile [sic], or whose rapid imagination, like the Peruvian torrents, when it brings down gold, mingles it with sand. (Quoted in Finegan, p. 21)

Exercise C

What do you think Johnson means when he states "like the Peruvian torrents, when it brings down gold, mingles it with sand"?

Johnson changed his views somewhat, however, as we can see from the Preface to the *Dictionary* (1755):

> Those who have been persuaded to think well of my design, require that it should fix our language, and put a stop to those alterations which time and chance have hitherto been suffered to make in it without opposition. With this consequence I will confess that I flattered myself for a while;

> but now begin to fear that I have indulged expectation which neither reason nor experience can justify. When we see men grown old and die at a certain time one after another, from century to century, we laugh at the elixir that promises to prolong life to a thousand years; and with equal justice may the lexicographer be derided, who being able to produce no example of a nation that has preserved their words and phrases from mutability, shall imagine that his dictionary can embalm his language, and secure it from corruption and decay. . . .
>
> With this hope, however, academies have been instituted, to guard the avenues of their languages, to retain fugitives, and repulse intruders; but their vigilance and activity have hitherto been vain; sounds are too volatile and subtile [sic] for legal restraints; to enchain syllables, and to lash the wind, are equally the undertakings of pride. . . . (Quoted in Finegan, p. 22)

Exercise D

Consider the preceding passage from Johnson.

a. How did Johnson's basic view change between 1747 and 1755?
b. What specifically is Johnson referring to when he states that academies have been instituted "to retain fugitives, and repulse intruders"?

Johnson continues:

> If the changes that we fear be thus irresistible, what remains but to acquiesce with silence, as in the other insurmountable distresses of humanity? It remains that we retard what we cannot repel, that we palliate what we cannot cure. Life may be lengthened by care, though death cannot be ultimately defeated: tongues, like governments, have a natural tendency to degeneration; we have long preserved our constitution, let us make some struggles for our language.
>
> In hope of giving longevity to that which its own nature forbids to be immortal, I have devoted this book, the labour of years, to the honour of my country, that we may no longer yield the palm of philology to the nations of the continent. (Quoted in Finegan, p. 22)

Prescriptive Grammars

Although the attempt to form an English academy was finally abandoned, numerous popular grammar books were published during the second half of the eighteenth century. Probably the best known, and certainly the most influential, was Robert

Lowth's *Short Introduction to English Grammar*, which first appeared in 1762. Lowth (1710–1787) was Bishop of Oxford and a professor of Hebrew poetry at the university there; he later became Bishop of London. Lowth intended his grammar to be used as a textbook: he states, "it was calculated for the use of the learner, even of the lower class" (p. xi). Moreover, it was essentially prescriptive. Lowth makes it clear that his interest is in correcting a perceived decline in standards among language users: "our best authors have committed gross mistakes, for want of a due knowledge of English grammar, or at least of a proper attention to the rules of it" (p. viii). Lowth's basic strategy was to lay down rules and illustrate them by "right" and "wrong" examples. He states that the purpose of a grammar is

> to enable us to judge of every phrase and form . . . , whether it be right or not. The plain way of doing this is, to lay down rules, and to illustrate them by examples. But, beside shewing [sic] what is right, the matter may be further explained by pointing out what is wrong. (p. viii)

Lowth's attitude and approach are characteristic of the prescriptive period. He used Latin models, largely disregarding the structural differences between Latin and English. He acknowledged the authority of usage—especially older usage—but begged the question of *whose* usage should be followed. For example, on the merger of **past tense** (e.g., *wrote*) and **past participle** forms (e.g., *written*), he commented, "This confusion prevails greatly in common discourse, and is too much authorised by the example of some of our best writers" (p. 60). In Milton's writing, for example, forms such as *have spoke*, *had rode*, and *was took* can be found; in Dryden, *have began*; in Pope, *The bard begun*; in Addison, *Mr. Milton has wrote* and *The men begun*; and in Swift, *had not arose*, *have stole*, and *have mistook*.

Exercise E

Explain how the following forms illustrate "confusion" of past tense and past participle forms.

a.† *have spoke*
b.† *The bard begun*
c. *Mr. Milton has wrote*
d. *had not arose*
e. *was took*

Exercise F

Consider the examples in Exercise E. Can you construct a simple principle that describes the distribution of past tense and past participle forms in standard Modern English?

Also, like the Greeks, Lowth assumed that "grammar" applied primarily to the written language. He makes an interesting comment in defining the sentence: "Sentences consist of words; words, of one or more syllables; syllables, of one or more letters" (p. 1). Note that in Lowth's mind the fundamental unit of language is the written *letter*, not the spoken *sound*.

Moreover, his rules were based primarily on personal preference (some might say prejudice). Lowth, it must be remembered, had no special license to decide matters of correctness; rather, he proceeded primarily on his own intuitions. In fact, the grammar writers of this period had for the most part very little training. One such author was Robert Baker, who published *Reflections on the English Language* in 1770. In it, he mentions that he knows no Greek and very little Latin, although such knowledge would be a minimum requirement for a writer of this period. He then goes on to state, "I have myself no books; at least, not many more than what a church-going old woman may be supposed to have . . ." (quoted in Baugh, p. 341). Perhaps the most important fact about Lowth's grammar, however, was its huge success. It went through 22 editions between 1762 and 1800 alone.

Not all language commentators during this period took a strictly prescriptive approach, however. Noteworthy for their contrast to Lowth were George Campbell and Joseph Priestley. Campbell's *Philosophy of Rhetoric* (1776) defined good usage as "reputable," "national," and "present"; he tried to distinguish between "verbal critics," such as Lowth, and true grammarians. In the following quote, Campbell explains his conception of grammar.

> It is no other than a collection of general observations methodically digested . . . by which the significations, derivations, and combinations of words in that language are ascertained. It is of no consequence here to what causes originally these modes or fashions owe their existence . . . ; they no sooner obtain and become general, than they are laws of the language, and the grammarian's only business is to note, collect, and methodize them. (Quoted in Finegan, p. 27)

Exercise G

Consider the preceding passage by Campbell.

a.† What do you think Campbell means by the "significations," "derivations," and "combinations" of words?

b. What evidence is there in this passage that Campbell is not a prescriptivist?

Another voice arguing against prescriptivism was Priestley, an English chemist as well known for his *Rudiments of English Grammar* (1761) as for his discovery of oxygen. He states that

> In modern and living languages, it is absurd to pretend to set up the compositions of any persons whatsoever as the standard of writing, or their conversation as the invariable rule of speaking. With respect to customs, laws, and every thing that is changeable, the body of a people . . . will certainly assert their liberty, in making what innovations they judge to be expedient and useful. The general prevailing custom where ever it happen to be, can be the only standard for the time that it prevails." (*Course*, p. 184)

In short, prescriptivists such as Lowth adopted a deductive approach to grammar: the grammarian's job is to set up rules and require that writers follow them. In contrast, the minority opinion, represented by Campbell and Priestley, preferred an inductive approach: the grammarian's job is to observe good writers and infer rules from their behavior.

IN THE UNITED STATES

While the primary impetus for the prescriptive movement came from England, it did not take long for its effects to cross the Atlantic. Two influential American authors were lexicographer Noah Webster and grammarian Lindley Murray. Both men were trained in the law; but, because of personal circumstance, turned to teaching and developed an interest in the English language. Webster's *A Grammatical Institute of the English Language* (1783–85) was ostensibly descriptive, but often quite prescriptive in practice. He wrote, for example, that

> Grammars should be formed on *practice*: for practice determines what a language is. . . . The business of a grammarian is not to examine whether or not national practice is founded on philosophical principles; but to *ascertain* the national practice. (*Dissertations*, pp. 204–205)

On the other hand, he argued that

> As an independent nation, our honor requires us to have a system of our own, in language as well as government. Great Britain . . . should no longer be *our* standard; for the taste of her writers is already corrupted, and her language on the decline. (*Dissertations*, p. 20)

Exercise H

> The two quotations by Webster might be said to exhibit mutually incompatible attitudes toward language. Point out the inconsistency between the two passages.

Most of us are probably more familiar with Webster's work not as a grammarian but as a lexicographer, which led to *A Compendious Dictionary of the English Language* (1806) and *An American Dictionary of the English Language* (1828). These works established differences between American and British varieties of English. For example, Webster established the double consonant in forms like *travelling* (British English has one *-l*) and the *-or* spelling in forms like *color* (British English has *-our*).

On the other hand, Lindley Murray's *English Grammar, Adapted to the Different Classes of Learners*, first published in 1795, was to the United States what Lowth's work was to Great Britain. Murray's book was intended for classroom use: as he states, it was "for the use of the schools and private learners" (1816, p. 5), and it was "designed for the instruction of youth" (p. 7). It eventually went into over 300 editions, selling 2 million copies. Because of its enormous popularity, Murray's work was very influential on subsequent views of grammar. Murray's basic approach was to rehash Lowth, with an emphasis on correctness. He linked good grammar with virtue and religious propriety. He was influential on subsequent views of grammar as "error-hunting" and adjudicating "right" and "wrong" usage.

Murray's dependence upon Lowth as a source cannot be overstated. Not only does Murray acknowledge that he borrowed directly from Lowth, as well as from Samuel Johnson and Joseph Priestley (p. 11), but he lifts passages from Lowth practically *verbatim*. For example, compare what the two men have to say about **double negatives**:

Lowth: "Two negatives in English destroy one another, or are equivalent to an affirmative." (p. 95)

Murray: "Two negatives, in English, destroy one another, or are equivalent to an affirmative." (p. 293)

The only difference between these two passages is the punctuation.

Also, compare the two men's condemnation of **preposition stranding** (i.e., leaving a preposition at the end of a clause):

Lowth: "The preposition is often separated from the relative which it governs, and joined to the verb at the end of the sentence . . . as, 'Horace is an author, *whom* I am much delighted *with*.' . . . This is an idiom which our language is strongly inclined to: it prevails in common conversation; and suits very well with the familiar style in writing: but the placing of the preposition before the relative, is more graceful, as well as more perspicuous; and agrees much better with the solemn and elevated style." (p. 96)

Murray: "The preposition is often separated from the relative which it governs: as, 'Whom will you give it to?' instead of, '*To whom* will

> you give it?' 'He is an author whom I am much delighted with;' . . . This is an idiom to which our language is strongly inclined: it prevails in common conversation; and suits very well with the familiar style in writing: but the placing of the preposition before the relative, is more graceful, as well as more perspicuous; and agrees much better with the solemn and elevated style." (pp. 294–295)

Exercise I

Consider the following sentences from the preceding passages.

Lowth: "This is an idiom which our language is strongly inclined to."
Murray: "This is an idiom to which our language is strongly inclined."

How strictly do these authors adhere to their own rule? Explain.

Coming into the nineteenth century, George Perkins Marsh (1801–1882) continued to build the connection between grammar and morality with his *Lectures on the English Language*. Referring to usages that he found unacceptable, Marsh wrote,

> To pillory such offences, to point out their absurdity, to detect and expose the moral obliquity which too often lurks beneath them, is the sacred duty of every scholar . . . who knows how nearly purity of speech, like personal cleanliness, is allied with purity of thought and rectitude of action. (pp. 644–645)

Another significant figure among nineteenth-century American grammarians was William Dwight Whitney (1827–1894). According to Finegan, Whitney was among the first to use sociological rather than linguistic criteria to distinguish "good" and "bad" usage, arguing that "bad English is simply that which is not approved and accepted by good and careful speakers" (Whitney, p. 3). In other words, he at least gave lip service to the idea that usage judgments should be based on observations about who uses which forms, rather than on *a priori* judgments about the forms themselves, without any regard for who uses them.

The dominant situation in nineteenth-century America, however, is summed up by Finegan as follows:

> Before 1875, grammatical popularizers commonly regarded usage items as intrinsically right or wrong; they did not formally recognize that circumstances alter cases. That appropriateness to an occasion ultimately governs linguistic propriety escaped them. Whitney alone grasped this

> insight, though his formulation failed to achieve useful explicitness. Americans had been nurtured on the absolutist dogmas of Murray . . . and disciplined by Webster's spelling books and dictionaries. No one had articulated a concept of functional varieties or classified their significance in determining correctness. Apparently, no one had sought, in examining English, to establish its varieties with their social, functional, and regional correlates. The notion of a monolithic grammatical English with bastardized offspring continued to prevail. (pp. 72–73)

Summary

Eighteenth-century England was emerging from social and political upheaval which, along with "vernacular nationalism," generated an intense interest in establishing rules for English usage. Thinkers such as Defoe, Dryden, and Swift attempted to establish an English Academy for this purpose. The failure to establish an Academy laid the field open to self-styled grammarians such as Lowth and Murray, whose writings were for the most part prescriptive, sometimes prejudiced, but nevertheless popular. By 1800 these writers had infiltrated the United States, and by the late nineteenth century, many of their ideas were firmly entrenched in the American educational system.

Time Line

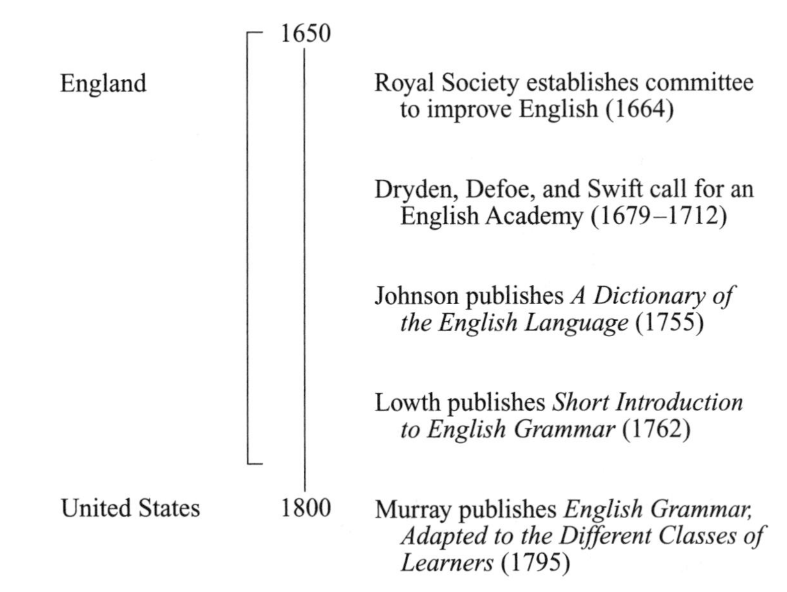

SUPPLEMENTARY EXERCISES

1. Which of the following quotations (taken from the Introduction on page 2) displays an attitude most sympathetic to Defoe's position on the English Academy? Explain.

a. There is, I believe, a morality of language: an obligation to preserve and nurture the niceties . . . .
b. Since grammar is a science, it must describe and analyze the basic facts of speech, and explain and interpret the laws governing the behavior of language.
c. Any interesting . . . grammar will be dealing . . . with mental processes that are far beyond the level of actual or even potential consciousness.

2. Consider the passage on page 25 from Johnson.

a. To what is Johnson referring in the final paragraph, when he hopes that England "may no longer yield the palm of philology to the nations of the continent"?
b. Why would Johnson feel that England had "yielded" this "palm" up to that point? (Hint: *palm* is used here in the sense of 'a medal or reward symbolizing victory or success.')
c. What metaphor does Johnson use to describe language change? (Hint: See the next-to-last paragraph.)

3. Consider the following quotation from Lowth:

> It doth not then proceed from any peculiar irregularity or difficulty of our language, that the general practice both of speaking and writing is chargeable with inaccuracy. It is not the language, but the practice that is in fault. The truth is, Grammar is very much neglected among us: and it is not the difficulty of the language, but on the contrary the simplicity and facility of it, that occasions this neglect. Were the language less easy and simple, we should find ourselves under a necessity of studying it with more care and attention. (p. vi)

a. What does Lowth mean when he states, "It is not the language, but the practice that is in fault"?
b. What does Lowth mean when he states, "it is not the difficulty of the language, but . . . the simplicity and facility of it, that occasions this neglect"?

4. Compare the following quotation to the passage on page 28 by Priestley.

> Grammar is very much neglected among us. . . . our best Authors for want of some rudiments of grammar have sometimes fallen into mistakes, and been guilty of palpable errors in point of Grammar.

a. Describe the difference(s) in attitude reflected in these two passages.
b. Who is the likely author of this quotation?

5. Examine the quotation on page 30 from Marsh.

a. What does *pillory* mean? When, and by whom, were pillories used in American history?
b. What does *obliquity* mean?
c. What does *rectitude* mean?
d. Discuss how this passage illustrates Finegan's claim that for Marsh, "linguistic propriety was *chiefly* a moral question" (p. 67).

▲▲▲ CHAPTER 3

Prescriptive Rules

In Chapter 2, we looked at some of the forces that led to the development of prescriptive grammar in England and the United States. In this chapter, we will focus on some specific rules developed by prescriptive grammarians during the eighteenth century. As you will probably recognize, many of these rules are still popular. However, when presented in grammar books today, the rules are generally simply stated as "do this" and "don't do that." By reading this chapter, you will become aware of the reasoning behind some of these rules, so that you can understand how they originally developed.

REPRESENTATIVE RULES

In this section, we treat 20 or so grammatical rules in some detail. The rules selected all have some syntactic component, rather than being those that deal solely with vocabulary (e.g., "*uninterested* means 'not interested' and *disinterested* means 'not biased'").

"Don't End a Sentence with a Preposition."

The prescriptive rule against ending a sentence with a preposition states that (1a) is acceptable but (1b) is not.

1. a. *To whom* did you speak?
   b. *Whom* did you speak *to*?

As discussed in Chapter 2, Lowth and Murray did not actually proscribe ending a sentence with a preposition, but rather stated their preference for keeping the preposition with its object (e.g., *the one to whom you spoke* vs. *the one whom you spoke to*).

This rule apparently is based on the fact that in Latin (as in all Romance languages), prepositions always precede a noun phrase and thus never appear in sentence-final position. In fact, the word *preposition* itself can be divided into *position* 'put' + *pre-* 'before.' That is, the term *preposition* gets its name from the fact that it is always 'put before' a noun phrase. Thus, the prescriptivists apparently reasoned that if a preposition always precedes a noun phrase, then it necessarily never ends a sentence.

Exercise A

Consider the following sentences. What problems would you run into if you tried to rephrase each one so that it does not end in a preposition?

a. I wonder what she's thinking about.
b. This is the man she used to work for.

"Don't Split an Infinitive."

The rule against splitting infinitives states that no word can come between the infinitive marker *to* and the uninflected verb form that follows. This rules states that (2a) is acceptable but (2b) is not.

2. a. Captain Queeg wanted *to understand* the problem completely.
   b. Captain Queeg wanted *to* completely *understand* the problem.

This rule seems once again to be based on a Latin model. It just so happens that infinitives in Latin consist of a single word, whereas in English they are made up of two. For example, the Latin infinitive *vidēre* corresponds to the English infinitive *to see*. Since *vidēre* cannot be "split," grammarians reasoned that in English *to see* should not be split.

Exercise B

Consider the following sentence: *John wants to win; he doesn't want to almost win.*

a. Identify the split infinitive in this sentence.
b. What problem would you run into if you tried to revise it to avoid the split infinitive?

"Use Shall *with First Person; Use* Will *with Second and Third."*

This rule states that *shall* is used with the subjects *I* and *we*, but *will* is used with any other subject (i.e., *you, he, she, it, they*, or any other noun phrase for which one of these can substitute). Thus, this rule states that (3a) is acceptable but (3b) is not.

3. a. *I shall* leave around 8:00.
   b. *I will* leave around 8:00.

This rule apparently never reflected actual usage. It was first laid down by John Wallis in his *Grammaticae Linguae Anglicanae* (1653). Over a century later, it was refined by Lowth (1762) to include questions and put into its final complex form by William Ward in his *Grammar of the English Language* (1765). Ward stipulated that Wallis's rule held only when the speaker intended to express a future act. On the other hand, Ward said that the opposite usage was correct (i.e., *will* with first person; *shall* with second and third), when the speaker intended to express determination or emphasis. Thus, according to Ward's revision, *I shall go* means something like 'I represent that I will go'; whereas *I will go* means something like 'I vow that I will go.'

As unlikely as it may seem, this rule is still current among some prescriptivists. For example, the 1980 edition of the *Oxford English Dictionary* states

> *shall* . . . 1. used with *I* and *we* to express future tense in statements and questions (but *will* is used with other words, *I shall arrive tomorrow* (but *they will arrive*)) . . . . 2. used with words other than *I* or *we* in promises or statements of intention or obligation, *You shall have it* (but *I will have it* = I intend to have it).

Interestingly, this rule confuses even the experts. For example, members of Congress were debating the wording of a bill to balance the budget by 2002. As they argued over the choice between *we shall* vs. *we will*, National Public Radio consulted an English professor, who said that *we shall* was the better choice because it was more emphatic. Actually, according to Ward's rule, *we will* should be used for emphasis.

Exercise C

a. In what year was the *shall/will* rule first spelled out?
b. In what year was the *shall/will* rule "extended" to cover questions?
c.† Why do you think questions, such as the following, were treated as a "special case" of the *shall/will* distinction?
   i. Shall we eat?
   ii. Will we eat?

"*Lie* Is Intransitive; *Lay* Is Transitive."

This rule states that *lie* cannot be used with a **direct object** (i.e., with a noun following it), but that *lay* must be used with a direct object. Thus, this rule states that (4a) is acceptable but (4b) is not.

4. a. *Lie* down and rest.
   b. *Lay* down and rest.

Unlike the *shall/will* rule, this one has some historical basis. *Lie* derives from the Old English intransitive verb *licgan*, and *lay* derives from the Old English transitive verb *lecgan*. The reason that these two verbs are easily confused derives from an overlap in their tensed forms:

Present tense	**Past tense**
lie	*LAY*
LAY	*laid*

Note that the present tense of *lay* (e.g., *The hens lay eggs everyday)* is identical to the past tense of *lie* (e.g., *I lay down yesterday*). This overlap accounts for the fact that many speakers stopped distinguishing between the two verbs as early as the Middle English period (1150–1500 A.D.), during the late Middle Ages.

Exercise D

Consider the verbs *raise, sit, rise,* and *set.* How do these verbs pattern with regard to *lie* and *lay*? (Consult a dictionary if necessary.)

"Use *like* as a Preposition; Use *as* as a Conjunction."

This rule, which applies to sentences making comparisons, states that *like* should be used when the following element is a noun phrase, while *as* should be used when the following element is a clause. According to this rule, (5a) is acceptable but (5b) is not.

5. a. He responded *as* I thought he would.
   b. He responded *like* I thought he would.

Some authorities allow more leeway in using *like* after linking verbs such as *sound, look, seem*, and *taste*, especially in informal usage (e.g., *This tastes like it hasn't been cooked long enough*).

Exercise E

> Around the early 1960s, the following slogan was used in advertisements for Winston cigarettes: *Winston tastes good like a cigarette should.* This ad spawned criticism from a number of usage authorities. What would be the reasoning behind their criticism?

"Use Nominative Case after the Verb be."

This rule states that (6a) is acceptable but (6b) is not.

6. a. It is I.
   b. It is me.

The appearance of nominative case after *be* is actually the result of reanalysis, occurring around 1500. Traugott (p. 126) gives the following history of this form.

500–1000:	*He it is*	*He* is subject (i.e., 'He is it' = 'He is the one').
1300–1400:	*It is he*	Word order change, but *he* is still subject.
1400–1500:	*It is he*	*It* reanalyzed as subject, so nominative case apparently follows *be*.
1500:	*It is I*	Nominative case following *be* extended to first person.
1600:	*It is me*	Objective case following *be* on analogy with other verbs.

According to Murray, the rule is a little more complicated:

> The verb *to be*, through all its variations, has the same case after it, expressed or understood, as that which next precedes it: "*It* may be . . . *he*, but *it* cannot be . . . *I*. . . ." The following sentences contain deviations from the rule, and exhibit the pronoun in a wrong case: "It might have been *him* . . . ." (pp. 269–70)

In other words, the pronoun following a form of *be* is always the same case as its subject.

Exercise F

> Murray cites the following sentences as containing errors in case (italicized). In each sentence, correct the error, and explain.
>
> a.† I saw one whom I took to be *she.*
> b.† She is the person *who* I understand it to have been.
> c. *Who* do you think me to be?
> d. *Whom* do men say that I am?
> e. And *whom* think ye that I am?

"Don't Use Double Negatives."

According to Dennis Baron, this rule originates with the sixteenth-century poet, Sir Philip Sidney, who states in his poem *Astrophel and Stella* that two negatives cancel each other out and make a positive (p. 84). The rule against double negatives states that (7a) is acceptable but (7b) is not.

7. a. Sven and Ole *don't* want any more pizza.
   b. Sven and Ole *don't* want *no* more pizza.

Unlike the other rules discussed in this section, this one actually does distinguish between standard (a) and nonstandard (b) usage in Modern English. (A **nonstandard** form is one that regularly draws negative attention to itself. Nonstandard forms are often referred to as **socially marked** forms.) During the eighteenth century, however, at the time the rule was established, usage was still in flux on this point. Indeed, double negatives were common up until the eighteenth century. (Both Chaucer's and Shakespeare's works are replete with double negatives.)

What's interesting here, however, is the reasoning which underlies this rule. Lowth states, "Two negatives in English destroy one another, or are equivalent to an affirmative" (p. 95). Lowth's reasoning may have been based upon logical systems such as mathematics, where the multiplication of one negative number by another results in a positive number. For example, (-3) x (-2) = 6. On the other hand, Lowth might have based his double-negative rule on sentences like (8) below.

8. Becky *didn't* want to be *not* chosen.

At first glance, this sentence appears to be paraphrasable as 'Becky wanted to be chosen.' This makes it look like the two negatives have canceled each other out. On closer examination, however, a better paraphrase is 'Becky didn't want to be overlooked.' In this case, *didn't* negates the main clause, whereas *not* negates only the single word *chosen*.

Regardless of the chain of reasoning by which Lowth arrived at his double-negative rule, the point is that two negatives do not always nullify each other. For example, sentence (7b) above, *Sven and Ole don't want no more pizza*, does not in fact mean 'Sven and Ole want more pizza.' Moreover, double negatives are not only allowed in other languages, but are sometimes even *required*. For example, the Spanish sentence *No quiero nada* '*not* I want *nothing*' is not paraphrasable as **Quiero nada*.

Exercise G

The following sentences all contain double negatives.

a. I couldn't eat nothing.
b. I couldn't hardly eat anything.
c. I couldn't scarcely eat anything.
d. I couldn't barely eat anything.

Identify the double negative in each sentence.

"Don't Use Ain't."

This negative contraction is, of course, shunned in prescriptive grammar. What is interesting, however, is the origin of the term *ain't*. Note that all but one of the following phrases have two contracted forms.

Uncontracted	Subject + Verb Contraction	Verb + *not* Contraction
I am not	I'm not	———
We are not	We're not	We aren't
You are not	You're not	You aren't
He/She is not	He's/She's not	He/She isn't
They are not	They're not	They aren't

The missing contraction would be something like *amn't* (from *am not*). The facts are, however, that two consecutive nasals (e.g., *mn*) cannot occur in the same syllable in English (note that the first *m* in *mnemonic* and the *n* in *damn* are not pronounced), and that in some varieties of English a vowel before a nasal is raised (note that *can't* rhymes with *paint* in some dialects). If we apply these principles to the form *amn't*, we first get *an't* (via loss of the *m*) and finally *ain't* (via vowel raising). The point is that even though *ain't* is clearly unacceptable in prestige varieties of English, it has evolved systematically from what was presumably an acceptable contraction of *am not*.

Exercise H

Consider the following quote taken from a grammar book published in 1950:

> A barbarism is a word or phrase that is not in good use. It may be a newly coined word, a slang expression, a vulgarism, a provincialism, or any illiterate or unauthorized expression. *Ain't*, *orate*, *aviate*, *complected*, *gym*, *woozy*, *nowheres*, *attackted*, *unbeknownst*, and *irregardless* are all barbarisms, because these expressions are not used by cultured writers and speakers. (House and Harman, p. 18)

Which of these expressions would not be considered "barbarisms" today?

"Don't Say Between You and I."

Prescriptive grammar requires that the object of a preposition be in objective case. Thus, in all varieties of English, we observe only phrases such as *Give that to me*, never **Give that to I*. Here *to* is a preposition and takes the objective case (*me*), not the nominative case (*I*).

What's interesting is that the prohibited nominative case occurs after a preposition only in coordinate constructions. For example, you might hear someone say *Do it for your mother and I*, but never **Do it for I*. One explanation for this phenomenon is that the second member of a coordinate structure is more distant from the preposition (which normally is followed by an objective case pronoun) and thus more likely to be replaced with the more prestigious nominative case, as illustrated below.

for you and *I* vs. for *I*
distant proximate

It's also interesting that the most common manifestation of this error contains the preposition *between* (as in *between you and I* rather than the preferred *between you and me*). Note that *between*, by virtue of its meaning, requires *two* semantic objects (i.e., *between X and Y*, never *between X* or *between Y*); thus the second object of *between* will always be a prime target for this error.

Exercise I

Consider the following quote from the same 1950 grammar book.

> *Solecism* is a term used to describe a blunder in grammar or a construction not sanctioned by good usage. Any word or combination of words deviating from the idiom of the language or from the rules of syntax may be called a *solecism*; as, *He don't* for *He doesn't*, and *between you and I* for *between you and me*. (House and Harman, p. 18)

a. What do you think is the essential difference between a "solecism" and a "barbarism"?
b. Which of these two types of errors is more likely to change over time? Explain.

"Don't Use Hopefully *to Mean 'I Hope.'"*

Prescriptive grammar dictates that *hopefully* is an adverb and as such must modify the action described by a verb, e.g., *The prisoner entered the room hopefully*. In contrast, prescriptivism prohibits such usages as *Hopefully, it won't rain*, where *hopefully* describes not the action of the verb but rather the state of mind of the speaker, meaning 'I am hopeful that . . . .' *Hopefully* is not the only adverb that is used to describe the mental state of the speaker; others include *frankly, truthfully, confidentially*, and *evidently, obviously, unfortunately,* meaning 'I'm being frank/truthful/confidential in saying that . . . ,' or 'I think it is evident/obvious/unfortunate that . . . .'

"Use Subjunctive for Hypothetical Situations."

Prescriptive grammar distinguishes three **moods** for verbs. **Indicative** mood is used for factual descriptions and is characterized by the third-person singular *-s* on present-tense verbs, e.g., *John walks home every day.* **Imperative** mood is used for directives (i.e., attempts to get the listener to do something) and is characterized by the absence of tense on the verb, e.g., *Be strong* (not **Are strong*). **Subjunctive** mood is used in some *that*-clauses which express intention and to express hypothetical meaning.

In *that*-clauses, the subjunctive is characterized by the absence of the third-person singular *-s* on present-tense verbs, e.g., *I insist that John walk home every day.* (Cf. *I know that John walks home everyday.*) The subjunctive forms for all verbs (except *be*) are exactly like the indicative forms except the third-person present singular has no *-s*. The subjunctive forms of *be* are contrasted with the indicative forms in the following table.

	Indicative		**Subjunctive**	
Present	I *am*	We *are*	I *be*	We *be*
	You *are*	You *are*	You *be*	You *be*
	He *is*	They *are*	He *be*	They *be*
Past	I *was*	We were	I *were*	We were
	You were	You were	You were	You were
	He *was*	They were	He *were*	They were

To express a hypothetical situation, then, prescriptive grammar would require the subjunctive form. Under this rule, (9a) is acceptable but not (9b).

9. a. If I *were* you, I wouldn't do that.
   b. If I *was* you, I wouldn't do that.

†Exercise J

Lowth states,

> Hypothetical, conditional concessive, and exceptive conjunctions seem in general to require the subjunctive mode after them: *as, if,*

> *though, unless, except, whether* . . . . Examples: "*If* thou *be* the Son of God." "*Though* he *flay* me . . . ." "*Unless* he *wash* his flesh." (p. 105)

In the examples Lowth gives, what would be the *indicative* form of each italicized verb?

"Don't Omit the Relative Pronoun."

Prescriptive grammar requires that the pronoun (i.e., *who(m), which, that*) introducing a **relative clause** always be included. This requirement dates back to Lowth, who states:

> The relative is often understood or omitted: as: "The man I love;' that is, "*whom* I love . . . . The construction is hazardous, and hardly justifiable . . . ." (p. 102)

†Exercise K

House and Harman state that it is acceptable to omit the relative pronoun in the sentence *Jones is the man I referred to,* because "a relative pronoun is clearly implied" (p. 356).

a. What is the implied relative pronoun in this sentence, and where would it occur?
b. What is it about this sentence that "implies" the presence of a relative pronoun?

"Don't Omit that *Introducing a Noun Clause."*

Prescriptive grammar requires the inclusion of the word *that* introducing a noun clause (e.g., *I think that she is wrong*). Once again, this prescription dates back to Lowth, who states, "The conjunction *that* is often omitted and understood: as, 'I beg you would come to me:' that is, '*that* you would' . . . (p. 109).

"Pronouns Must Agree with Their Antecedents."

Murray states,

> Pronouns must always agree with their antecedents . . . in gender and number: as, . . . 'The king and the queen had put on *their* robes.' . . .

> Of this rule there are many violations to be met with . . . . "Can any one, on their entrance into the world, be fully secure that they shall not be deceived?" "on *his* entrance," and "that *he* shall." (pp. 232–33)

Exercise L

> Consider the sentence *Everybody must leave their notebook.* This sentence appears to violate number agreement. What are some of the problems you might run into with each of the following "corrections"?
>
> a. Everybody must leave their notebooks.
> b. Everybody must leave his notebook.
> c. Everybody must leave his or her notebook.

*"***Either/Or** *and* **Neither/Nor** *Take Singular Verbs."*

Murray has this to say:

> these constructions must be in the singular number: as, "Ignorance or negligence *has* caused this mistake." . . .
>
> The following sentences are variations from this rule. "Neither character nor dialogue were yet understood;" "*was* yet." (p. 229)

Exercise M

> For each of the following sentences, supply a present tense form of the verb *to be* (i.e., *am, are, is*). What problem do you run into?
>
> a. Either you or I __________ responsible.
> b. Either he or they __________ responsible.
> c. Either he or I __________ responsible.

Case Following **As/Than**

These conjunctions introduce not just a single noun but an entire clause; thus, the case of the noun is determined by its role in the clause. Murray gives the following examples:

> "Thou art wiser than I;" that is, "than I am." "They loved him more than me;" i.e. "more than they loved me." "The sentiment is well expressed by Plato, but much better by Solomon than him;" that is, "than by him." . . .

> The propriety or impropriety of many phrases, in the preceding as well as in some other forms, may be discovered, by supplying the words that are not expressed; which will be evident from the following instances of erroneous construction. "He can read better than me." "He is as good as her." . . . "Who did this? Me." (p. 315*)*

Exercise N

Use Murray's test of "supply the words that are not expressed" to correct each of the "erroneous" constructions which he cites:

a.† He can read better than me.
b. He is as good as her.
c. Who did this? Me.

Subject-Verb Agreement

It is a truism of prescriptive grammar that subject and verb must agree in number (e.g., *This is* *broken* vs. *These are* *broken*). This rule is easy to apply as long as the simple subject and the verb are contiguous, as in the preceding examples. However, the rule is more difficult to apply when the simple subject and the verb are separated by other words (e.g., *The memory requirements for each program is/are listed in Table 2).* In this example, *are* is correct since it is plural and agrees with *requirements*; however, *is* is a common mistake since the word to its immediate left is *program*, which is singular.

It's interesting that this point of grammar was in dispute as early as two centuries ago. Here is what Murray had to say:

> It has been advanced as a rule of grammar, that "When the nominative [i.e., subject] consists of several words, and the last of the nouns is in the plural number, the verb is commonly plural:" as, "A part of the exports *consist* of raw silk;" "A number of men and women *were* present;" "The train of our ideas *are* often interrupted." The support of this rule has been ingeniously attempted, by the following observations: "The whole of the words, in the first part of each of the preceding sentences, or the noun and its adjuncts, are the actual [subject]. Separate the words *part* and *exports*, in the first example, and the affirmation of the verb cannot with truth be applied to either: and as the whole must be considered as the [subject], the verb is very naturally connected in number with the last noun."

> This reasoning, how plausible soever it may, at first sight, appear, is certainly destitute of solidity. It would counteract some of the plainest principles of grammar; and would justify the following constructions, and a multitude of others of a similar nature. "The truth of the narratives *have* never been disputed;" "The virtue of these men and women, *are* indeed exemplary:" "A fondness for such distinctions, *render* a man ridiculous." (p. 224)

Exercise O

Consider the last three sentences in the preceding quotation from Murray. In each sentence, what does the verb agree with? What *should* it agree with, according to Murray?

Parallelism

Prescriptive grammar requires that items in a series be of the same grammatical form. This rule dates back at least to Murray, who states,

> Conjunctions connect the same moods and tenses of verbs, and cases of nouns and pronouns: as, "Candour is *to be approved and practised;*" "If thou sincerely *desire*, and earnestly *pursue* virtue, she *will* assuredly *be found* by thee, *and prove* a rich reward;" "The master taught *her and me* to write;" "*He and she* were school-fellows."
>
> A few examples of inaccuracy respecting this rule, may further display its utility. "If he prefer a virtuous life, and is sincere in his professions, he will succeed;" "if he *prefers*." "To deride the miseries of the unhappy, is inhuman; and wanting compassion towards them, is unchristian;" "and *to want* compassion." "The parliament addressed the king, and has been prorogued the same day;" "and *was* prorogued." "His wealth and him bid adieu to each other;" "and *he*." "He entreated us, my comrade and I, to live harmoniously;" "comrade and *me*." "My sister and her were on good terms;" "and *she*." "We often overlook the blessings which are in our possession, and are searching after those which are out of our reach:" it ought to be, "and *search* after." (p. 301)

Exercise P

Identify any violations of parallelism among the items in the following list.

Beach Regulations

- Alcoholic beverages and glass containers are not permitted.
- Motorized vehicles (except for wheelchairs) are prohibited.
- Boaters may not anchor or launch their craft on public beaches.
- Sleeping on the beach is prohibited between midnight and 6:00 a.m.
- Dogs are not permitted on public beaches between 9:00 a.m. and 6:00 p.m. from Memorial Day to Labor Day.
- Picking sea oats or other dune vegetation and harassing or disturbing sea turtles and their nests are all punishable offenses.
- Discharging fireworks, shark fishing, flying stunt kites or using sand sailers are prohibited.
- Fires (except for cooking on portable liquid fueled stoves) are not permitted.
- Nudity and indecent exposure are prohibited.
- Do not wear lifeguard emblems or insignias if you are not a lifeguard.
- Littering is a punishable offence.

ASSUMPTIONS UNDERLYING PRESCRIPTIVE RULES

So far, we have looked at a number of specific prescriptive rules. In this section we will try to analyze some of the assumptions that underlie these rules.

Latin Grammar Is an Appropriate Model for English

As noted, several prescriptive rules (e.g., against ending a sentence with a preposition or splitting an infinitive) attempt to apply the rules of Latin to English. However, such attempts are problematic for several reasons.

- Latin is an Italic language, whereas English is Germanic. Although they are genetically related, they have not been mutually intelligible for approximately 5000 years.
- Latin is a synthetic language (one with many inflections), whereas English is analytic (with few inflections). For example, directionality in Latin is indicated primarily by suffixes on nouns, whereas directionality in English is indicated primarily by prepositions. Thus, *puero* in Latin corresponds to *to the boy* in English; the *-o* suffix on *puero* here serves the same function as the preposition *to.*
- Latin is basically an OV language (i.e., the direct object normally precedes the verb), whereas English is basically a VO language (i.e., the direct object normally follows the verb). This distinction is important since it correlates

with a number of other mirror-image patterns in the two languages: for instance, prepositions (e.g., *in here*) correlate with VO order, and postpositions (e.g., *herein*) correlate with OV.

The point is that Latin and English display significant structural differences that prevent a direct transfer of rules from one language to the other. Because of Latin's prestige as a language of learning, however, grammarians during the prescriptive period found it worthy of emulation as they constructed their grammars of English.

Different Forms Imply Different Meanings

This assumption is apparently what underlies several prescriptive rules, such as the *lie/lay* distinction, the *like/as* distinction, and Wallis' *shall/will* rule. For example, Wallis seems to have reasoned that since *shall* and *will* are different words (i.e., different forms), they must have different meanings. If they have different meanings, they cannot be used interchangeably in a single context. Thus, *shall* must be for use with the first person and *will* for use with the second and third. Such reasoning, however, is suspect. English, like other languages, appears to have numerous forms that are interchangeable in a single context. Consider, for example, the sentences in (10), all of which seem to have essentially the same meaning.

10. a. Tiny Abner *leaves* for Chicago tomorrow.
    b. Tiny Abner *is leaving* for Chicago tomorrow.
    c. Tiny Abner *will leave* for Chicago tomorrow.
    d. Tiny Abner *is going to leave* for Chicago tomorrow.

Moreover, the converse of such reasoning is also found in prescriptive grammars; that is, if two forms appear to be synonymous, one of them must be superior to the other. Consider, for example, the forms in (11) and (12).

11. a. Fred thinks *that* Ethel is crazy.
    b. Fred thinks Ethel is crazy.

12. a. Rudy hates people *that* smoke.
    b. Rudy hates people *who* smoke.

Even though some argue for the superiority of one form over the other in such cases, there's no compelling evidence for this position.

Language Change Represents Decay

The present-day adherence to prescriptive rules that were established hundreds of years ago reflects a general assumption that older forms of the language are preferable and should be preserved. (Recall the similar impulse during the prescriptive period to "fix" the language.) In fact, however, language change appears to be a perfectly natural process that is difficult to halt. First, note, for example, that the French Academy has been unsuccessful in keeping foreign words (e.g., *le by-pass*) out of French for the last 300 years, as long as it's been in existence. Second, note that English has changed dramatically and systematically over the last 1000 years, despite all attempts to turn back the hands of time. Old English (the language of *Beowulf*) changed into Middle English (the language of Chaucer), which evolved into Early Modern English (the language of Shakespeare), which in turn became Modern English. Third, note that so-called "dead languages" only give the appearance of being unchanged. Latin, for example, evolved into Spanish, Italian, French, and the other Romance languages. The fact that Latin has been preserved as a religious language in essentially an unchanged form is more an artifact of human history than a reflection of the nature of language.

Language Is "Logical"

The fact is that language *is* "logical" in the sense that it is a self-contained, rule-governed system. However, English is not subject to "common sense" logic, such as Lowth's insistence that two negatives make a positive. Consider, for example, the sentences in (13).

13. a. Tector is *eager* to please.
    b. Tector is *easy* to please.

Note that even though these two sentences are superficially similar, they have quite different and mutually exclusive interpretations. In (13a) *Tector* is interpreted as the subject of *please* (i.e., 'Tector pleases others'), but in (13b) Tector is interpreted as the object of *please* (i.e., 'Others please Tector').

These sentences illustrate two points. First, neither English nor any other language is subject to analysis via "common sense" logic (i.e., identical superficial structures = identical interpretations). Second, each of these sentences is an example of a more general class of English predicates. The predicate *be eager* behaves like *be sure*, *be certain*, *be likely*, *be crazy*, *be stupid*, *be smart*, and others. The predicate *be easy*, on the other hand, behaves like *be hard*, *be impossible*, *be fun*, *be tough*, *be a breeze*, *be a snap*, and others. The subject of any predicate in the first group will be interpreted as the *subject* of the infinitive, whereas the subject of any predicate in the second group will be interpreted as the *object* of the infinitive, as in (13c) and (13d) below.

13. c. Tector *is sure* to please. (i.e., 'Tector pleases others')
    d. Tector *is hard* to please. (i.e., 'Others please Tector')

DEGREES OF "CORRECTNESS"

One shortcoming of the prescriptive approach, especially as it has sometimes been integrated into applied areas such as the teaching of writing, has been its tendency to label particular structures as either "correct" or "incorrect." This binary distinction, however, tends to oversimplify the complexities of actual language use.

For example, consider the following sentences:

14. Who did you talk to?
15. I didn't talk to nobody.

Both (14) and (15) violate prescriptive rules and hence could be labeled as "incorrect" by a prescriptive grammarian. However, most of us probably have quite different reactions to these sentences. While (14) violates a prescriptive rule, we nevertheless would not be surprised to hear it uttered by a speaker of **standard English**—that is, by a speaker of that variety used in broadcasting, newspapers, and so on. Such a structure would be especially unremarkable in informal spoken discourse. By comparison, (15) is not a sentence we would expect to hear uttered by a speaker of standard English. Instead, it is characteristic of a socially stigmatized variety, **nonstandard English**. The main point is that "correct" and "incorrect" are probably best regarded not as a binary distinction, but rather as points along a continuum. To use an analogy, some violations, like (14), are mere misdemeanors; others, like (15), carry more serious penalties.

Exercise Q

In a 1981 article, Maxine Hairston reported results of a survey of 100 professional people such as business executives, realtors, and social workers (no English teachers!). She asked them to rate 66 sentences as "Does not bother me," "Bothers me a little," or "Bothers me a lot," according to how the respondent would react to encountering each sentence in someone else's writing.

Below are some of the items from Hairston's survey. First, try to identify the prescriptive rule violated by each item. (Some of the rules are discussed in this chapter; others are not.) Next, rate each item according to Hairston's categories. Then compare your ratings to one or two of your classmates' ratings. Your instructor can then provide you with information about how Hairston's respondents rated the items.

a. The situation is quite different than that of previous years.
b. People are always impressed by her smooth manner, elegant clothes, and being witty.
c. The small towns are dying. One of the problems being that young people are leaving.

d. Having argued all morning, a decision was finally reached.
e. If the regulating agency sets down on the job, everyone will suffer.
f. The data supports her hypothesis.
g. Him and Richards were the last ones hired.
h. The reporter paid attention to officers but ignores enlisted men.
i. If I was in charge of that campaign, I would be worried about opinion polls.
j. There has never been no one here like that woman.
k. The worst situation is when the patient ignores warning symptoms.
l. When Mitchell moved, he brung his secretary with him.
m. Three causes of inflation are: easy credit, costly oil, and consumer demand.
n. The lieutenant treated his men bad.
o. He went through a long battle. A fight against unscrupulous opponents.
p. We direct our advertising to the young prosperous and sports-minded reader.
q. That is her across the street.
r. Calhoun has went after every prize in the university.
s. Its wonderful to have Graham back on the job.
t. When we was in the planning stages of the project, we underestimated costs.

Summary

The rules touted in prescriptive grammars were sometimes based on questionable assumptions, for example, that Latin grammar is an appropriate model for English, that different forms imply different meanings, that language change indicates decay, and that language is subject to common-sense logic. While prescriptive grammar tends to classify forms as "correct" or "incorrect," actual language use reflects various grades of acceptability.

SUPPLEMENTARY EXERCISES

1. In a study reported by Fasold (1984, pp. 258–259), college freshmen were tested to see whether they would use *is* or *are* in the frame *There* __________ *about five minutes left.* Following this performance test, they were asked to self-report on which verb they had used and also to judge one of the verbs as more "correct." The following graph shows the results (P = performance test, R = self-report, and C = judgment as correct).

Based on the graph, answer the following questions.

a. T-F The form judged "correct" by most speakers is the same one actually used by most speakers.
b. T-F Most speakers think that they actually use an "incorrect" form.
c. T-F The form judged "correct" is more formal than the form actually used by most speakers.
d. T-F It appears that most speakers are able to give a reliable report of the forms that they themselves use.

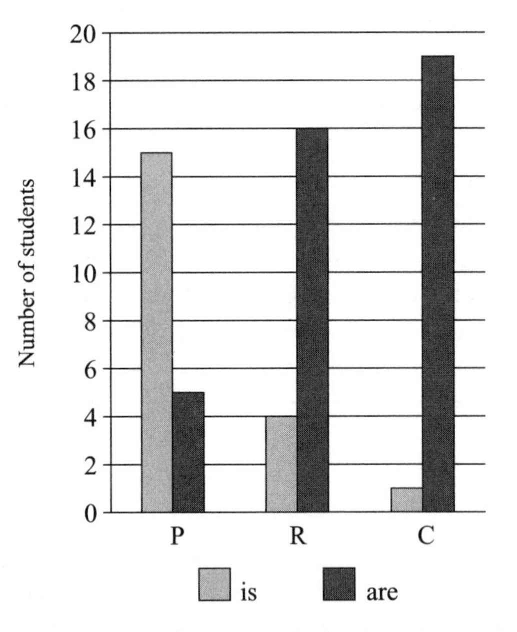

Number of subjects who used *is/are* in performance tests (P), who reported *is/are* as the form they used (R), and who considered *is/are* correct (C).

FIGURE 3-1 Results of performance test, self-reported usage, and judgments as correct.

2. In his 1981 article "The Phenomenology of Error," Joseph Williams, a professor of English and linguistics at the University of Chicago, begins with the following point:

> I am often puzzled by what we call errors of grammar and usage, errors such as *different than*, *between you and I*, a *which* for a *that*, and so on. I am puzzled by what motive could underlie the unusual ferocity which an *irregardless* or a *hopefully* or a singular *media* can elicit. In his second edition of *On Writing Well*, William Zinsser, an otherwise amiable man I'm sure, uses, and quotes not disapprovingly, words like *detestable vulgarity*, *garbage*, *atrocity*, *horrible*, *oaf*, *idiot*, and *simple illiteracy* to comment on usages like *OK*, *hopefully*, the affix *-wise*, and *myself* in *He invited Mary and myself to dinner*.
>
> The last thing I want to seem is sanctimonious. But as I am sure Zinsser would agree, what happens in Cambodia and Afghanistan could more reasonably be called horrible atrocities. The likes of Idi Amin qualify as legitimate oafs. Idiots we have more than enough of in our state institutions. And while simple illiteracy is the condition of billions, it does not characterize those who use *disinterested* in its original sense. (p. 152)

a. Based on what Williams says, what theory of grammar does Zinsser seem to adhere to? (Hint: Consult the Introduction for choices.)
b. What theory of grammar does Williams apparently adhere to?
c. Several of the usages that Williams refers to are covered in this chapter; others are not. Look up the ones that are *not* covered in this chapter by consulting a dictionary or college writing handbook such as the *Harbrace Handbook* or the *St. Martin's Handbook.* Briefly summarize each of the rules that cover these points of usage.

3. Williams further argues:

> . . . if we read any text the way we read freshman essays, we will find many of the same kind of errors we routinely expect to find and therefore do find. But if we could read those student essays unreflexively, if we could make the ordinary kind of contact with those texts that we make with other kinds of texts, then we could find many fewer errors. (p. 159)

a. Speculate on what Williams means by "the way we read freshman essays." (Hint: Who reads freshman essays, and what expectations about error do those readers bring to the essays?
b. What "reflex" typically characterizes readers of freshman essays (i.e., what do those readers automatically start doing when they read a freshman essay)?
c. Based on your answer to (b), what would it mean to read such an essay "unreflexively"?

4. Williams argues that we should define categories of error based on "the nature of our response to violations of grammatical rules":

> At the most basic level, the categories must organize themselves around two variables: Has a rule been violated? And do we respond? Each of these variables has two conditions: A rule is violated or a rule is not violated. And to either of those variables, we respond, or we do not respond. We thus have four possibilities:
>
> 1a. A rule is violated, and we respond to the violation.
> 1b. A rule is violated, and we do not respond to the violation.
>
> 2a. A rule is not violated, and we do not respond.
> 2b. A rule is not violated, and we do respond. (p. 159)

a. Williams writes, "I appreciate that many of you believe that you notice split infinitives as quickly as you notice a subject-verb error, and that both should be equally condemned in careful prose." Williams himself, however, does not agree that the two errors are equally noticeable or of equal seriousness. Into which category do you think Williams would place the split infinitive? What about a subject-verb error (e.g., *He walk to school every day*)?

b. Where do you think Williams's system would place a text that adheres to highly conservative prescriptive rules, like the following: "I shall not attempt broadly to define specific matters of evidence on which one might rest one's case"?

c. Consider the following passage:

> Since the members of the committee had discussed with each other all of the questions which had been raised earlier, we decided to conduct the meeting as openly as possible and with a concern for the opinions of everyone that might be there. And to ensure that all opinions would be heard, it was suggested that we not limit the length of the meeting. By opening up the debate in this way, there would be no chance that someone might be inadvertently prevented from speaking, which has happened in the past. (p. 161)

This passage contains a number of usages that Williams classifies as type (1b): "errors" whose violations we do not notice. What are some of those usages? Rewrite the passage to "correct" them.

5. Williams observes that those who make the rules sometimes break the rules themselves. Among the examples he cites are some from the respected essayist E. B. White. For example, White's *Elements of Style* (a short handbook for writers) prescribes the following rules:

> Express coordinate ideas in similar form. This principle, that of parallel construction, requires that expressions similar in content and function be outwardly similar. *That, which. That* is the defining or restrictive pronoun, *which* [is] the non-defining or nonrestrictive . . . The careful writer . . . removes the defining *whiches*, and by so doing improves his work.

Yet White's essay "Death of a Pig" contains the following passage:

> . . . the premature expiration of a pig is, I soon discovered, a departure which the community marks solemnly on its calendar . . . I have written this account in penitence and in grief, as a man who failed to raise his pig, and to explain my deviation from the classic course of so many raised pigs. The grave in the woods is unmarked, but Fred can direct the mourner to it unerringly and with immense good will, and I know he and I shall often revisit it, singly and together, . . .

a. Identify any instances of faulty parallelism in White's passage.
b. Identify any instances of "defining *whiches*" in White's passage.
c. Speculate on why these "errors" would go unnoticed by most of us. (Hint: Consider the expectations that a reader might bring to an essay by a famous writer.)
d. Speculate on why these "errors" apparently went unnoticed by White himself (and, presumably, his editor). How do you think White might respond if these "errors" were pointed out to him?

6. Consider the following passage from Williams.

> It may be that to fully account for the contempt that some errors of usage arouse, we will have to understand better than we do the relationship between language, order, and those deep psychic forces that perceived linguistic violations seem to arouse in otherwise amiable people. But if we cannot yet fully account for the psychological source of those feelings, or why they are so intense, we should be able to account better than we do for the variety of responses that different "errors" elicit. It is a subject that should be susceptible to research. And indeed, one kind of research in this area has a long tradition: In this century, at least five major surveys of English usage have been conducted to determine how respondents feel about various matters of usage. . . .
>
> The trouble with this kind of research, though, with asking people whether they think *finalize* is or is not good usage, is that they are likely to answer. As William Labov and others have demonstrated, we are not always our own best informants about our habits of speech. Indeed, we are likely to give answers that

> misrepresent our talking and writing, usually in the direction of more rather than less conservative values. Thus when the editors of the *American Heritage Dictionary* asks its Usage Panel to decide the acceptability of impact as a verb, we can predict how they will react: Merely by being asked, it becomes manifest to them that they have been invested with an institutional responsibility that will require them to judge usage by the standards they think they are supposed to uphold. So we cannot be surprised that, when asked, Zinsser rejects *impact* as a verb, despite the fact that *impact* has been used as a verb at least since 1601. (pp. 153–154)

a. By rejecting *impact* as a verb, what category does Zinsser place it into? (See question [4] for a description of the categories.)
b. Williams suggests that *impact* actually belongs in a different category. Which one?
c. The "punchline" of Williams's essay is that he incorporates about 100 errors into his own essay. Toward the end of the piece, he asks readers the following question: "If you had to report right now what errors you noticed, what would they be? Don't go back and reread, looking for errors, at least not before you recall what errors you found the first time through" (p. 165). Without looking at the passage at the beginning of this question, can you recall any errors that you noticed in it? (There are at least five violations of prescriptive rules.)
d. Now go back and reread the passage, deliberately looking for errors. Do you obtain a different result from your answer to (c)? How would Williams account for this difference?

Part II

Descriptive Grammar

This section of the book focuses on the descriptive approach to English grammar, which developed largely from early twentieth-century structuralist theory. The primary technical concepts introduced in this section have to do with parts of speech, constituent structure, and descriptions of the basic phrase and sentence patterns in English.

▲▲▲ CHAPTER 4

The Descriptive Period

Descriptive grammar developed from so-called "structuralist" theory, which itself was an extension of the historical–comparative period.

THE HISTORICAL–COMPARATIVE PERIOD (1800–1900)

During the nineteenth century, a new emphasis in language study arose, known as the historical–comparative approach. This term reflects the two main types of efforts undertaken by scholars during this period: chronicling the historical development of languages, and comparing similarities and differences among various languages. It was during this period that European scholars began to apply **descriptive** (rather than prescriptive) methodologies. That is, analysts became concerned primarily with collecting and cataloguing data, rather than with establishing rules governing usage. A good example of this new orientation is House and Harman's statement that "grammar is a science," which was cited in the Introduction.

One consequence of the new knowledge acquired during this period was a greater understanding of the relationship between English and other languages. Recall that eighteenth-century grammarians, based on what was known at the time, could reasonably assume that English descended from Latin and Latin from Greek. By the end of the nineteenth century, however, analysts had arrived at a much fuller understanding of the relationship among these three languages. Greek and Latin were classified as sister languages, rather than mother and daughter. Latin was identified as the historical antecedent of the Romance languages, a group that includes French, Italian, Portuguese, and Spanish. In contrast, English was classified as a member of the Germanic family, which also includes Danish, Dutch, German, Norwegian, and Swedish.

The following chart shows the relationship among some of the members of Indo-European (IE), one of the world's major families of languages. The basic division within IE is between the Centum and Satem branches, each of which reflects a different pronunciation of the word for 'hundred.' (Latin and Sanskrit appear in parentheses to reflect their status as "dead" languages.)

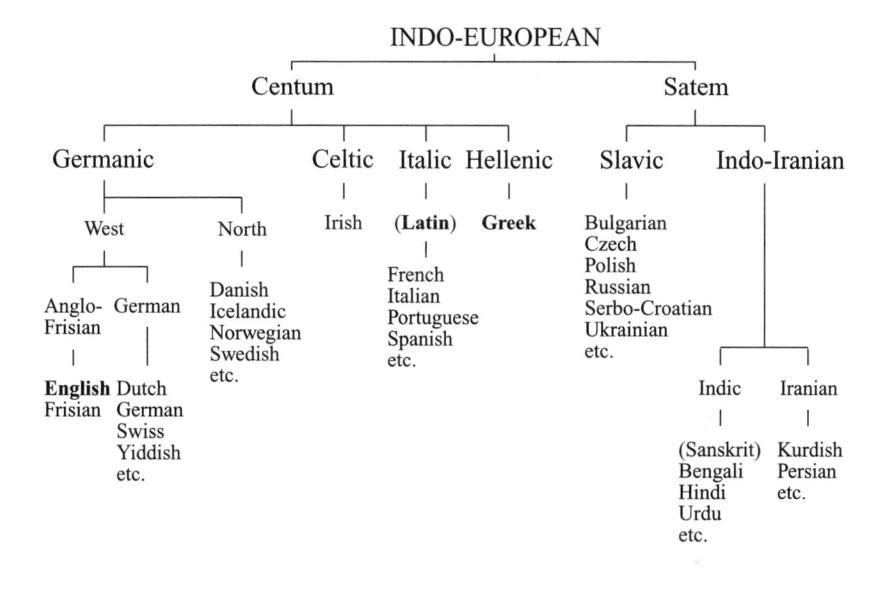

Two of the major figures during the historical–comparative period were Sir William Jones (1746–1794) and Jacob Grimm (1785–1863). Jones was an English judge in Calcutta during the British colonization of India. He became interested in studying Sanskrit, now recognized as the oldest Indo-European language for which records actually exist. (The study of Sanskrit was aided by its status as an important religious and literary language, since written records of it were available. In addition, the Indian scholar Panini had produced a descriptive grammar of Sanskrit around 500 B.C.) While studying Sanskrit, Jones noted similarities between it and other languages. For example, compare the Latin and Sanskrit forms below.

	Latin	**Sanskrit**
'god'	deus	deva
'two'	duo	dvau
'three'	tres	trayas
'five'	quīnque	pañca
'eat'	edō	atti

Correspondences such as these eventually led to the establishment of the IE "family tree" depicted above.

Within linguistics, Jacob Grimm is best known not for fairy tales but for Grimm's Law, which he formulated in his *Deutsche Grammatik* (1822). Grimm's Law is a set of principles that describe how consonants in Germanic languages relate to those in other IE languages. One principle is that **voiceless stops** in other IE languages (/p, t, k/) became voiceless **fricatives** in Germanic (/f, θ, h/) (/θ/ = first segment in *think*). This correspondence can be seen by comparing the items on the left (each containing (/p, t, k/) with those on the right (each containing /f, θ, h/).

Other IE forms	**Germanic (e.g., English)**
*p*ater (Latin)	*f*ather
*p*ēs (Latin)	*f*oot
*t*res (Spanish)	*th*ree
*t*u (French)	*th*ou
*k*ardiakós (Greek)	*h*eart
*c*entum (Latin)	*h*undred

Exercise A

Use Grimm's Law to determine the Modern English word containing a Germanic root that corresponds to each of the following words with non-Germanic roots (consult a good dictionary): *pisces* (Latin), *pyre* (Greek), *canine* (Latin), *unicorn* (Latin), *tornado* (Spanish).

A second principle of Grimm's Law is that **voiced** stops in other IE languages (/b, d, g/) became voiceless stops in Germanic (/p, t, k/). The following forms illustrate this correspondence.

Other IE forms	**Germanic (e.g., English)**
kánna*b*is (Greek)	hem*p*
*d*os (Spanish)	*t*wo
gi*g*nōskein (Greek)	*k*now [*k* was pronounced in Old and Middle English]
*g*enu (Latin)	*k*nee

Exercise B

Use Grimm's Law to determine the Modern English word containing a Germanic root that corresponds to each of the following words with non-Germanic roots (consult a good dictionary): *gynecologist* (Greek), *genus* (Latin), *grain* (Latin), *December* (Latin), *dental* (Latin), *cardiac* (Greek). Hint: Note that the symbols used to represent sound segments may correspond to various spellings; for example, /k/ may be spelled in English as *k, c,* or *qu.*

The advances by Jones, Grimm, and others reflect several general trends in the intellectual atmosphere in Europe during the nineteenth century. One was romanticism, which coincided with nationalistic pride in Germany. This motivated Grimm's investigation of his own native tongue. A second was Darwinism, reflected by a general interest in studying the history and "evolution" of languages. A third was what might be called "scientism," an emphasis on natural sciences and scientific investigation. The trend toward scientism stimulated interest in the collection of details about living languages and classification of languages into groups. This trend is reflected in the following passage from Max Müller's *Lectures on the Science of Language* (1861):

> the language which we speak, and the languages that are and that have been spoken in every part of our globe since the first dawn of human life and human thought, supply materials capable of scientific treatment. We can collect them, we can classify them, we can reduce them to their constituent elements, and deduce from them some of the laws that determine their origin, govern their growth, necessitate their decay; we can treat them, in fact, in exactly the same spirit in which the geologist treats his stones and petrifactions,— nay, in some respects, in the same spirit in which the astronomer treats the stars of heaven or the botanist the flowers of the field. There *is* a Science of Language as there is a science of the earth, its flowers and its stars. (vol. 2, p. 1) (Quoted in Harris & Taylor, p. 168)

Exercise C

> In Chapter 2, we said that one assumption underlying prescriptive grammar was that language change is a form of decay. How does Müller's use of the term "decay" in line 5 of the preceding passage differ from the prescriptivist use of the term?

In summary, the nineteenth century saw the beginning of descriptive linguistics, precipitated by Jones's recognition of the genetic relationship among Greek, Latin, and Sanskrit. This discovery led to a mapping of the entire IE family of languages and the statement of the sound laws (e.g., Grimm's Law) relating various branches of the family. However, the earlier eighteenth-century emphasis on the prescription of correct usage was not replaced by the nineteenth-century emphasis on the description of language change. Prescriptivists were not transformed into descriptivists; in fact, the major figures in the two periods were mutually exclusive groups. Rather, prescriptivism flourished in the school system under the rubric *grammar*, while descriptivism developed within universities under the name *linguistics*.

Exercise D

Compare the following quotation from George Campbell's *The Philosophy of Rhetoric* to the preceding one by Müller:

> [Grammar] is no other than a collection of general observations. . . . It is of no consequence here to what causes . . . these modes or fashions owe their existence . . . , they no sooner obtain and become general, than they are laws of the language, and the grammarian's only business is to note, collect, and methodize them." (Quoted in Finegan, p. 27)

Is the attitude toward language expressed in these two passages the same or different? In what respect? What is surprising about this fact?

STRUCTURALISM (1900–1950)

The historical–comparative studies of the nineteenth century led quite naturally to the evolution of **structuralism**. This view of language rests on two powerful ideas concerning language which were developed in the first half of the twentieth century. The first is that a language can be studied irrespective of its history and genetic relationship to other languages. The second is that linguistics is properly viewed as a physical science.

The first of these ideas derives from Ferdinand de Saussure (1857–1913), a Swiss professor of linguistics at the University of Geneva at the turn of the century. He published little during his lifetime; in fact, the work for which he is best known, *Course in General Linguistics*, was compiled posthumously from his students' notes and published in 1916, three years after his death. Nonetheless, his impact on the development of linguistics as a field of study has been so great that he might be called the "father of structural linguistics." The idea that has had the most impact in the field is his differentiation of diachronic and synchronic linguistics.

Diachronic linguistics is another term for historical linguistics: the study of a language at two different points in time. For example, we might compare Old English (450–1150) and Middle English (1150–1475), in order to chronicle the changes undergone by the language and to infer regularities of language change. Thus, diachronic linguistics, along with comparative linguistics, constituted the entire methodology for studying language during the nineteenth century. (Comparative linguistics is the study of two related languages at one point in time, for example, a comparison of Middle High German [1100–1500] and Middle English [1150–1475], in order to infer characteristics of the parent language.)

Synchronic linguistics, on the other hand, is the study of a language irrespective of its history or its genetic relationship to other languages. In other words, synchronic linguistics is the study of language as a self-contained system. Saussure states,

> *Synchronic linguistics* will be concerned with the logical and psychological relations that bind together coexisting terms and form a system in the collective mind of speakers. *Diachronic linguistics*, on the contrary, will study relations that bind together successive terms not perceived by the collective mind but substituted for each other without forming a system. (pp. 99–100)

In other words, Saussure viewed the relation between two items in a single language as part of a psychological system or "structure"—hence the term *structuralism*. At the same time, he viewed the relation between two items in two separate languages (or in one language at two points in time) as *outside* the psychological system of speakers. This was a new idea.

†Exercise E

From Saussure's point of view, would Grimm's Law be an instance of diachronic or synchronic linguistics? Explain.

The second important idea in structural linguistics was the view that language was a purely physical phenomenon. The most important proponent of this view was the American linguist Leonard Bloomfield (1887–1949). If Saussure was the father of structural linguistics, Bloomfield could legitimately be called the "father of *American* structuralism." Bloomfield's major work, *Language* (1933), exhibited two of the major influences on his view of linguistics. First was the fact that much of Bloomfield's work had involved the analysis of American Indian languages. (For example, he published *Menomini Texts* in 1928 and *Plain Cree Texts* in 1934.) This is important because such languages are superficially extremely different from English, which led Bloomfield to focus on the differences among languages rather than on their underlying similarities.

Second was the fact that he was influenced by behaviorist psychology, championed by the American psychologist J. B. Watson (1878–1958). **Behaviorism** is "The system of psychology that admits as its subject matter overt, *observable*, and measurable behavior. . . . [It] denies the admission of traditional issues of mental events" (Brennan, p. 353). The exclusion of the mind as an object of scientific inquiry and the insistence on studying only observable events led Bloomfield and his followers to reduce the study of language to the study of physical speech. After all, the only things that met the criteria of behaviorism were the physical speech produced by a human being and the physical forces acting on the speaker as he or she spoke (e.g., speaker's blood pressure, temperature of ambient air, etc.).

Bloomfieldian structuralists viewed language as a "habit"—an overlearned response, mastered by imitation and reinforcement. In essence, these linguists viewed human beings as uncomplicated organisms who learned sentence patterns and words to fill them by means of vaguely defined powers of memory and association. This position was probably most thoroughly articulated by the American psychologist B. F. Skinner (1904–1990) in his 1957 book *Verbal Behavior*, which applies the theory of stimulus–response conditioning to language. Under this view, something in the environment serves as a stimulus, which then acts upon the speaker, causing him or her to issue a response. This response in turn acts as another stimulus, and the cycle is repeated. In other words, language is essentially a conditioned response to external stimuli.

It's important to note, however, that not all American structural linguists were behaviorists. In contrast to Bloomfield and his followers, Edward Sapir (1884–1939) and the group he represented came out of anthropology and never adhered to rigid behaviorism. In fact, Sapir laid the groundwork for the study of language as a mental reality in his paper "La Réalité Psychologique des Phonemes" ("The Psychological Reality of Phonemes"), published in the *Journal de Psychologie* in 1933.

Sapir was trained by Franz Boas (1858–1942), whose major work was *Handbook of American Indian Languages*, published in 1911. Boas's main contribution to linguistics was to point out that the languages of primitive peoples are just as complex and systematic as European languages. Likewise, one of Sapir's best-known students was Benjamin Whorf (1897–1941). Whorf was intrigued by American Indian languages and spent years in the Southwest studying Aztec and Hopi. Based on his observations of American Indian languages, he and Sapir formed what has become known as the **Sapir–Whorf Hypothesis**: that the structure of a person's language (especially syntax and morphology, or word structure) influences nonlinguistic activity and the person's view of reality. This idea was developed in a series of articles written between 1936 and 1938. Even though now largely discredited, the Sapir–Whorf Hypothesis helped establish linguistics as a branch of the study of mind.

†Exercise F

One phenomenon often cited in support of the Sapir–Whorf Hypothesis is cross-linguistic differences in vocabulary. For example, Eskimo has many more words for snow than English does, and Arabic has many more words pertaining to sand. According to the Sapir–Whorf Hypothesis, we can conclude from such phenomena that Eskimo and Arabic allow speakers to make distinctions that English does not. What is a more plausible explanation of the same phenomena?

In short, Bloomfield and Sapir had dramatically different views of the role the mind played in language. Whereas Bloomfield felt the mind was essentially unstudiable, Sapir believed that the organization of perception was fundamental to the study of language. On the other hand, the parallels between the two men's careers are striking. Both published books entitled *Language*—Sapir in 1921 and Bloomfield in 1933. Moreover, both men taught at Yale, although their respective tenures did not overlap; Sapir was there from 1931 until his death in 1939, and Bloomfield was there from 1940 until his death in 1949.

†Exercise G

Consider the following quote:

> We sometimes hear it said that . . . the series of shifts . . . which have become celebrated under the name of "Grimm's Law" are merely mechanical processes, consummated by the organs of speech and by the nerves that control them. . . . It is my purpose . . . to indicate that the sounds and sound processes of speech cannot be properly understood in such simple, mechanical terms.

Who is more likely to have written this passage: Bloomfield or Sapir? Explain.

Exercise H

Consider the following quote:

> Every child acquires . . . habits of speech and response in the first years of his life. . . . Under various stimuli the child utters and repeats vocal sounds. . . . Suppose he makes a noise which we may represent as *da*. . . . The sound-vibrations strike the child's eardrums while he keeps repeating the movements. This results in a habit: whenever a similar sound strikes his ear, he is likely to make these same mouth-movements, repeating the sound *da*. . . . [Then] the mother . . . says *doll*. When these sounds strike the child's ear, his habit comes into play and he utters his nearest babbling syllable, *da*. We say that he is beginning to "imitate."

Who is most likely to have written this passage: Bloomfield or Sapir? Explain.

DESCRIPTIVISM VS. PRESCRIPTIVISM

The twentieth century in the United States saw an increased division between adherents to the traditional prescriptive approach and proponents of more descriptive, relativistic studies. Here we look at some representative studies of this type.

Exercise I

Consider the following quotation:

> The discrimination of elegant or "correct" speech is a by-product of certain social conditions. The linguist has to observe it as he observes other linguistic phenomena. . . . It is part of his task to find out . . . why, for example, many people say that *ain't* is "bad" and *am not* is "good." . . . Strangely enough, people without linguistic training devote a great deal of effort to futile discussions of this topic.

a. What is the topic of this quote?
b. What is the likely linguistic orientation of the author?

One of the earliest studies of usage in America was *Modern English: Its Growth and Present Use* by George Philip Krapp (1872–1934). Edward Finegan, in his book *Attitudes Toward English*, identifies four areas in which Krapp broke ground. First, his work provided the first systematic view of the relativity of correctness—that is, the notion that usage can be judged as "appropriate" or "inappropriate" for a particular speaker in a particular situation, rather than as a matter of absolute right or wrong. Under this view, for example, *It is I* would be appropriate in a highly formal situation, while *It is me* would be appropriate in a more casual situation. Second, Krapp argued for the primacy of spoken language over written language. (Recall that the prescriptivists assumed the opposite.) Third, he argued for the **doctrine of usage**, stating that "the grammarian has no more power of legislating in the rules of grammar than the scientist has in the physical laws of nature" (Krapp, p. 322). He also raised the question of whose usage is standard.

Fourth, and perhaps most important, Krapp distinguished between "good" English and "standard" English. Good English was defined as the effective, appropriate use of the language that was comfortable for the speaker. This concept stood in contrast to standard, conventional English, that form which has been elevated to "conscious legalized use" (p. 331). Under this distinction, for example, usages such as *It is me* and *Who did you talk to?* would be considered "good" English, even though they violate prescriptive rules. Krapp further argued that "standard English must continually refresh itself by accepting the creations of good English. . . . If the standardizing tendency were carried to its fullest extent, it would result in a complete fixity of language" (p. 333).

Exercise J

Examine the last quotation from Krapp.

a. How does his view compare to that of the eighteenth-century prescriptive grammarians?

b. One could argue that Krapp's views reflect a more "American" approach to grammar. How so?

Another group of important usage studies in the twentieth-century United States were those sponsored by the National Council of Teachers of English (NCTE), founded in 1911. We will examine two of these in some detail, again basing our discussion on the data examined by Finegan.

Current English Usage, by Sterling Leonard, was significant because it based its findings on a usage survey. In particular, 102 debated usage items were sent to seven types of respondents: linguistics experts, leading businessmen, authors, editors of influential publications, NCTE members, members of the Modern Language Association (MLA), and speech teachers. Respondents were asked to classify items according to their observations about actual usage, placing the items into three categories:

(1) "literary," or formally correct, English;

(2) "standard," cultivated colloquial English;

(3) "naive," popular, uneducated English.

Categories (1) and (2), in other words, were deemed acceptable for use by educated people.

Based on the responses, Leonard placed the usage items into three categories:

- **"Established"** items were those judged as (1) or (2) by at least 75 percent of the respondents.
- **"Disputable"** items were those judged as (1) or (2) by an intermediate number of respondents, between 25 and 75 percent.
- **"Illiterate"** items were those judged as (1) or (2) by fewer than 25 percent.

Exercise (3) in the Supplementary Exercises at the end of this chapter includes some of the items surveyed by Leonard.

Another important work commissioned by the NCTE, with support from MLA and the Linguistic Society of America, was Charles C. Fries's *American English Grammar*. Fries's method of collecting data was different from Leonard's in several ways. First, Fries based his study on actual letters written by Americans who were corresponding with the government; he examined 3000 letters or excerpts in all. Second, Fries began by using independent (i.e., nonlinguistic) grounds to classify the writers into three social groupings.

- **Speakers of "Standard English":** college graduates engaged in professions (professors, physicians, lawyers, judges); Army officers above the rank of lieutenant; school superintendents and newspaper editors from cities of 25,000 or more.

- **Speakers of "Common English":** those having completed between one year of high school and one year of college or technical school; neither professionals nor unskilled laborers (e.g., businessmen, electricians, police chiefs, nurses, Army sergeants, shop foremen).
- **Speakers of "Vulgar English":** persons who had not gone past eighth grade and who held strictly manual or unskilled jobs.

Fries's methodology was important because he inferred the linguistic traits of each group only after examining the group's educational and professional traits. Thereby, according to Finegan, "The vicious circle of defining correct English as the usage of the cultured and defining the cultured by their usage was finally broken" (p. 98).

Some of Fries's findings, as summarized by Finegan, include the following. First, all three groups used singular sentence openers such as *There is/There was/There has* before plural nouns. Second, constructions such as *these kind of/those sort of* were used by writers of Standard English, although such structures had been labeled as "disputable" in Leonard's survey. Third, Fries found no cases of *whom* as an interrogative (e.g., *Whom should we contact?*). However, Standard English writers used *whom* in about two-thirds of the appropriate relative pronoun constructions (e.g., *I have one child <u>whom</u> I have not seen*). Fourth, structures such as *she don't* and *it don't* were used by about 30 percent of the Common English writers and more often by Vulgar English writers, but never by writers of Standard English.

A final work that deserves our attention is the NCTE volume *The English Language Arts*, published in 1952. This work represents an official endorsement of the principles established by Krapp, Leonard, Fries, and other descriptive linguists: namely, language changes constantly; change is normal; spoken language *is* the language; correctness rests upon usage; and all usage is relative. Not surprisingly, however, the response by many to this document was one of alarm and antagonism:

> Such was the protest against *The English Language Arts*, . . . so truculent and widespread the dissent, that we may seriously question whether the influence of Council leaders reached significantly into the membership ranks; and if it did, then we must doubt that these teachers transferred their views to their students. (Finegan, p. 109)

Indeed, speculates Finegan, the backlash against this work and others promoting the doctrine of usage has continued into the second half of the twentieth century.

Exercise K

Writing in 1960, Professor John C. Sherwood, director of Freshman Composition at the University of Oregon, described the "new grammar" (i.e., the view espoused by *The English Language Arts*) as follows:

> . . . it stands for democracy; for spontaneity, self-expression, and permissiveness; for nominalism; for skepticism; for a social-scientific view of life; for progress and modernity; for nationalism and regionalism. It is "other-directed," seeing the proper standard of conduct as conformity to the mores of the group. It represents a linguistic Rousseauism, a belief that man's language is best and most real when most spontaneous and unpremeditated and that it is somehow tainted by the efforts of educational systems to order and regularize it. Just as the old grammar tried to take its values from above, the new tries to deduce them, in the manner of Dr. Kinsey, from the facts. (p. 277)

a. Does Sherwood seem to endorse or condemn the "new grammar"? What is your evidence?

b.† Look up *nominalism* and *Rousseauism*. What is the meaning of each of these words? In what way do these words apply to the "new grammar"?

c. If you are not familiar with Dr. Alfred Charles Kinsey, consult an encyclopedia to find out who he was and what the subject of the "Kinsey Report" was. What message and attitude does Sherwood convey by comparing *The English Language Arts* to the Kinsey Report?

Summary

The study of language became "scientific" in the late eighteenth century with William Jones's discovery that Sanskrit was genetically related to Latin and Greek. This discovery led to numerous historical–comparative studies where relationships among the Indo-European languages, such as Grimm's Law, were observed. In contrast to such diachronic studies, Saussure developed synchronic linguistics: the idea that each language constituted a self-contained system or "structure," whose fundamental psychological unit was the sign. Bloomfield developed structuralism within the context of behaviorist psychology, while Sapir developed it within the context of cultural anthropology. As structuralism developed within "theoretical" linguistics, descriptivism developed as its "applied" side. Descriptivist studies concentrated on questions of usage and focused on the following points: (1) usage is relative: "appropriate" or "inappropriate" according to context, not right or wrong; (2) usage varies among social groups; and (3) usage changes over time.

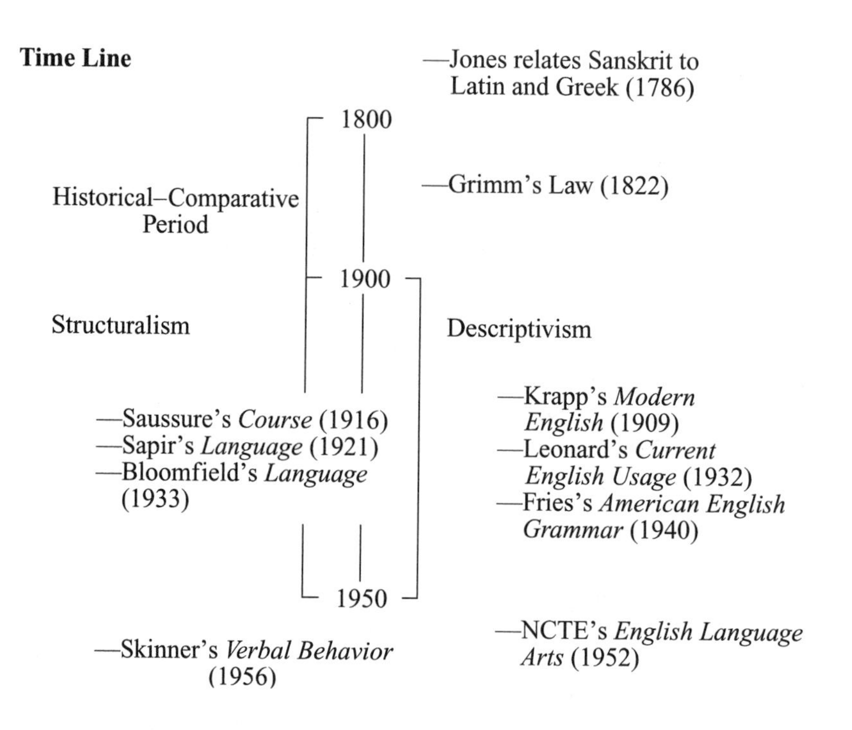

SUPPLEMENTARY EXERCISES

1. Characterize the difference between a course called "Modern English Grammar" and one called "History of the English Language" in terms of Saussure's distinction between diachronic and synchronic linguistics.
2. Finnish has no grammatical contrasts reflecting natural gender (i.e., sex differences between males and females). According to the Sapir–Whorf Hypothesis, what would this fact about the Finnish language say about Finnish speakers?
3. Below are some of the usage items that Leonard asked respondents to judge.

   a. Determine exactly what it is about each item that might be subject to dispute.
   b. Use Leonard's categories (1), (2), and (3) to rate each item.
   c. Pool your results with those of your classmates. Based on group percentages, determine if each item should be labeled as "established," "disputable," or "illiterate."
   d. Compare the results that you and your classmates arrive at with the ratings arrived at by Leonard's respondents. (Your instructor will provide these for you.) How, if at all, do the two sets of results differ?

1. John had awoken much earlier than usual.
2. A woman whom I know was my friend spoke next.
3. Everybody bought their own ticket.
4. It don't make any difference what you think.
5. A treaty was concluded between the four powers.
6. It is me.
7. That's a dangerous curve; you'd better go slow.
8. I enjoy wandering among a library.
9. One rarely likes to do as he is told.
10. The British look at this differently than we do.
11. Who are you looking for?
12. None of them are here.
13. The data is often inaccurate.
14. Everyone was here, but they all went home early.
15. Invite whoever you like to the party.
16. They swang their partners in the reel [square dance].
17. Neither of your reasons are really valid.
18. She sung very well.
19. He dove off the pier.
20. Martha don't sew as well as she used to.
21. It says in the book that . . .

▲▲▲ CHAPTER 5

Identifying Parts of Speech

Throughout this book, we have been using grammatical terms such as *noun*, *verb*, and *preposition*; however, we have not always identified a systematic procedure for placing a given word into a particular grammatical category. This chapter offers a number of tests for identifying the category, or part of speech, that a word belongs to. We will start by looking at the general kinds of evidence that descriptive grammarians use to classify a word into a particular category. Then we will look at specific tests used to place words into particular parts of speech.

THE NEED FOR STRUCTURAL TESTS

In studying grammar prior to this course, you probably encountered a semantic, or meaning-based, definition of the different parts of speech. This approach to classifying words is generally associated with prescriptive grammar. For example, some commonly used semantic definitions for **noun** and **verb** are given below.

> Noun: a word used to name anything
> Verb: a word used to express action or being
> (Adapted from House & Harman, pp. 20 and 93)

Some words seem to fit neatly within these definitions. For example, words like *shirt, horse*, and *Frank* easily fit the semantic definition of noun, since they name specific entities in the real world. Similarly, words like *run* and *hit* easily fit the semantic definition of verb, since they express actions.

On the other hand, we run into problems with semantic definitions when we move beyond these clear-cut cases. For example, consider the words *love*, *honesty*, and *determination*. All these words are classified as nouns, yet they name a "thing" only in the broadest interpretation of the term. In fact, including the word "anything" in the definition of *noun* renders the definition so vague that it is virtually useless. Likewise, is a word like *jogging* best classified as a noun, or as a verb? It names a "thing" that many people do, yet it also expresses an "action."

Moreover, semantic definitions fail to account for our intuitive ability to classify new words as nouns, verbs, or other parts of speech, since we may not even know the meaning of a new word. The following excerpt from Lewis Carroll's poem "Jabberwocky" is often used to illustrate this point.

> 'Twas brillig, and the slithy toves
> Did gyre and gimble in the wabes

A native speaker of English who is familiar with basic grammatical terminology can intuitively classify *toves* as a noun and *gyre* as a verb. We can do this even if we cannot identify the "thing" that *toves* names or the "action" that *gyre* expresses. Clearly, then, we must be relying on something besides semantic information to classify words into categories.

Exercise A

> Referring again to the "Jabberwocky" passage, what part of speech does each of the following words seem to be: *brillig, slithy, gimble, wabes*? What sort of reasoning can you use to defend your analysis of each one?

In short, the semantic definitions associated with prescriptive grammar work in some cases, but are too limited and imprecise for classifying a great many other words. For this reason, descriptive grammarians have devised a different approach for classifying words into parts of speech. Instead of focusing on the meaning of a word, the descriptive approach tends to focus more on the word's form and behavior: properties such as the endings that can be attached to the word, its ability to occur in the same phrase as certain other words, and so on. The underlying assumption is that if two words behave the same way under the same test, they should be classified as the same part of speech. For example, if two words can both take an ending that is associated with nouns, then we have evidence that they should be classified as nouns.

With this general principle in mind, let's look at some of the structural tests used to identify particular parts of speech.

IDENTIFYING THE FORM CLASSES

One useful concept introduced by the descriptive grammarians is the distinction between form classes and structure classes. The **form classes** are those that carry the primary meaning in a sentence: nouns, verbs, adjectives, and adverbs. They are called *form classes* because they change "form" (e.g., *boy/boys*). In contrast, the **structure classes** are those whose primary function is to build grammatical structure rather than convey meaning. The structure classes include pronouns, conjunctions, auxiliary verbs, determiners, and prepositions. They are called *structure* *classes* because they provide supporting "structure" for the form classes (e.g., *from boys, with boys, to boys*). An often used analogy is that the form classes are the "bricks" of a sentence, while the structure classes are the "mortar" that holds the bricks together.

In this section we will focus on four types of tests used to identify the form classes: inflection, derivation, co-occurrence, and pro-forms.

Inflection

An **affix** is a form that can be attached to the beginning or end of a word, typically a noun, verb, adjective, or adverb. An affix attached to the beginning is called a **prefix**; an affix attached to the end is called a **suffix**. An **inflection** is a suffix that modifies the form of a noun, verb, or adjective, without changing the class of the word. English has eight **inflectional affixes**:

Noun +	
plural	*boys*
possessive	*boy's*

Adjective +	
comparative	*taller*
superlative	*tallest*

Verb +	
3rd-person singular	*he walks*
past tense	*he walked*
past participle	*he has walked*
present participle	*he is walking*

The inflectional affixes provide one test for classifying a word as a noun, verb, or adjective. For example, a word that permits the plural inflection is a noun; a word that permits the present participle inflection is a verb; a word that permits the comparative inflection is an adjective; and so on.

Note that the examples given above represent **regular** cases of the inflectional affixes. English also has a number of **irregular** cases in which a noun, verb, or adjective undergoes the effect of inflection without displaying a predictable change in form. For example, while the plural of *girl* is *girls* (a regular case), the plural of *woman* is *women* (not **womans*). Likewise, while the past tense of *talk* is *talked* (a regular case), the past tense of *sing* is *sang* (an irregular case). Despite their unpredictable form, irregular cases are nevertheless treated as analogous to regular cases, for the purposes of identifying the category of a word. For example, one piece of evidence that *woman* is a noun is that it has a plural form, even though that form is not inflected with an *-s*.

Inflection is a fairly good test for some parts of speech. For example, all verbs accept the present participle inflection. However, the test is not foolproof. For example, consider the words *honesty* and *determination*. Although these words are traditionally classified as nouns, they cannot be pluralized: compare **honesties* and **determinations*. (Recall that an asterisk designates a form that is unacceptable to native speakers for some reason.) On the other hand, they do not pass the structural tests for any other parts of speech. For example, the forms **honestier* and **determinationing* are likewise unacceptable; thus *honesty* and *determination* are neither adjectives nor verbs. Because of cases like these, we need additional evidence beyond the inflection test.

Exercise B

Which of the following nouns can or cannot be made plural?

a. information	f. money
b. Marilyn Monroe	g. dollar
c. product	h. advice
d. research	i. suggestion
e. evidence	

Derivation

A second type of evidence useful for classifying words comes from **derivational affixes**. Any suffix that is not inflectional is, by process of elimination, derivational. In addition, all prefixes are derivational. It turns out that derivational affixes offer two kinds of evidence for classifying parts of speech.

Unlike inflectional suffixes, derivational suffixes frequently change the category of the word they are attached to. For example, *critic* is a noun, but *criticize* is a verb. In some cases, we can identify a word as a particular part of speech because of the presence of a certain derivational affix. For example, the suffixes {-ion} and {-ment} occur only on nouns: *production*, *accomplishment*, and so on. Likewise, the suffix {-able} (or {-ible}) occurs only on adjectives: *likeable, flexible,* and so on.

In other cases, we can identify a word as a particular part of speech because it accepts a certain derivational affix. For example, {-ment} attaches only to verbs (changing them into nouns, e.g., *pavement*); {-ness} attaches only to adjectives (changing them into nouns, e.g., *happiness*); {-ful} attaches only to nouns (changing them into adjectives, e.g., *peaceful*). We can say with certainty that a word to which we can attach {-ment} is a verb; a word to which we can attach {-ness} is an adjective; and a word to which we can attach {-ful} is a noun.

However, like the inflection test, the derivation test is not foolproof. For example, the suffix {-ly} can be added to both adjectives (e.g., *noisy/noisily*) and nouns (e.g., *man/manly*). In the first case, it yields an adverb; in the second case, an adjective. Therefore, it's useful to have additional tests.

Exercise C

a. What's the evidence that *do-able* as in *That's just not do-able* is an adjective?
b. What part of speech is *friendly*? Provide evidence.

Co-occurrence

In addition to inflection and derivation, which change the actual form of a word, descriptive grammarians also introduced the idea of co-occurrence as a test for categorizing a word. **Co-occurrence** refers to the items that can precede or follow the word under question. For example, only a noun can occur in the following frame:

Article ______________ verb phrase

For example, only a noun (e.g., *sofa*) can fit in the frame *The* ________ *is here.* Likewise, only a verb can occur in the following test frames:

Don't ______________ .

You must ______________ .

Again, however (as you may have guessed by now), we must note that not all co-occurrence tests are foolproof. For example, the following looks like a good co-occurrence test for adjectives:

Article ______________ Noun

This test frame does, indeed, allow for adjectives: for example, *the red sofa, a cold drink*). However, other categories will also fit into this slot: for example, nouns (e.g., *a stone wall, a horse trailer)*. We can conclude that all adjectives will fit into this test frame, but the opposite is not true: a word is not necessarily an adjective because it fits into this frame. Instead, it may be an **adjectival**: a word that is not necessarily an adjective but that appears in a position normally occupied by an adjective. (Adjectivals are discussed in more detail in Chapter 8.)

Exercise D

Consider the phrase *a brick house.*

a. Provide structural evidence that *brick* is or is not an adjective.
b. Explain why a semantically based definition of "adjective" is inadequate for answering this question.

Exercise E

Walk is both a noun and a verb.

a.† What part of speech is it in the sentence *He walked home*? What is your evidence?

b. What part of speech is it in the sentence *He might walk home*? What is your evidence?
c.† What part of speech is it in the sentence *A walk is good exercise*? What is your evidence?
d. What part of speech is it in the sentence *We used to go for long walks*? What is your evidence?

Pro-forms

There is a fourth type of evidence that can be used to place a given item into a particular category: whether a particular pro-form can be substituted for the item. A **pro-form** is a word that replaces another part of speech, usually an antecedent that occurred earlier in the same sentence or stretch of discourse (e.g., earlier in the same paragraph or conversation). The affix *pro-* means 'for,' so a pro-form is a form that stands in "for" another word or phrase.

One pro-form you are probably familiar with is the **pronoun**. Unfortunately, the term *pronoun* is not quite accurate, for a pronoun actually substitutes for a noun phrase (NP) rather than for a noun (N). For example, consider the following sentence.

1. That mysterious man from the CIA was looking for you, but he left.

If *he* were truly a "pro-noun," it would substitute for the noun in the preceding phrase, *man*. However, we get an ungrammatical sentence if we change the second clause to reflect this substitution.

1a. *That mysterious man from the CIA was looking for you, but that mysterious he from the CIA left.

Nor does *he* seem to substitute for the string *mysterious man*, as shown by (1b).

1b. *That mysterious man from the CIA was looking for you, but that he from the CIA left.

Nor does *he* seem to substitute for the string *That mysterious man*, as shown by (1c).

1c. *That mysterious man from the CIA was looking for you, but he from the CIA left.

Instead, *he* substitutes for the entire string *That mysterious man from the CIA*, as shown in our original sentence (1). In other words, *he* substitutes for an entire NP, not just for a noun. A more accurate name for pronouns, then, would be "pro-NPs."

You may be wondering how to reconcile this interpretation of pronouns with the following data.

2. John was looking for you, but he left.

Here *he* does appear to substitute for a noun, *John*. We are faced with something of a dilemma. Do we want to say that pronouns sometimes substitute for NPs, but other times substitute for nouns? The problem with this approach is that it does not predict which type of substitution will occur when.

An alternative approach is to say that pronouns always substitute for NPs, and that *John* is, in fact, an NP. The latter claim may seem counter-intuitive, because we are used to thinking of phrases as necessarily containing more than one word. However, it is possible to define **phrase** so that it can include both *John* and *that mysterious man from the CIA*. We can define a phrase as a unit that must contain a **headword** and that may also (optionally) contain **pre-** and **post-modifiers** of the headword (i.e., modifiers that precede or follow the headword). The headword of a phrase, in turn, is defined as the part of speech for which the phrase is named. For example, the head of a noun phrase (NP) is a noun (N); the head of a prepositional phrase is a preposition; and so on. We can think of the headword as the "nucleus" of the phrase; other items can occur before or after it, but the headword is the only essential element in the phrase.

In the case of *John*, the NP consists solely of the headword *John*; there are no pre- or post-modifiers. In the case of *that mysterious man from the CIA*, the NP consists of the headword *man*, along with pre-modifiers (*that mysterious*) and post-modifiers (*from the CIA*).

It turns out that English contains a number of other pro-forms which, like pronouns, actually substitute for phrasal categories. Some of these are listed below.

- Pro-Verb Phrase: *do; do so; so*
  3. John wants to <u>close early</u>, but I don't think we should <u>do so</u>.
  4. If those people can <u>pass this course</u>, <u>so</u> can you.
- Pro-Adjective Phrase: *so*
  5. We were afraid the weather would be <u>too hot</u>, but we didn't find it <u>so</u>.
- Pro-Prepositional Phrase: *then, there*
  6. Bring in your homework <u>on Monday</u> and I'll look at it <u>then</u>.
  7. Put the car <u>in the garage</u> and leave it <u>there</u>.

As these examples illustrate, pronouns are a special case of a more general category, pro-form. English allows for pro-forms to substitute for a number of phrasal categories, not only for NPs.

Exercise F

a. Consider the sentence *Some woman on the bus this morning said she was being followed*. What's the antecedent for *she*? What type of category is it?

b.† Consider the sentence *She went to the library, and I did too*. What's the antecedent for *did*? What type of category is it?

c. Consider the sentence *She went to the library, and I went there too.* What's the antecedent for *there*? What type of category is it?
d. Consider the sentence *She went to the library, and so did I.* What's the antecedent for *did*? What type of category is it?

General Characteristics of the Form Classes

In addition to the properties just discussed, form class words (i.e., nouns, verbs, adjectives, and adverbs) display several other characteristics that distinguish them from structure class words (i.e., prepositions, pronouns, conjunctions, interjections, determiners, and auxiliary verbs).

- **Form classes are open sets.** New members can be added by borrowing from other languages (e.g., *chic* comes from French) or by word-formation methods such as compounding (e.g., *sightsee* from *sight* + *see*), clipping (e.g., *bra* from *brassiere*), and blending (e.g., *smog* from *smoke* + *fog*). However, it is difficult to find a structure class word, such as a preposition, that we have borrowed from another language.
- **Form classes often undergo functional shift.** For example, a noun may function adjectivally, as in the phrase *a <u>stone</u> wall.* However, it is hard to find a structure class word, such as a conjunction, functioning as another part of speech.
- **Form class words need not co-occur with structure class words.** For example, not all nouns require an article (e.g., *honesty*); likewise, not all verbs require an auxiliary (e.g., *drove*). However, articles always require nouns, and auxiliary verbs always require main verbs.

Exercise G

Consider the italicized forms in the following sentences. For each one, provide at least two types of evidence (inflection, derivation, co-occurrence, or pro-form substitution) to determine what part of speech it is.

a. We were *outfoxed* by our opponents.
b. They *decorated* their front door with a wreath, and so did their neighbors.
c. He is one of the most *decorated* soldiers in history.
d. She sings *beautifully*.

IDENTIFYING THE STRUCTURE CLASSES

In this section we will concentrate on the so-called "function words" or structure classes: pronouns, conjunctions, auxiliary verbs, determiners, and prepositions.

The first three of these will be dealt with in later chapters; for now, we will focus on some of the properties of determiners and prepositions.

All structure classes comprise closed sets with a fairly small number of members. For this reason, we do not have to worry so much about developing tests that allow us to identify new members of these classes. Instead, we will survey some of the general traits that the structure classes share and look more closely at determiners and prepositions.

General Characteristics of the Structure Classes

In the previous section we looked at some general characteristics of form class words. We can start here by surveying the general characteristics of the structure classes.

- **Structure classes are closed sets.** In contrast with the form classes, the structure classes rarely add new members. While form classes are large (and, in fact, have a potentially infinite size), structure classes have a relatively small and finite number of members (e.g., conjunctions include *and, but, or,* and a handful of other words).
- **Structure classes generally do not change form.** The conjunction *and,* for example, takes no inflectional or derivational affixes. (The exception to this general rule is the auxiliary verbs, which can have both tensed and participial forms.) In contrast, as we have seen, form class words can undergo changes in form by means of inflection and derivation.
- **Structure classes occur in a limited and fixed position with respect to the associated form class words.** For example, determiners normally occur only as the first item in a noun phrase (e.g., *the coffee*).
- **Structure class words do not tend to undergo functional shift.** A form class word like *horse* can function not only as a noun (*That horse is fast*) but also as an adjectival (*We bought a horse trailer*) or a verbal (*They are horsing around*). In contrast, structure class words tend to serve only their primary function.
- **Structure classes must co-occur with form class words.** For example, although not all nouns require an article, all articles require a noun.

Let's now take a closer look at two structure classes: determiners and prepositions.

Determiners

The most important members of the determiner category are **articles** (*the, a/an*), **demonstratives** (*this, that, these, those*), **possessives** (*my, our, your, his, her, its*), and **quantifiers** (*each, every, all, some*). In this section we will focus on some properties of the articles.

Most of us are used to classifying articles as **definite** (*the*) and **indefinite** (*a/an*). The definite article is used when the referent of an NP is thought to be uniquely identifiable, for one reason or another. One reason is that the referent has been previously introduced in the discourse. For example, consider (8).

8. They own a Thoroughbred and a Quarter Horse. *The Thoroughbred* used to be a racehorse.

The definite NP *the Thoroughbred* refers to a particular referent that has been previously introduced in the first sentence in (8).

Definite articles are also used when the speaker treats the NP as having a unique referent and assumes that the listener will share this understanding. For example, compare (9a) and (9b):

9a. Their horse won *the Kentucky Derby.*
9b. Their horse won *a valuable horse race.*

In (9a) the definite article *the* is used as part of the NP *the Kentucky Derby*, since there is only one Kentucky Derby—the NP has a unique referent. In contrast, (9b) uses the indefinite article *a*. This sentence is not part of a larger stretch of discourse, so no referent for *a valuable horse race* has been previously introduced. In addition, there is not a unique referent for this NP, since there are many valuable horse races to which the speaker could be referring.

The definite article is also used when the speaker treats the NP as referring to an entity that is unique in a particular context. For example, consider a situation in which a speaker and listener are in a room containing one cat and one sofa. In this context, the sentence *Get the cat off the sofa* would be appropriate, since there is a uniquely identifiable referent for both *cat* and *sofa* (note that the definite article can be used for both of those NPs). In contrast, a sentence like *Get me a pillow from the sofa* would be appropriate for a context containing one sofa with more than one pillow.

Finally, the definite article is used when an NP is identifiable as part of a larger whole, which in turn has been previously mentioned in the discourse or is identifiable from the context. For example, consider the sentence *We looked at a used car on Sunday, but the body needed too much work.* The use of the definite article in the NP *the body* is appropriate because the body is identifiable as part of the larger whole—the car itself—which in turn has been mentioned earlier in the discourse.

Exercise H

Fill in each blank with the article that sounds most natural to you (*a, an,* or *the*). (Do not spend a lot of time making this decision; just use your "gut reaction.") Then identify the principle that accounts for each of your choices. If two choices are possible for any of the blanks, try to identify the information you would need to make a choice between them.

a. You shouldn't stare at ________ sun during ________ eclipse.
b. Here comes Beverly, acting like ________ Queen of Sheba.
c. On Sunday we looked at ___________ house that's on ___________ market, but ________ back yard was too small.
d. Waiter, there's ________ fly in my soup!
e. We'll need ________ chain saw to cut down that tree.

When dealing with indefinite articles, it is useful to make a further distinction between **specific** and **nonspecific** reference. Consider the following sentences.

10a. Annie wants to buy *a horse*; so far, she has looked at several.
10b. Annie wants to buy *a horse*; it's a very nice Thoroughbred.

Both sentences contain an indefinite NP, *a horse*. However, (10a) contains a **nonspecific** NP, since the phrase *a horse* does not refer to a particular entity. In contrast, (10b) contains a **specific** NP, since the phrase *a horse* does refer to a particular entity. Therefore, we would label *a horse* in (10a) as indefinite and nonspecific; we would label *a horse* in (10b) as indefinite and specific.

The following sentences contain further examples of NPs that are indefinite yet specific:

11. *A candidate for the job* called up and withdrew his application.
12. There is *a new novel by P.D. James* at the library.
13. I know I have *a corkscrew* around here somewhere.

As these examples illustrate, an indefinite NP is specific if the speaker has a particular referent in mind.

Exercise I

a.† Consider the sentence *John is looking for a dog*. Discuss *a dog* from the perspective of both definiteness and specificity.

b. Consider the sentence *John is looking for that dog*. Discuss *that dog* from the perspective of both definiteness and specificity.

c. Consider the sentence *John is looking for a dog*. Discuss *John* from the perspective of both definiteness and specificity.

Prepositions

Prepositions form a fairly extensive, but still finite, group of words that usually indicate location, direction, or time. Some of the more common prepositions are listed below:

about	below	in	past
above	between	into	under
after	by	of	until
along	down	off	up
around	for	on	with
at	from	over	without
before			

A **prepositional phrase** (PP) consists of a preposition followed by a noun phrase (NP). Thus, the headword of a PP is a preposition, just as the headword of an NP is a noun. For example, the PP *up a big hill* consists of the preposition *up* followed by the NP *a big hill.* The headword of the PP is *up*; the object of the preposition is *a big hill.*

Exercise J

> According to House and Harman, a preposition is a "word . . . used with a noun or pronoun . . . to form a phrase" (p. 174). In light of this definition, consider the phrase *tall weeds*. What's the problem with House and Harman's definition of preposition?

Some words used as prepositions also serve another role: as particles. A **particle** is a word that looks like a preposition but that actually forms part of a verb phrase. For example, consider the following two sentences, both containing the word *up*.

14. John ran *up* a big hill.

15. John ran *up* a big bill.

Both sentences appear to contain a PP, since *up* is followed by a noun phrase in both cases. Actually, though, *up* is a preposition only in sentence (14). In sentence (15), it's a particle. Fortunately, there are several structural tests for differentiating a preposition from a particle.

First of all, particles can generally be moved to the right of any noun phrase that follows them; prepositions cannot. This is shown by the contrast between (14a) and (15a) when we try this operation.

14a. *John ran a big hill *up.*

15a. John ran a big bill *up.*

Second, a prepositional phrase can generally be **fronted**, that is, moved to the initial position in its sentence. A sequence of **particle-direct object**, in contrast, cannot. Compare (14b) and (15b).

14b. *Up a big hill* John ran.

15b. **Up a big bill* John ran.

Third, a prepositional phrase can generally be replaced by a pro-form such as *there* (if the phrase describes a place) or *then* (if the phrase describes a time). A particle-direct object string, on the other hand, cannot. For example, compare (14c) and (15c).

14c. John ran *there.*

15c. *John ran *there.*

Although (15c) is the same sentence as (14c), (15c) is marked as ungrammatical to indicate that it is not an acceptable substitute for (15), *John ran up a big bill.*

In short, prepositions and particles may have the same external form, but they behave like two different parts of speech.

Exercise K

Consider the italicized words in the following sentences. Identify each as a particle or preposition. Give evidence for your answers.

a.† i. John wrote *down* my address.
ii. John walked *down* my street.

b. i. Throw *out* the trash.
ii. Walk *out* the door.

c. i. Did he turn *in* the driveway?
ii. Did he turn *in* his paper?

Summary

The main points covered in this chapter are outlined in the following table.

Parts of Speech

Form Classes (e.g., noun, verb, adjective)	Structure Classes (e.g., conjunction, preposition)
• open sets	• closed sets
• change form	• do not change form
• undergo functional shift	• do not undergo functional shift
• occurs independently of structure words	• occur only with form class words

Identifying Form Classes

Inflection: Does the word take a characteristic inflection for a particular form class? (e.g., the plural inflection indicates a noun)

Derivation: Does the word take a characteristic derivation for a particular form class? (e.g., *-able* indicates an adjective)

Co-occurrence: Does the word fit a characteristic frame for a particular form class? (e.g., *Don't* ______ indicates a verb)

Pro-form: Can the word be replaced by a pro-form characteristic of a particular form class? (e.g., *He* indicates an NP)

Identifying Structure Classes

Determiners: articles (e.g., *the*), demonstratives (e.g., *this*), possessives (e.g., *my*), quantifiers (e.g., *every*)

Definite: unique referent (e.g., *The Earth*)

Specific: particular referent (e.g., *I married a Norwegian*)

Prepositions: Cannot move to the right of a direct object (e.g., **run a street down*)

Particles: Can move to the right of a direct object (e.g., *run an informant down*)

SUPPLEMENTARY EXERCISES

1. Aphasia is a brain disorder that affects language. In one type of disorder called Wernicke's aphasia, patients substitute **neologisms,** or nonsense words, for form class words. For example, one patient with Wernicke's aphasia was heard to say, *"That's a bangahochapee. That's what that is, isn't it?"* What part of speech is *bangahochapee*? What can you use as evidence?

2. Definite articles regularly appear in titles of books, plays, and movies (e.g., *The Spy Who Came in from the Cold, The Man Who Knew Too Much, The Best Years of Our Lives, The 39 Steps*). Can such usages be accounted for by any of the principles discussed in this chapter related to the use of definite and indefinite articles? If so, which ones? If not, what other principles would you suggest to account for such usages?

3. Review your answers to Exercise H. Identify each article as definite or indefinite. Further classify any indefinite articles as specific or nonspecific.

4. In experiments conducted by Warden (1976), subjects of different ages were asked to look at drawings and construct a story from them. Over half of the 3-year-olds began their stories with structures like the following:

A. *The* cat was chasing *the* bird. *The* bird flew away from *the* cat.

In contrast, over 80 percent of the 9-year-olds and 100 percent of the adults began their stories with structures like the following:

B. *A* cat was chasing *a* bird. *The* bird flew away from *the* cat.

What principle about the use of definite articles has been acquired by the older subjects, but not by the 3-year-olds?

5. Use the tests described in this chapter to decide if the italicized phrase in each of the following sentences is a verb-particle combination or a verb followed by a preposition.

a. Bill *fell over* the trash can.
b. *Turn over* the trash can.
c. How many of us have the luxury of *turning down* a job offer?
d. We should have *turned down* the last street.
e. Jim is *heading up* the new committee.
f. Jim was *heading up* the stairs the last time I saw him.

6. Judy Reilly of UCLA recorded the following interchange between 6-year-old Jamie and his mother (cited in Moskowitz, 1979, p. 94):

Jamie:	Why are you doing that?
Mother:	What?
Jamie:	Why are you writing what I say down?
Mother:	What?
Jamie:	Why are you writing down what I say?

What syntactic principle has Jamie acquired?

7. Consider the following data:

A. I drive a Toyota and a Ford.	D. *I drive a Toyota and to school.
B. I drive to work and to school.	E. I drive carefully and slowly.
C. I drive to work and school.	F. *I drive carefully and to work.

Based on these data, what generalization can you make about whether two items (words or phrases) can be conjoined with *and*? (Your generalization should account for why D and F are ungrammatical.)

▲▲▲ CHAPTER 6

Nouns and Pronouns

In Chapter 5 we looked at a range of tests for classifying words into parts of speech. In this chapter we will look more closely at various types of nouns and pronouns.

SUBCLASSES OF NOUNS

Nouns in English can be divided into several subcategories that, while semantically based, also correspond to structural differences.

Proper vs. Common

One preliminary distinction we can make among nouns is to classify them as either proper or common. **Proper nouns** are names of unique, specific entities: for example, *President Roosevelt, Thursday, Los Angeles, Asia, Fred.* **Common nouns**, in contrast, do not refer to unique entities: for example, *cat, honesty, computers*, and *mail* are all common nouns.

While the distinction between proper and common nouns is in one respect a semantic one (i.e., based on the meaning of the noun), it also corresponds to some differences in how the two subcategories behave. Generally speaking, proper nouns do not co-occur with determiners: for example, phrases such as **the President Roosevelt, *an Asia,* and **the Fred* are all ungrammatical. Likewise, proper nouns cannot generally be inflected for plurality, a fact that stems from their reference to a unique (and therefore presumably one-of-a-kind) entity.

English being the complex language that it is, of course, not all proper nouns adhere to these generalizations. For example, some geographical names and names of buildings can co-occur with determiners: *the Alps, the Atlantic, the Smithsonian Institute.*

Exercise A

The sentences below contain proper nouns.

a. Make a judgment in each case as to whether the determiner *the* can precede the proper noun. If so, write *the* in the appropriate space. If not, leave the space blank. Try to make your judgments as quickly as possible, based on your immediate reaction.

b. After you have worked through all the sentences, go back and examine the ones that can co-occur with *the.* Can you construct any principles that might explain why the determiner can be used for these cases? (You may need more than one principle to account for all the cases.)

i. Would you rather go to ______ Europe or ______ Bahamas on your vacation?

ii. ______ United States is experiencing severe thunderstorms. ______ East Coast was hit especially hard, as were many towns along ______ Mississippi River.

iii. Usually I work on ______ Wednesday, but ______ Wednesday after next is my birthday, so I'm taking the day off.

iv. We saw a play by ______ Arthur Miller at ______ Kennedy Center; ______ Clintons were there, too.

v. If you want to splurge, get a room at ______ Plaza Hotel in ______ New York City overlooking ______ Central Park.

vi. Their oldest son went to ______ Harvard, but their daughter is attending ______ University of Michigan, and their youngest son will be going to ______ Michigan State.

Count vs. Noncount

Common nouns may be further subdivided into count and noncount nouns. Like the distinction between proper and common nouns, we can discuss the distinction between count and noncount nouns from both a semantic and a structural perspective. **Count** nouns are those that can be pluralized and can co-occur with *many, these*, and *those*, all of which indicate plurality: for example, *those cats, these computers, many opinions*. On the other hand, **noncount** nouns (also known as **mass** nouns) cannot be pluralized and cannot co-occur with plural determiners such as *many, these*, and *those*: for example, **many information(s), *these furniture(s), *those coffee(s)*. However, mass nouns can co-occur with *much, little*, and *a great deal of*: *He didn't find much information; She has too little furniture; I drank a great deal of coffee last night.*

Exercise B

> The nouns *coffee, bread, flour, sugar,* and *water* are typically considered to be noncount nouns. However, consider the following usages. How can you account for the plural forms of these words in these examples? Consider in particular passage (b), which contains both singular and plural forms of *bread.*
>
> a.† "Read about our full range of coffees on page 22."
>
> b. "We literally lived on bread for weeks, but to our surprise, none of us gained an ounce. Why? Because unlike breads made from refined flours, which the body quickly converts into sugars, whole grain breads digest more slowly, and their rich flavors make high-fat spreads unnecessary." (Pizzorno, p. xv)
>
> c. "Mineral waters are growing in popularity in the United States."

As the preceding exercise illustrates, some nouns can function as both count and noncount nouns. Other examples of nouns with this capability include *time, personality, experience, exercise*, and *work.*

Exercise C

> Make up two sentences for each of the five nouns just listed: one in which the noun is used as a count noun, and one in which it is used as a mass noun.

Singular count nouns (e.g., *book*), plural count nouns (e.g., *books*), and mass nouns (e.g., *knowledge*) display some further distinctions when we look at other determiners. For example, all three types of nouns can co-occur with the definite article *the*. On the other hand, not all three can co-occur with the so-called "zero" article (i.e., in the absence of any article). A singular count noun cannot co-occur with the zero article: **Book is a bestseller*. However, plural count nouns and mass nouns can co-occur with the zero article: *Books are expensive these days; Knowledge is not the same as wisdom.*

Exercise D

Listed down the lefthand side of the chart below are six different determiners. Decide whether each determiner can co-occur with each noun type (singular count, plural count, and mass noun). If the determiner cannot co-occur with the noun type, construct an ungrammatical sentence to show this restriction. If the determiner can co-occur with the noun type, construct a grammatical sentence to illustrate the co-occurrence. You should end up with a total of 18 sentences (the first three are done as examples).

	Singular count noun (e.g., *book*)	**Plural count noun (e.g., *books*)**	**Mass noun (e.g., *knowledge*)**
indefinite article (*a/an*)†	*I bought a book about Ireland.*	**A books are expensive these days.*	May be grammatical with post-modifier: *A knowledge of grammar is useful* (cf. **A knowledge is useful*).
possessive pronoun (*my, your, his,* etc.)			
this/that			
every/each			
all			
such			

Regular vs. Irregular

As mentioned in Chapter 5, the regular process by which nouns in English are pluralized is signaled in spelling by adding the inflectional suffix *-s* or *-es*: for example, *cats, dogs, horses, glasses, matches*. Evidence that this is the regular process is the fact that new nouns in English are pluralized using this inflection (e.g., *That Mazda dealer has three Miatas for sale*).

Some English nouns, however, are pluralized irregularly. For example, *deer, sheep,* and *fish* exhibit "zero inflection," meaning that no suffix is added to signal the plural form. Still other Latinate words, such as *basis, cactus*, and *datum*, signal their plural via a change of form: *bases, cacti, data*.

PRONOUNS

As briefly explained in Chapter 5, pronouns are actually a special type of pro-form; they are words that substitute for NPs. In this section we will look in more detail at some of the types of pronouns in English.

Personal Pronouns

The most common pronouns in English are the **personal pronouns**. The personal pronouns, in turn, can be subdivided by case, number, and person, as shown below.

		1st person	**2nd person**	**3rd person**
Subjective	Singular	*I*	*you*	*he/she/it*
	Plural	*we*	*you*	*they*
Objective	Singular	*me*	*you*	*him/her/it*
	Plural	*us*	*you*	*them*

Case refers to the form that the pronoun takes depending on its function within a sentence. Subjective (or nominative) case is the form used when the pronoun substitutes for a subject NP: e.g., *He was yelling at Sally*. Objective case is the form used when the pronoun occurs as the object of a verb or preposition: e.g., *Harry was yelling at her*. **Number** refers to the form that the pronoun takes depending on whether it refers to one entity (singular) or more than one entity (plural). Finally, **person** refers to the form that the pronoun takes depending on whether it refers to the speaker (first person), the addressee (second person), or some other entity (third person).

Taken together, these three variables are used to identify each personal pronoun. For example, *me* is the first-person, singular, objective case personal pronoun. The third-person, singular pronouns can further be distinguished according to **gender**: masculine (*he/him*), feminine (*she/her*), or neuter (*it*).

Exercise E

Try to answer the following questions without referring to the chart above.

a. Specify the person, number, and case of each of the following pronouns: *we, she, her, them.*
b. Identify the pronoun(s) described by each set of terms.
   i. 2nd person, singular, objective case
   ii. 3rd person, plural, subjective case
   iii. 1st person, singular
   iv. 3rd person, singular, objective case, neuter

In addition to the subjective and objective case personal pronouns, we can also identify two types of possessive case (or genitive) personal pronouns, as shown below.

		Person		
		1st	**2nd**	**3rd**
Possessive (NP Function)	Singular	*mine*	*yours*	*his/hers/its*
	Plural	*ours*	*yours*	*theirs*
Possessive (Determiner Function)	Singular	*my*	*your*	*his/her/its*
	Plural	*our*	*your*	*their*

The first group of possessives pattern more like true pronouns, since they substitute for NPs and occur in NP positions: e.g., *Mine is the last office on the left*; *They still have some sandwiches, but we ate ours*. The second group of possessives, on the other hand, while commonly referred to as possessive pronouns, actually pattern more like determiners: they occur as part of an NP (rather than substituting for an NP), before the required head noun and before any optional adjectives: e.g., *my brilliant career, our mutual friend, its furry coat.*

Reflexive Pronouns

Reflexive pronouns are characterized by the suffix *-self* (singular) or *-selves* (plural). English contains eight reflexive pronouns.

	1st person	**2nd person**	**3rd person**
Singular	*myself*	*yourself*	*himself/herself/itself*
Plural	*ourselves*	*yourselves*	*themselves*

Generally speaking, reflexive pronouns occur in object position, having an **antecedent** earlier in the same clause. For example, a reflexive may serve as **direct object**, **indirect object**, or **object of a preposition**, as shown in the following examples. (The subscript numbers indicate the co-reference between the antecedent and the reflexive pronoun.)

1. Fred$_1$ nominated *himself*$_1$ for department head. (direct object)
2. Joan$_1$ threw *herself*$_1$ a party after she was promoted. (indirect object)
3. They$_1$ are drawing attention to *themselves*$_1$ with their rude behavior. (object of a preposition)

Reciprocal Pronouns

The reciprocal pronouns in English are *each other* and *one another*. Like reflexive pronouns, reciprocal pronouns generally occur only in object position.

4. Bob and I know *each other* well. (direct object)
5. The members of the committee argued with *one another* all morning. (object of a preposition)

Reciprocal pronouns can also be used in the possessive case, in which instance the possessive form functions like a determiner.

6. Do you have *each other's* phone numbers?

Prescriptive grammarians sometimes reserve *each other* for two referents and *one another* for more than two referents. For example, this rule would require *Bob and I know <u>each other</u> well* but *Bob, Amanda, and I know <u>one another</u> well.*

Demonstrative Pronouns

The demonstrative pronouns in English are *this, that, these*, and *those*. Demonstrative pronouns are subdivided according to number and proximity to the speaker:

	Close proximity	**Distant proximity**
Singular	*this*	*that*
Plural	*these*	*those*

Although normally referred to as demonstrative pronouns, these words can actually function as either determiners (i.e., pre-modifiers of nouns) or pronouns (i.e., substitutes for nouns). The following sentences illustrate their use as determiners.

7. <u>*This*</u> *ham* is good, but <u>*that*</u> *chicken* tastes spoiled.
8. I wouldn't recommend <u>*those*</u> *books*; <u>*these*</u> *articles* contain more up-to-date information.

In contrast, the demonstrative pronouns in the following sentences are being used as true pronouns.

9. *These* are the times that try men's souls.
10. It was stupid of you to do *that.*

Indefinite Pronouns

The indefinite pronouns in English comprise a group of words that generally indicate quantity or amount. They are call "indefinite" because they do not refer to a specific antecedent. Some of the more common members of this class include the following.

all	most
any	much
both	neither
each	no
either	nobody/no one
every/everyone/ everybody/everything	none
	nothing
few/fewer	one
little	several
many	some
more	somebody/someone/something

Like demonstratives, indefinite pronouns do not always function as true pronouns (i.e., as substitutes for NPs); some can serve as pre-noun modifiers: *The museum contains <u>many valuable objects</u>*. An indefinite pronoun functioning in this capacity is known as a **quantifier**, reflecting the fact that it indicates "quantity" or amount. In contrast, in the sentence *<u>Many</u> are called, but <u>few</u> are chosen*, *many* and *few* function as heads of their NPs.

A few additional points need to be made about these examples. First, note that we introduced the term *quantifier* to describe the function of *many* in phrases like *many valuable objects.* Since determiners and adjectives can also function as pre-noun modifiers, this raises the question of why we need an additional category. Recall the general principle of descriptive grammar introduced in Chapter 5: if two items behave differently under the same test, this is evidence that they should be classified as different parts of speech. In a phrase like *many valuable objects*, it would not be accurate to classify *many* as a determiner because it violates one of the co-occurrence patterns associated with that category. Only one determiner can occur per NP; however, we can have phrases like *the many valuable objects* or *these many valuable objects*, in which *many* co-occurs with a determiner. Therefore, *many* itself does not appear to be a determiner.

Why not classify *many* as an adjective, another category that can also appear before a noun? One piece of evidence in favor of this analysis would be that an NP can contain more than one adjective; thus, we might simply claim that *many* and *valuable* are both adjectives. However, there are some other pieces of evidence against classifying *many* as an adjective. First, it does not inflect for comparative or superlative the way that adjectives do (e.g., *larger, largest; more valuable, most valuable*). Second, other adjectives can occur in varying orders before a noun (e.g., *large, old, valuable objects; old, large, valuable objects*), but *many* (and other quantifiers) must occur in a fixed position after any determiners and before any adjectives (e.g., *the many large, old, valuable objects* is permissible, but not **the large, many, old valuable objects*). These tests make it fairly clear that *many* and other indefinite pronouns cannot be classified as either determiners or adjectives. For these reasons, it seems justifiable to place them instead into a separate quantifier category when they are serving as pre-noun modifiers.

Moreover, it is important to recognize a subtle distinction between the indefinite pronouns (e.g., *few*) and personal pronouns (e.g., *they*). We have established that personal pronouns substitute for entire NPs; in contrast, indefinite pronouns seem to substitute for *parts* of NPs. One piece of evidence for this is that indefinite pronouns (just like nouns) can follow a determiner and an adjective: for example, *A select few have been chosen.*

†Exercise F

In the sentence *A select few will be chosen*, what part of speech would you assign to *few* (i.e., for what part of speech is it substituting)?

The behavior of the indefinite pronoun *one* adds another layer of complexity to this analysis. Consider the following sentence.

11. I want a red *balloon,* not a blue *one.*

In this sentence, *one* appears to be substituting for *balloon* and hence would best be analyzed as a noun. However, consider another sentence.

12. This *red balloon* is bigger than that *one.*

What item is *one* replacing in sentence (12)? The answer is that we cannot tell with certainty. It could be that *one* is replacing *balloon* as it was in (11), in which case it would appear that *one* is functioning as a noun. However, it could also be that *one* is replacing the entire phrase *red balloon.* The problem is that we have not yet defined any phrasal unit that would include just the words *red balloon* (where *red* is an adjective and *balloon* is a noun), but not the accompanying determiner. (An NP would include all three words.) We will take up the problem of how to classify phrases like *red balloon* in Part III.

Exercise G

If you are having trouble seeing the two readings of the sentence *This red balloon is bigger than that one*, try reading it aloud with stress in two different places.

a. First, put heavier stress on *This.* Under this reading, what word(s) does *one* appear to substitute for?

b. Second, put heavier stress on *red*. Under this reading, what word(s) does *one* appear to substitute for?

Summary

The main points of this chapter are summarized in the following table.

Nouns
- Inflected for number (*boys*) and case (*boy's*)

Proper (*John*) vs. **common** (*man*)
Count (*pebble*) vs. **noncount** (*sand*)

Pronouns
- inflected for number (*I/we*), case (*I/me*), person (*I/you*), and gender (*he/she*)

Personal (*she*)
Reflexive (*herself*)
Reciprocal (*each other*)
Demonstrative (*these*)
Indefinite (*someone*)

SUPPLEMENTARY EXERCISES

1. Earlier, we stated that proper nouns cannot generally be inflected for plurality. Now consider the sentence that contradicts this generalization: *There are two Parkers in the class that meets on Thursday.* How do you account for the pluralized proper nouns in this sentence?

2. Consult a good dictionary to determine the plural forms of the following words. Are any alternate forms listed? If so, what is their nature?

alumna
alumnus
addendum
criterion
emphasis
octopus
seraph
spectrum
stratus
symposium

3. The following message was printed on a chopsticks wrapper:

Welcome to Chinese Restaurant

Please try your Nice Chinese Food with Chopsticks,

the traditional and typical of Chinese glorious history and cultual.

PRODUCT OF CHINA

Chinese Restaurant should be *this Chinese Restaurant* (or something similar). What principle of English has not been acquired by the writer of this message (apparently a nonnative speaker of English)?

4. Some nonstandard dialects of English use the following set of reflexive pronouns.

	1st person	**2nd person**	**3rd person**
Singular	*myself*	*yourself*	*hisself/herself/itself*
Plural	*ourselves*	*yourselves*	*theirselves*

a. Which forms in this set are different from the forms used in standard varieties of English?

b. List the pronouns to which *-self/-selves* is attached in the nonstandard dialect. Do they have anything in common?

c. List the pronouns to which *-self/-selves* is attached in the standard dialect. Do they have anything in common?

d. Based on your answers, can you draw any conclusions about why the nonstandard dialect uses different reflexive forms from the standard dialect? (Hint: Is the nonstandard dialect more consistent in any way than the standard dialect?)

5. One problem that sometimes occurs in writing is ambiguous, unclear, or inconsistent pronoun reference. For each of the following passages, explain the nature of the pronoun reference problem. Then revise each passage to eliminate the problem. Note: There is more than one way to revise each passage.

a. The client sued the broker after he invested unwisely.

b. If you try to connect the computer to the printer with the wrong cable, you may damage it.

c. Karen had the art department design three new layouts. She then spent an hour discussing them with the client. This probably kept us from losing the account.

d. The committee was asked to design a more cost-effective plan. It met once a week for a month. They also interviewed six plant managers.

e. A printer driver can allow a user to print fonts that their printer supports, but that their word processor does not.

6. Traditionally, the singular masculine pronouns (*he, him,* and *his*) have been used to refer to indefinite pronouns and generic antecedents, as in the examples below.

A. *Each student* should bring *his* book to the final.

B. *A manager* needs to meet regularly with *his* employees.

C. *The average American* saves 5.7% of *his* salary.

Understandably, however, many readers object to the implied gender bias in such usage. As a result, many publications and professional organizations have adopted guidelines for gender-neutral language. The following strategies can be used to avoid the singular masculine pronoun when the antecedent may include female referents.

- Replace *his* with *a, the,* or no pronoun at all.
- Use *his or her* (note: this option can become tedious over stretches of text longer than a sentence or two).
- Pluralize the antecedent.

Use these strategies to revise sentences (A-C) in several different ways.

7. In addition to the determiners discussed in Chapter 5, English also contains **predeterminers.** As the term indicates, these items occur before a determiner (e.g., *both (of) the young girls*). Predeterminers include *all, both, such, what,* and fractions such as *half.*

a. Construct NPs containing the predeterminers listed above.

b. What arguments exist for classifying these words as a type of determiner, rather than as an adjective? (Hint: Review the analysis of quantifiers in this chapter.)

▲▲▲ **CHAPTER 7**

Verbs and Verb Phrases

This chapter examines the major categories of verbs and verb phrases in English from three different perspectives. First, we examine the forms that main verbs can take. Second, we review the primary predicate types in English and introduce a method for diagramming, or visually representing, them. Third, we look at the English auxiliary system.

MAIN VERB FORMS

The **main verb** is always the rightmost verb in a simple sentence. For example, in the sentence *Jenny should have finished her homework*, *finished* is the main verb. Main verbs in English have five forms (sometimes called the **principal parts** of the verb).

Infinitive

The infinitive form of a verb can be thought of as its basic or "pure" form. It is easy to identify an **infinitive** because it is the form that follows *to*, as in *They want to go/win/walk/finish*. As we will see below, the other forms typically involve adding an inflection: e.g., *going, winning, walked, finished*. For this reason, the infinitive form is also called the **uninflected** form.

Exercise A

Below are some inflected verb forms. Identify the infinitive form of each verb.

a. brought
b. bought
c. sang
d. broken
e. had
f. did
g. ate
h. improving

Present Tense

The present tense of a verb in English has two forms, depending on the subject of the verb. With a third-person singular subject (e.g., *that woman, John, he, she, it*), the present tense has an *-s* inflection: e.g., *That woman raises horses, John jogs, She plays basketball, He does his homework, It often rains in April.* With other types of subjects, however, the present tense form of a verb is the same as the infinitive form: e.g., *They raise horses, I jog, You play basketball.* The present tense form of a verb can be identified by using the following frames: *She always* ______________, *I always* ______________.

The exception to these patterns is found in forms of the main verb *to be.* Unlike other main verbs, *to be* has three present tense forms, all of them distinct from its infinitive form. Its present tense forms are as follows.

	Singular	**Plural**
1st Person	I *am*	We *are*
2nd Person	You *are*	You *are*
3rd Person	She/He/It *is*	They *are*

It is interesting to note, nonetheless, that the third-person singular form of *to be* ends in an *-s*, in keeping with the general pattern displayed by other main verbs.

Past Tense Forms

The past tense form of a verb can be identified by using the following frame: *Yesterday, I* ________________. Unlike the present tense, which has two predictable forms (uninflected or *-s*), past tense forms vary much more widely. This variation is due largely to historical reasons having to do with the evolution of English. Like those in other Germanic languages, modern English verbs fall into two categories. The so-called **weak** or **regular** verbs form their past tense by adding an *-ed* inflection: e.g., *walked, mailed, married, avoided.* The so-called **strong** or **irregular** verbs typically signal their past tense by an internal vowel change, rather than by the addition of a suffix—e.g., *sang* (from *sing*), *ran* (from *run*), *fell* (from *fall*).

There are a few verbs that do not seem to fit neatly into either of these categories. For example, *brought* (from *bring*) and *bought* (from *buy*) display both a vowel change and an ending change. Finally, there are a few verbs that do not undergo any formal change in the past tense: e.g., *put* and *cut.* Historically, though, all these verbs descended from strong verbs.

†Exercise B

Main verb *be* has two past tense forms.

a. Identify the two past tense forms of *be.*

b. Can you make any generalizations about when each form will be used? (Hint: Does the past tense of *be* show any correspondences with the present tense?)

Present Participle

The present participle of a verb is easy to identify: it always ends in *-ing: running, walking, telecommuting, being*. Thus we can refer to *-ing* as the present participle inflection. The present participle form can also be identified by using the following frame: *I am* _______________.

It is technically incorrect, by the way, to refer to the present participle form (or the past participle form, discussed in the next section) as a "tense." Strictly speaking, a verb has only two tenses—present and past.

Past Participle

The past participle of a verb can be identified by using the following frame: *I have* _______________. If you try this test on a few verbs—*walk, bring, take*—you will quickly discover that past participle forms vary widely. This variation corresponds, by and large, to the distinction between regular and irregular verbs. For regular verbs, the past participle form is the same as the past tense form: e.g., *Yesterday I walked to school* (past tense); *I have walked to school every day this week* (past participle).

Other verbs behave like regular verbs, in the sense that their past participle form is identical to their past tense form; yet these forms do not end in *-ed*, the characteristic past participle suffix for regular verbs. Examples include *I have brought my lunch/bought a new car/read that book/cut my hair/put the car in the garage.*

For irregular verbs, the case is more complicated. One generalization we can make is the following: If a verb form ends in *-en*, it is a past participle. In other words, all *-en* forms are past participle forms: for example, *given, been, driven, eaten, taken*. Unfortunately (for it would make the identification of past participles much simpler), the converse is not true. Not all past participles end in *-en*. For example, we have already seen that the past participle form of regular verbs is the same, superficially, as their past tense form: both end in *-ed* (e.g., *walked, climbed, breathed*). In fact, the identical forms for both the past tense and past participle is one characteristic of regular verbs.

Other verbs behave like irregular verbs, in that their past participle is distinct from their past tense form; yet these forms do not end in *-en*, the characteristic past participle suffix for irregular verbs. Examples include *I have run a mile/sworn my oath/sung a song/rung a bell*).

The following chart outlines the means by which the past participle of various verbs is formed.

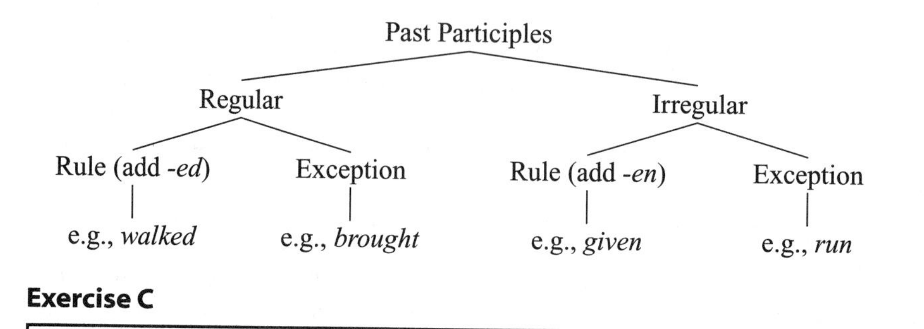

Exercise C

Complete the following table by filling in the present tense, past tense, present participle, and past participle forms of each verb. When using the frames, add an object after the verb if needed.

Infinitive	Present	Past	Pres. part.	Past part.
	(Every day she ___)	(Yesterday I ___)	(I am ___)	(I have ___)
do	______	______	______	______
arrest	______	______	______	______
drive	______	______	______	______
dive	______	______	______	______
think	______	______	______	______
read	______	______	______	______
write	______	______	______	______
ride	______	______	______	______
see	______	______	______	______
vacuum	______	______	______	______
sew	______	______	______	______
drink	______	______	______	______
bake	______	______	______	______
staple	______	______	______	______
bathe	______	______	______	______
speak	______	______	______	______
take	______	______	______	______

PREDICATE TYPES IN ENGLISH

Verbs in English can be classified according to the types of items that can follow them. For example, some verbs permit (or require) a direct object, while others do not. The **predicate** of a sentence is defined as the verb plus its object (direct or indirect), or complement, and their various modifiers. Therefore, rather than speaking of verb types, it is really more accurate to speak of predicate types. The following sections define the main predicate types in English: **transitive**, **intransitive**, and **linking**.

This chapter also introduces a method of sentence diagramming that is generally referred to as the **Reed–Kellogg** system. It was first introduced in 1878 in Reed and Kellogg's *Higher Lessons in English*, making it the oldest diagramming system still widely used in American schools.

To construct a Reed-Kellogg diagram, always begin by placing the subject and predicate on a horizontal line and bisecting them with a vertical line. For example, the sentence *Frank jogs*, which consists of a one-word subject and a one-word predicate, would be diagrammed as shown at right:

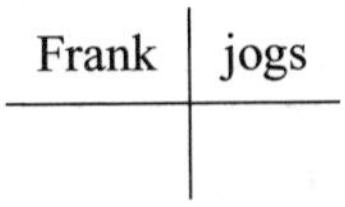

Frank | jogs

In this chapter we will focus primarily on variations within the predicate section of the diagram.

Transitive Verbs

Most verbs in English fall into one of two categories: transitive or intransitive. Transitive verbs are those that occur with a **direct object**; intransitive verbs are those that do not. For example, *hit* is a transitive verb (*John hit Ed in the nose* is grammatical; **John hit* and **John hit in the nose* are not). In contrast, *sleep* is an intransitive verb; *Mary is sleeping* (no object) is grammatical, as is *Mary is sleeping in the living room* (verb followed by a prepositional phrase), but **Mary is sleeping the bed* is ungrammatical, reflecting the fact that *sleep* cannot be followed by a direct object.

At this point we need to review the definition of direct object. In semantic terms, the direct object is the entity or thing that is affected by the action described by the verb. In structural terms, the direct object NP immediately follows the verb and moves to subject position in the corresponding **passive** sentence, a structure that we will look at in more detail later in this chapter. (However, these structural observations may also apply to an **indirect object**, as discussed in the next section.) For example, in the sentence *John hit Ed in the nose*, *Ed* is the direct object. It immediately follows the verb *hit*; and it becomes the subject of the corresponding passive sentence *Ed was hit in the nose by John*. (By the way, *hit* is still a transitive verb in this sentence, even though its direct object has been moved into subject position.)

Verbs like *hit* and *sleep* are clear-cut cases of transitive and intransitive verbs, respectively. The verb *hit* requires an object; *sleep* cannot have one. However, other verbs do not exhibit such clear-cut behavior. For example, *eat* can appear with or without an object: *I already ate* (no object) is grammatical, but so is *I already ate the last cookie* (direct object). The question arises, then, as to whether *eat* should be classified as transitive or intransitive. There is some lack of consistency in how various grammarians answer this question. Some analysts (ourselves included) classify such verbs on a sentence-by-sentence basis. Under this view, the verb in the sentence *I already ate* is intransitive, while that in the sentence *I already ate the last cookie* is transitive. You should be aware, though, that other analysts classify *eat* as a transitive verb, since it is capable of co-occurring with an object.

To diagram a verb phrase with a direct object, place the direct object on a horizontal line after the verb. Separate the verb from the object with a vertical line perpendicular to the horizontal line. In the adjacent example, the direct object *the last cookie* contains not just a noun (*cookie*) but also two **modifiers,** *the* and *last*. A modifier is generally placed on a slanted line below the item that it modifies. (We will deal with modifiers in more detail in later chapters.)

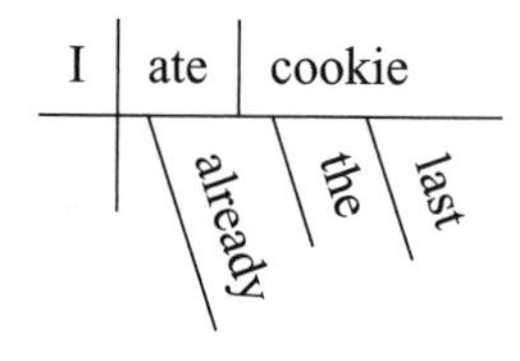

Exercise D

Diagram each of the following sentences using Reed–Kellogg diagrams.

a.† Tim punched Ed.
b. We saw a good movie.
c. Your friend called.

So far we have looked at some transitive verbs that co-occur with single objects. However, other transitive verbs co-occur with double objects (i.e., they are followed by two NPs). Some verbs in this category can be followed by a sequence of **indirect object–direct object**, as illustrated in the following sentence:

1. The IRS sent <u>Mary</u> <u>a refund check</u>.
   I.O. D.O.

In terms of its meaning, the indirect object identifies the recipient or beneficiary of the action described by the verb. In terms of its structural behavior, the indirect object can be paraphrased so that it becomes the object of a preposition (typically *to* or *for*) following the direct object: e.g., *The IRS sent a refund check <u>to Mary</u>.* Note that an indirect object never occurs without a direct object: for example, **The IRS sent Mary* or **The IRS sent to Mary*.

Exercise E

Other verbs that can take indirect objects include *give, sell, buy, write,* and *tell.*

a. Construct sentences using these verbs followed by the indirect object-direct object sequence.

b. Paraphrase the sentences that you constructed for (a) by changing the indirect object into the object of a preposition.

c. Based on your answer to (b), what two prepositions are permitted in paraphrases of indirect objects?

To diagram a verb that contains an indirect and a direct object, begin with the same kind of diagram that you would use with just a direct object. The indirect object is placed on an angled line under the verb. For example, to the right is a diagram of the sentence *She sent Martha a present.*

If the indirect object has been made into the object of a preposition, the preposition is placed on the line above the indirect object. For example, to the right is a diagram of the sentence *She sent a present to Martha.*

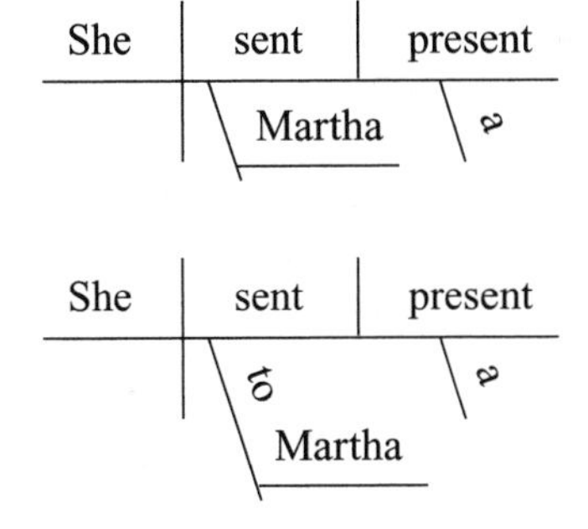

Exercise F

Diagram each of the following sentences using Reed–Kellogg diagrams.

a.† His parents gave Jeff a new car.

b. My mother wrote me a long letter.

c.† I wrote a short note to her.

d. Kim sold her old car to Kevin.

e. She bought herself a new Toyota.

In addition to verbs that can take an indirect and a direct object, other transitive verbs can be followed by a direct object and an **objective complement**. As the term indicates, an objective complement is an item that "completes" or "fills in" information about the direct object. The objective complement can be either an NP (as in sentence 2 below) or an adjective (as in sentence 3):

2. John considers Mary a genius.
3. John considers Mary intelligent.

Some verbs of this type can appear with or without an objective complement, as shown here.

4. They christened the baby Miranda.
5. They christened the baby.

Exercise G

Here are some additional verbs that can take direct objects and objective complements: *name, call, make, elect, appoint, find* (in the legal sense). For each one, construct a sentence in which the verb is followed by a direct object and an objective complement.

To diagram this type of predicate, place the objective complement after the direct object and separate it from the direct object by a left-slanted line. (Note that the line slants toward the object being modified by the complement.)

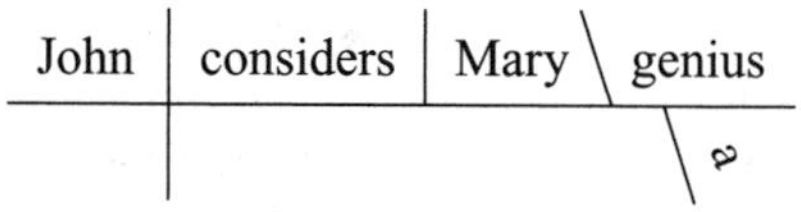

John | considers | Mary \ genius
a

Exercise H

Diagram the following sentences.

a.† The committee elected Frieda chair.
b. We find the defendant guilty.
c. The court declared him temporarily insane.
d. Courtney named the kitten Jumbo.

To summarize, the class of transitive verbs can be broken down into single-object and double-object categories. The double-object category can be further subdivided into verbs that take an indirect object and those that take an objective complement. These categories are illustrated in the following diagram.

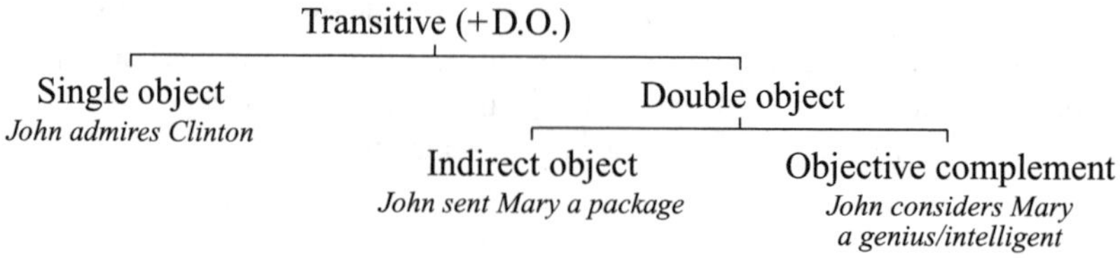

Transitive (+D.O.)

Single object
John admires Clinton

Double object

Indirect object
John sent Mary a package

Objective complement
John considers Mary a genius/intelligent

Intransitive Verbs

As mentioned earlier, intransitive verbs are those that do not require a complement of any sort (i.e., a direct object, indirect object, objective complement, etc.). Examples include *sleep, read,* and *disappear*.

6. When I can't sleep, I read.
7. My wallet has disappeared.

Diagramming predicates with intransitive verbs is quite simple, since all that needs to be placed on the predicate line is the verb itself. For example, the sentence *My wallet has disappeared* would be diagrammed as shown at right:

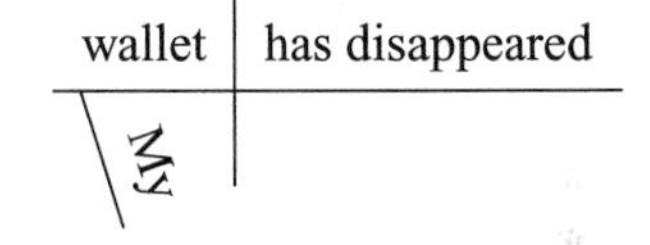

Linking Verbs

Linking verbs comprise a finite group; they include forms of the verb *to be* as well as the following verbs: *seem, feel, look, appear, taste, smell*, and *sound*. Linking verbs are so-called for semantic reasons. Rather than representing an action, they instead "link" the subject and the predicate, which describes some characteristic of the subject. The item following the linking verb is known as the **subjective complement**, and can be an adjective phrase, a noun phrase, or a prepositional phrase. Linking verbs are sometimes called **copular** or **copulative** verbs, since they "couple" or unite two sentence elements, the subject and the subjective complement. All linking verbs can be followed by an adjective phrase, as shown in the following examples. Note that the adjective phrase in each case describes the subject NP.

8. That woman is intelligent.
9. She seems very angry.
10. Those dogs look hungry.
11. The weather appears cold.
12. The car sounded funny.
13. The food at that restaurant smells delicious.
14. His soup doesn't always taste good.

Exercise I

A few verbs in English lead a "double life" as both linking and non-linking verbs. Identify the italicized verb in each sentence as linking, transitive, or intransitive.

a.† This coffee *tastes* bitter.

b.† I can *smell* her perfume from the next county.

c. After the chef *tasted* the soup, she added salt.
d. I can't *smell* anything with this cold.
e. That candy *looks* tempting.
f. That course *appears* easier than it is.
g. He *seems* less sure of himself than he used to be.
h.† A new student *appeared* in the class.
i. I *looked* under the hood, but didn't see anything unusual.

In diagramming, linking verbs (like transitive and intransitive verbs) are separated from the subject by a vertical bisecting line. The subjective complement is placed on the horizontal line after the verb and is separated from the verb by a left-slanting line (i.e., a line that points back toward the subject). For example, to the right is a diagram of the sentence *That woman is intelligent.*

woman | is \ intelligent
That

Exercise J

Diagram the following sentences.

a.† She seemed angry.
b. Those dogs looked hungry.
c. The weather appears cold.
d. This coffee tastes bitter.
e.† I can't smell anything.
f. That candy looks tempting.
g. The car sounds funny.
h. The food smells delicious.
i. I can smell her perfume.

Forms of the linking verb *be* can be followed not only by an adjective phrase but also by a noun phrase or prepositional phrase.

15. The suspect is a known felon.
16. Beth was in her office.

Each of these elements is diagrammed differently. If the linking verb *be* is followed by a noun phrase, the noun phrase is considered a subjective complement and is placed on the horizontal line after a line slanted back toward the subject. For example, to the right is a diagram of (15).

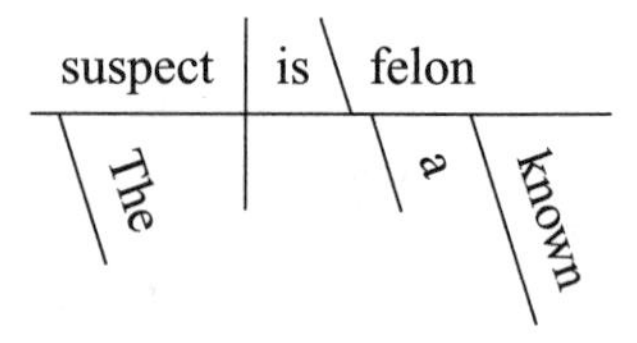

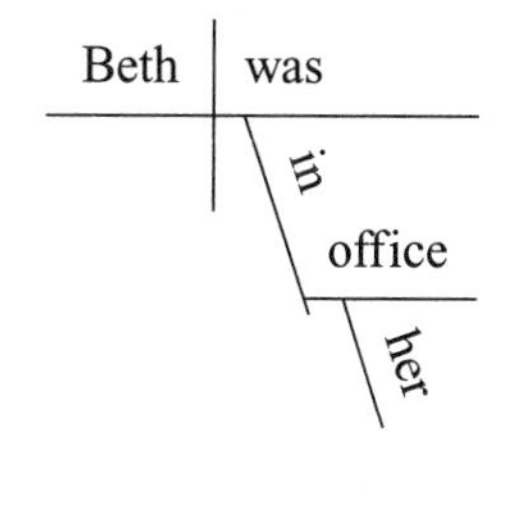

Prepositional phrases following linking verb *be* can be diagrammed in two different ways, depending on their function. For example, to the right is a diagram of (16).

In sentence (16), the PP *in her office* has an **adverbial** function, meaning that it modifies the main verb. (Adverbials are discussed in more detail in Chapter 9.) However, some PPs that follow linking verbs have an **adjectival** function. For example, consider the following sentences.

17. Beth was in a hurry.
18. He is out of breath.
19. I feel under the weather.

Note that the PPs in these examples describe the subject's state of mind (an adjectival function) rather than the subject's location (an adverbial function). Adjectival PPs are diagrammed differently from their adverbial counterparts. Since an adjectival PP represents a subjective complement, it is placed in the same part of the diagram that a subjective complement would be, to the right of the linking verb and separated by a left-slanting line. The PP itself is place on a pedestal in this position. For example, to the right is a diagram of (17).

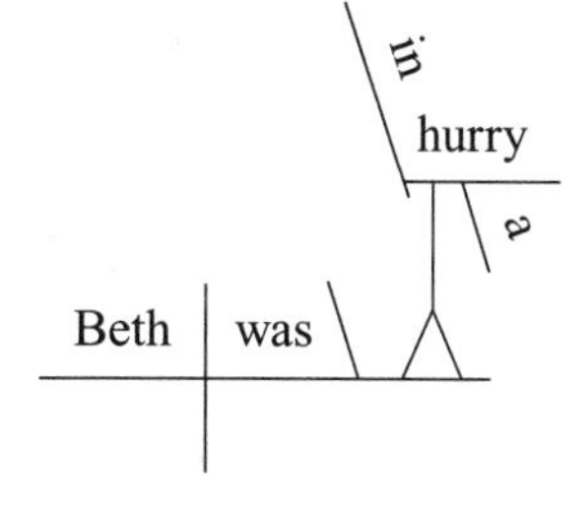

There is not always a single foolproof way to tell if a PP is adverbial or adjectival, but there are several tests you can try. Adverbial PPs that indicate location can often be replaced by *there* or questioned by *where*. For example, the sentence *Beth was there* is a logical paraphrase of *Beth was in the office*; likewise, *Beth was in the office* is a logical answer to the question *Where was Beth?* In contrast, *Beth was there* is not a logical paraphrase of *Beth was in a hurry*; nor is the latter sentence a logical answer to the question *Where was Beth?*

Second, an adjectival PP can usually be replaced by a one-word adjective, and can often be modified by *very*. For example, *Beth was in a hurry* can be paraphrased as *Beth was frantic*. Likewise, the PPs in (18) and (19) can be modified by *very*: *He is very out of breath*; *I feel very under the weather*.

Exercise K

Decide if each PP is adjectival or adverbial; then diagram each sentence accordingly.

a.† You weren't on time.

b.† The suitcases are on the train.

c. His request seems within reason.
d. The dog was under the table.
e. Her books are in that box.
f. Anna is in a snit.

Phrasal Verbs

Some transitive and intransitive verbs combine with other elements, called **particles**, to constitute phrasal verbs. The following sentences contain phrasal verbs (italicized).

20. I don't think they have *decided on* a name.
21. She *made up* the quiz.
22. He *brought up* an unpleasant subject at the meeting.
23. Why don't you *call up* your mother?
24. She may *call on* that student for the answer to the next question.
25. They're not going to *get over* the accident.
26. Who *knocked over* the trash can?

We can distinguish two patterns of behavior among phrasal verbs. In some phrasal verbs, the particle can be moved to the right of the direct object (the direct object in the following sentences is underlined).

27. She *made* the quiz *up*.
28. He *brought* an unpleasant subject *up* at the meeting.
29. Why don't you *call* your mother *up*?
30. Who *knocked* the trash can *over*?

As we saw in Chapter 5, the particle in such verbs can occur grammatically either before or after the direct object.

However, other phrasal verbs do not allow the particle to move. In some cases, the result is an ungrammatical sentence.

31. *I don't think they have *decided* a name *on*.
32. *She may *call* that student *on* for the answer to the next question.
33. *They're not going to *get* the accident *over.*

Exercise L

Identify the phrasal verb and the direct object in each of the following sentences. Then decide whether or not the particle can be moved grammatically to the right of the direct object.

a.† Frank might bring in the mail.
b. I will find out the answer by tomorrow.
c.† They have settled on a fair price for the house.
d. The police will turn over their information to the FBI.
e. I looked up that word in the dictionary.
f. She ran into a friend of hers at the mall.

Phrasal verbs are diagrammed like one-word verbs. For example, to the right is a diagram of (21), which contains the phrasal verb *made up*.

She | made up | quiz
the

Exercise M

Diagram the verb phrases (verb + direct object) in Exercise L.

Summary

Main verbs in English have five principal parts: the infinitive, present tense, past tense, present participle, and past participle forms. Main verbs in English can be classified into three types: transitive, intransitive, and linking verbs. Further subgroups within these types are included in the following diagram.

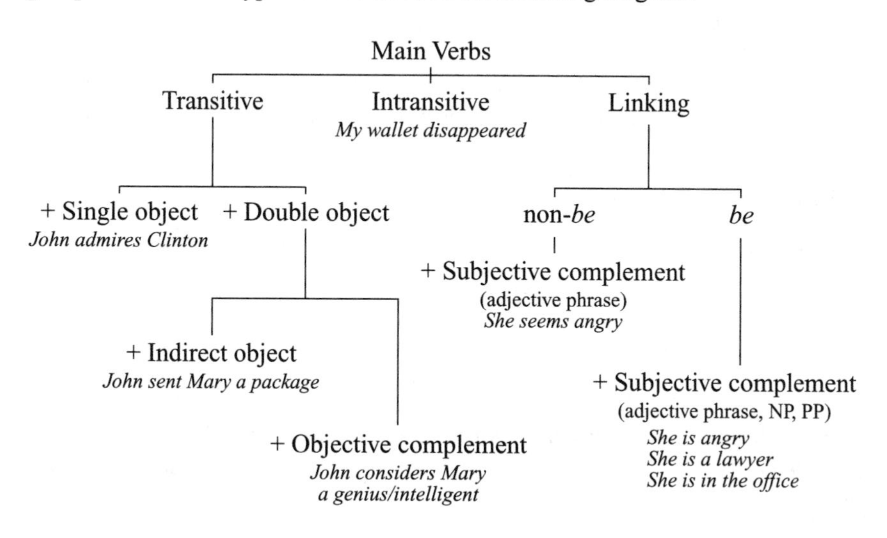

THE AUXILIARY SYSTEM

So far our discussion has centered on the properties of main verbs in English: their principal parts and the items that can follow them. In this section we turn our attention to **auxiliary verbs** (sometimes called "helping" verbs). English contains three main types of auxiliary verbs; we will take these up one at a time.

Modals

English contains five modal auxiliaries, all but one of which occur in a present and past tense form.

Present	**Past**
can	could
may	might
—	must
shall	should
will	would

(There is no present-tense form of *must* in Modern English, although the form *muss* filled that role as late as Middle English [c. 1150–1500] and occurs in German.) Keep in mind that the term **tense** simply refers to the form of a verb, not necessarily to its time reference. For example, the sentence *Theresa might come with us* contains a past-tense verb form (*might*) but refers to a future time.

We can make several other observations about modal auxiliaries. First, unlike other verbs, modals cannot be inflected for either the past participle or present participle form (e.g., **maying, mayen*). Second, modals do not take the *-s* inflection that normally occurs with a third-person singular subject (e.g., *John runs*, but not **John mays run*).

The verb form following a modal is always an infinitive (uninflected) form. For example, the sentence *John can be silly* is grammatical, but not **John can is silly.*

Auxiliary have

In its role as an auxiliary verb, *have* can occur in either present or past tense.

Present	**Past**
has	had
have	

The verb form following auxiliary *have* is always a past participle form: for example, *John has <u>been</u> sick; We have <u>given</u> a donation to that charity; They have <u>called</u> three times.*

Keep in mind that *have* can function as either an auxiliary verb or a main verb. If it is the rightmost verb in the verb phrase, it is a main verb; otherwise it is an auxiliary verb. In its role as a main verb, *have* can occur in the five principal parts displayed by other main verbs.

Infinitive:	have
Present:	has, have
Past:	had
Present participle:	having
Past participle:	had

Exercise N

Identify each occurrence of *have* as either an auxiliary verb or a main verb. Then identify the form of each occurrence of *have* and any other verbs (i.e., infinitive, past tense, present tense, past participle, present participle). Note that the first verb will always be either present or past tense; the form of any subsequent verbs will depend on the auxiliary verb that precedes them.

a.† I had three bad hair days last week.

b. You can have another cup of coffee.

c.† You should have had another cup of coffee.

d. It had rained three days before it stopped.

e. She has captured America's heart.

Auxiliary be

In its role as an auxiliary verb, *be* can occur in either the present tense, past tense, or past participle form.

Present	Past	Past participle
am	was	been
are	were	
is		

The verb form following auxiliary *be* is always a present participle form: for example, *John was acting sick*; *We are giving regular donations to that charity; They have been calling all day*.

Like *have*, *be* can function as either an auxiliary verb or a main verb. If it is the rightmost verb in the verb phrase, it is a main verb; otherwise it is an auxiliary verb. In its role as a main verb, *be* can occur in the five principal parts displayed by other main verbs.

Infinitive:	be
Present:	am, are, is
Past:	was, were
Present participle:	being
Past participle:	been

Exercise O

Identify each occurrence of *be* as either a main verb or an auxiliary verb. Then identify the form of each occurrence of *be* and any other verbs (i.e., infinitive, past tense, present tense, past participle, present participle). Note that the first verb will always be either present or past tense; the form of any subsequent verbs will depend on the auxiliary verb that precedes them.

a.† He is being a jerk.
b. They should be watching the child.
c. I could have been a contender.
d.† It was hot yesterday.
e. You are acting foolishly.

Co-occurrence Restrictions on Auxiliary Verbs

As the term implies, auxiliary verbs supplement the main verb. It is possible to have a grammatical verb phrase that contains a main verb and no auxiliary verb (e.g., *John ate the last cookie*), but the opposite is not true: an auxiliary verb cannot occur without a main verb (e.g., **John might the last cookie*).

Elliptical structures are an apparent exception to this generalization. For example, in the sentence *John didn't eat the last cookie, but I might*, it appears that *might* occurs in the absence of a main verb. However, notice that the main verb can be **recovered**, that is, reconstructed from the preceding discourse (i.e., *John didn't eat the last cookie, but I might eat the last cookie*). Thus, we can maintain the generalization that an auxiliary verb never occurs without a (recoverable) main verb.

The auxiliary verbs discussed so far—modals, *have*, and *be*—can co-occur in a number of combinations, as illustrated below.

Auxiliary elements	Example
modal	John might take a nap.
modal + *have*	John might have taken a nap.
modal + *be*	John might be taking a nap.
modal + *have* + *be*	John might have been taking a nap.
have	John has taken a nap.
have + *be*	John has been taking a nap.
be	John is taking a nap.

Based on these examples, we can see that the auxiliary portion of a verb phrase can contain up to three auxiliary verbs. Furthermore, if more than one auxiliary verb occurs, they must occur in a particular order:

- If a modal occurs with the other auxiliary verbs, it is always first (e.g., *might have been*).
- If *have* occurs with the other two auxiliary verbs, it is always second (e.g., *might have been*).
- If *be* occurs with the other two auxiliary verbs, it is always third (e.g., *might have been*).
- The main verb always follows any auxiliary verbs (e.g., *might have been taking*).

Auxiliary do

In addition to the three auxiliary verbs already discussed, English contains a fourth element, auxiliary *do*. In its role as an auxiliary verb, *do* can occur in the present and past tense forms.

Present	Past
do	did
does	

Auxiliary *do* and the other three auxiliary verbs are in a relationship known as **complementary distribution**. This means that auxiliary *do* never co-occurs with any of the other auxiliary verbs. Instead, auxiliary *do* occurs only in three specific environments.

One use of auxiliary do is to form a *yes-no* question from a declarative sentence that has no auxiliary verb. Normally, to form such a question, the first auxiliary verb is inverted with the subject NP. For example, a question based on the declarative *She has seen John* would be formed as *Has she seen John?* However, when the declarative contains no auxiliary verb, the question is formed by adding a form of *do*. For example, a question based on the declarative *She saw John* would be formed as *Did she see John?*

A second use of auxiliary *do* is to form a negative sentence from a positive sentence that has no auxiliary verb. Normally, to form a negative sentence, the word *not* is placed after the first auxiliary verb (or contracted with it). For example, the negative version of *She has seen John* would be *She has not/hasn't seen John.* However, when the sentence contains no auxiliary verb, the negative counterpart is formed by adding a form of *do*. For example, the negative counterpart of *She saw John* would be *She did not/didn't see John.*

A third use of auxiliary *do* is to form an emphatic sentence from a declarative that has no auxiliary verb. Normally, to form an emphatic sentence, the first auxiliary verb is stressed. For example, the emphatic version of *She has seen John* would be *She HAS seen John*. However, when the declarative contains no auxiliary verb, an emphatic version is formed by adding a form of *do*. For example, the emphatic version of *She saw John* would be *She DID see John*.

When auxiliary *do* occurs in a verb phrase, it occurs as the first verb and therefore is either present or past tense. The verb form following auxiliary *do* is always an infinitive (uninflected) form.

Exercise P

From each of the following sentences, construct (i) a *yes/no*-question, (ii) a negative declarative, and (iii) an emphatic declarative. Based on your new sentences, what generalization can you make about the tense of auxiliary *do*? That is, given a declarative sentence, can you make any predictions about the form that auxiliary *do* will take if it is added?

a.† The committee needs a new chair.
b. The Senate passed the bill on Friday.
c. Most Americans support health care reform.

ASPECT AND VOICE

In this final section, we will look at two properties of the verb phrase that can be expressed through the use of tense and auxiliary verbs.

Aspect

The aspect of a verb refers to the relation between the time that a sentence is uttered and the time that the situation described in the sentence occurred. The **perfect aspect**, expressed through a form of auxiliary *have*, indicates that the situation described in the sentence began at some point earlier than the utterance time. The present perfect indicates an activity or situation that began in the past and extends to the present. It is formed by using a present-tense form of auxiliary *have*.

34. The committee *has debated* the bill for three weeks.
35. We *have reached* a decision.

The past perfect indicates an activity or situation that ended earlier than some other past time. The past perfect is formed by using a past-tense form of auxiliary *have*.

36. The children *had eaten* when I got home.
37. The expedition *had waited* for three days before help arrived.

The future perfect indicates an activity or situation that will be completed from the viewpoint of some time in the future. The future perfect is formed by using *will* (uncontracted or contracted) followed by *have* and a past participle.

38. The movie *will have started* by the time we get there.
39. At this time tomorrow, *we'll have driven* 400 miles.

The **progressive aspect**, expressed through a form of auxiliary *be*, indicates an activity in progress. The present progressive indicates that the activity is concurrent with the time of the utterance, or will take place in the near future. The present progressive is formed by using a present-tense form of auxiliary *be*.

40. They *are replacing* the windows in all the classrooms.
41. You *are upsetting* the dog.

The past progressive indicates an activity that was in progress in the past. The past progressive is formed by using a past-tense form of auxiliary *be*.

42. They *were walking* out the door when the phone rang.
43. I *was grading* papers until midnight.

The future progressive indicates an activity that will take place in the future. The future progressive is formed by using *will* followed by *be* and a present participle.

44. Jeff *will be calling* you tonight.
45. Congress *will be voting* on the bill tomorrow.

In addition to the perfect and progressive aspects, English also allows for the perfect progressive aspects. As you might surmise, these are formed by combining forms of auxiliary *have* and auxiliary *be*. The present perfect progressive aspect indicates states or activities leading up to the present time (i.e., the time of utterance).

46. We *have been hoping* that he will resign.
47. They *have been running* the same story on all the news broadcasts.

The past perfect progressive indicates states or activities that were in progress up to some past time.

48. I *had been meaning* to call you when I got your letter.
49. Before he finally got a job, he *had been interviewing* for three weeks.

The future perfect progressive indicates progressive states or activities that will end in the future.

50. They *will have been driving* for eight hours by the time they reach Nashville.
51. The groceries *will have been sitting* in the car for too long by the time we get home.

The aspects and their meanings are summarized below, along with an example of each.

Perfect

present (*has eaten*): activity begun in past
past (*had eaten*): activity begun in past and ending in past
future (*will have eaten*): activity ending in future

Progressive

present (*is eating*): ongoing current activity
past (*was eating*): ongoing past activity
future (*will be eating*): ongoing future activity

Perfect progressive

present (*has been eating*): activity begun in past and ongoing in present
past (*had been eating*): activity begun in past, ongoing in past, and ending in past
future (*will have been eating*): activity ongoing in future and ending in future

Exercise Q

Identify the aspect of the verb phrase in each sentence as one of the following:

(i) present perfect
(ii) past perfect
(iii) future perfect
(iv) present progressive
(v) past progressive
(vi) future progressive
(vii) present perfect progressive
(viii) past perfect progressive
(ix) future perfect progressive

a.† It has been raining for two hours.
b. The prisoner had asked for a stay of execution.
c.† Her show is gaining in popularity.
d. She will have been working for 40 years when she retires.
e. I had been wondering about his judgment.
f. The car will have used a tank of gas by the time we get home.
g. The dog was sleeping on the sofa.
h. You are heading down a dangerous path.
i. The new James Bond movie will be opening tomorrow.

Voice

The distinction between **active** and **passive** voice is limited to transitive verbs. A sentence is said to be in the active voice when the subject NP serves as the **agent** of the verb (i.e., the entity responsible for the action), and the object NP follows the verb.

52. The police arrested a suspect.
53. Simon & Schuster is publishing her memoirs.
54. The National Weather Service has issued a tornado warning.

In a passive voice sentence, the subject of the sentence is not the agent of the verb but rather the **patient** (i.e., the thing affected by the verb). The following sentences are the passive counterparts of (52–54).

55. A suspect was arrested by the police.
56. Her memoirs are being published by Simon & Schuster.
57. A tornado warning has been issued by the National Weather Service.

Passive sentences are distinguished by several structural characteristics. First, note that the agent of the verb appears in a *by*-phrase in the passive sentences. English also allows an **agentless passive**, in which the *by*-phrase is omitted.

58. A suspect was arrested.
59. Her memoirs are being published.
60. A tornado warning has been issued.

Because of this possibility, the agentless passive is sometimes associated with questionable rhetorical strategies such as avoiding responsibility for action—as in the famous quotation by former President Ronald Reagan, "Mistakes were made."

Second, when a sentence is converted from active voice to passive voice, a form of auxiliary *be* is introduced immediately before the main verb, and the main verb always carries the past participle inflection (e.g., *The cake <u>was</u> eat<u>en</u> by Mary*).

As a final note, be aware that the voice of a verb has nothing to do with its tense. A passive voice sentence can be in the present tense; conversely, a past tense sentence can be in the active voice. (Recall once more that tense is identified by examining the first verb form.) For example, the sentence *The last cookie has been eaten by John* is a passive sentence, but the first verb (*has*) is inflected for present tense. Conversely, the sentence *John ate the last cookie* is an active voice sentence, but the first verb is inflected for past tense.

Exercise R

Identify each sentence as active or passive; then change it to the opposite voice. (In changing an agentless passive to the active voice, you will have to supply an agent.)

a.† The car hit a telephone pole.
b.† Electricity was wiped out for three hours by the storm.
c. A French author has written a new translation of that book.
d. They might have seen the accident.
e. You can claim your luggage in the Customs area.
f. A new instructor is teaching that course.
g. A package was left at our door.

Summary

The material covered in this chapter is outlined in the following table.

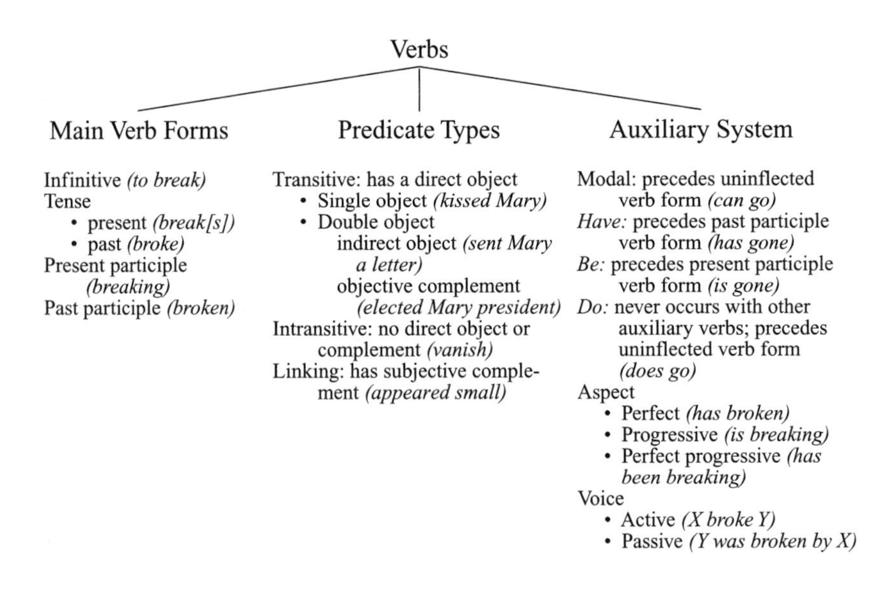

SUPPLEMENTARY EXERCISES

1. It is common in nonstandard dialects to hear *brang* used as a past tense form.

a. In what way is this form consistent with the past tenses of other irregular verbs?

b. Can you think of any verbs that rhyme with *bring*? How do they form their past tense?

2. Here are some verbs that have gained widespread use in English only fairly recently: *fax, telecommute, downsize, download, outsource, dis* (meaning 'disrespect'). Identify the past tense and past participle forms of these verbs. What class of verbs do they seem to fall into?

3. Several years ago, one of the authors employed a gardener who left the following note: *I weedeated the yard.* ("Weedeater" is a brand name for a tool used to edge lawns.) Speculate on why the gardener used the form *weedeated* rather than *weedate.*

4. Go back to the sentences that you constructed for Exercise E. Try substituting the following synonyms for some of the verbs: *donate* (for *give*), *purchase* (for *buy*), *compose* (for *write*), *communicate* (for *tell*).

a. What happens when you substitute synonyms for the verbs in the sentences that you constructed for exercise (a)?

b. Consult a dictionary about the history of the words *give, buy, write,* and *tell.* Do they have anything in common?

c. Consult a dictionary about the history of the words *donate, purchase, compose,* and *communicate.* Do they have anything in common?

d. What can you conclude about the type of verb that can appear with an indirect object?

5. a. Consider the following jokes. How can you explain them with reference to various predicate types?

(From an episode of *M*A*S*H.*)
Houlihan: "Did you call me, doctor?"
Hawkeye: "Why should I call you 'doctor'? I'm the surgeon."

Bob: "Call me a taxi."
Ray: "O.K. You're a taxi!"

b. Diagram the two readings of *Call me a taxi* that account for the humor in that joke.

6. Earlier in this chapter we stated that the particle in a verb-particle sequence can be moved to the right of the direct object. Now consider the following sentences containing the verb-particle sequence *make up.*

a. You need to make up that quiz.
b. You need to make that quiz up.
c. *You need to make up it.
d. You need to make it up.

Based on these examples, what restriction needs to be placed on particles with certain types of direct objects?

7. Examine the past-tense modal forms.

a. What pattern do they have in common in terms of their endings?
b. How does this pattern relate to the past–tense ending found on regular main verbs?

8. Like *have* and *be, do* can function as both an auxiliary verb and a main verb. In its role as a main verb, it occurs in the five principal parts shown below.

Infinitive:	do
Present:	do, does
Past:	did
Present participle:	doing
Past participle:	done

Identify each occurrence of *do* as either a main verb or an auxiliary verb. Then identify the form of each occurrence of *do* and any other verbs (i.e., infinitive, past tense, present tense, past participle, present participle).

a. Did he see that movie?
b. She doesn't have a clue.
c. You should have done your homework.
d. I DID do my homework!
e. Did he bring a present?
f. Does he do a good job?
g. They aren't doing the right thing.

9. Examine the following active sentence and its passive counterpart.

A. *Simon & Schuster is publishing her memoirs.*
B. *Her memoirs are being published by Simon & Schuster.*

a. Can a sentence contain more than one instance of auxiliary *be*? Explain.
b. Review the way that the non-passive auxiliary *be* differs from the auxiliary *be* introduced by passive, in terms of how each verb affects the following verb form.

▲▲▲ CHAPTER 8

Modifiers of Nouns

So far we have looked at noun phrases and verb phrases, which fill the essential syntactic roles of subject and predicate. In this and the next chapter we will look at **modifiers**: elements that typically add nonessential detail to a noun phrase, verb phrase, or sentence. We will also look at ways to diagram these modifiers.

ADJECTIVES

The prototypical modifier of a noun is an **adjective**. As we saw in Chapter 5, adjectives can be identified by several structural tests. First, since adjectives are a form class, they are subject to inflection. Adjectives can typically be inflected for degree, usually by adding a **comparative** (*-er*) or **superlative** (*-est*) affix:

warm, warmer, warmest   red, redder, reddest

Note, however, that some adjectives are **derived** from another part of speech. For example, the adjective *ridiculous* is formed from the verb *ridicule*; the adjective *expensive* is formed from the noun *expense*. These derived adjectives are typically made comparative and superlative not by adding an inflection but by using them in a phrase with *more* or *most*: for example, *more ridiculous*, *most expensive*.

Note also that two of our most common adjectives, *good* and *bad*, are made comparative and superlative by using **suppletive forms** (i.e., words that developed historically from another root). Thus we have the series *good, better, best* and *bad, worse, worst*.

A second test for classifying a word as an adjective is its ability to co-occur with an **intensifier** such as *very, extremely*, and *too*. Thus we have phrases such as *extremely warm, very good,* and *too rich.*

Third, many adjectives accept certain derivational suffixes that convert them into other parts of speech. For example, the suffixes *-ness, -ity,* and *-th* attach to adjectives to form nouns: *goodness, density, warmth.*

Fourth, certain derivational affixes appear only on adjectives that have been derived from other parts of speech. For example, the *-able* and *-ible* suffixes appear on adjectives derived from verbs: *variable, flexible*. Likewise, the *-al* and *-ar* suffixes denote adjectives derived from nouns: *nuclear, popular*. And the *-ish* suffix denotes an adjective derived from another adjective or from a noun: *reddish, boyish, foolish*.

Exercise A

Analyze each of the following words by identifying (i) each word's part of speech, (ii) the components of each word (root and derivational affix(es)), and (iii) the root's part of speech. Consult a dictionary if necessary.

a.† Oedipal	f.† toxic
b.† edible	g.† monstrosity
c. gullible	h. curiosity
d. tubular	i. generosity
e. porous	j. breadth

By way of review, you might recall some basic contrasts between adjectives and determiners.

- Determiners, unlike adjectives, cannot be inflected. (This follows from the fact that determiners are a structure class, and structure classes generally do not undergo inflection.) Thus, while forms like *warmer* and *warmest* are permitted, we have no forms like **thiser* or **thatest.*
- An NP can contain more than one adjective, but only one determiner. For example, the phrase *a rich, fat, stupid man* is permitted, but not **a the man.*
- If an NP contains both a determiner and an adjective, the determiner must precede any adjective(s). For example, the phrase *a rich, fat, stupid man* is permitted, as is *a fat, stupid, rich man,* but not **fat a rich, stupid man.* Typically, by the way, adjectives occur as **pre-nominal modifiers**, meaning that they occur before the noun that they modify. (There are a few exceptions, notably in some legal phrases derived from French such as *attorney general* and *court martial.*)

Diagramming Adjectives

Although clear structural differences exist between determiners and adjectives, Reed–Kellogg diagramming does not distinguish between them. (This is one weakness of that diagramming system.) Both are diagrammed on diagonal lines below the noun that they modify. If an NP contains more than one modifier, the items are placed on parallel lines in the order that reflects the actual sentence structure. For example, to the right is a diagram of the sentence *The little dog laughed.*

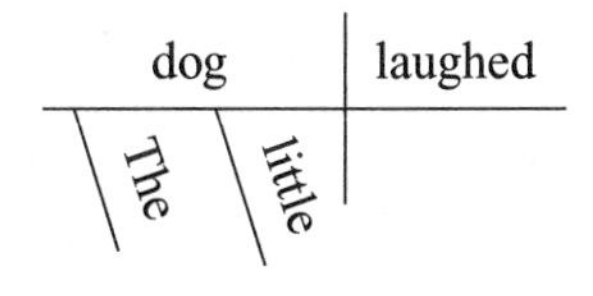

Since NPs can occur in several sentence slots—subject, direct object, indirect object, object of a preposition, objective complement, and subjective complement—adjectives can also occur as modifiers of those slots. The principle for diagramming adjectives remains the same, regardless of the role played by the noun that they modify. For example, to the right is a diagram of the sentence *Our new neighbors bought their youngest son a red motorcycle.*

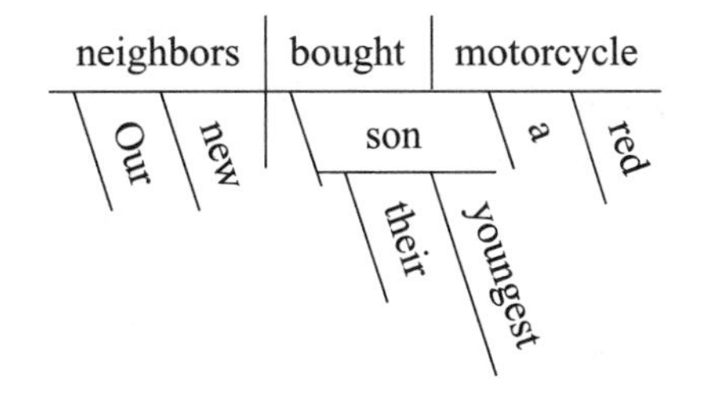

Exercise B

Diagram the following sentences.

a.† A good secretary is an invaluable asset.
b. She sent a funny card to her best friend.
c. I gave those old red shoes to a local charity.

ADJECTIVAL NOUNS

So far we have looked in some detail at adjectives, which are the "default" modifiers of nouns. However, at this point we need to introduce a distinction between **form** and **function**. Consider the following sentence:

1. The new legislation will have a small effect on the automobile industry.

This sentence contains two words whose form would lead us to classify them as adjectives: *new* and *small.* These words can be inflected for degree (*newer, smaller*), and they also can be intensified (*very new, too small*). Clearly, then, these words are adjectives; and we can make this judgment by looking at the form in isolation. We can further say that these words function as modifiers in the particular NPs in which they appear. That is, when we look at the NPs *the new legislation* and *a small effect,* we can see that *new* modifies *legislation,* and *small* modifies *effect.* In order to capture this fact, we can say that *new* and *small* are adjectives (in form) that are functioning adjectivally (i.e., that fit into an adjective slot) within this particular sentence.

If we were to limit ourselves to adjectives functioning adjectivally (i.e., modifying a noun) it might not be immediately clear why we even need to distinguish between form and function. However, now consider the word *automobile.* In terms of its form, this word would be classified as a noun. For example, it can be made plural and possessive (e.g., *automobiles, automobile's*), and it can co-occur with a determiner (e.g., *the/a/this automobile*). The same argument could be made for the word *industry*—it shows all the formal properties of being a noun. However, in the phrase *the automobile industry,* these two nouns play different roles. *Industry* is the headword of the NP; it is the noun that comprises the structural center of the NP. *Automobile*, on the other hand, is functioning as an **adjectival**—a word or phrase that modifies a noun. Thus, in this particular phrase, we can say that *automobile* is a noun (in form) functioning as an adjectival.

It is crucial to note that we are *not* calling *automobile* an adjective. To call something an adjective (or a noun) is to make a claim about its form, and by extension about the types of inflectional, derivational, and co-occurrence patterns to which it adheres. Under these tests, *automobile* is clearly not an adjective; for example, we have no forms like **very automobile* or **automobileest*. In contrast, to call something an adjectival is simply to make a claim about its function within a particular phrase. In the case of the phrase *the automobile industry*, we are simply observing that *automobile* modifies the noun *industry*; adjectivals are elements that modify nouns; therefore, *automobile* is an adjectival.

This example leads us to several generalizations about form and function:

- The form of a word can be identified by examining it in isolation (e.g., *automobile* is identifiable as a noun even when it does not appear in a phrase or sentence).
- The function of a word can be identified by examining its position in a phrase or sentence (e.g., depending on the sentence, *automobile* could be an adjectival or a **nominal**—a word serving a noun function such as subject or direct object).
- One function can typically be filled by a number of different forms. For example, the adjectival function can be filled by an adjective (e.g., *the <u>largest</u> industry*), but it can also be filled by a noun (e.g., *the <u>automobile</u> industry*).
- One form can often fill a number of functions. For example, among the functions that a noun can fill are subject, modifier, direct object, indirect object, object of a preposition, subjective complement, and objective complement.
- Certain functions are characteristically associated with certain forms, although they can be filled by other forms as well. For example, the characteristic form that fills the adjectival slot is that of adjective (e.g., *the <u>largest</u> industry*), although other forms can fill this slot as well (e.g., *the <u>automobile</u> industry*).

In order to avoid confusion and develop accuracy in your analytical skills, it's important to use form and function terminology precisely. For example, in analyzing the term *the automobile industry*, it would be accurate to refer to *automobile* as a noun (an accurate description of its form) or an adjectival (an accurate description of its function). It would be inaccurate to refer to it as an adjective (an inaccurate description of its form).

Diagramming Adjectival Nouns

An adjectival noun is diagrammed exactly like an adjective: it is placed on a slanted line below the noun that it modifies. So, for example, the sentence *That gas station doesn't accept credit cards* would be diagrammed as shown here.

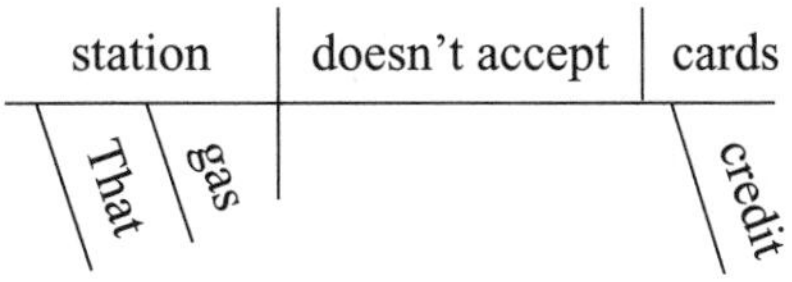

Exercise C

Identify any adjectival nouns in the following sentences. Then diagram the sentences.

a.† Our horse trailer has two feed mangers.
b. His last e-mail message upset the secretarial staff.
c. We found your address book.
d. Their dinner menu doesn't offer many low-fat choices.

ADJECTIVAL PREPOSITIONAL PHRASES

A **prepositional phrase** consists of a preposition followed by a noun phrase. Prepositional phrases are common as **post-nominal** adjectivals (i.e., following nouns), although they can also appear pre-nominally (i.e., preceding nouns). It is easy to find examples of prepositional phrases serving as post-nominal adjectivals: *the book on the table, the man in the moon, a play by Harold Pinter, the shop around the corner*. Pre-nominal prepositional phrases are less common, but do occur: *on-the-job training*, an *off-the-wall idea, the over-the-hill gang, an under-the-table agreement, an off-the-charts hit.* Note that when pre-nominal prepositional phrases appear in writing, they are typically hyphenated. This provides the reader with a visual cue that the hyphenated phrase is to be interpreted as a single unit, serving as a single adjectival modifying the following noun.

Note that not all post-nominal prepositional phrases are adjectival. As we will see in the next chapter, it is also possible for a prepositional phrase to function as an **adverbial**, i.e., as the modifier of a verb. For example, consider the following sentence: *The police arrested a suspect on Thursday.* The prepositional phrase *on Thursday* follows immediately after the nominal *a suspect*, yet it is not functioning adjectivally in this sentence.

There are several types of evidence for this. One is our intuition about what *on Thursday* modifies: it tells when the suspect was arrested. Since it tells us something about the verb, it is best classified as an adverbial. Another test is to construct a passive version of the sentence: *A suspect was arrested by the police on Thursday*. Notice that the two underlined parts of the sentence, *A suspect* and *on Thursday*, now occupy separate parts of the sentence. *A suspect* appears in subject position, but *on Thursday* remains in the predicate. This is further evidence that *on Thursday* is not a modifier of *A suspect*; if it were, if would have moved along to subject position when we converted the sentence to a passive. However, moving *on Thursday* into subject position yields an ungrammatical sentence: **A suspect on Thursday was arrested by the police.*

Exercise D

Decide if the prepositional phrase in each of the following sentences is functioning as an adjectival or as an adverbial. Supply evidence based on your intuitions about what the prepositional phrase modifies and, where possible, the passive test.

a.† The police arrested a suspect in the robbery.
b. Marilyn found the key to the door.
c. Marilyn put the key in the door.
d. The voters elected a person with great ambition.
e. Our neighbor down the street owns that car.

Diagramming Adjectival Prepositional Phrases

An adjectival prepositional phrase is diagrammed below the noun that it modifies. The preposition is placed on a right-slanting line, connected to its object on a horizontal line. For example, the sentence *We saw a revival of a play by George Bernard Shaw* is diagrammed below. This sentence contains two adjectival prepositional phrases: *of a play* (which modifies *revival*) and *by George Bernard Shaw* (which modifies *play*).

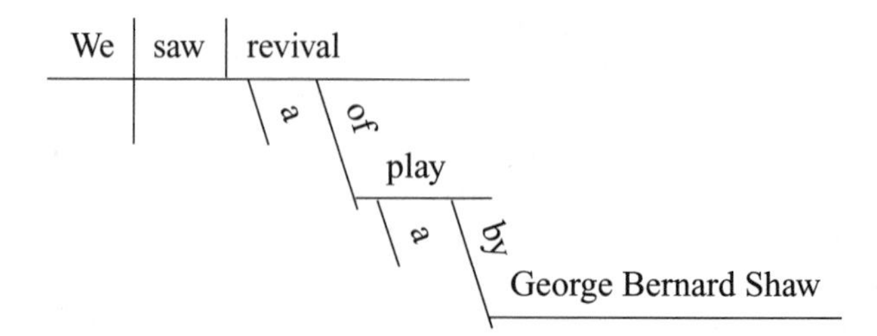

Exercise E

Diagram those sentences from Exercise D containing adjectival prepositional phrases.

ADJECTIVALS BASED ON VERB FORMS

So far we have looked at three forms that can function as adjectivals: adjectives, nouns, and prepositional phrases. In this section we will examine adjectivals based on various verb forms.

Participles

As explained in Chapter 7, a participle is a verb carrying the past participle or present participle inflection. The present participle verb in English is easy to identify, because it always ends in *-ing*: *moving, amusing,* and so forth. These forms can appear as pre-nominal adjectivals, in phrases such as *a moving target* and *an amusing book*, or they can appear post-nominally, as in *I find his jokes amusing,* for example. They can also appear in other adjectival slots such as subjective complement. Thus, in the sentence *John is annoying, annoying* is a subjective complement that modifies *John*.

As we saw in Chapter 7, past participles are somewhat trickier to identify than present participles. Recall that some verbs have a distinctive *-en* suffix that marks the past participle: *the broken window*, *a badly shaken victim*, and so forth. Other verbs, however, have a less predictable past participle form: *the torn dress*, *a fried potato*, *those cut flowers*. The best test for finding the past participle form is to construct an active sentence with auxiliary *have* in it. The verb form following *have* in such a sentence is always a past participle: for example, *She has torn her dress*, *They have cut all the flowers.*

Like present participles, past participles can serve as pre-nominal adjectivals (as in the examples in the previous paragraph) or as post-nominal adjectivals, as in *He likes his potatoes fried*. They can also serve as subjective complements, as in *Her dress is torn*, where *torn* modifies the noun *dress*.

Exercise F

For each of the following verbs, identify the past participle form. Remember to use the *have*-frame as a test if you need to. Then use each past participle in a phrase or sentence in which it functions adjectivally. Vary your phrases and sentences among pre-nominal and post-nominal adjectivals and subjective complements.

a.† type
b. injure
c.† write
d. use
e. prohibit
f. rest
g. age
h. lose

Infinitives

The infinitive verb form consists of the infinitive marker *to* followed by an uninflected verb form and any items that complement or modify the verb (e.g., a direct object). For example, consider the sentence *The best place to buy vegetables is the farmers' market*. The phrase *to buy vegetables* is an infinitive phrase which, in turn, functions adjectivally by modifying the noun *place*.

Exercise G

Identify those adjectivals based on verbs in the following sentences. Also identify the noun being modified.

a.† A rolling stone gathers no moss.
b. The five living Presidents attended the ceremony.
c.† James Bond has a license to kill.
d. One of the most popular places to vacation is Hawaii.
e.† I'd like some crushed ice.
f. She could be mistaken.
g. We left no stone unturned.

Diagramming Adjectivals Based on Verbs

Like other adjectivals, those based on verbs are diagrammed below the noun that they modify. Beyond this similarity, though, participles and infinitives are each diagrammed somewhat differently. A participle is placed on an angled line below the item that it modifies. For example, the following diagram shows the sentence *The badly shaken victim left the burning wreckage*, which contains two adjectival participles (*shaken* and *burning*).

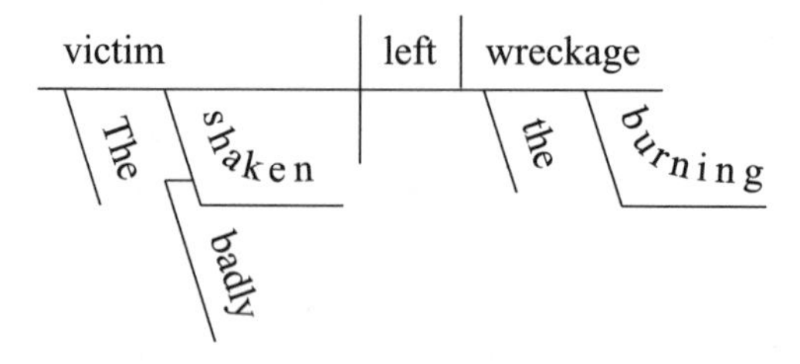

Note also that in this sentence, the adverb *badly* is attached to the item that it modifies, *shaken*.

An infinitive is diagrammed with *to* on a slanted line (like a preposition), followed by the infinitive verb form on a horizontal line (like the object of a preposition). For example, consider the sentence *A good place to eat is the Chinese restaurant at the mall.* In this sentence, *to eat* is an adjectival infinitive phrase modifying *place*, and thus is diagrammed as follows.

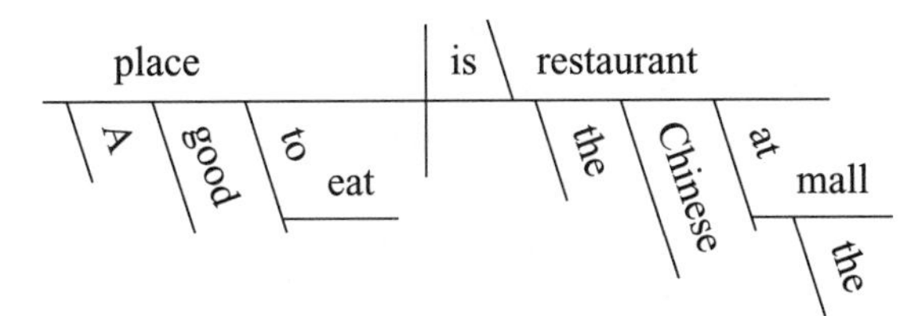

Exercise H

Diagram the sentences in Exercise G.

RELATIVE CLAUSES

A relative clause is a **dependent clause** (i.e., a group of words containing a subject and a predicate) that modifies a noun. For this reason, relative clauses are also sometimes referred to as **adjectival clauses**. Examples of relative clauses are shown in the italicized portions of the following sentences:

2. The police caught the man *who robbed the bank.*
3. The man *who robbed the bank* was carrying a gun.
4. The bank *that the man robbed* is near my house.
5. My friend works at the bank *that the man robbed.*

These examples show that a relative clause can modify any noun. For example, the relative clause in (2) modifies an object in the **main clause**, as does the relative clause in (5). The relative clause in (3) modifies the subject of the main clause, as does the relative clause in (4).

These examples also show that a relative clause may contain a **relative pronoun** that refers back to the noun being modified by the clause. Since relative clauses always occur post-nominally, we can refer to the noun as the antecedent of the relative pronoun. English contains five relative pronouns: *who, whom, that, which*, and *whose*. The relative pronoun may be omitted in some relative clauses: for example, *My friend works at the bank* <u>the man robbed</u>. However, you can confirm that this is a relative clause by reinserting a relative pronoun (*that* or *which*).

Exercise I

Underline the relative clause in each of the following sentences. Circle any relative pronouns. Double-underline the item that the relative clause modifies. (Two of the sentences do not contain relative pronouns.)

a.† The latest book that he wrote is a best-seller.
b. I didn't understand the question that she asked.
c.† Do you know the person who owns this car?
d. The next person who calls will win a free ticket.
e. The store doesn't have the brand I usually buy.
f. I can't decide between the two applicants we interviewed.
g. Every person whose child is an honors student received a bumper sticker.

Function of the Relative Pronoun

A relative clause has the essential elements of a sentence, namely a subject and a predicate. In turn, the relative pronoun—which is, after all, a "pro-noun," an element substituting for a nominal—fills one of the slots in the relative clause normally filled by a noun: subject, subjective complement, direct object, objective complement, indirect object, or object of a preposition. (The exceptions are *whose*, which functions as a determiner, and *where*, which functions as an adverbial.)

Exercise J

Examine the relative pronouns that you identified in Exercise I (repeated here). What is the function of each of these relative pronouns within the relative clause?

a.† The latest book that he wrote is a best-seller.
b. I didn't understand the question that she asked.
c.† Do you know the person who owns this car?
d. The next person who calls will win a free ticket.
e. The store doesn't have the brand I usually buy.
f. I can't decide between the two applicants we interviewed.
g. Every person whose child is an honors student received a bumper sticker.

From Exercises I and J, you should be able to confirm the following:

- A relative clause modifies a noun in the main clause.
- A relative pronoun functions as a noun within the relative clause.

These principles may combine in a number of ways. For example, consider the following possibilities:

- Relative clause modifying a subject; relative pronoun functioning as subject. Example: *The man <u>who robbed the bank</u> was carrying a gun.*
- Relative clause modifying an object; relative pronoun functioning as subject. Example: *The police caught the man <u>who robbed the bank</u>.*
- Relative clause modifying a subject; relative pronoun functioning as object. Example: *The bank <u>that the man robbed</u> is on the corner.*
- Relative clause modifying an object; relative pronoun functioning as object. Example: *My friend works at the bank <u>that the man robbed</u>.*

Diagramming Relative Clauses

To diagram a relative clause, begin by isolating the relative clause from the rest of the sentence (the main clause) and then analyze the internal structure of the relative clause. The relative pronoun is diagrammed to reflect its function within the relative clause. Then the relative pronoun is linked by a dashed line to the noun that the relative clause modifies.

For example, consider the sentence *The bank that the man robbed is on the corner.* We can make the following observations about this sentence.

- *That the man robbed* is a relative clause
- Within the relative clause, the relative pronoun *that* functions as the object of *robbed*
- The relative clause modifies the subject of the main clause, *bank*

Based on this analysis, we would diagram this sentence as follows.

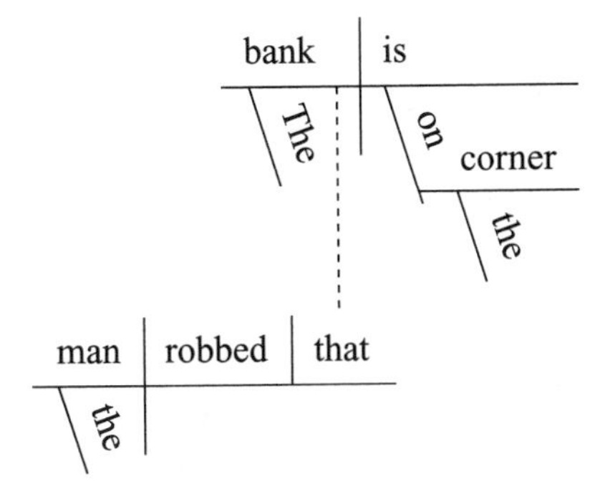

In a relative clause containing *whose*, the relative pronoun is diagrammed to reflect its function as a determiner. For example, the sentence *I know someone whose brother is a movie actor* would be diagrammed as follows.

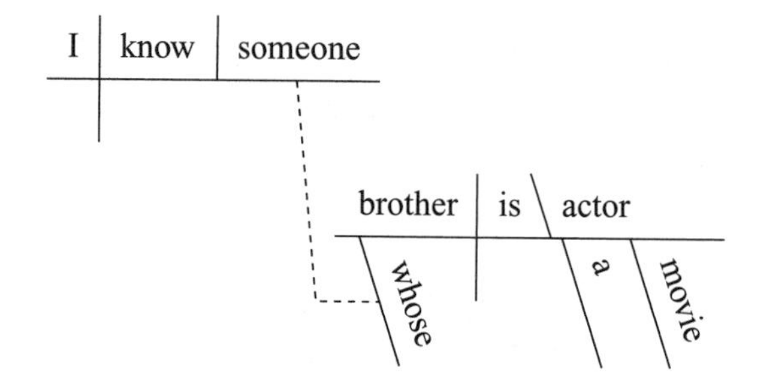

Likewise, in a relative clause containing *where*, the relative pronoun is diagrammed to reflect its function as an adverbial. Consequently, such items are sometimes called **relative adverbs**. For example, the adjacent diagram shows the sentence *The store where I bought this jacket is closed.*

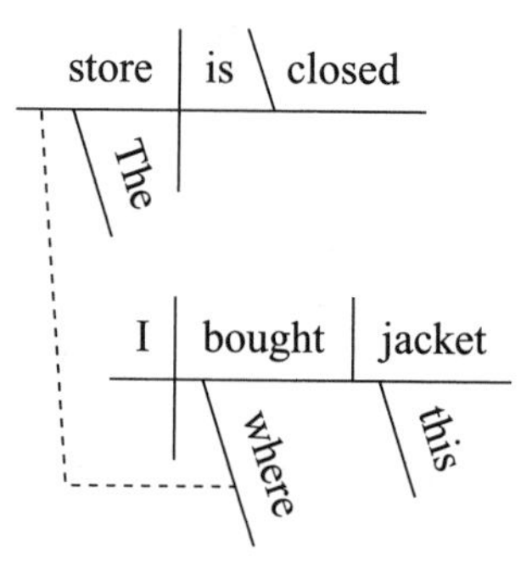

If the relative pronoun is omitted, the missing pronoun (e.g., *that, who*) is placed in parentheses in the slot that the relative pronoun would otherwise occupy. For example, the sentence *The bank the man robbed is near my house* would be diagrammed as follows.

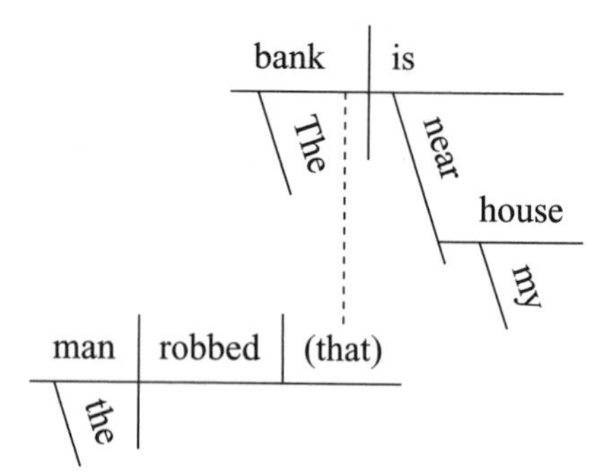

Exercise K

Diagram the sentences in Exercise J.

Restrictive and Nonrestrictive Relative Clauses

Before leaving the topic of relative clauses, let's look briefly at two subgroups of relative clauses: restrictive and nonrestrictive. These terms refer to whether or not the relative clause provides information that is needed to uniquely identify the noun being modified by the relative clause.

All our examples up to this point have been **restrictive relative clauses**. In each case, the writer assumes that the reader would not be able to identify the referent of the modified noun without the information supplied by the relative clause. In this sense, then, the relative clause "restricts" the possible interpretations that the reader might put on the sentence: for example, *Hand me the book that is on the table* (i.e., not the one on the desk).

Let's turn to some examples of **nonrestrictive relative clauses**. Like a restrictive relative clause, a nonrestrictive relative clause supplies additional information about the noun that it modifies. However, by using a nonrestrictive clause, the writer assumes that even without this information, the reader could still identify the referent of the modified noun. The information supplied by the relative clause is the type of information that we might preface with "incidentally." The following sentences contain examples of nonrestrictive clauses.

6. President Clinton, who left for Camp David on Sunday, is expected to win the primary.
7. The book, which he published last summer, is on the best-seller list.
8. The workers at this company, who belong to a powerful union, are negotiating a new contract.

Notice the difference between how restrictive and nonrestrictive relative clauses are punctuated. A nonrestrictive relative clause is set off with a pair of commas at the beginning and end of the clause.

In general, relative clauses that modify proper nouns (e.g., *President Clinton*) are punctuated as nonrestrictive. The reasoning behind this convention is that proper nouns are generally considered to refer to unique entities; therefore, any additional descriptive material is not necessary for their identification.

In many other cases, however, a relative clause cannot be punctuated as restrictive or nonrestrictive without considering the context in which it occurs or the writer's assumptions. For example, consider the following sentences.

9. Teenagers who constantly listen to loud music are likely to suffer permanent damage to their hearing.
10. Teenagers, who constantly listen to loud music, are likely to suffer permanent damage to their hearing.

Sentence (9) assumes that there are at least two groups or types of teenagers: those who constantly listen to loud music and those who don't. This assumption is signaled by the use of a restrictive relative clause: *who constantly listen to loud music* identifies a particular subset of the antecedent *teenagers*. In contrast, (10) conveys a different assumption: that *all* teenagers constantly listen to loud music. This assumption is signaled by the use of a nonrestrictive relative clause. When this type of relative clause is used, the message conveyed by the writer/speaker is that the main clause would still be true even without the "incidental" material supplied by the relative clause: *Teenagers are likely to suffer permanent damage to their hearing*. Clearly, then, (10) makes a generalization that (9) doesn't.

Exercise L

Identify the relative clauses in the following sentences as restrictive or nonrestrictive. Then change each restrictive relative clause to a nonrestrictive, and vice-versa. When you make this change, what differences arise in how you interpret the sentence, or in the attitudes, beliefs, or assumptions that you attribute to the writer of the sentence?

a.† Men who rely on women to cook for them often go hungry.
b.† The suspect, who was arrested by the police on Thursday, is a known felon.
c. The greatest benefits from his tax reform bill will go to members of the upper class who currently pay lower taxes anyway.
d. I made the mistake of falling in love with a suede coat which I could not afford.
e. The workers at that company, who belong to a powerful union, are negotiating a new contract.

Summary

Modifiers of nouns are known as adjectivals. As shown in the diagram below, this class includes not just adjectives but also other categories that can serve to modify nouns. Thus *adjectival* describes a general function rather than a specific form.

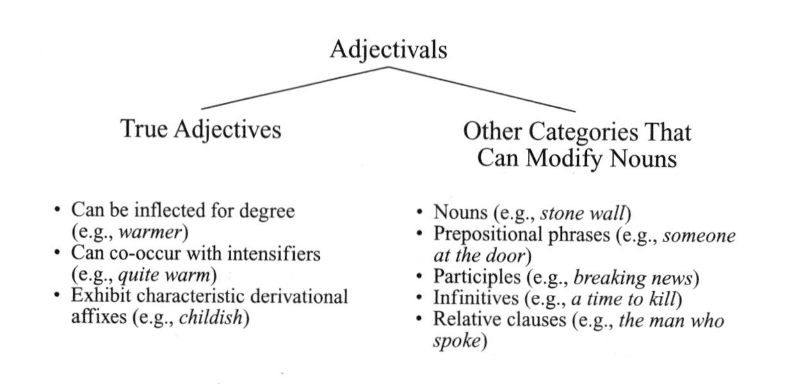

SUPPLEMENTARY EXERCISES

1. Earlier we observed that adjectives can be made comparative and superlative and can co-occur with intensifiers such as *very*. However, some people argue that comparative, superlative, or intensified forms of *unique* should not be used.

a. Does this mean that *unique* is not an adjective?
b. Do you think *unique* is an adjective? If so, what is your evidence? If not, what part of speech do you think it is?
c. What is the rationale behind the prohibition of comparative, superlative, and intensified forms of *unique*?
d. When you have heard such forms used, what meaning do you think was intended by their users?
e. What type of grammar subscribes to this prohibition?

2. Examine the sentences from Exercise I. Identify any sentences in which the relative pronoun is omitted, or from which it could be omitted. Can you draw any generalizations about when a relative pronoun can be omitted?

a. The latest book that he wrote is a best-seller.
b. I didn't understand the question that she asked in class.
c. Do you know the person who owns this car?
d. The next person who calls will win a free ticket.
e. The store was out of the brand I usually buy.
f. I can't decide between the two applicants we interviewed.
g. Every person whose child is an honors student received a bumper sticker.

3. Earlier in this chapter we said that proper nouns are followed by nonrestrictive, rather than restrictive, relative clauses. However, consider the sentence *The Baltimore that I knew as a child has changed over the past several decades*. How would you account for the acceptability of the restrictive relative clause (*that I knew as a child*) following *Baltimore*?

4. Ambiguity can sometimes arise in the use of noun modifiers. First, identify the ambiguity in each of the following sentences. Second, diagram each sentence in two different ways, to demonstrate where the ambiguity arises. Third, revise each sentence in two different ways (each revision should reflect a different interpretation).

a. Gifts may not include tobacco or perfume costing more than $5.00.
b. The newspaper reported the results of the vote on Thursday.
c. The police arrested our neighbor down the street.

5. Modifiers often occur in compound form, especially in scientific and technical writing. Several principles govern their punctuation:

- Hyphenate the parts of a compound adjectival when it precedes a noun. However, don't hyphenate between the compound adjectival and the noun (e.g., *well-organized proposal*).
- Do not hyphenate compounds composed of an adverb-adjectival if the adverb ends in *-ly* (e.g., *recently remodeled facilities*).

Based on these principles, decide whether each modifying phrase needs hyphenation.

a. a 30 second alarm
b. those computer generated images
c. that poorly written proposal
d. a nineteenth century invention
e. this badly needed renovation
f. a newly developed theory
g. a 2 inch pipe
h. twelve 18 month calendars
i. the company's earnings per share ratio
j. their overly complicated form

6. According to Clark and Clark (pp. 355–56), children acquiring relative clauses find them easier to interpret if the relative pronoun cannot be deleted and if the relative clause does not interrupt the main clause. Based on these principles, which one of the following sentences should be easiest for a child to interpret? Most difficult?

A. The girl that ran after the boy caught the dog.
B. The girl that the boy ran after caught the dog.
C. The girl caught the dog that ran after the boy.
D. The girl caught the dog that the boy ran after.

▲▲▲ CHAPTER 9

Modifiers of Verbs

In the previous chapter we looked at modifiers of nominals. In this chapter we will look at four modifiers of verbs: adverbs, prepositional phrases, verb phrases, and adverbial clauses. Just as adjectives are the prototypical modifiers of nouns, so adverbs are the prototypical modifiers of verbs. Hence we can use the cover term **adverbial** to describe all types of verb modifiers.

ADVERBS

An adverb is a word that modifies a verb, typically by telling how, when, where, or why the action expressed by the verb happened. Adverbs can be identified by several structural tests. First, many adverbs consist of an adjective with an *-ly* suffix: *She ran quickly, He plays wonderfully, I don't fully understand.*

Second, in addition to *-ly*, there are several other derivational suffixes that signal an adverb formed from another part of speech, most notably *-ward(s)* and *-wise*. The suffix *-ward(s)* forms an adverb from a preposition or noun, as in *We ate lunch and went swimming afterwards*, *My thoughts turned inward as I walked homeward*. The suffix *-wise* forms an adverb from a noun, as in *Cut the cloth lengthwise*.

Third, adverbs (like adjectives) can usually be intensified: *She ran very quickly, He plays more wonderfully than I expected, I don't quite fully understand*. Notice that adverbs and adjectives share the same set of intensifiers; some of the more common ones are *very, more, less, quite, almost, extremely,* and *too*.

Be aware that, while the *-ly* suffix is characteristic of adverbs, there are a number of common adverbs that do not end in *-ly*, including *fast, hard, late, high, long, straight*, and *wrong*. For example, we have sentences like the following: *You're driving too fast*, *He didn't try very hard, We arrived late*, *She aims high, We have stayed too long*, *I can't see straight*, and *Something went wrong*. Note that all these words can also be used as adjectives: *a fast ball, a hard test, a late arrival, a high* *grade, a long drive, a straight arrow*, and *a wrong answer.* And even though some of them can occur with an *-ly* suffix, the suffix alters the meaning of the root. For example, *lately*, as in *Have you seen him lately?*, means 'recently'; *hardly*, as in *I've hardly begun*, means 'barely.'

Exercise A

The following words all end in *-ly.* Are all of them adverbs? If a word is not an adverb, what category does it belong to? Are there any cases where the category cannot be determined with certainty?

a.† silly	e. harmfully
b.† utterly	f. basically
c. heavenly	g. outwardly
d. seemingly	h. intensely

Diagramming Adverbs

An adverb is diagrammed on a slanted line below the verb that it modifies. Any intensifier of the adverb is diagrammed as a modifier of it. For example, consider the sentence *I don't quite fully understand.* In this instance, *fully* is an adverb modifying *understand*, while *quite* is an intensifier modifying *fully*. This sentence would be diagrammed as shown at right.

Uncontracted negative words (e.g., *not, never*) are also considered adverbs and therefore are also diagrammed as modifiers of the main verb. For example, consider the sentence *I almost never read biographies*. In this instance, *never* is an adverb modifying *read*, and *almost* modifies *never*. This sentence would be diagrammed as shown at right.

Finally, if a verb is modified by more than one adverb, they are placed on parallel lines in the order in which they occur in the sentence. For example, the sentence *I walked homeward quickly* would be diagrammed as shown at right.

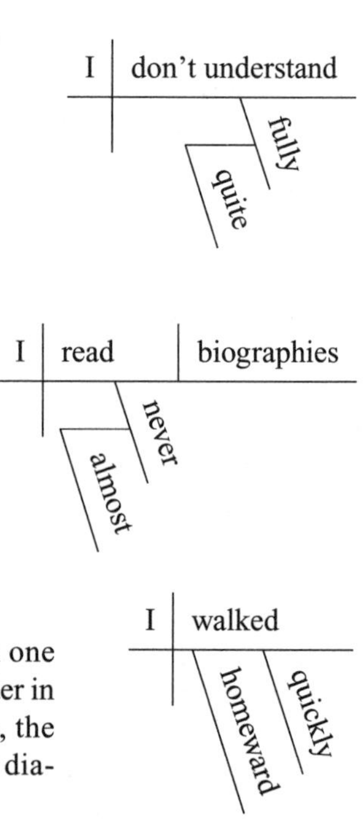

Exercise B

Diagram the following sentences.

a.† He speaks French very fluently.
b.† You're always driving too fast.
c. The people in my Shakespeare class seldom raise their hands.
d. A number of faculty have just recently joined the union.
e. That truck almost crashed.

ADVERBIAL PREPOSITIONAL PHRASES

Prepositional phrases are a common type of verb modifier. They may be used to provide any of the general types of information associated with adverbials. For example, a PP may indicate manner (*She speaks with a French accent*), place (*They are campaigning in Iowa)*, time (*I'll meet you at three o'clock*), or reason (*I'm saving for a new car*).

Exercise C

Identify the adverbial PP in each of the following sentences. Describe the type of information provided by the adverbial.

a.† He left in a hurry.
b.† They studied for three hours.
c. They studied for the French test.
d. Call me on Wednesday.
e. We must have driven through a foot of mud.

As explained in Chapter 8, PPs can also function as adjectivals. Since a predicate can contain both a verb and a noun (e.g., a direct object), a predicate can also contain both types of PPs—adverbial (one that modifies the verb) and adjectival (one that modifies the noun).

As an example, consider the sentence *I saw a student from my class at the movies.* This sentence contains two PPs: *from my class* and *at the movies*. The first PP, *from my class*, is an adjectival modifying *student* (it provides information about which student was seen). The second PP, *at the movies*, is an adverbial modifying *saw* (it tells where the action expressed by the verb happened). In addition, the same predicate could contain more than one adverbial PP: for example, *I saw a student from my class at the movies on Thursday*. In this case, both *at the movies* and *on Thursday* are adverbials modifying *saw*. This sentence is diagrammed below.

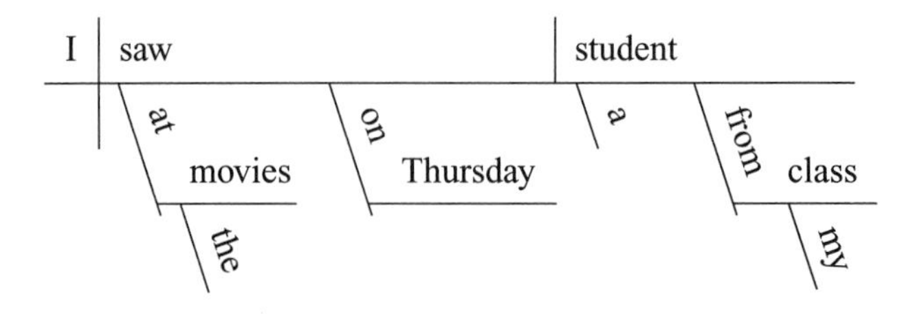

Exercise D

Identify each PP as adjectival or adverbial. Supply evidence based on your intuitions about what the PP modifies and, where possible, the passive test described in Chapter 8. Are any sentences ambiguous—i.e., are there any cases where a PP can be interpreted as both an adjectival and an adverbial? What changes can you make in the position of some of the adverbial PPs?

a.† Marilyn put the key to the door in her purse.

b.† The path through the woods was blocked by the snowstorm on Tuesday.

c. The storm stranded a boat in the middle of Lake Superior.

d. They went to Mexico over spring break.

e. The teacher gave us the answers to the test on Monday.

You probably observed that some adverbial PPs can be separated from the predicate and moved to the beginning of the sentence. Adverbials are, in general, more flexible in their position than are adjectivals. For example, a sentence like *They went to Mexico over spring break* can be paraphrased *Over spring break, they went to Mexico.*

Related to adverbial PPs are a small group of noun phrases that can function adverbially: for example, *Call me <u>Wednesday</u>, I'm leaving <u>today</u>, He writes <u>every morning</u>, We're going <u>home</u>.* Note that in some cases a preposition can be reinserted before the adverbial NP (e.g., *Call me <u>on Wednesday</u>*); in the case of *today* and *tomorrow*, the adverbial NP derives historically from the merger of a preposition (*to*) and a noun (*day, morrow*). In other cases, the preposition cannot be reinserted idiomatically (*I write during every morning, He's going to home*). Nevertheless, such phrases seem to function analogously to adverbial PPs and are probably best considered a variation on them, or perhaps a truncated version of them.

Diagramming Adverbial PPs

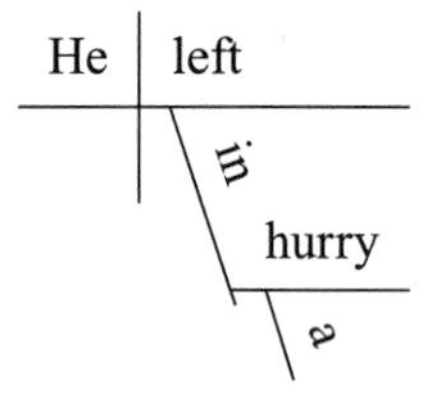

An adverbial PP is diagrammed below the main verb that it modifies. For example, consider the diagram of the sentence *He left in a hurry*, where *in a hurry* is an adverbial PP modifying *left.*

A truncated PP is diagrammed like a PP, but the preposition itself is omitted. For example, in the sentence *He writes every morning, every morning* is a truncated PP modifying *writes*. In turn, *every* modifies *morning*. This sentence would be diagrammed as shown at right.

As we saw in the previous section, sentences containing more than one adverbial are diagrammed with the adverbials in sequence. For example, consider the sentence *They studied diligently for the French test*. Both *diligently* and *for the French test* are adverbials modifying *studied*. The diagram of this sentence is to the right.

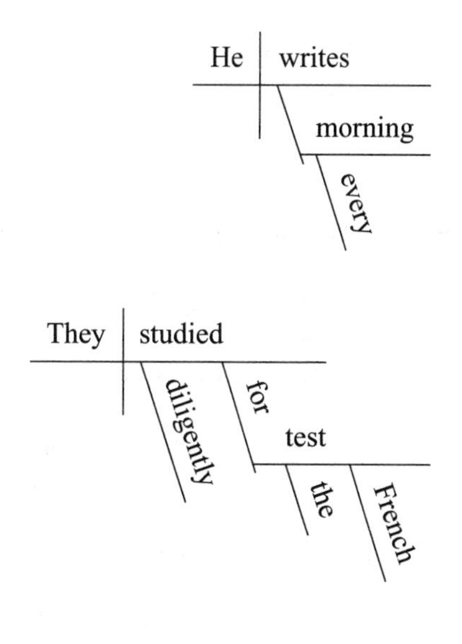

Exercise E

> Diagram the sentences in Exercises C and D, paying particular attention to whether modifiers are functioning adverbially or adjectivally.

ADVERBIAL VERB PHRASES

Three types of verb phrases can function as adverbials. The most common is the **infinitive phrase**, consisting of *to* followed by a verb form. An infinitive phrase typically tells how or why an action is performed: for example, *She plays <u>to win</u>, I often read mysteries <u>to relax</u>*. Since infinitive phrases contain verbs, they can also contain complements, objects, and adverbials: for example, *I bought a book <u>to teach myself French in three days</u>*.

Exercise F

> Analyze the function of the following elements in the sentence *I bought a book to teach myself French in three days.*
>
> a. *to teach myself French in three days*
> b. *myself*
> c. *French*
> d. *in three days*

Although less common than infinitives as adverbials, present participles can also function as adverbials: for example, *Horses sleep standing up*, *They hit the ground running*. Likewise, past participles can also serve as adverbials: for example, *I slept fully dressed*.

Diagramming Adverbial Verb Phrases

Verb phrases functioning adverbially are all diagrammed below the main verb that they modify. An infinitive is diagrammed using a structure similar to a PP, with *to* filling the preposition slot. For example, consider the diagram of the sentence *I often read mysteries to relax*.

An adverbial participle is placed on an angled line below the verb that it modifies. For example, the adjacent diagram shows the sentence *They hit the ground running*.

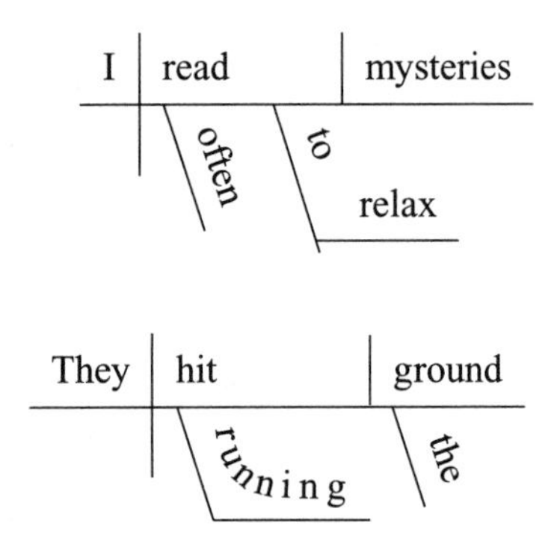

Exercise G

Identify the function of the infinitive and participial verb phrases in the following sentences. In particular, be sure that you can distinguish items that are functioning adverbially from those that are functioning adjectivally. Then diagram each sentence. (Hint: Be careful not to confuse the preposition *to* with infinitival *to*. The preposition *to* always precedes a noun or noun modifier, and infinitival *to* always precedes a verb or verb modifier.)

a.† She was dressed to kill.

b. I went to the store to get a carton of milk.

c. The cab driver knows the best way to get to Carnegie Hall.

d.† The falling stock market alarmed many investors.

e. He stood in line for three hours to get tickets for that show.

f.† Her son hit a stop sign driving home.

g. I slept fully dressed.

ADVERBIAL CLAUSES

A fourth type of verb modifier is the adverbial clause. This is a **subordinate** (i.e., dependent) **clause** introduced by a **subordinating conjunction**. A sentence consisting of a subordinate clause and a **main** (i.e., independent) **clause** is called a **complex sentence**. The most common subordinating conjunctions are listed below, with a brief explanation of the type of relationship each one denotes.

Cause-effect:	*because, if, since*
Chronology:	*after, as long as, as soon as, before, once, until, when*
Comparison:	*as, just as*
Contrast:	*although, despite the fact that, even though, in spite of the fact that, though*

Adverbial clauses can either precede or follow the main clause, as illustrated below.

1. *Even though* sand colic is a common disorder in areas having sandy soils, little information exists about its clinical signs, treatment, and prognosis.
2. Little information exists about the clinical signs, treatment, and prognosis of sand colic, *even though* it is a common disorder in areas having sandy soils.

In standard written English, an adverbial clause must be punctuated as part of a sentence containing an independent clause. Otherwise the adverbial clause constitutes a sentence fragment, like the italicized material in the following example.

3. Little information exists about the clinical signs, treatment, and prognosis of sand colic. *Even though it is a common disorder in areas having sandy soils.*

When the adverbial clause precedes the main clause, the standard punctuation calls for a comma after the adverbial clause, as in the following example:

4. Because many residents are failing to put their garbage in plastic bags, dogs have been creating a mess around the trash containers.

When the adverbial clause follows the main clause, it is separated by a comma if it signals comparison or contrast, but not if it illustrates cause–effect or chronology. The following sentences are punctuated according to this principle.

5. A transition helps the reader follow your prose, *just as* a road sign helps a traveler decide which way to go. (Comparison)
6. Little information exists about this disorder, *in spite of the fact* that it is so common. (Contrast)

7. He didn't do well on the test *because* he hasn't been coming to class. (Cause–Effect)

8. I will grade these papers *after* I eat dinner. (Chronology)

Exercise H

Combine each pair of clauses into a single sentence, using a subordinating conjunction to do so. You may make slight revisions, but be sure to retain the complete intended meaning. Punctuate each sentence according to the principles described in this section.

a. Being self-insured is quite tempting to companies trying to cut costs. The risks involved in such a decision can be quite serious.

b. These components are slightly more expensive initially. Their use greatly reduces your overall system cost in the long run.

c. I have experience working in a busy retail store. I believe I am a good candidate for your internship.

d. We review the candidates on Monday. We will announce our decision on Tuesday.

e. Many people make investment decisions without adequate information. They do not know how to acquire sound investment advice.

Diagramming Adverbial Clauses

To diagram an adverbial clause, begin by separating it from the main clause. The adverbial clause is diagrammed like a simple sentence and placed below the main clause. The main verbs of the two clauses are then linked by a dotted line containing the subordinating conjunction. For example, the sentence *If you drive too fast, you'll get a ticket* is diagrammed as shown here.

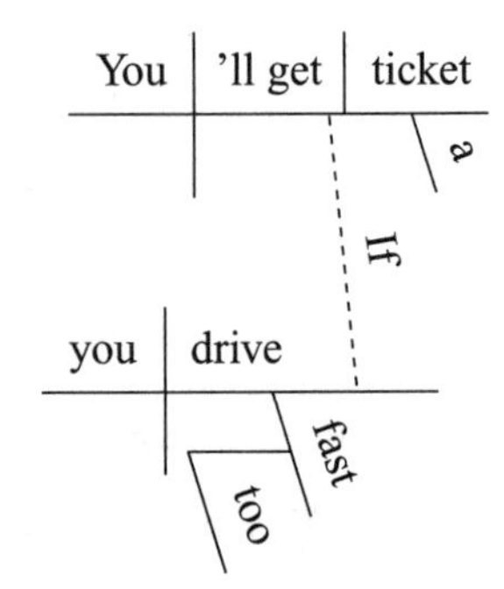

Likewise, the sentence *The unemployment rate rose dramatically when the factory closed* would be diagrammed as follows.

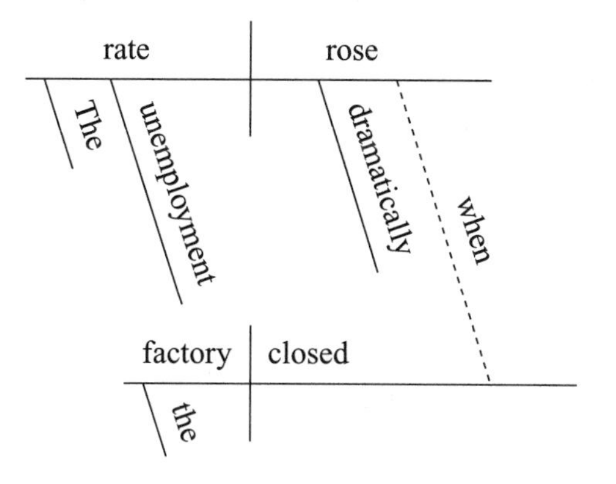

Exercise I

Diagram the following sentences.

a. Because I could not stop for Death, he kindly stopped for me. (Emily Dickinson)
b.† Although the house has a big yard, it doesn't have enough bedrooms.
c. I will grade these papers after I eat dinner.
d. We won't catch the plane unless we leave now.
e.† When the Democrats introduced a bill to raise spending, they didn't consider its effects on the domestic economy.
f. Little information exists about the clinical signs of sand colic, even though it is a common disorder in areas having sandy soils.

Summary

Modifiers of verbs are known as adverbials. As shown in the diagram below, this class includes not just adverbs but also other categories that can modify verbs. Thus the term *adverbial* describes a general function rather than a specific form.

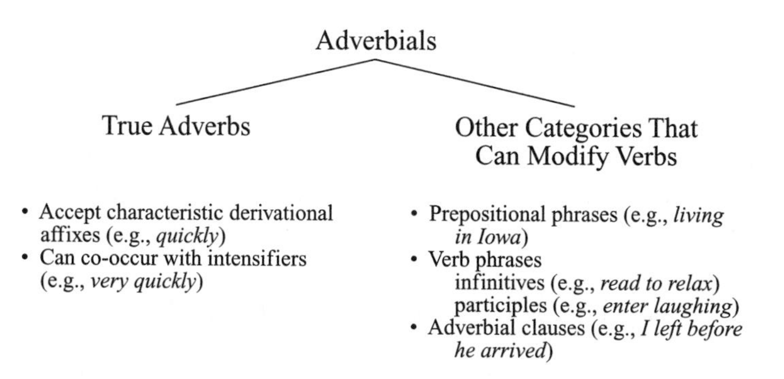

SUPPLEMENTARY EXERCISES

1. There is a classic Groucho Marx joke that goes as follows: "One morning I saw an elephant in my pajamas. How he got in my pajamas I don't know." What is the source of the humor in this joke? (Hint: Draw two diagrams of *I saw an elephant in my pajamas.*)

2. "Dangling" modifiers result from a combination of two conditions:

- A sentence begins with an introductory participial phrase that does not contain a subject for the participle, and
- The subject of the sentence's main clause is not a logical agent for the participle.

For example, the following sentence begins with a dangling modifier: *While inspecting the plant, several safety violations were noted.*

One way to revise a dangling modifier is to add an agent for the participle into the introductory phrase (e.g., *While <u>the engineers</u> were inspecting the plant, several safety violations were noted*). Another way is to make a logical agent of the participle the subject of the main clause (e.g., *While inspecting the plant, <u>the engineers</u> noted several safety violations*).

Based on these principles, identify and revise any dangling modifiers in the following sentences. (Note: you will need to figure out a logical agent in some cases.)

a. By filling out the enclosed forms, the changes you are requesting can be made in your policy.

b. When using Universal Price Codes, errors due to incorrect pricing are greatly reduced.

c. After evaluating the software packages on three criteria, a clear winner became apparent.

d. By assuming a pipe diameter of 4 inches, the total size of the reactor was calculated to be 164 feet.

e. By having more products in stock, our shipping accuracy should improve to 97.5 percent.

3. One common type of sentence fragment results from punctuating a phrase or subordinate clause as an independent clause (i.e., as a sentence). For example, the italicized portion of the following passage is a sentence fragment:

> Student retention has risen. *Although new student enrollment has declined.*

The simplest way to correct a subordinate clause fragment is to join it to the beginning or end of the main clause that usually comes before it (e.g., *Student retention has risen, although new student enrollment has declined*).

Identify the fragment in each of the following passages. (If possible, also identify the type of phrase or clause that constitutes the fragment.) Then revise each passage so that it no longer contains a fragment. Note: There is usually more than one way to revise each passage.

a. Student retention has risen. Because of increased advising efforts.
b. We should encourage employee participation in cost control. For example, an award for the best money-saving idea.
c. Many new companies have entered the industry. Making it more difficult to gain market share.
d. This material has many uses. For instance, to repair tissue.
e. The mail-order industry has several advantages. One of those being the ability to target catalogs at specific demographic groups.
f. The company has hired a number of employees over the past six months. Who may be laid off after the merger.
g. The meeting will be simulcast from the Twin Cities. Which will allow viewers in Duluth to watch.
h. Each program makes different use of the input devices. Some uses being more logical than others.

▲▲▲ CHAPTER 10

Nominals

In previous chapters we have looked at both the form and function of nouns and NPs. In this chapter we will look at various types of clauses and phrases that can substitute for NPs.

Our discussion in this chapter builds upon the basic distinction between form and function introduced in Chapter 8. In that chapter we distinguished between adjectives and adjectivals, the latter being words or phrases that function as adjectives but that do not themselves display the characteristic forms associated with adjectives.

A similar situation holds with the structures we will be examining in this chapter: phrase and clause types that, while not NPs themselves, can fill the role of an NP. Just as we used the label *adjectival* to describe other categories that function as adjectives, so we use the label **nominal** to describe other categories that function as NPs. Nominals, like NPs, can appear in a variety of slots: subject, direct object, indirect object, subjective complement, objective complement, and object of a preposition.

THAT-CLAUSES

The word *that* serves several different functions in English. One of these is to introduce a nominal clause (i.e., a clause that can fill a nominal slot), as in *I think that you're sick*. Nominal clauses are also known as **noun clauses**. In this role, *that* is known as a **complementizer** or as **expletive *that*.** However, as you will recall from previous chapters, *that* can also function as a demonstrative pronoun (e.g., *I know that man*) and as a relative pronoun (e.g., *I saw a dog that was wearing a sweatshirt*). At this point, it might be useful to get some practice in distinguishing the three types of *that*.

The demonstrative pronoun *that* is fairly easy to identify. Try substituting another demonstrative pronoun (*this, these*, or *those*) for *that*; if you can do so, you are dealing with the demonstrative form of *that*. For example, in the sentence *I know that man*, we can substitute *this, these,* and *those* (*I know this/these/those men*).

It can be a bit trickier to distinguish between expletive *that* (which introduces a nominal clause) and relative pronoun *that* (which introduces a relative clause). For example, the following sentences contain clauses beginning with *that*; some of them are nominal clauses, while others are relative (i.e., adjectival) clauses.

1. I know *that I turned out the lights.*
2. *That I might not want his help* had not occurred to him.
3. It had not occurred to him *that I might not want his help.*
4. You need to replace the fuse *that I bought.*
5. The paint *that she bought for the living room* clashes with the rug.

However, there are several principles we can use to tell them apart.

Function of the Clause

A nominal clause has an NP function within the larger sentence. For example, in (1), the clause functions as the direct object of *know*. In (2), the clause functions as the subject of the sentence. In (3), the clause functions as an **appositive** (i.e., material that renames another noun in the sentence—in this case, the subject *it*). All these functions are nominal in nature.

In contrast, a relative clause does not have an NP function within the larger sentence; rather it is adjectival in nature. For example, in (4), the relative clause modifies the direct object *the fuse*; in (5), the relative clause modifies the subject *the paint*.

Location of the Clause

Relative clauses generally follow NPs. However, we cannot assume that every *that*-clause following an NP is a relative clause. A nominal clause can also immediately follow an NP. This type of structure is illustrated in (6).

6. The idea *that I might not want his help* never occurred to him.

Even though the italicized phrase immediately follows the NP *the idea*, it does not modify that NP. Instead, it serves as an appositive clause, one that renames an NP in the same syntactic position. (In this case, *that I might not want his help* renames *The idea*, and both occur in subject position.) Such appositive clauses generally follow NPs that refer to concepts or ideas: for example, *the idea*, *the fact, the notion*, *the rumor*, *the proposal*. However, the mere presence of such an NP does not guarantee that you are dealing with an appositive. Compare (6) with (7).

7. The idea *that she proposed at the meeting* should be investigated further.

In (7), the italicized phrase is a relative clause modifying the noun phrase *the idea*. Note: *that she proposed at the meeting* does not rename *the idea*; rather it identifies which idea it was—the one she proposed at the meeting, not the one she proposed, say, in a memo.

Another way of distinguishing between nominal clauses like (6) and relative clauses like (7) is to put *is* between the NP and the clause. If the clause is nominal, the result will be grammatical: *The idea is that I might not want his help.* If the clause is a relative clause, the result will be unacceptable: **The idea is that she proposed at the meeting.*

Deletion Test

If a relative clause is deleted, we still have a grammatical sentence (e.g., [4] *You need to replace the fuse*). However, a nominal clause generally cannot be deleted without destroying the grammaticality of the sentence (e.g., [2] **Had not occurred to him*). This difference in behavior follows from the fact that adjectivals are typically optional elements (and thus deletable); however, nominals (except for appositives) are generally required elements (and therefore not deletable).

Function of That

Expletive *that* serves no function within the nominal clause; instead, the nominal clause is a complete sentence without *that*. For example, in (1) (*I know that I turned out the lights*), the nominal clause *I turned out the lights* constitutes a complete sentence. On the other hand, the relative pronoun *that* does fill a function within the relative clause. If you remove the relative pronoun *that*, the remaining material does not constitute a complete sentence. For example, in (4) (*You need to replace the fuse that I bought*), the sequence *I bought* does not constitute a complete sentence.

Substitution Test

In general, the relative pronoun *that* can be replaced by another relative pronoun such as *which* or *who*; for example, *You need to replace the fuse which I bought; The paint which she bought for the living room clashes with the rug.* In contrast, the complementizer *that* cannot be replaced by *which* or *who*: compare **I know which I turned out the lights*, **Which I might not want his help had not occurred to him*, and **It had not occurred to him which I might not want his help.*

Finally, keep in mind that a single sentence may contain all three types of *that*: demonstrative, complementizer, and relative pronoun. For example, consider the following sentence:

8. I'm stunned by the fact *that* the popcorn at *that* theater *that* we went to cost $4.00.

Exercise A

For sentence (8), classify each instance of *that* according to type and provide evidence for your classification.

Diagramming That-*Clauses*

Start by identifying the clause and its function in the sentence. Apart from the word *that*, the nominal clause itself is diagrammed like a simple sentence. A pedestal is used to link the clause to the nominal slot that it occupies. (The pedestal allows us to see both the internal structure of the clause and the function of the clause in the larger sentence.) The complementizer *that* is linked to the verb of the nominal clause by a dotted line.

As an example, consider the sentence *I think that the Senate will pass the bill.* To the right is the diagram for this sentence.

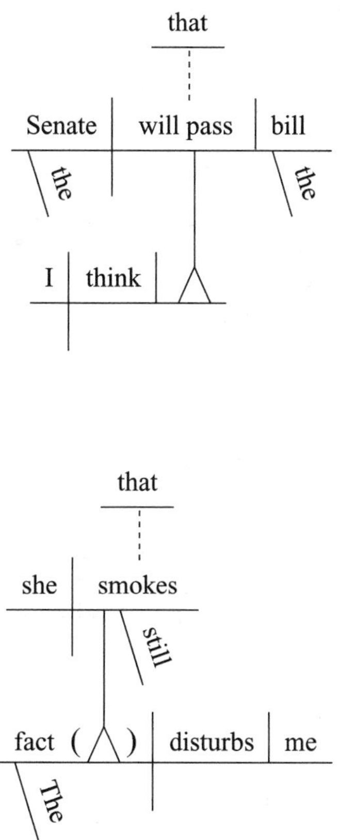

Note that the complementizer *that* is optional when the *that*-clause functions as an object (e.g., *I think* ______ *the Senate will pass the bill*). If *that* is omitted from the sentence, *that* is placed in parentheses on the line normally occupied by *that*.

That-clauses serving an appositive function are diagrammed in a similar manner. Consider the diagram of *The fact that she still smokes disturbs me*, shown at right.

In this sentence, *that she still smokes* functions as an appositive to the subject NP *The fact*. Note that the pedestal for the appositive terminates in the subject slot. The parentheses around the pedestal symbolize the optional nature of the appositive. Structurally, we have a complete sentence (subject and predicate) without the appositive (*The fact* ____ *disturbs me*), although certainly we lose some crucial meaning by omitting the appositive.

Likewise, in the sentence, *It had not occurred to him that I might not want his help*, the clause, *that I might not want his help* functions as an appositive to the subject NP *It.* Therefore, the nominal *that*-clause would be diagrammed in a similar way, enclosed in parentheses in the subject slot.

Exercise B

Diagram sentences (1–3), (6), and (8), repeated below.

a. I know that I turned out the lights.
b. That I might not want his help had not occurred to him.
c. It had not occurred to him that I might not want his help.
d. The idea that I might not want his help never occurred to him.
e. I'm stunned by the fact that the popcorn at that theater that we went to cost $4.00.

INTERROGATIVE CLAUSES

A second type of clause that can serve a nominal function is the interrogative clause. As the term implies, **interrogative clauses** are related to questions, in that they begin with a ***wh*-word** (*who, whom, whose, what, where, when, why, which, how*). Like nominal *that*-clauses, interrogative clauses serve a nominal function within the larger sentence. For example, the interrogative clause (italicized) serves as the subject of sentence (9).

9. *Where he gets his money* is a mystery.

On the other hand, the same clause functions as direct object in sentence (10).

10. I don't know *where he gets his money.*

An interrogative clause can also function in other NP roles, especially subjective complement and object of a preposition. These possibilities are illustrated in examples (11) and (12), respectively.

11. Bermuda is *where they're going on their honeymoon*. (subjective complement)
12. He interrogated me about *who was at the party*. (object of a preposition)

Exercise C

Identify the function played by the interrogative clause in each of the following sentences (subject, subjective complement, direct object, or object of a preposition).

a.† St. Alban's is where their child goes to school.
b. She is writing a book about why some women stay in abusive relationships.
c.† I can't remember where I put my keys.
d. Thursday is when many people go to the grocery store.
e. How they met is an interesting story.

Just as *that* can introduce both a nominal clause and a relative clause, so certain *wh*-words, especially *who* and *which*, can introduce both an interrogative clause and a relative clause. Therefore, we need a way to distinguish between these two functions. For example, consider the following sentences.

13. I know the woman *who got the job.*
14. I know *who got the job.*

In (13), *who got the job* is an adjectival (relative) clause. In (14), *who got the job* is a nominal (interrogative) clause. The clause in (13) can be identified as a relative clause because another relative pronoun, *that*, can be substituted for *who*: *I know the woman that got the job*. No such substitution can be made in (14): **I know that got the job.*

Function of the Wh-*Word*

Typically, *who, whom,* and *what* play a nominal role (i.e., subject, object, or complement) within the interrogative clause. For example, in (14), *who* functions as the subject of the nominal clause. Now consider the following sentences.

15. I don't know *who I should talk to.*
16. I don't know *who the supervisor is.*

In (15), the nominal clause *who I should talk to* functions as the direct object of the verb *know*. Within the nominal clause, *who* functions as the object of the preposition *to*. This may be somewhat difficult to see at first, since the two items are separated in this sentence. However, it is easier to see if we isolate the clause and move *who* after the preposition:

__________ I should talk to *who*

Although this clause cannot function as a free-standing sentence, we can see that it contains the essential elements of a sentence: *I* is the subject, and *should talk to who* is the predicate. (Note that in a more formal style, the preposition may be "fronted," i.e., moved to the front of the clause. This would probably be accompanied by a more formal *wh*-word, *whom*: *I don't know to whom I should talk.)*

Other *wh*-words play different roles within the nominal clause. *Where, when, why,* and *how* typically serve adverbial functions within the *wh*-clause (e.g., *I don't know where he gets his money; When you find the time to exercise is a mystery; She told him why she was leaving*). In contrast, *whose* and *which* generally serve determiner functions: *The children argued about which TV show they would watch; I don't know whose book this is.*

Exercise D

Label each *wh*-clause as either an adjectival (relative) clause or a nominal clause. Then identify the role that the *wh*-word plays within each clause.

a.† He wouldn't tell me who he bought the present for.

b. Do you know who's coming to the party?

c.† Many people who have children shouldn't.

d. She had an idea which didn't appeal to me.

e. Which picture do you like?

f. We haven't decided whose essay should win the award.

Diagramming Interrogative Clauses

Start by isolating the clause and identifying its function in the sentence (e.g., in [14] the noun clause is the direct object of the verb in main clause). Then analyze the internal structure of the interrogative clause, making sure to identify the function of the *wh*-word correctly. Then place the entire nominal clause on a pedestal to reflect its function within the larger sentence. For example, consider the sentence *Where he gets his money is a mystery.* In this sentence, *Where he gets his money* is the subject. Within that clause, *where* functions as an adverbial. Therefore, this sentence would be diagrammed as follows.

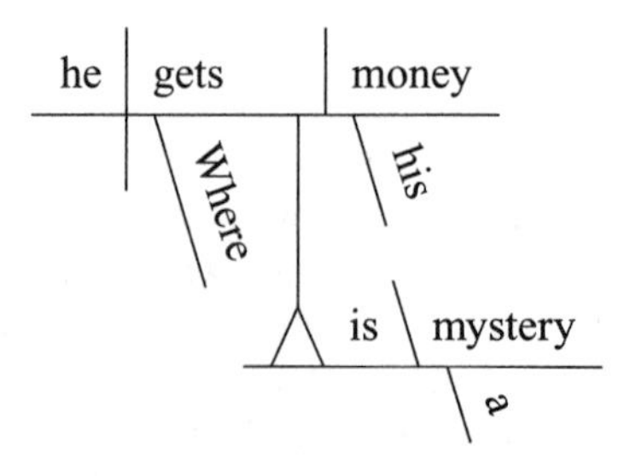

Consider another example. In the sentence *The committee can't decide who the best candidate is*, the interrogative clause serves as the object of the main clause. *Who,* in turn, is the subject complement of the noun clause. Therefore, this sentence would be diagrammed as follows.

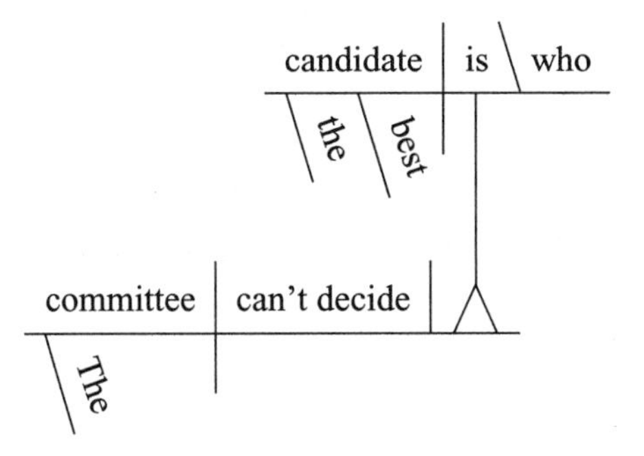

Exercise E

Diagram sentences (11–16), repeated below.

a.† Bermuda is where they're going on their honeymoon.

b. He interrogated me about who was at the party.

c.† I know the woman who got the job.

d. I know who got the job.

e. I don't know who I should talk to.

f.† I don't know who the supervisor is.

INFINITIVES

A third type of structure that can serve as a nominal is the infinitive clause or phrase. Infinitives are easy to identify; they nearly always contain *to* followed by an uninflected verb form.

Infinitive Clauses

Infinitive clauses resemble sentences in that they contain a subject NP and a predicate (i.e., a main verb plus any objects or complements). However, the verb is never inflected for tense. Verbs inflected for tense are called **finite verbs**, and those not inflected for tense are called **nonfinite verbs**; hence the term *infinitive*.

Compare the clauses in (17—finite) and (18—infinite).

17. I would hope *that Jill is selected for the award.* (tensed)
18. I would prefer *for Jill to be selected for the award.* (nontensed)

Unlike finite clauses, infinitive clauses cannot contain modals, although they can contain auxiliary *have* and auxiliary *be.*

19. *I would prefer *for Jill to will win the award.*
20. I would prefer *for Jill to have won the award.*
21. I would prefer *for Jill to be receiving the award.*

Moreover, as shown in sentences (18–21), an infinitive clause may be introduced by the word *for*. This use of *for* is classified as a preposition by some analysts, since it assigns objective case to any pronoun that follows it. Compare (22) and (23).

22. I would prefer *for her to win the award.* (*her*=objective case)
23. *I would prefer *for she to win the award.* (*she*=nominative case)

On the other hand, *for* patterns like the complementizer *that,* which introduces a nominal *that*-clause. For this reason, *for* is sometimes classified as a complementizer when it introduces a clause.

Not all infinitive clauses, however, are introduced by *for*. Consider, for example, the infinitive clause in (24).

24. I want *Jill to win the award.*

Whether or not *for* appears in the infinitive clause seems to be a function of the verb in the main clause: *prefer* seems to require *for*; *like* allows it; and *want* disallows it.

The primary nominal functions served by infinitive clauses are subject, direct object, and subjective complement. These possibilities are illustrated in the following sentences.

25. *For Jill to win the award* would be wonderful. (subject)
26. We would like *for Jill to win the award.* (direct object)
27. What everyone wants is *for Jill to win the award.* (subjective complement)

Exercise F

Identify the infinitive clause in each of the following sentences; then identify its function in the main clause.

a.† The best solution might be for them to move.
b. For Bill to get into medical school would require divine intervention.
c. We'd like Jeff to be our waiter.
d.† I need you to go to the store for me.

Infinitive Phrases

An infinitive phrase consists of just the predicate portion of an infinitive clause—that is, the infinitive marker *to*, followed by the untensed verb and any complements—but without a subject. Like infinitive clauses, infinitive phrases can appear in a variety of nominal positions, as illustrated by the following sentences.

28. *To compete in the Olympics* requires years of training. (subject)
29. No one likes *to be rejected.* (direct object)
30. My goal is *to lose 10 pounds in two months*. (subjective complement)

Exercise G

Identify the function of the infinitive phrase in each of the following sentences.

a. Don Quixote vowed to dream the impossible dream.
b.† To err is human.
c. His plan is to apply to law school in the spring.
d. I want to be alone.
e.† Amanda wants to sleep in the living room.

Diagramming Infinitives

Start by isolating the infinitive clause or phrase and identifying its function in the sentence. An infinitive clause is diagrammed much like a simple sentence, with *for* and *to* diagrammed on slanted lines, like prepositions. A pedestal is used to link the infinitive to the nominal slot that it occupies. (This is a somewhat simplified version of the original Reed–Kellogg method.)

Consider a sentence with an infinitive clause as subject: *For Jill to win the award would be a wonderful surprise.* Following is the diagram of this sentence.

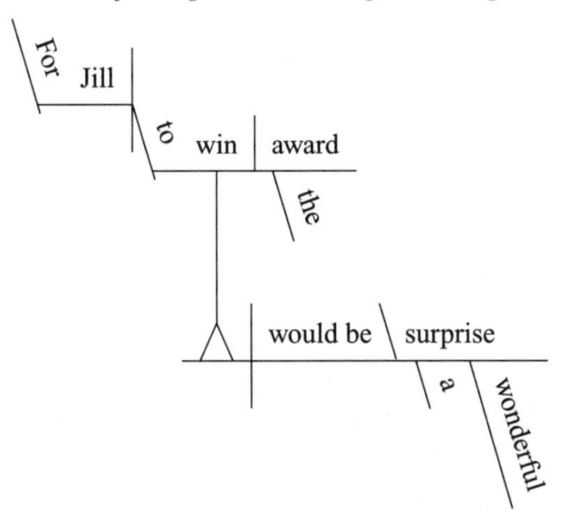

An infinitive phrase is diagrammed exactly the same way, except the infinitive has no subject. For example, the following is a diagram of *My goal is to lose 10 pounds in two months.*

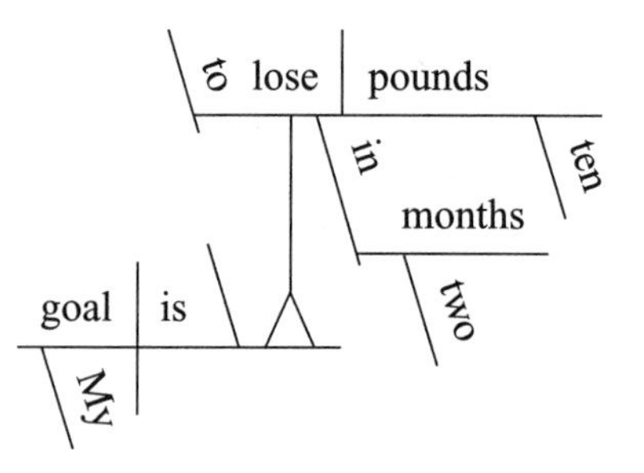

Exercise H

Diagram the sentences in Exercises F and G.

GERUNDS

A fourth type of structure that can serve as a nominal is the gerund clause or phrase. Like infinitive clauses, gerund clauses resemble sentences in that they contain a subject and a predicate. However, instead of being uninflected, the main verb carries the present participle (*-ing*) inflection: for example, *I appreciate your getting that book for me.*

Gerund clauses can serve a variety of nominal functions, as illustrated in the following sentences.

31. *Meg's choosing Ralph as her assistant* shocked us. (subject)
32. I resent *his having a bigger office than me.* (direct object)
33. We heard about *Bill's trying to get a raise.* (object of a preposition)
34. The latest surprise was *Linda's granting him a paternity leave.* (subjective complement)

Note that the subject of a gerund clause (e.g., *Meg's, his, Bill's, Linda's*) is typically inflected for possessive case, especially in more formal styles. However, the objective clause may be heard in less formal registers: e.g., *I resent him having a bigger office than me; We heard about Bill trying to get a raise.*

Gerund phrases are essentially gerund clauses without the subject. They, too, can serve a variety of nominal functions.

35. *Drinking beer* will not help your waistline. (subject)

36. Most people enjoy *relaxing on the beach.* (direct object)
37. Her advice about *getting a grant* was very useful. (object of a preposition)
38. Her favorite pastime is *riding horses*. (subject complement)

Exercise I

Identify the gerund clause or phrase in each of the following sentences, as well as the function of the clause or phrase. (Hint: Keep in mind that not all forms ending in *-ing* are gerunds.)

a.† Being department head is keeping her busy.
b. He regrets burning his bridges with that company.
c.† Those kids are crazy about reading.
d. Rollerblading seems to have replaced skateboarding.
e. I admire Jane's keeping her grace under pressure.
f. *Newsweek* just published an article about his losing the election.

Diagramming Gerunds

First, separate the gerund from the main clause. The gerund is diagrammed on a broken line, and the subject of the gerund (if it has one) is diagrammed as a modifier. Then the entire gerund is placed on a pedestal to reflect its role in the main clause. For example, in sentence (31) *Meg's choosing John as her assistant shocked us*, the gerund clause serves as the subject of the main clause. This sentence is diagrammed as follows.

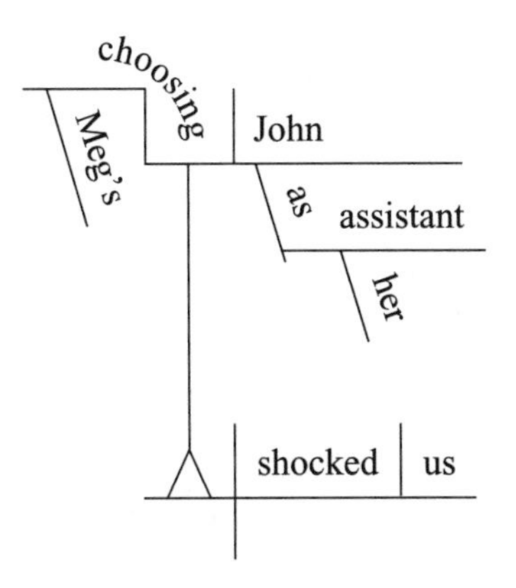

In sentence (32), *I resent his having a bigger office than me*, the gerund clause serves as the direct object of the verb in the main clause. This sentence is diagrammed as follows.

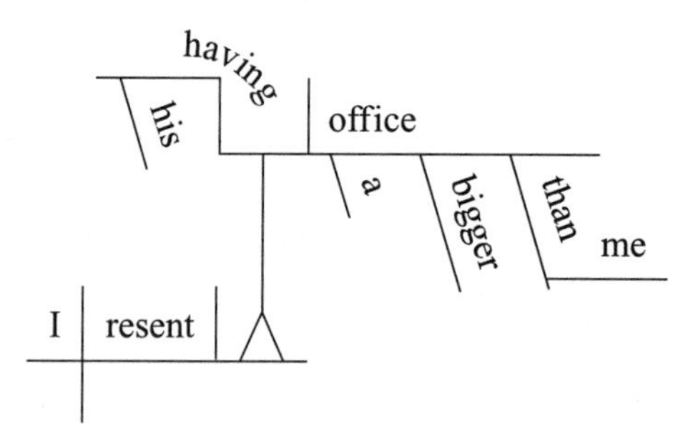

A gerund phrase is diagrammed exactly the same way, except that the gerund has no subject. For example, the following is a diagram of (35), *Drinking beer will not help your waistline*.

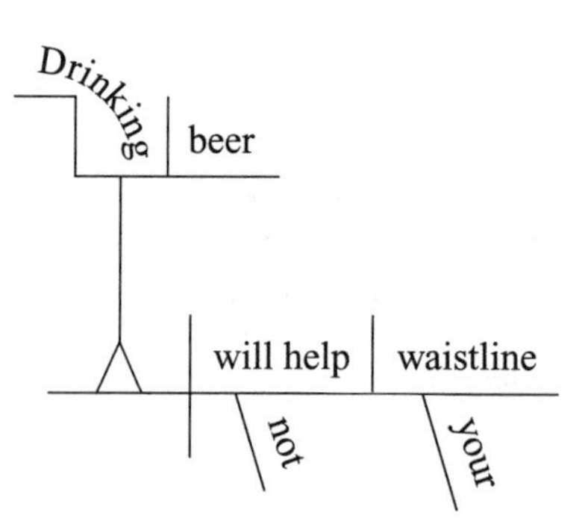

Exercise J

Diagram sentences (33–34) and (36–38), repeated here.

a.† We heard about Bill's trying to get a raise.

b. The latest surprise was Linda's granting him a paternity leave.

c. Most people enjoy relaxing on the beach.

d. Her advice about getting a grant was very useful.

e.† Her favorite pastime is riding horses.

Summary

Clauses and phrases that can function as NPs are known as nominals. Nominals can occupy any of the NP slots: subject, object, complement, etc. The following table summarizes some of the main characteristics of the nominals discussed in this chapter.

***That*-Clauses**

- Expletive *that* has no syntactic function within the clause (e.g., *The idea that you might kiss me is revolting*)
- Expletive *that* cannot be replaced by a relative pronoun (e.g., **The idea which you might kiss me is revolting*)

Interrogative Clauses

- Contain a *wh*-word but no antecedent within the main clause (e.g., *I will vote for whoever runs*)

Infinitives

- Infinitive clause contains a subject and a predicate with an uninflected verb (e.g., *For Jill to win the award would be an honor*)
- Infinitive phrase consists of the predicate portion of an infinitive clause (e.g., *To win the award would be an honor*)

Gerunds

- Gerund clause contains a subject and a predicate with a present participle verb (e.g., *Your smoking offends me*)
- Subject of the clause is usually inflected for possessive case
- Gerund phrase consists of the predicate portion of a gerund clause (e.g., *Smoking offends me*)

SUPPLEMENTARY EXERCISES

1. Consider the following line from Robert Frost's poem "Stopping by Woods on a Snowy Evening": *Whose woods these are I think I know.*

a. The word order in this line has been inverted for poetic effect. What would the normal word order be?
b. Once you've returned this line to its normal word order, identify the interrogative clause.
c. What is the syntactic function of the interrogative clause within the larger clause?

2. Diagram the following sentences from Exercises C and D in this chapter.

a. St. Alban's is where their child goes to school.
b. She is writing a book about why some women stay in abusive relationships.
c. I can't remember where I put my keys.
d. Thursday is when many people go to the grocery store.
e. How they met is an interesting story.
f. He wouldn't tell me who he bought the present for.
g. Do you know who's coming to the party?
h. Many people who have children shouldn't.
i. She had an idea which didn't appeal to me.
j. Which picture do you like?
k. We haven't decided whose essay should win the award.

3. Diagram the following sentences from Exercise I in this chapter.

a. Being department head is keeping her busy.
b. He regrets burning his bridges with that company.
c. Those kids are crazy about reading.
d. Rollerblading seems to have replaced skateboarding.
e. I admire Jane's keeping her grace under pressure.
f. *Newsweek* just published an article about his losing the election.

4. Earlier we said that the subject of a gerund clause (if it has one) is normally in possessive case, e.g., *I can't imagine <u>his</u> going to Japan.* However, sometimes an objective case pronoun will appear instead of the possessive: *I can't imagine <u>him</u> going to Japan.*

a. Can you think of a way of diagramming this sentence that will preserve the generalization that only possessive pronouns can serve as the subject of a gerund? (Hint: Diagram it so that *him* is not the subject of going.)
b. Now consider the sentence *<u>Him</u> going to Japan is out of the question.* Is there any way to diagram this sentence so that *him* is not the subject of *going*?
c. Based on your answers to (a) and (b), revise the statement: The subject of a gerund is normally in the possessive case.

5. One type of sentence fragment results from punctuating an interrogative clause as an independent clause (i.e., as a sentence), as in the following passage:

> The task force will recommend recycling procedures. In particular, *what steps we can take to reduce paper waste.*

An interrogative clause fragment can be revised in several ways:

- Join the interrogative clause to the main clause that precedes it (often with a colon or a dash) (e.g., *The task force will recommend recycling procedures—in particular, what steps we can take to reduce paper waste*).
- Make the interrogative clause the object of a verb or of a preposition (e.g., *The task force will recommend recycling procedures. In particular, we need to know what steps we can take to reduce paper waste*).
- Change the interrogative clause to a direct question by placing the first auxiliary verb after the *wh*-item (e.g., *The task force will recommend recycling procedures. In particular, what steps can we take to reduce paper waste*?).

Identify and revise the fragments in the following passages. Some are interrogative clauses, while some are other types of nominal clauses. Note: There are several ways to revise each passage.

a. Also known as stockholders' equity, book value is the difference between the company's assets and its liabilities. In other words, what the shareholders own after the company's debts have been paid.
b. Cash register software can be used for a number of new functions. For example, to issue rebate coupons.
c. It was completely unexpected. For the stock to fall ten points.
d. She has several hobbies. Riding horses, sewing, and reading mystery novels.
e. The story left an important question unanswered. Why the police waited until the next day to search the crime scene.

Part III

Generative Grammar

This section of the book emphasizes the generative approach to English grammar, begun in the 1950s and epitomized by what is popularly known as "transformational grammar." The development of generative grammar can be divided into two stages: standard theory, dealing with phrase structure grammar and transformations, and government and binding theory, dealing with X-bar syntax, constraints on movement, and binding.

CHAPTER 11

Generative Theory

The field of linguistics since mid-century has been shaped almost entirely by the ideas of Noam Chomsky (b. 1928), a linguistics professor at MIT. It's impossible to overestimate the impact Chomsky has had not only in linguistics but in such diverse fields as psychology, philosophy, anthropology, folklore, composition, and even computer science. This is not to say that practitioners in these fields all accept Chomsky's ideas, but the way they view the world has in one way or another been affected by Chomsky. It is probably not far off to say that if there were a Nobel Prize for linguistics or philosophy, Chomsky would have won it by now.

STANDARD THEORY (1950–1980)

In the early 1950s Chomsky was a graduate student at the University of Pennsylvania working on his Ph.D. in linguistics under one of the most influential structuralists of the time, Zellig Harris (b. 1909), and trying unsuccessfully to work within the structural paradigm (i.e., language is a habit learned through imitation and reinforcement). In his spare time, almost as a hobby, he developed what came to be known as "transformational grammar." (Interestingly, the term *transformation* was introduced into linguistics by Harris, but his understanding of the concept was quite different from Chomsky's.) Not surprisingly, Chomsky had difficulty getting his innovative ideas accepted by American journals, and eventually a Dutch company, Mouton, published his theory of transformational grammar in 1957 under the title *Syntactic Structures*. In this work Chomsky introduced the idea that every language has a set of basic or **kernel** sentences, consisting essentially of simple (one-clause), active, declarative, positive sentences. All other sentences in the language could be described as reflecting systematic changes or **transformations** of the structure underlying one of these basic sentences. Consider, for example, sentences (1a–e).

1a. Chris won the fellowship.
1b. The fellowship was won by Chris.
1c. Did Chris win the fellowship?
1d. Chris did not win the fellowship.
1e. Wasn't the fellowship won by Chris?

According to Chomsky, sentence (1a) is a kernel because it is simple, active, declarative, and positive. However, sentences (1b–e) are not kernels: (1b) is not active; (1c) is not declarative; (1d) is not positive; and (1e) is neither active, declarative, nor positive.

In Chomsky's view kernel sentences would be described directly by a relatively simple set of **phrase structure** (PS) rules (i.e., rules that describe the basic structure of simple, active, declarative, positive sentences), and each of the non-kernel sentences would be described by one or more transformations (i.e., systematic changes of a basic structure). Under this analysis, sentences (1a–e) all have the same basic structure, but (1b–e) have additionally undergone one or more transformations, as indicated in (2a–e).

2a. Chris won the fellowship.
2b. Chris won the fellowship. + Passive Transformation
2c. Chris won the fellowship. + Question Transformation
2d. Chris won the fellowship. + Negative Transformation
2e. Chris won the fellowship. + Passive + Question + Negative Transformations

By conceptualizing syntax in this way, standard theory allows us to make an important observation about groups of sentences like (1a–e). On the one hand, (1a–e) are obviously different sentences. On the other hand, (1a–e) are the same on a more abstract level, in that they share the same proposition—that is, the same **agent**, or "doer of the action" (*Chris*), the same action (*won*), and the same **patient**, or "thing affected by the action" (*the fellowship*). Thus, one of Chomsky's breakthroughs was in developing a theory that would simultaneously accommodate the "same–different" relationship among sets of sentences like (1a–e).

Exercise A

For each of the following sentences, state whether it is a kernel sentence (simple, active, positive, declarative) or not. If not, state how it differs from a kernel sentence (e.g., passive rather than active; negative rather than positive; question rather than declarative). Some sentences may differ in more than one way.

a.† Will the voters re-elect the president?
b. Has the president been re-elected by the voters?
c. The voters won't re-elect the president.

d.† The president may not be re-elected by the voters.
e. Shouldn't the voters have re-elected the president?
f. The voters will re-elect the president.

Chomsky's conception of a language as a system of interacting rules that generate structures represents a major break from the structuralist tenet that a language is a superficial habit. The structuralist view was embodied in B. F. Skinner's 1957 work *Verbal Behavior*. Skinner's position had numerous intractable problems:

- First, children acquiring their native language produce novel forms. For example, they say *goed* for *went, foots* for *feet,* and *Why I can't go?* for *Why can't I go?* If the child is merely imitating the adult, it is not clear what serves as the model for these novel forms, since adults don't speak this way.
- Second, children don't acquire the most frequent items first. For example, the articles *the* and *a,* the conjunction *and,* and prepositions such as *in* and *on* are extremely common in the speech children are exposed to. Yet articles, conjunctions, and prepositions are among the *last* words that a child acquires. If the strength of a stimulus increases with repetition, then these function words would serve as very strong stimuli, and we would expect the child to learn them relatively early.
- Third, humans are able to produce and interpret sentences they have never heard before. Consider, for example, the first sentence in Excercise A. Chances are you have never seen this sentence before, yet you have no trouble interpreting it. For that matter, pick any book off any bookshelf and open to any page, and point to any sentence. Once again, you probably haven't seen that particular sentence before. Nonetheless, if the book you have chosen is in English, you are able to interpret the sentence without effort.

These facts are inexplicable within behaviorist theory. Instead, these examples suggest that the interpretation of a sentence involves not a simple response to a stimulus, but rather a system of rules for analyzing sentences. The rules are finite, but the structures they generate are infinite—just as the rules of addition are finite, but they can be used to add an infinite number of numbers.

In 1959, Chomsky published a devastating review of Skinner's *Verbal Behavior* in the journal *Language*. Shortly thereafter, in 1965, Chomsky codified his ideas in *Aspects of the Theory of Syntax*, which articulates what has come to be known as **standard theory**. It was here that Chomsky introduced the idea, again contrary to the structuralist view, that the mind (i.e., knowledge of language) was not only a reasonable object of study in linguistics, but really the most interesting object of study. In particular, Chomsky drew his now-famous distinction between linguistic **competence** (i.e., the unconscious knowledge that *underlies* a speaker's ability to produce sentences) and linguistic **performance** (i.e., the actual production of those sentences). In his own words,

> We thus make a fundamental distinction between *competence* (the speaker-hearer's knowledge of his language) and *performance* (the actual use of language in concrete situations). . . . linguistic theory is mentalistic, since it is concerned with discovering a mental reality [i.e., competence] underlying actual behavior [i.e., performance]. (p. 4)

Perhaps an analogy might make the point clearer. Even people who know how to add and subtract often make errors in balancing their checkbooks. These errors (performance) do not indicate that such people do not know the rules of arithmetic (competence). In Chomsky's terms, the mathematician studies the rules of arithmetic that people presumably follow in balancing their checkbooks; likewise, the linguist studies the rules of language that people presumably follow in uttering everyday sentences of their language. For Chomsky, the interesting question is "What is the knowledge that *underlies* the behavior?"

Exercise B

Explain the role of competence and performance in each of the following situations.

a. A typist types *biew* for *view.*
b. A monkey at a keyboard types *bnvi.*
c. A contestant on *Jeopardy* is asked who starred in the movie *Philadelphia.* The contestant saw the movie, knows Tom Hanks, but can't recall his name.

In short, Chomsky redefined both the goal and methodology of linguistics. The goal was to characterize the speaker's unconscious knowledge of language, and the methodology was to draw inferences from the speaker's judgments about sentences. Let's take a look at an example of how this methodology works. Grammar books found in the public schools often state that imperative sentences such as *Watch out* have an "understood subject," *you.* Chomsky's approach actually establishes evidence for this claim. Consider the following sentences. (Recall that an asterisk indicates a sentence that is unacceptable for one reason or another.)

3. **Fred* took a picture of *Fred.*
4. *Fred* took a picture of *himself.*
5. **Himself* took a picture of *Fred.*

The fact that sentence (3) is unacceptable allows us to infer that two identical noun phrases referring to the same entity cannot occur in a simple sentence. Sentence

(4) allows us to infer that one of the two NPs must appear as a compatible reflexive pronoun, one having the same person, number, and gender. Sentence (5) allows us to infer that it is the second occurrence of the identical NP that appears as the reflexive, not the first. In other words, we can infer the following Reflexive rule: whenever two identical NPs occur in a simple sentence, the second one is manifested as a compatible reflexive pronoun. Put another way, a reflexive pronoun implies the presence of an antecedent somewhere in the sentence.

Consider now sentence (6) below.

6. Watch out for *yourself.*

Note that (6) contains a reflexive pronoun (*yourself*). Thus, there must be an antecedent somewhere in the sentence. The only spot such an antecedent could occupy is subject position, which appears to be empty. The presence of the reflexive, however, suggests that the subject position is not empty but rather contains *you* covertly. Thus, we have established some evidence that imperative sentences actually do have the "understood subject," *you*.

Furthermore, we can explain the occurrence of sentences such as *Watch out for yourself* in terms of a *system* of rules (i.e., imperative sentences have a covert *you* subject which serves as a trigger for the Reflexive rule, and is later deleted by an Imperative rule that deletes the subject of the imperative). Consider the following **derivation**, in which one rule operates on the output of the preceding rule.

	you - watch out - for you
REFL:	you - watch out - for yourself
IMP:	Ø - watch out - for yourself

In this derivation of the sentence *Watch out for yourself*, the source structure contains two identical noun phrases (*you*). This triggers the Reflexive rule, which turns the second occurrence of *you* into a compatible reflexive (*yourself*). Then the Imperative rule applies, which deletes the subject of the imperative (*you*). This yields *Ø - watch out - for yourself.*

GOVERNMENT AND BINDING THEORY (1980–PRESENT)

Generative grammar (i.e., a rule–system for generating derivations of sentences) has undergone two major changes since 1965. These changes have resulted in a second major stage in Chomsky's ideas, which has come to be known as **government and binding theory**. The first milestone beyond standard theory appears in Chomsky's 1973 paper entitled "Conditions on Transformations." Essentially, what Chomsky tried to demonstrate was that properties of several individual rules of English were in fact the result of a more general principle, one which could be applied universally to other languages as well. For example, in the 1960s it was generally accepted that English contained two distinct transformations: Passive and Subject Raising. Passive described the relationship between active and passive structures, as illustrated by the sentences in (7) and (8).

7. Hussein attacked Kuwait.
8. Kuwait was attacked by Hussein.

The Passive transformation consisted of three steps: (a) interchange subject and object; (b) insert *by* before the new object; (c) insert a form of *be* before the main verb, as follows.

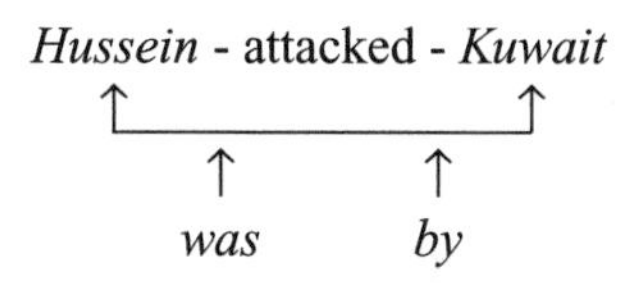

Subject Raising, on the other hand, described the relationship between the structures underlying sentences such as (9) and (10).

9. It is certain for Hussein to attack Kuwait.
10. Hussein is certain to attack Kuwait.

The Subject Raising transformation consisted of three steps: (a) move the subject of the infinitive clause to subject position of the main clause; (b) delete *for*; (c) delete *it*, as follows.

It - is certain - *for* - *Hussein* to attack Kuwait

↓ ↓

Ø Ø

Chomsky, however, suspected that this type of analysis was overlooking a fundamental similarity between the two rules, namely, that they both involved moving a "lower" NP to a "higher" NP position. (Higher and lower are defined in structural terms. For example, the subject of a sentence is higher than the object; the subject of the main clause is higher than the subject of the dependent clause; and so on.) He extracted this common denominator and formalized it as **Noun Phrase (NP) Movement**: move any NP to any empty NP position higher in the structure. Under this analysis, the passive sentence (8) and the subject raised sentence (10) would be derived as follows:

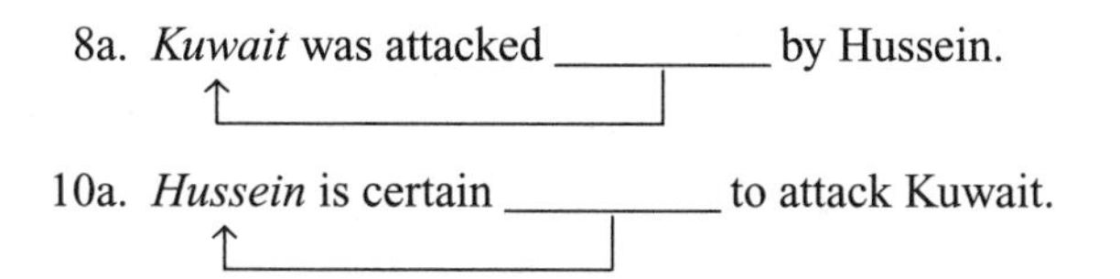

At the same time, doing away with idiosyncratic properties of individual transformations and reducing them all to NP Movement allowed the grammar to wildly overgenerate. That is, it allowed the grammar to generate a lot of unacceptable sentences, e.g., **Hussein was attacked Kuwait by* or **Kuwait is certain Hussein to attack.* To make up for this deficit, Chomsky hypothesized a set of **constraints on transformations**, where each constraint prohibited a particular type of movement. For example, the **Specified Subject Condition** states, in oversimplified terms, that a direct object cannot be moved out of a clause containing a subject. Consider sentence (11), which is derived as indicated in structure (12).

11. *Kuwait is certain Hussein to attack.

12. *Kuwait* is certain Hussein to attack ________.
    ↑________________________________|

Sentence (11) violates the Specified Subject Condition because the direct object (*Kuwait*) has been moved out of a clause containing a subject (*Hussein*). Thus, the rule of NP Movement plus the Specified Subject Condition would prohibit the grammar from generating unacceptable derivations like (12).

By extracting the common denominator from two rules of English (Passive and Subject Raising), Chomsky had once again changed the goal of linguistics: from constructing grammars of particular languages to hypothesizing rules common to all languages.

Exercise C

For each of the following rules, state whether you think it is language-specific (i.e., applies only to English) or universal (i.e., might apply to all languages). (Hint: You don't need to know any languages other than English to do this exercise. Instead, consider whether each rule mentions an English word.)

a.† Move any NP to any NP position higher in the structure.

b.† Insert *not* following tense and a modal, *have,* or *be.*

c. Attach *do* to the left of tense.

d. Insert *it* into any empty NP in subject position.

e. Interchange a direct object (if not a pronoun) and an indirect object (if preceded by *to* or *for*).

f.† No rule can move an item out of a coordinate structure.

g. No rule can move a category out from under an identical category.

h. Move the subject to the right of *be* and insert *there* into subject position.

The second major milestone in the development of government and binding theory came with Chomsky's 1980 article "On Binding." Here Chomsky argued for a unified treatment of dependencies and their antecedents. Consider the following examples. (In each case, the dependency is underlined and the antecedent is in italics.)

13. *John* said that <u>he</u> was sick.
14. *John* hurt <u>himself</u>.
15. *John* tried _________ to breathe.
16. *John* seemed _________ to be sick.
17. *Who* did John hurt _________?

The dependency in such cases can be either a word (e.g., a pronoun) or a "gap" (i.e., a site from which something is missing or has been moved). Heretofore, constructions like those in (13–17) were thought to have little to do with each other; however, Chomsky pointed out several things they have in common. Most importantly, he noted that in each case the antecedent is higher in the structure than the dependency, as illustrated below.

18. *John* hurt <u>himself</u>.
19. *<u>Himself</u> hurt *John*.

Moreover, he hypothesized that there were essentially two types of dependencies: anaphors and pronominals. An **anaphor** (e.g., <u>himself</u>) must have its antecedent within the same clause, whereas a pronominal (e.g., <u>him</u>) cannot. This is illustrated below.

18. *John* hurt <u>himself</u>.
20. *John* hurt <u>him</u>.

In (18) the anaphor *himself* must refer to *John* (which is in the same clause). On the other hand, in (20) the pronominal *him* cannot refer to *John* (which is in the same clause).

Moreover, a **pronominal** can have an antecedent in another clause, whereas a lexical NP (e.g., <u>John</u>) cannot. This is illustrated below.

21. *John* said that <u>he</u> saw Mary. (<u>He</u> can refer to *John*)
22. **John* said that <u>John</u> saw Mary. (<u>John</u> cannot refer to *John*)

Chomsky called the relationship between a dependency and its antecedent **binding**; that is, a dependency and its antecedent are said to be **bound**. An anaphor must be bound within its clause; a pronominal cannot be bound within its clause; and a lexical NP cannot be bound anywhere.

Exercise D

Consider the following sentence: *Mary realized that she and John loved each other.*

a. Is *each other* an anaphor or a pronominal? What is its antecedent? Explain.
b. Is *she* an anaphor or a pronominal? What is its antecedent? Explain.

Summary

In the mid-1950s, Chomsky broke with his structural predecessors by claiming that language was a system of rules rather than simply a set of habitual responses to environmental stimuli. Moreover, he treated the mind as the primary object of study within linguistics rather than as something inaccessible to rational inquiry. Chomsky's theory of linguistic structure has passed through at least two identifiable stages since the 1950s. These are illustrated below.

Standard Theory (*Aspects*, 1965)	**Government and Binding** ("Conditions," 1973) ("On Binding," 1980)
PS Rules + Complex, Language–Specific Transformations	PS Rules + Simple, Universal Transformations + Constraints on Movement + Binding Conditions

SUPPLEMENTARY EXERCISES

1. A four-year-old boy says to his father: "I *lefted* my hat in the house." How does this child's use of *lefted* serve as evidence against a behaviorist conception of language learning?
2. For each of the following sentences, state whether it is a kernel sentence (simple, active, positive, declarative) or not. If not, state how it differs from a kernel sentence (e.g., passive rather than active; negative rather than positive; question rather than declarative). Some sentences may differ in more than one way.

   a. The boss should have given Alice a raise.
   b. Should the boss have given Alice a raise?

c. Alice should have been given a raise by the boss.
d. The boss is giving a raise to Alice.
e. Alice wasn't given a raise by the boss.
f. Alice isn't being given a raise by the boss.
g. Isn't Alice being given a raise by the boss?

3. Explain the role of competence and performance in each of the following situations.

a. You're taking a geometry test and are asked what πr^2 is the formula for. You have no idea.
b. Your favorite song comes on the radio; you can't carry a tune in a bucket, but you can tell that the song is not being performed by the original group.
c. A college student is trying to take notes and writes *the* for *they* in his notebook.

4. Consider the following sentences, all of which contain **tag questions** at the end.

A. I was invited, wasn't I?
B. You were invited, weren't you?
C. She was invited, wasn't she?

How can these data be used to argue that an imperative sentence such as *Come in* actually has an underlying *you* subject?

5. For each of the following rules, state whether you think it is language-specific (i.e., applies only to English) or universal (i.e., might apply to all languages). (Hint: You don't need to know any languages other than English to do this exercise. Instead, consider whether each rule mentions an English word.)

a. Interchange subject and object; put a form of *be* before the main verb and *by* before the newly created object.
b. Move any question-word to clause-initial position.
c. No rule can move an item across two clause boundaries.
d. Delete the agent if it is *by someone* or *by something*.
e. No rule can move an item out of a tensed clause.

▲▲▲ CHAPTER 12

Standard Theory

This chapter outlines the two basic components of Chomsky's earlier version of generative grammar: a phrase structure (PS) grammar and a set of transformations describing English.

PHRASE STRUCTURE GRAMMAR

As briefly explained in Chapter 11, PS rules describe "kernel" sentences: simple, active, positive, declarative structures. The rules presented below do not constitute a complete description of kernel sentences in English. However, they do constitute a reasonable first attempt to *define* five phrase types: sentence (S), noun phrase (NP), verb phrase (VP), prepositional phrase (PP), and adjective phrase (AP).

Sentences

The following examples illustrate two basic properties of English sentences.

1. Ice floats.
2. *Floats ice.
3. *Ice.
4. *Floats.

Sentence (1) is made up of a subject NP (*Ice*) and a VP (*floats*). Sentence (2) illustrates that the NP must precede the VP. Sentences (3–4) illustrate that both components (NP and VP) are necessary for a sentence. These basic properties of sentences are formalized in the following rule:

S → NP - VP

This PS rule can be translated as follows: "All grammatical 'kernel' sentences in English consist of an NP followed by a VP." Think of this rule as essentially a *definition* of sentence. This rule, in turn, is said to **generate** the adjacent structure:

Such a structure is known as a **tree diagram**. On the other hand, this same rule does *not* generate (i.e., defines as ungrammatical) the adjacent structure:

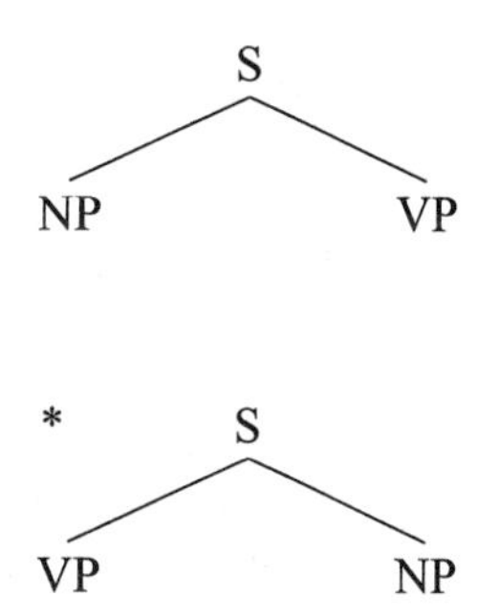

Noun Phrases

The following examples illustrate two basic properties of NPs in English.

5. children
6. the children
7. *children the

The NP in (5) is made up of a single noun (*children*). Example (6) illustrates that an NP may have an optional **determiner** (*the*). Recall that *determiner* (D) is a cover term for articles (e.g., *a, the*), demonstratives (e.g., *this, that*), possessives (e.g., *my, their*), and quantifiers (e.g., *some, many*). Example (7) illustrates that if an NP contains a D, then it must precede the N. These basic properties of NPs are formalized in the following rule.

NP → (D) - N

This PS rule can be translated as follows: "All grammatical NPs in English consist of an optional D followed by an N." (An optional element in a PS rule is indicated by putting it in parentheses.) This rule, in turn, generates the two adjacent structures:

On the other hand, this same rule defines as ungrammatical the adjacent structures:

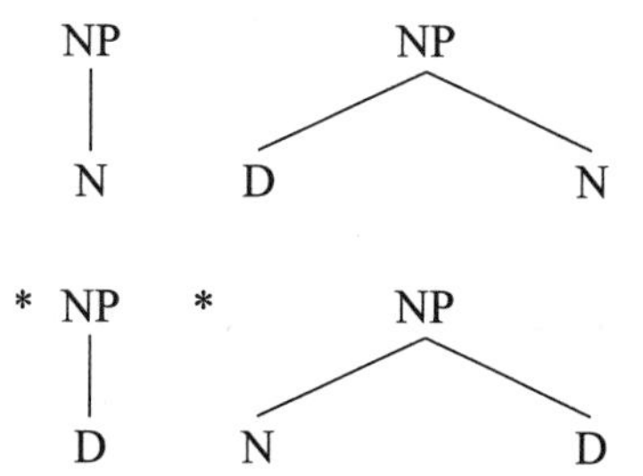

This rule illustrates some basic properties of PS rules in general. First, note that the PS rule consists of two parts. The item to the left of the single-shafted arrow is the phrasal category (e.g., NP) being defined. The material to the right of the arrow shows the items that can appear in an expansion of the phrasal category. Second, note that the left-to-right ordering of theses items indicates the sequence in which they must appear (e.g., if an NP expands into D-N, those items must appear in that order).

Verb Phrases

The following examples illustrate two basic properties of VPs in English:

8. Someone ate.
9. Someone ate cake.
10. Someone ate in the kitchen.
11. Someone ate cake in the kitchen.
12. *Someone ate in the kitchen cake.

The VP in (8) contains a single V (*ate*); the VP in (9) contains a V followed by an NP (*cake*); the VP in (10) contains a V followed by a prepositional phrase (*in the kitchen*); and the VP in (11) contains a V followed by both an NP and a PP. These sentences illustrate that a VP must contain a head V, which *may* be followed by either a direct object NP or a PP or both. Sentence (12) further illustrates that if the VP contains both an NP and a PP, then they must occur in that order. These basic properties of VPs can be formalized in the following rule.

VP → V - (NP) - (PP)

This PS rule can be translated as follows: "All grammatical VPs in English consist of a V followed by an optional NP followed by an optional PP." This rule, in turn, generates the following four structures:

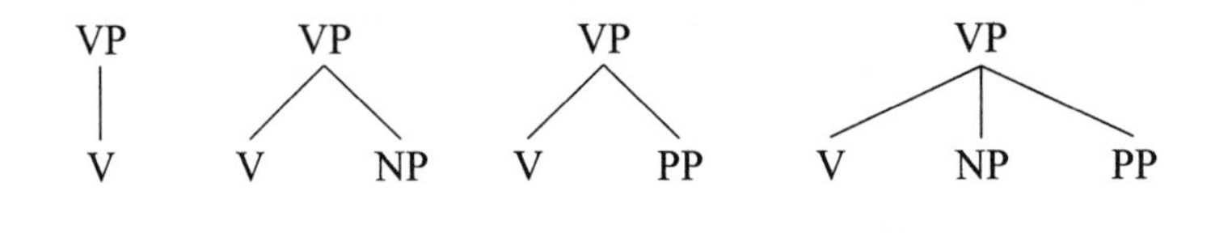

On the other hand, this same rule defines as ungrammatical the adjacent structure, thereby ruling out the ungrammatical sentence (12).

* VP

V PP NP

Prepositional Phrases

The following examples illustrate two basic properties of PPs in English.

13. at home
14. *home at

Example (13) illustrates that a PP consists of two elements: a preposition (*at*) followed by an NP (*home*). Example (14) illustrates that, within a PP, the preposition (P) must precede the NP. These generalizations are captured in the following rule.

PP → P - NP

We have now constructed PS rules for four types of structures: S, NP, VP, and PP. Each of these rules constitutes a *definition* of a particular phrase type. For example, an S is any structure that contains an NP followed by a VP; a PP is any structure that contains a P followed by an NP; and so on. Taken together, these rules constitute a PS grammar of English. Although this grammar is obviously incomplete (e.g., it does not define adverb phrases), it constitutes a rudimentary definition of "kernel" sentences in English. We repeat this grammar below.

S → NP - VP

NP → (D) - N

VP → V - (NP) - (PP)

PP → P - NP

Exercise A

Some of the following sentences *cannot* be described by this grammar. In those cases, explain how the sentence is ruled out by one of the PS rules. Draw trees for any sentences that *can* be described by the PS rules. Example: *That guy pushed Fred.*

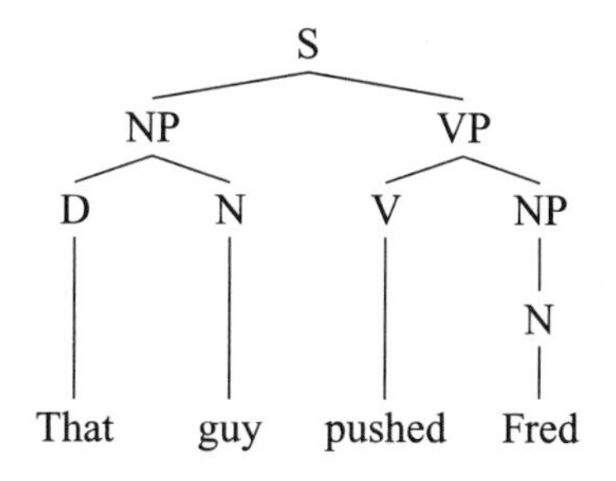

a.† Several people stumbled.
b. He shoved my sister down the stairs.
c.† Maxine put the key in the lock.
d. Maxine found the key to the door.
e. Sidney tasted the spaghetti.
f.† The fish tasted quite salty.
g. Chris was a very poor employee.
h. Those people were in the library.
i.† Those women are dancers.
j. The man on the phone was a telemarketer.
k. Some guy walked into the office.
l. Some guy walked in.

Exercise B

a. Which of the preceding sentences are not defined as grammatical by our PS grammar?

b. What new phrase type is introduced in sentences (f) and (g)?

c. Construct a PS rule for this phrase type. (Recall that *quite* and *very* are intensifiers (I).)

d. How would the VP and NP rules have to be revised to accommodate this new phrase type?

e. How would the NP rule have to be revised to account for sentence (j)?

f. Compare sentences (k) and (l). How could the PP rule be revised to accommodate them both?

Exercise A introduces a new phrase type: an adjective phrase (e.g., *quite salty*) made up of an intensifier (*quite*) followed by an adjective (*salty*). Adjective phrases can appear before a noun within an NP (e.g., *a very poor subject*) or following a linking verb (*tasted quite salty*). Exercise A also introduces adjectival PPs (e.g., *the guy on the phone*).

In order to generate, or define as grammatical, all of the sentences in Exercise A, our PS grammar would have to be revised along the following lines.

$S \rightarrow NP - VP$

$NP \rightarrow (D) - (AP) - N - (PP)$

Translation: a noun phrase consists of an optional determiner, followed by an optional adjective phrase, followed by an optional prepositional phrase.

$VP \rightarrow V - (\begin{Bmatrix} NP \\ AP \end{Bmatrix}) - (PP)$

Translation: a verb phrase consists of a verb, followed by an optional noun phrase or adjective phrase, followed by an optional prepositional phrase. (When items are stacked within braces, only one of the items may be chosen.)

$PP \rightarrow P - (NP)$

Translation: A prepositional phrase consists of a preposition followed by an optional noun phrase.

$AP \rightarrow (I) - A$

Translation: An adjective phrase consists of an optional intensifier followed by an adjective.

Notice the process we have been going through. Our goal was to define the concept of "kernel" sentence. We attempted to do this by examining some very simple sentences and trying to formalize rules for constructing them. After establishing some rudimentary rules, we observed slightly more complicated sentences and revised our rules to accommodate the new sentences while still accurately describing the original ones. This process was essentially that used by linguists in constructing PS grammars of English within Standard Theory.

Before leaving this topic, let's consider two final sentences from Exercise A above. Take a look at sentences (c) and (d), repeated here.

c. Maxine put the key in the lock.
d. Maxine found the key to the door.

These two sentences seem to have identical structures, as shown at right.

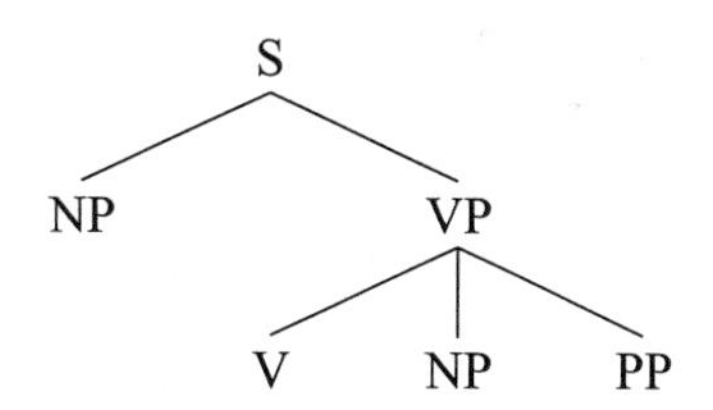

There is evidence, however, that they do not. One of the fundamental tenets of generative grammar is the following: *Sentences that behave differently under the same operation have different structures*. One such operation is passive, which moves the direct object NP of the active sentence to subject position of the passive sentence. When this operation is applied to (c–d), it yields (c_1–d_1), not (c_2–d_2).

c. Maxine put *the key* in the door.
c_1. *The key* was put in the door by Maxine.
c_2. **The key in the door* was put by Maxine.

d. Maxine found *the key to the door.*
d_1. *The key to the door* was found by Maxine.
d_2. **The key* was found to the door by Maxine.

This illustrates that the direct object NP in (c) is *the key*, whereas the direct object NP in (d) is *the key to the door*. This, in turn, means that (c–d) have different structures, as follows.

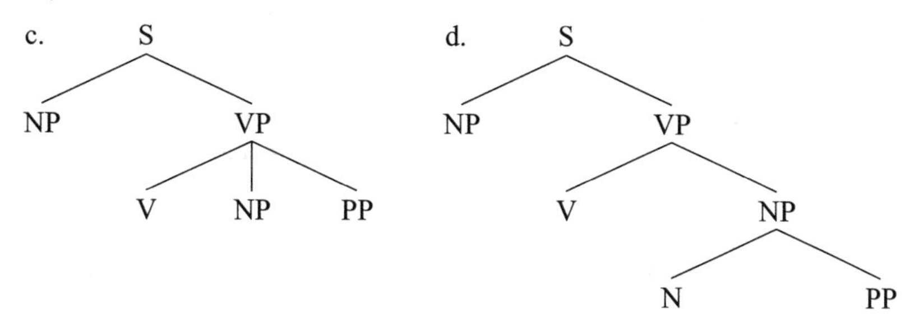

Both of these structures are generated by our revised PS grammar: in (c) the PP *follows* the direct object NP, and in (d) the PP *is part of* the direct object NP.

Exercise C

Draw tree diagrams for each of the following sentences. (Hint: Two of the sentences are ambiguous. Draw two diagrams for those sentences, one for each interpretation.)

a. John put the car in the street.
b. John repaired the car in the street.
c. Jane hid the letter to Dan.
d. Jane hid the letter from Dan.

TRANSFORMATIONS

As explained in the preceding chapter, one of the early and fundamental insights of generative grammar was that non-kernel sentences (i.e., non-active, non-declarative, non-positive sentences) could be described as reflecting systematic **transformations** (i.e., permutations) of kernel sentences. A diagram of this view of grammar is given below.

PS Grammar generates kernel sentences	+	Transformations operate on kernel sentences to generate non-kernel sentences
e.g., *John has driven the car.*		e.g., *The car has been driven by John.* *Has John driven the car?* *John has not driven the car.*

This section describes some elementary transformations in English and their interaction.

Affix Hopping

One of Chomsky's earliest insights was the structure of the auxiliary (AUX) system in English. You will recall that English has three auxiliary verbs that can occur together in the same sentence: the modals (M), forms of *have*, and forms of *be*. Now consider the following "kernel" sentences, which include all possible combinations of M, *have,* and *be.*

15a. He drives.
15b. He *will* drive.
15c. He *has* driven.
15d. He *is* driving.
15e. He *will have* driven.

15f. He *will be* driving.
15g. He *has been* driving.
15h. He *will have been* driving.

Here are some observations we can make about the auxiliary system based on these examples.

- If there is a modal, it occurs first.
- If there is a form of *be,* it occurs last.
- If there is a form of *have,* it occurs in the middle.
- A modal is followed by an uninflected verb form.
- Aux *have* is followed by a past participle (*en*) verb form.
- Aux *be* is followed by a present participle (*ing*) verb form.

What's most interesting about AUX is the fact that each auxiliary verb tells us something about the form of the *following* verb: if an M occurs in a kernel sentence, it will always be *followed* by an uninflected verb form; if a form of *have* occurs, it will always be *followed* by a past participle verb form; and if a form of *be* occurs, it will always be *followed* by a present participle verb form. These generalizations about the auxiliary system in kernel sentences can be incorporated into our PS grammar by revising it as follows.

S → NP - AUX - VP — **Translation:** a "kernel" sentence consists of an NP followed by AUX followed by a VP.

AUX → TNS - (M) - (have-en) - (be-ing)

Translation: the AUX must contain TNS. It may also contain an M and/or *have* and/or *be,* in that order. If it contains *have,* it also contains the past participle marker *en*; if it contains *be,* it also contains the present participle marker *ing*.

$$\text{TNS} \rightarrow \begin{Bmatrix} \text{pres} \\ \text{past} \end{Bmatrix}$$

Translation: TNS is either present or past.

Note that the revised PS rules introduce the auxiliary verbs and their associated affixes. The way Chomsky devised to get affixes like *en* and *ing* attached to the *following* verb form is through a transformation called Affix Hopping:

AFFIX - V-form ⇛ V-form + AFFIX

This transformation can be translated as follows: "Any time an affix (i.e., present, past, *en*, *ing*) is immediately followed by a verb-form (M, *have*, *be*, or any main verb), attach the affix to the right of the verb form." (Note: a plus sign (+) means one form has been attached to another.)

The Affix Hopping rule illustrates some basic properties of transformational rules in general. Note that the rule consists of two main parts. The material to the left of the double-shafted arrow describes the structure that provides the input to the transformational rule. The material to the right of the arrow describes the way the structure is changed by the application of the rule. In general, transformational rules either add to, delete, or change the order of elements in the input structure (Affix Hopping, for example, changes the order of the affix and the verb form).

Our grammar now consists of two types of rules: PS rules and transformational rules (e.g., Affix Hopping). Together, these two elements can be used to construct a **derivation**. The purpose of a derivation is to show the relationship between the **underlying structure** of a sentence (i.e., the elements described by the PS rules) and its **surface structure** (i.e., the sequence of elements in the actual sentence, as affected by any transformational rules that have applied). Thus a derivation is essentially a "history" of a sentence, described in terms of PS rules and transformations. For example, consider the derivation of *You should have seen that movie*. The PS grammar assigns the following underlying structure to this sentence:

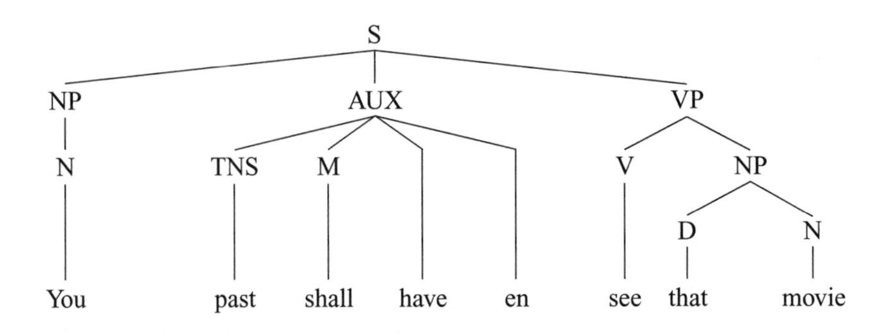

The Affix Hopping transformation changes this underlying structure into the following **surface structure**:

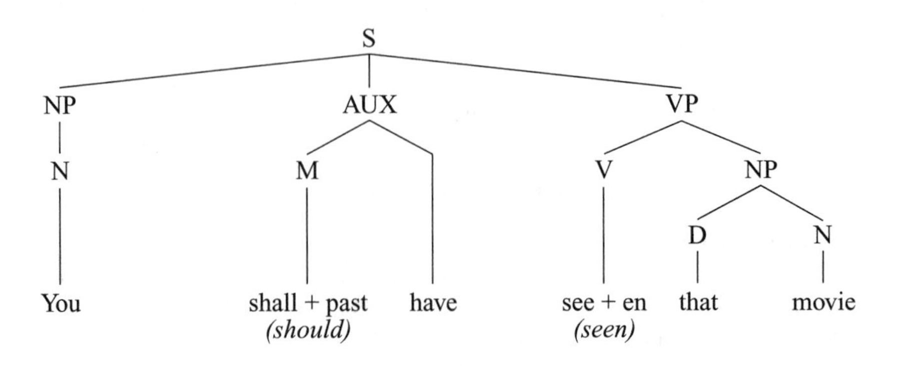

You'll note that, for example, there are four lines depending from AUX in the underlying structure, but only two in the surface structure. This change is the result of **tree pruning**: deleting any **non-terminal node** (i.e., any node represented by a capital letter) that dominates nothing. For example:

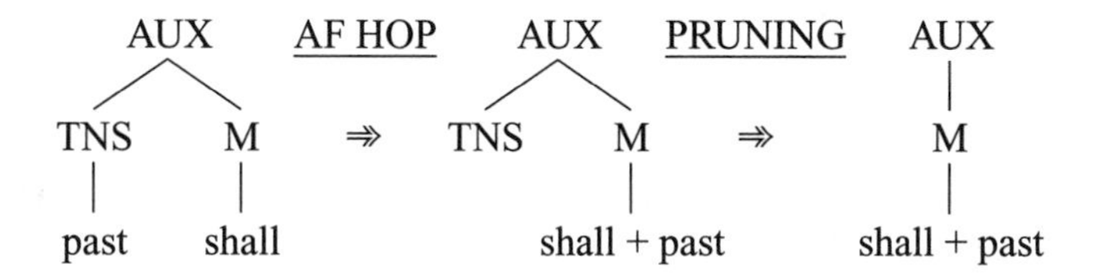

After Affix Hopping has applied, then TNS (a non-terminal node) no longer dominates anything; thus TNS is deleted via the convention of tree pruning.

The PS grammar and transformations, as far as we have developed them, are summarized below.

PS Rules

S → NP - AUX - VP

NP → (D) - (AP) - N - (PP)

$\text{VP} \rightarrow \text{V} - (\begin{Bmatrix} \text{NP} \\ \ \end{Bmatrix}) - (\text{PP})$

AP → (I) - A

PP → P - (NP)

AUX → TNS - (M) - (have-en) - (be-ing)

$\text{TNS} \rightarrow \begin{Bmatrix} \text{pres} \\ \text{past} \end{Bmatrix}$

Transformations

AFFIX HOPPING: AF - V-form ⇛ V-form + AF

Exercise D

For each of the following sentences, use the PS grammar to draw the underlying structure (US) tree. Then draw the surface structure (SS) tree, showing the results of AFFIX HOPPING.

a.† Pete might be leaving.
b. Missy has gone.
c. Melonie should have finished her work.
d.† That old guy is being a fool.

e. The man in the lake could have been drowning.
f. Gladstone had been coming to class.
g. Hazel might have been at home.
h. That car can move.
i. Sidney must be quite crazy.

Indirect Object Movement

One structure that early generative grammarians tried to derive transformationally is the indirect object construction. Indirect objects can serve as the complement to only a limited set of verbs (e.g., *send, give, mail, sell, make*) and can appear as the object of only two prepositions (*to* and *for*). Consider the following pairs.

16a. John gave a present *to Mary.*
16b. John gave *Mary* a present.

17a. John baked a cake *for Mary.*
17b. John baked *Mary* a cake.

Note that the VPs in the (a) examples contain an NP followed by a PP (i.e., *a present to Mary, a cake for Mary*), whereas the VPs in the (b) examples contain two NPs (i.e., *Mary a present, Mary a cake*). Note further that the VP expansion rule (VP → V - ({NP/AP}) - (PP)) describes the structure of the (a) sentences but not the (b) sentences. Thus, the (a) sentences were assumed to directly reflect the US of each pair, and the (b) sentences were assumed to be derived by way of a transformation called Indirect Object Movement:

$$V - NP_1 - {}_{PP}[P - NP_2] \Rightarrow V - NP_2 - NP_1$$

This rule can be translated as follows: "If an NP is followed by a PP within the VP, then delete the P and reverse the two NPs." Consider the derivation of (16b):

John gave Mary a present.

US (assigned by PS Grammar):

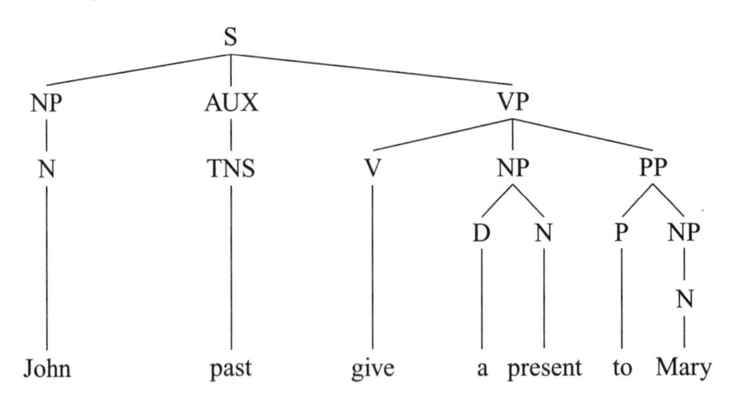

The INDIRECT OBJECT MOVEMENT transformation changes this structure into the following **derived structure:**

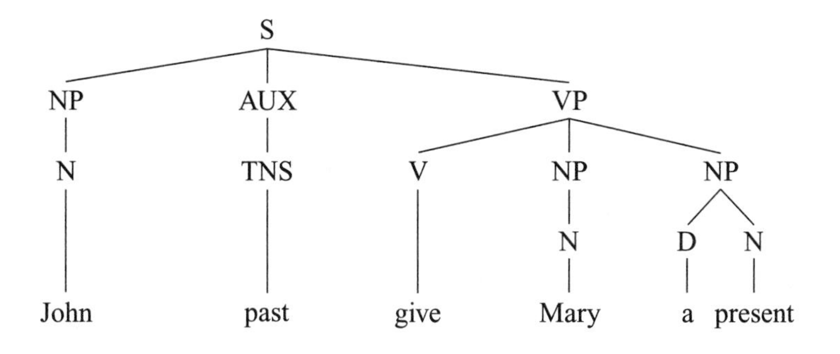

Then the AFFIX HOPPING transformation changes this structure into the following surface structure:

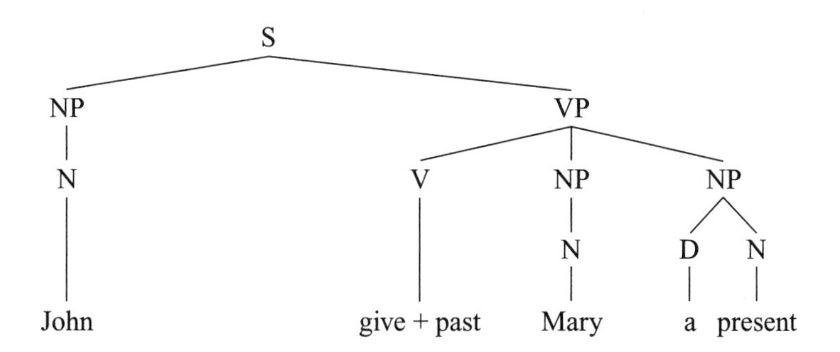

Note that we needed two transformations to derive this sentence, since the surface structure (*John gave Mary a present*) shows the effects of both INDIRECT OBJECT MOVEMENT and AFFIX HOPPING.

Exercise E

Show the derivation for the following sentences. This includes showing the US assigned by the PS grammar and the application of any transformations. (All sentences will require AFFIX HOPPING; some will also require INDIRECT OBJECT MOVEMENT. If both rules apply, do INDIRECT OBJECT MOVEMENT first.)

a.† Mary is sending John an e-mail.
b. Harry told that silly fellow a joke.
c. Alex should have written a letter to his mother.
d. He has mailed them a rubber check.
e. Hazel may have been at home.

f. Gladstone has been coming to this class.
g. Jones can levitate.

Passive

The structural relationship between active and passive sentences was one of the first correspondences Chomsky noticed. Consider the following pairs of sentences. Each pair is made up of an active sentence and its passive counterpart.

18a. Kramer ate the corndog.
18b. The corndog *was* eaten *by* Kramer.

19a. Kramer is eating the corndog.
19b. The corndog is *being* eaten *by* Kramer.

20a. Kramer has eaten the corndog.
20b. The corndog has *been* eaten *by* Kramer.

21a. Kramer could have eaten the corndog.
21b. The corndog could have *been* eaten *by* Kramer.

22a. Kramer must eat the corndog.
22b. The corndog must *be* eaten *by* Kramer.

Transformational grammarians assumed the passive member of each pair could be derived transformationally from the active member. There are four steps in deriving the passive from the active:

- move the direct object NP into subject NP position.
- move the original subject NP to the end of the VP.
- insert *be - en* before the main verb.
- insert *by* before the (original) subject NP.

These four steps can be formalized into the PASSIVE transformation, as follows.

$$NP_1 \text{ - AUX - V - } NP_2 \Rightarrow NP_2 \text{ - AUX - be - en - V - by } NP_1$$

(Examine the rule to confirm that it incorporates the four steps just described.)

Let's now consider the derivation of *The corndog was eaten by Kramer.*
US (assigned by PS Grammar):

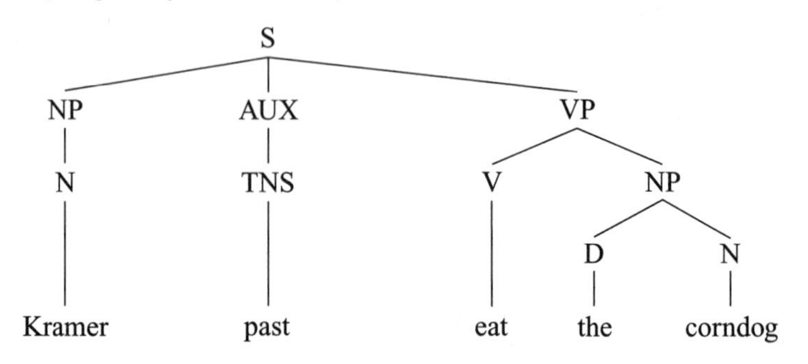

Recall that the PS grammar generates an active structure. The PASSIVE transformation changes this structure into the following derived structure:

S
NP AUX VP
D N TNS V PP
P NP
N
the corndog past be en eat by Kramer

Then the AFFIX HOPPING transformation changes this structure into the following surface structure:

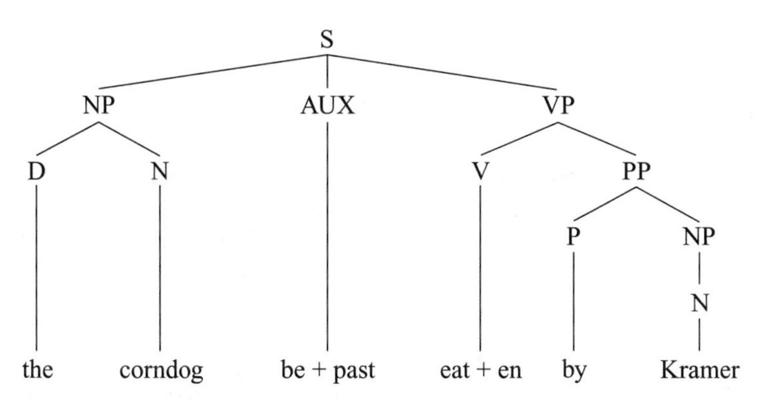

Note that it is necessary to perform PASSIVE before AFFIX HOPPING. This is because PASSIVE introduces a verb form and an affix (*be-en*) that are then affected by AFFIX HOPPING.

It's cumbersome to draw an entire tree structure for each stage of a derivation; therefore, generative grammarians developed a **shorthand notation** for derivations. The following is shorthand notation for deriving the same sentence we derived above: *The corndog was eaten by Kramer.*

US:	Kramer - past - eat - the corndog
PASSIVE:	the corndog - past - be - en - eat - by Kramer
AFFIX HOP:	the corndog - be+past - eat+en - by Kramer

In this shorthand notation, we show only the terminal elements of the tree (i.e., the words) with dashes to separate constituents (i.e., NP, AUX, VP, etc.); we do not show the tree itself.

Exercise F

Derive the following sentences using shorthand notation. Show the US and then apply any necessary transformations in the following order: PASSIVE, AFFIX HOPPING.

a. John was standing by Mary.

b.† The tree might have been struck by lightning.

c.† Sidney got a brand new truck.

d. That story was told to Bob by an old man.

e. The IRS should have mailed a check to Mindy.

f. The suspect might be caught by the police.

Interaction of INDIRECT OBJECT MOVEMENT and PASSIVE

So far we have considered three transformations: AFFIX HOPPING, INDIRECT OBJECT MOVEMENT, and PASSIVE. We have derived sentences where only AFFIX HOPPING has applied, sentences where INDIRECT OBJECT MOVEMENT and AFFIX HOPPING have applied, and sentences where PASSIVE and AFFIX HOPPING have applied, as follows:

23a. An old man told that story to Bob. (AFFIX HOPPING)

23b. An old man told Bob that story. (INDIRECT OBJECT MOVEMENT + AFFIX HOPPING)

23c. That story was told to Bob by an old man. (PASSIVE + AFFIX HOPPING)

Let's now consider the derivation of a sentence where all three apply: *Bob was told that story by an old man*.

US:	An old man - past - tell - that story - to Bob
IOM:	An old man - past - tell - Bob - that story
PASSIVE:	Bob - past - be - en - tell - that story - by an old man
AFFIX HOP:	Bob - be+past - tell+en - that story - by an old man

Notice what happens in this situation: *that story* is the direct object NP in the US. The INDIRECT OBJECT MOVEMENT transformation moves the indirect object *Bob* into direct object position (i.e., first NP following V). Then the PASSIVE transformation moves *Bob* into subject position.

Exercise G

Derive the following sentences using shorthand notation. Show the US and then apply any necessary transformations in the following order: INDIRECT OBJECT MOVEMENT, PASSIVE, AFFIX HOPPING.

a.† A check was mailed to Mindy by the IRS.

b. Mindy was mailed a check by the IRS.

Question

The formation of questions from declaratives is another transformation early formalized by Chomsky. Consider the following pairs of sentences. Each pair consists of a declarative sentence and its corresponding question.

24a. Fred can eat.

24b. *Can* Fred eat?

25a. Fred has eaten.

25b. *Has* Fred eaten?

26a. Fred is eating.

26b. *Is* Fred eating?

27a. Fred could have been eating.

27b. *Could* Fred have been eating?

It's clear from these examples that in forming a question, the first auxiliary verb (M, *have*, or *be*) is being moved to the left of the subject NP. Moreover, since the first verb-form in all simple sentences is inflected for tense, the formation of questions involves moving TNS as well as the first auxiliary. These operations are formalized in the QUESTION transformation as follows.

$$\text{NP - }\left[\text{TNS - }\begin{Bmatrix}\text{M}\\\text{have}\\\text{be}\end{Bmatrix}\right] \Rightarrow \left[\text{TNS - }\begin{Bmatrix}\text{M}\\\text{have}\\\text{be}\end{Bmatrix}\right]\text{ - NP}$$

The square brackets indicate that the enclosed items must be moved as a unit.

Now consider the derivation of *Has Fred eaten?*

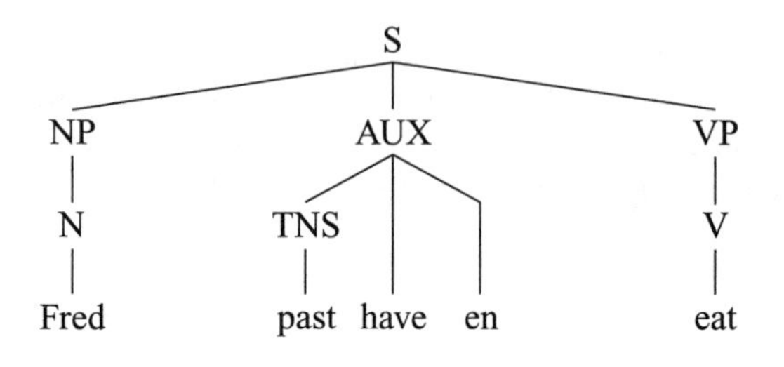

QUESTION:

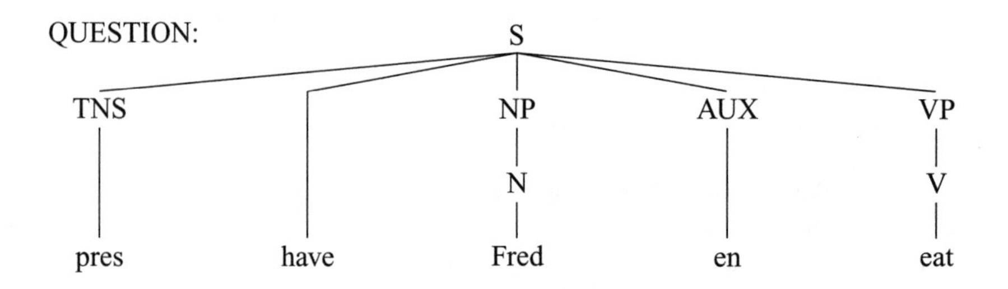

AFFIX HOP:

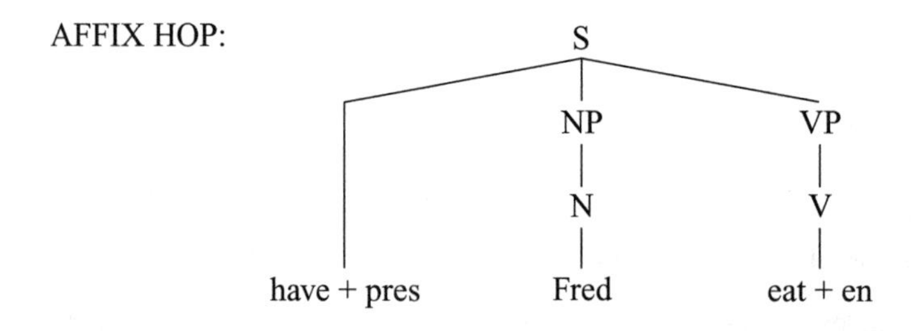

Shorthand notation:

US:	Fred - pres - have - en - eat
QUESTION:	pres - have - Fred - en - eat
AFFIX HOP:	have+pres - Fred - eat+en

Exercise H

Derive the following sentences using shorthand notation. Show the US and then apply any necessary transformations in the following order: QUESTION, AFFIX HOPPING.

a.† Can you help me?

b. Have you been drinking?

c. Will you be coming to the party?

d. Could Fred have been eating?

Negative

Early generative grammarians were quick to see the structural correspondences between positive and negative sentences. Consider the following pairs, the first member of which is positive and the second of which is negative.

28a. Raoul is eating.
28b. Raoul is *not* eating.

29a. Raoul has eaten.
29b. Raoul has *not* eaten.

30a. Raoul will eat.
30b. Raoul will *not* eat.

31a. Raoul could have eaten.
31b. Raoul could *not* have eaten.

32a. Raoul had been eating.
32b. Raoul had *not* been eating.

In each case, *not* is inserted after the first auxiliary verb, which is also inflected for tense. This pattern can be formalized in the NEGATIVE transformation, as follows.

$$\left[\text{TNS - }\begin{Bmatrix}\text{M}\\ \text{have}\\ \text{be}\end{Bmatrix}\right] \Rrightarrow \left[\text{TNS - }\begin{Bmatrix}\text{M}\\ \text{have}\\ \text{be}\end{Bmatrix}\right]\text{ - not}$$

Now consider the derivation of *Raoul has not eaten*.

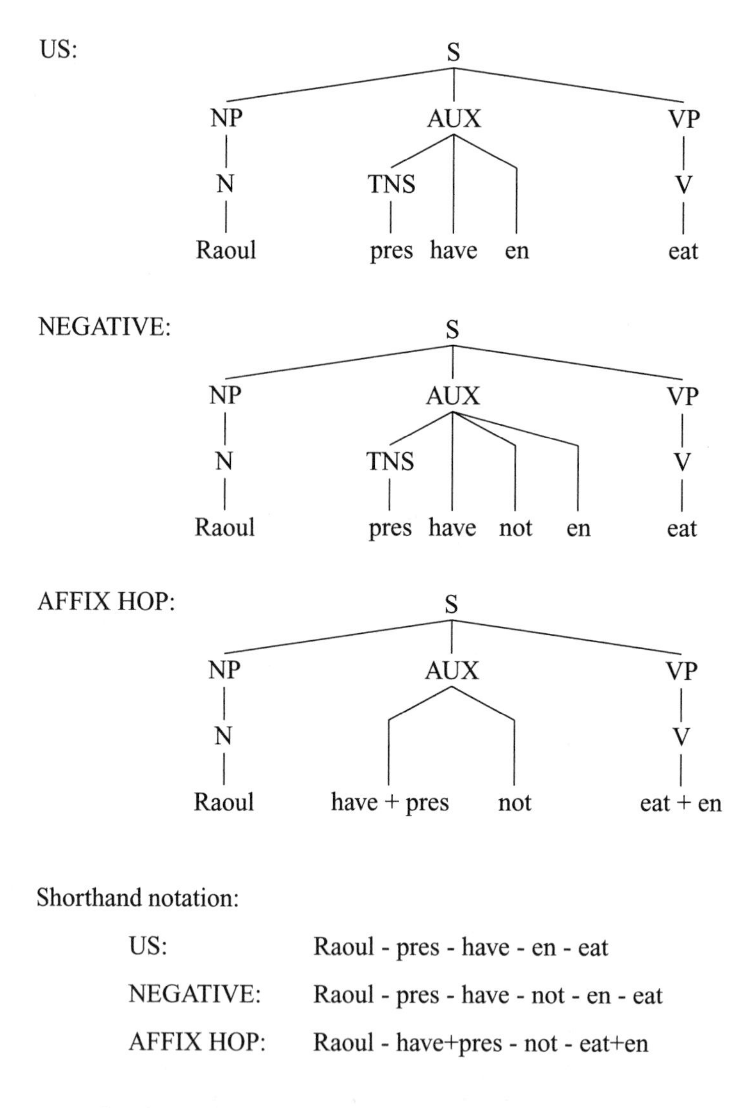

Shorthand notation:

US:	Raoul - pres - have - en - eat
NEGATIVE:	Raoul - pres - have - not - en - eat
AFFIX HOP:	Raoul - have+pres - not - eat+en

Exercise I

Derive the following sentences using shorthand notation. Show the US and then apply any necessary transformations in the following order: NEGATIVE, AFFIX HOPPING.

a.† You should not have been doing that.
b. Sue must not be going.

c. The man in the front row may not leave.
d. Your investment has not been successful.

Auxiliary Do

Note that the questions and negatives we have derived so far all have an overt auxiliary verb. For example,

Juan *will* eat.

Will Juan eat? (Question)

Juan *will* not eat. (Negative)

Something interesting happens when we create a question or a negative from a structure that does *not* contain an auxiliary verb: a form of the verb *do* appears in place of the "missing" auxiliary. For example,

Juan ate.

Did Juan eat? (Question)

Juan *did* not eat. (Negative)

We will not go into the actual mechanics of how auxiliary *do* is inserted into such structures, because it would involve revising both the QUESTION and NEGATIVE transformations. Suffice it to say that, as explained in Chapter 7, the auxiliary verb *do* is in complementary distribution with all the other auxiliary verbs. That is, auxiliary *do* only appears in environments where the other auxiliaries don't. (Review Chapter 7 for more details.)

Interaction of NEGATIVE and QUESTION

We have derived sentences where *either* NEGATIVE *or* QUESTION has applied. Let's now consider sentences where *both* apply: *Have you not seen that movie?* This sentence is derived as follows:

US:	you - pres - have -en - see - that movie
NEGATIVE:	you - pres - have - not - en - see - that movie
QUESTION:	pres - have - you - not - en - see - that movie
AFFIX HOP:	have+pres - you - not - see+en - that movie

Note that when both rules apply in the derivation of a sentence, then NEGATIVE must apply before QUESTION. Applying them in the opposite order would result in an unacceptable sentence, in this case, **Have not you seen that movie?*

Exercise J

Derive the following sentences using shorthand notation. Show the US and then apply any necessary transformations in the following order: NEGATIVE, QUESTION, AFFIX HOPPING.

a.† Can he not read the fine print?
b. Has Sara not been sleeping?
c. Will Chuck not be coming to the celebration?
d. Should they not have been so pushy?

Interaction of PASSIVE and NEGATIVE

We have derived sentences where *either* PASSIVE *or* NEGATIVE has applied. Let's now consider a sentence where *both* apply: *You were not selected by the committee.* In this sentence, PASSIVE has to apply before NEGATIVE, because PASSIVE inserts a form of *be* that NEGATIVE needs in order to apply. The derivation of this sentence would be as follows.

US:	the committee - past - select - you
PASSIVE:	you - past - be - en - select - by the committee
NEGATIVE:	you - past - be - not - en - select - by the committee
AFFIX HOP:	you - be+past - not - select+en - by the committee

Exercise K

Derive the following sentences using shorthand notation. Show the US and then apply any necessary transformations in the following order: PASSIVE, NEGATIVE, AFFIX HOPPING.

a.† Muffy has not been located by the police.
b. The police have not been questioning Muffy.
c. Muffy was not found in her house by the police.

Interaction of PASSIVE and QUESTION

We have derived sentences where *either* PASSIVE *or* QUESTION has applied. Let's now consider a sentence where *both* apply: *Were you selected by the committee?* In this sentence, PASSIVE has to apply before QUESTION, because PASSIVE inserts a form of *be* that QUESTION needs in order to apply. The derivation of this sentence would be as follows.

US:	the committee - past - select - you
PASSIVE:	you - past - be - en - select - by the committee
QUESTION:	past - be - you - en - select - by the committee
AFFIX HOP:	be+past - you - select+en - by the committee

Ordering Summary

We have shown that INDIRECT OBJECT MOVEMENT must apply before PASSIVE, that NEGATIVE must apply before QUESTION, and that PASSIVE must apply before both NEGATIVE and QUESTION. The ordering of all the transformations we have discussed can be summarized as follows.

1. INDIRECT OBJECT MOVEMENT	INDIRECT OBJECT MOVEMENT creates a new direct object NP; PASSIVE moves the direct object.
2. PASSIVE	PASSIVE inserts form of *be*; NEGATIVE and QUESTION can move *be*.
3. NEGATIVE	NEGATIVE inserts *not* after first auxiliary; QUESTION moves first auxiliary.
4. QUESTION	
5. AFFIX HOPPING	

Exercise L

Derive the following sentences using shorthand notation. Show the US and then apply any necessary transformations in the order INDIRECT OBJECT MOVEMENT, PASSIVE, NEGATIVE, QUESTION, AFFIX HOPPING.

a.† Had the children been frightened by the movie?
b. Has Eraserhead written a letter to his mother?
c. The heckler was not being recognized by the chairman.
d. Were the presents not given to the children by the YMCA?
e. Gonzo has not mailed the IRS his check.
f. Could Bush have been re-elected by the voters?
g. Was the package not left by the messenger?
h. Should the extra homework not have been assigned by the teacher?

It should be emphasized that speakers of English have no need to think about these rules consciously while they are speaking; they just apply them automatically.

At the same time, it is worthwhile to look at English as a logical system of interacting rules, rather than relying on our intuitions that a sentence "just sounds right." The perspective of generative grammar is especially useful when dealing with speakers of other languages, who need reassurance and a demonstration that English, like their own language, follows a system of interacting rules.

Summary

A "standard theory" model of generative grammar consists of two components: a phrase structure grammar, which describes the "kernel" sentences of a language, and a transformational component, which transforms the structures underlying these basic sentence types into "non-kernels," such as passives, negatives, and questions. The model we have discussed here generates the following types of sentences, and more.

	Transformations
The IRS will send a check to Mindy.	= AH
The IRS will send Mindy a check.	= IOM + AH
A check will be sent to Mindy by the IRS.	= PASS + AH
Mindy will be sent a check by the IRS.	= IOM + PASS + AH
Will the IRS send a check to Mindy?	= QUES + AH
A check will not be sent to Mindy by the IRS.	= NEG + AH
Will the check not be sent to Mindy by the IRS?	= NEG + QUES + AH
Will Mindy not be sent a check by the IRS?	= IOM + PASS + NEG + QUES +AH

SUPPLEMENTARY EXERCISES

1. Consider the following passive sentences.

A. Mr. Matuzak *got* eaten by piranhas.
B. Mr. Matuzak has *gotten* eaten by piranhas.
C. Mr. Matuzak is *getting* eaten by piranhas.
D. Mr. Matuzak will *get* eaten by piranhas.

a. How do these sentences differ from ordinary passives discussed earlier?
b. How would the PASSIVE transformation have to be revised to generate these new passives?
c. Use the revised PASSIVE transformation to derive sentence (C) above. (Use shorthand notation.)

2. Derive the following sentences using shorthand notation. Show the US and then apply any necessary transformations in the order INDIRECT OBJECT MOVEMENT, PASSIVE, NEGATIVE, QUESTION, AFFIX HOPPING.

a. Was the movie good?
b. Ron showed me his blue ribbon.
c. Were the packages delivered by UPS?
d. The stock was not recommended by her broker.
e. Have you been appointed to the committee by the dean?
f. Could you give a message to your sister?

3. The following forms were produced by a native speaker of German acquiring English as a second language.

A. Can you go with me?
B. Has he drunk the beer?
C. Came you home early?

Based on these data, how does German appear to differ from English in terms of question formation? How would you describe the German rule for forming a *yes/no*-question?

4. In this chapter we established that PASSIVE must apply before NEGATIVE if both rules are needed in the same derivation. Try to derive *You were not selected by the committee* by applying NEGATIVE before PASSIVE. Why won't the derivation work if the rules are applied in this order?

5. The following sentences illustrate the way that various *yes/no*-questions are formed in **standard** (SE) and **nonstandard** (NSE) varieties of English.

A. Are they sick? (SE)
B. Do they be sick? (NSE)
C. Are they going? (SE)
D. Do they be going? (NSE)
E. Do they have a car? (SE and NSE)
F. Do they need money? (SE and NSE)

Label the following generalizations about *yes/no*-questions as true or false. For each response, explain how the data support your answer.

a. T - F Main verb *be* behaves like other main verbs in SE.
b. T - F Main verb *be* behaves like other main verbs in NSE.
c. T - F Auxiliary *be* behaves like a main verb in NSE.
d. T - F Main verb *have* behaves like an auxiliary verb in SE.

▲▲▲ CHAPTER 13

Government and Binding Theory

This chapter outlines four basic components of Chomsky's more recent version of generative grammar, popularly known as "GB Theory": X-bar syntax (PS grammar), *Wh*-Movement and NP-Movement (transformations), constraints on movement, case theory, and binding conditions. It concludes with a brief description of Chomsky's program for future research, which he calls "minimalism."

X-BAR SYNTAX

X-bar syntax extends traditional PS grammars in two ways. First, it recognizes a structural unit intermediate in size between a phrasal category (e.g., NP) and a lexical category (e.g., N). This intermediate category is called a "bar" (e.g., N-bar) category and is symbolized by the category with a bar over it (e.g., $\bar{N}$) or with a prime mark following it (e.g., N'). Second, X-bar syntax makes the claim that all phrase types (e.g., NP, VP, AP, etc.) have essentially the same internal structure. Thus, this system of representation (e.g., N, N', NP) can be generalized to any phrase type (e.g., X, X', XP), where X stands for any category (e.g., N, V, A, etc.). Hence, the term *X-bar syntax*.

In standard theory, Chomsky assumed that phrases such as *the redheaded student* have the internal structure shown here.

That is, *the redheaded student* can be interpreted as an NP; and *student* can be interpreted as an N; but *redheaded student* is not a **constituent** (i.e., structural unit) of any sort.

However, as we saw in Chapter 5, one piece of evidence for the internal structure of phrases is **pro-form substitution**. A pro-form is a word which can substitute for a phrase that forms a constituent. With this in mind, consider the following data.

1a. I know this *redheaded student* better than that *one.*
1b. *I know *this redheaded student* better than *one.*

In (1a), the pro-form *one* substitutes for *redheaded student,* which means that *redheaded student* is a constituent of some sort. This constituent is intermediate in size between the NP *this redheaded student* and the N *student*. Moreover, (1b) illustrates that *one*-substitution is a good test for picking out such intermediate categories, since *one* will not substitute for the entire NP *this redheaded student.*

Generative grammarians concluded that the internal structure of a phrase such as *the redheaded student* must be something like the following.

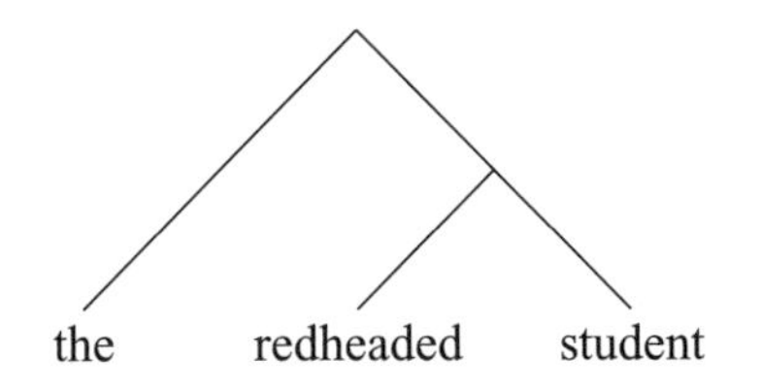

That is, *the redheaded student* is an NP; *redheaded student* is an N'; and *student* is an N. In short, this tree diagram reflects one important basic inference that X-bar theorists have drawn about phrases such as *redheaded student*: *redheaded student* is a separate identifiable structural unit. This represents a major step forward from standard theory.

Exercise A

> Consider the sentence *Employers prefer an industrious worker to a lazy one.* Is *worker* in this phrase an N or an N' or both? Explain.

When it comes to actually labeling the categories in X-bar syntax, however, the situation is more complex. Nonetheless, X-bar theorists developed the following tests to help them draw inferences about the internal structure of NPs.

Pro-form Substitution

The pro-form *one* is unique in English in that it substitutes for N', but not for NP or N. The evidence for this is the fact that *one* is the only pro-form in English that can have a determiner (e.g., *I want this one, not that one*). Since the determiners (i.e., *this/that*) are part of the NP, then *one* cannot be substituting for the entire NP. (X-bar theorists use the term **specifier** for the position filled by a determiner.)

Let's see how this fact is used to infer the categories of the words in phrases such as *this redheaded student* and *this music student*. Consider the following sentences:

1c. I know [the redheaded student] better than [the blonde one]
1d. *I know [the music student] better than [the drama one]

Since *one* substitutes for *student* in (1c), then *student* in the phrase *the redheaded student* must be an N'. However, since *one* does not substitute for *student* in (1d), then *student* in the phrase *the music student* must not be an N' (instead, it's an N). Thus, the structures of the relevant phrases in (1c) and (1d) are as follows.

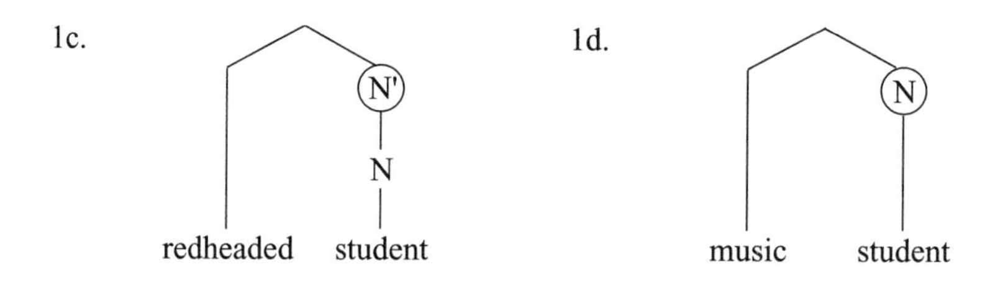

These same structures are preserved when the modifiers are moved from pre-nominal to post-nominal position, as in *the student with red hair* and *the student of music*. Consider the following sentences.

2a. I know [the student with red hair] better than [the one with blonde hair]
2b. *I know [the student of music] better than [the one of drama]

Once again, since *one* substitutes for *student* in (2a), then *student* in the phrase *the student with red hair* must be an N'. However, since *one* does not substitute for *student* in (2b), then *student* in the phrase *the student of music* must not be an N' (instead, it's an N). Thus, the structures of the relevant phrases in (2a) and (2b) are as follows.

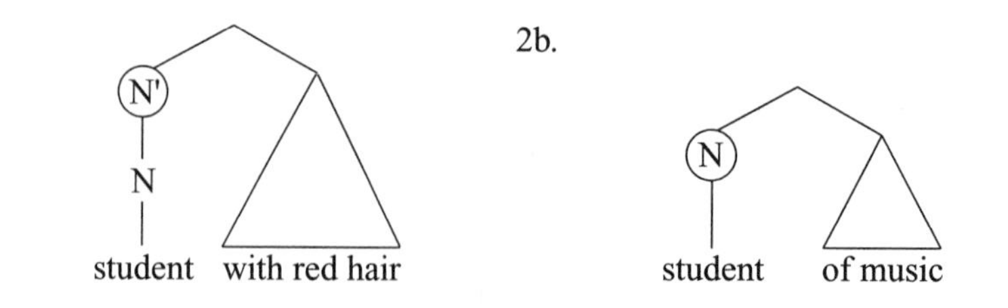

X-bar theorists call modifiers of N' (e.g., *redheaded* and *with red hair*) **adjuncts**, and modifiers of N (e.g., *music* and *of music*) **complements**.

Reversibility

When two adjuncts occur in an NP, they can occur in either order (i.e., they are reversible). However, an adjunct and a complement within an NP occur in a fixed order (i.e., they are not reversible). Consider the following phrases.

3a. the *redheaded bearded* student
3b. the *bearded redheaded* student

3c. the *redheaded music* student
3d. *the *music redheaded* student

In (3a–b) *redheaded* and *bearded* are both adjuncts and thus can occur in either order. However, in (3c–d) *redheaded* is an adjunct and *music* is a complement; thus, their order is fixed. The structures of (3a) and (3c) are as follows.

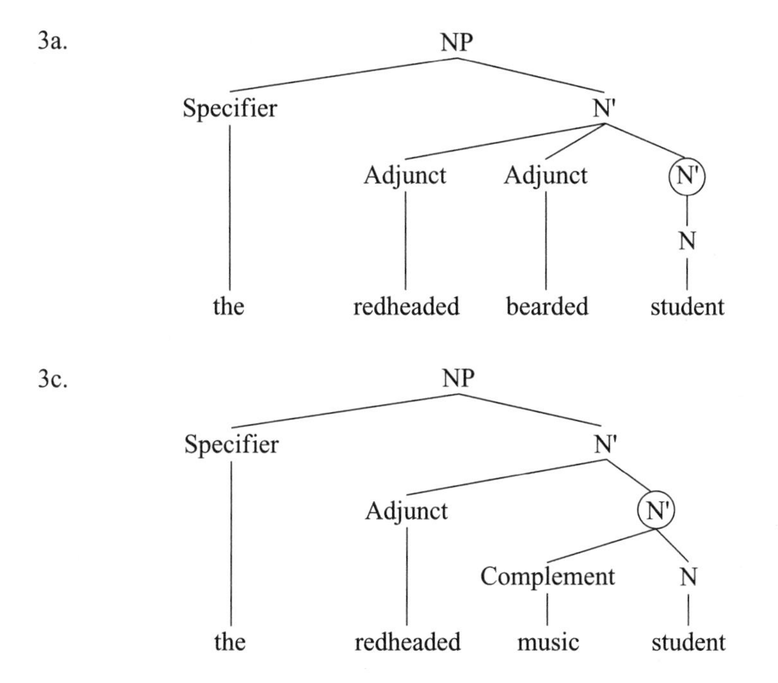

In (3a), *redheaded* and *bearded* both modify the circled N'; thus, they can occur in either order. In (3c), however, *redheaded* modifies the circled N', and *music* modifies the N. (In X-bar terminology, *redheaded* is a **sister** of N', and *music* is a **sister** of N.) Note that this analysis predicts the fact that *redheaded* (an adjunct) must precede *music* (a complement) when they both occur pre-nominally. Since an adjunct always modifies an N', it will always be farther away from the head of the phrase than a complement, which always modifies an N.

Note that this relative ordering of adjunct and complement holds even in post-nominal modifers, as follows.

4a. the student *with a beard* *with red hair*
4b. the student *with red hair* *with a beard*
4c. the student *of music* *with red hair*
4d. *the student *with red hair* *of music*

In (4a–b), *with red hair* and *with a beard* are both adjuncts and can occur in either order. However, in (4c–d) *of music* is a complement and *with red hair* is an adjunct; thus their order is fixed, with the adjunct (*with red hair*) occurring farther from the head (*student*) than does the complement (*of music*).

Exercise B

Draw diagrams for (4a) and (4c). (Use diagrams (3a) and (3c) as models.)

Coordination

Two adjuncts can be coordinated (i.e., connected by *and* or *or*); likewise, two complements can be coordinated. However, an adjunct and a complement cannot. Consider the following phrases:

5a. the *redheaded and bearded* student
5b. *the *redheaded and music* student

(5a) is acceptable because *redheaded* and *bearded* are both adjuncts and thus can be coordinated. (5b) is unacceptable because *redheaded* is an adjunct but *music* is a complement, and thus cannot be coordinated.

Exercise C

For each of the following phrases, state whether X-bar theory predicts it will be acceptable or unacceptable. In each case, explain why.

a.† the student with red hair and with a beard
b.† the student of music and with a beard
c. the student with a beard and red hair
d. the student with red hair and of drama
e. the student of music and of drama
f. the student of drama and of music

The tests discussed so far are summarized in the following table.

TABLE 13-1

Test	Data	Inference
One-substitution: *One* substitutes for N', but not for NP or N.	I know this redheaded *student* better than that blonde *one*	*student* = N' in *redheaded student*
	*I know this music *student* better than that drama *one*	*student* = N in *music student*
	I know the *student* with red hair better than the *one* with blonde hair	*student* = N' in *student with red hair*
	*I know the *student* of music better than the *one* of drama	*student* = N in *student of music*
Reversibility: Like modifiers can be reversed; unlike modifiers cannot.	the *redheaded music* student *the *music redheaded* student	*redheaded* = adjunct (sister of N') *music* = complement (sister of N)
	*the student *with red hair of music* the student *of music with red hair*	*with red hair* = adjunct *of music* = complement
Coordination: Like modifiers can be coordinated; unlike modifiers cannot.	the *redheaded and bearded* student *the *redheaded and drama* student	*bearded* = adjunct *drama* = complement

Summary

The following tree diagrams summarize what X-bar theorists have inferred about the internal structure of NPs.

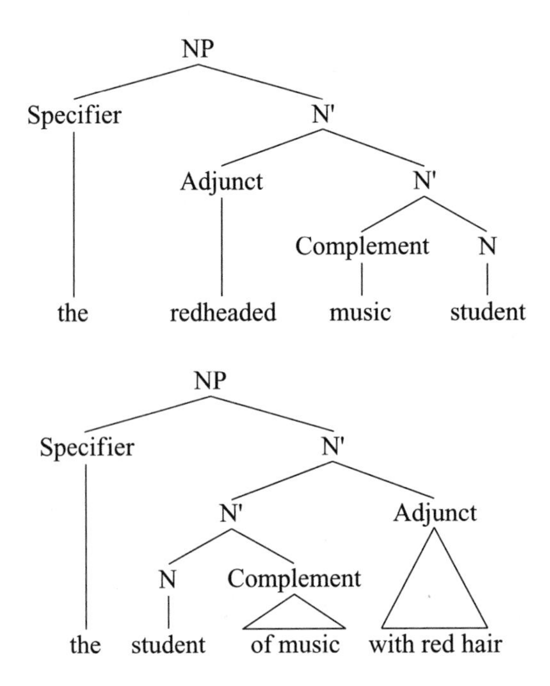

These X-bar diagrams account for a number of properties which were overlooked in earlier models of PS grammar:

- NPs contain intermediate constituents. For example, we have not only *the redheaded music student* but also *redheaded music student* and *music student.*
- Adjuncts and complements can occur before or after the head of an NP (e.g., *music student* or *student of music*).
- NP modifiers are of three different types: specifier (daughter of NP), adjunct (sister of N'), and complement (sister of N).
- Complements are always closer to the head than are adjuncts.

WH-MOVEMENT AND NP-MOVEMENT

Standard theory postulated numerous language-specific transformations (e.g., Indirect Object Movement, Passive, Negative); in fact, standard theory attempted to *maximize* the number of surface forms it could generate transformationally: the more transformations the better. GB theory, in contrast, attempts to *minimize* the number of transformations and to investigate only those thought to apply in all languages. There are two such transformations: *wh*- Movement and NP-Movement.

***Wh*-Movement** (WHM) moves any *wh*-phrase (i.e., one containing *who, what, which, when, where, why, how*, etc.) to clause-initial position (called "COMP" for *complementizer*) and leaves a **trace** (*t*) in the position from which it was moved. Thus, the derivation of a sentence like *Who did you hit?* would be as follows.

6a. US [[$_{\text{COMP}}$] did you hit *who*]
↑___________|

6b. SS [[$_{\text{COMP}}$*who*] did you hit *t*]

The motivation for WHM in this situation is that *hit* is a transitive verb and requires a direct object (*who*) adjacent to it in the US. When the object is not next to the verb, it is assumed to have been moved out of that position by a transformation.

NP-Movement (NPM) moves any NP to any *empty* NP position (*e*) and leaves a trace in the position from which it was moved. Thus, the derivation of a passive sentence like *John was hit* is as follows.

7a. US [[$_{\text{COMP}}$] *e* was hit *John*
↑ NPM |

7b. SS [[$_{\text{COMP}}$] *John* was hit *t*]

The motivation for NPM in this situation is identical to that for WHM: *hit* is a transitive verb and requires a direct object (*John*) adjacent to it in the US. When the object is not next to the verb (as in a passive sentence), it is assumed to have been moved out of that position by a transformation.

NPM is also required in subject raising sentences, where the subject of a dependent infinitive clause is "raised" to subject position of the main clause. Thus, the derivation of a sentence such as *You are sure to hit yourself* is as follows.

8a. US [[$_{\text{COMP}}$] *e* are sure [[$_{\text{COMP}}$] *you* to hit yourself]]
↑___________|

8b. SS [[$_{\text{COMP}}$] *You* are sure [[$_{\text{COMP}}$] *t* to hit yourself]]

The motivation for NPM in this situation is somewhat different. One piece of evidence that *you* must originate in the dependent clause is the fact that a reflexive pronoun (*yourself*) requires an antecedent (*you*) within the same clause. Thus, *you* must originate in the dependent clause, so it can serve as the antecedent for *yourself*. All sentences containing so-called "raising predicates" (e.g., *be sure, be certain, be likely, seem*, etc.) are assumed to be derived via NPM.

Finally, if a *wh*-question like *Who did you hit?* requires WHM, and if a passive like *John was hit* requires NPM, then a passive *wh*-question like *Who was hit?* requires both, as follows.

9a. US [[$_{COMP}$] *e* was hit *who*
↑WHM ↑NPM

9b. SS [[$_{COMP}$*who*] *t* was hit *t*]

Since *who* is both an NP and a *wh*-word, it undergoes both NPM and WHM in (9). NPM moves *who* into the empty NP position *e*; then WHM moves *who* into COMP.

A summary of movement prototypes is as follows.

10a. [[$_{COMP}$] [Smith kissed Jones.]] (No movement)
10b. [[$_{COMP}$] [*Jones* was kissed ______ .]] (Passive)
↑ NPM

10c. [[$_{COMP}$] *Smith* is likely [______ to kiss Jones.]]] (Raising)
↑ NPM

10d. [[$_{COMP}$ *Who*] [______ kissed Jones?]] (Movement of subject)
↑WHM

10e. [[$_{COMP}$ *Who*] [did Smith kiss ______ ?]] (Movement of object)
↑ WHM

Exercise D

Which of the following most clearly corresponds to the underlying structure of *Who did you say you saw?*

a. [did you say [you saw who]]
b. [did you say who [you saw]]
c. [[$_{COMP}$] [did you say who [[$_{COMP}$] [you saw]]]]
d. [[$_{COMP}$] [did you say [[$_{COMP}$] [you saw who]]]]
e. [[$_{COMP}$ who] [did you say [[$_{COMP}$] [you saw]]]]

CONSTRAINTS ON MOVEMENT

A GB grammar with two transformations that can essentially move any *wh*-phrase to COMP (WHM) and any NP to any empty NP position is extremely unconstrained and thus is capable of generating an infinite number of unacceptable surface structures, as follows.

11. **John* is believed [_____ is incompetent]
↑____________________|

This derivation generates the surface structure **John is believed is incompetent* rather than *John is believed to be incompetent.* To avoid this "overgeneration" by the grammar, Chomsky extended the theory of transformational grammar to include **constraints** on transformations. Each constraint is not part of a particular transformation but rather a restriction on what transformations in general can do.

Empty Node

This constraint states that a constituent can be moved only to an empty node (*e*), as follows.

12a. [*e* was hit *John*]
↑__NPM__|

12b. *[Mary was hit *John*]
↑__NPM___|

Trace

This constraint states that every moved constituent leaves a **co-indexed** trace (t_n), as follows.

13a. US [*e* was hit *John*]
↑________|

13b. SS [$John_1$ was hit t_1]

Cycle

This constraint states that transformations must apply to the most deeply embedded clause before applying to a higher clause, as follows: *When will he reveal who he saw?*

14. [[*e*] will he reveal [[*e*] he saw *who*] *when*]
↑1st cycle|
↑____________2nd cycle____________|

Unit-Movement

This constraint states that only a constituent (i.e., a word or phrase dominated by a single node) can be moved by a transformation. Consider the following examples of how the unit-movement constraint works.

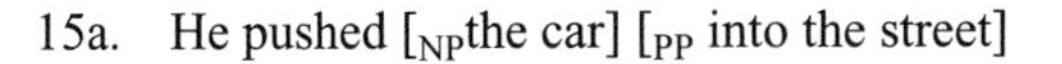

15a. He pushed [$_{NP}$the car] [$_{PP}$ into the street]

15b. [$_{NP}$ *the car*] was pushed *t* [$_{PP}$ into the street]

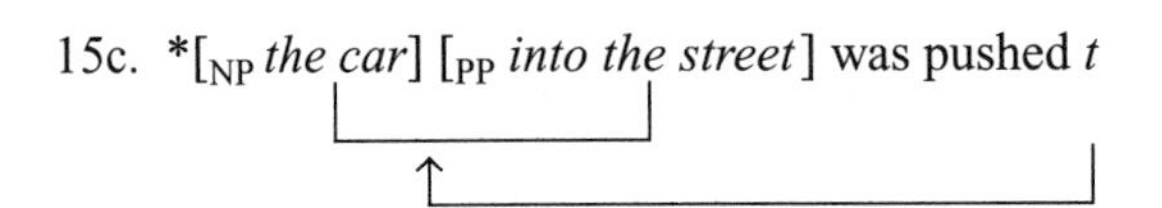

15c. *[$_{NP}$ *the car*] [$_{PP}$ *into the street*] was pushed *t*

The car is a constituent, so it can be moved as a unit. *The car into the street* is not a constituent, so it cannot be moved as a unit.

A-over-A

This constraint states that a constituent (A) dominated by an identical category (A) cannot be moved out from under that category. Consider the following examples.

16a. He jumped [$_{PP}$ *out* [$_{PP}$ *of which window*]]?

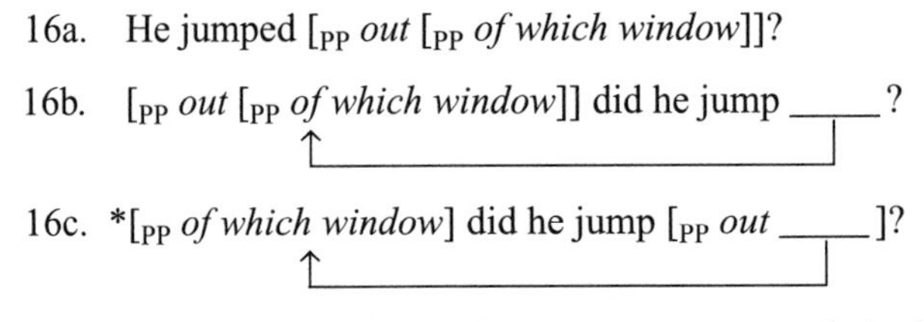

16b. [$_{PP}$ *out* [$_{PP}$ *of which window*]] did he jump _____?

16c. *[$_{PP}$ *of which window*] did he jump [$_{PP}$ *out* _____]?

Of which window is a PP dominated by another PP, *out of which window*. Therefore, the lower PP cannot be moved out from under the higher one.

Subjacency

This constraint states that no constituent can be moved across more than one bounding node (NP or IP) by a transformation. (IP stands for 'inflectional phrase,' which is what a sentence is called in GB theory. A phrase that contains a verbal inflection [i.e., tense, present participle, past participle] is an IP.)

17a. He doesn't remember that [$_{IP}$ he bought *which gun*]

17b. *Which gun* doesn't he remember that [$_{IP}$ he bought _____]

18a. He doesn't remember [$_{NP}$ the fact that [$_{IP}$ he bought *which gun*]]

18b. **Which gun* doesn't he remember [$_{NP}$ the fact that [$_{IP}$ he bought ____]]

Subjacency allows the movement in (17b) because *which gun* crosses only one bounding node (IP). However, it prohibits the movement in (18b) because *which gun* crosses two bounding nodes (NP and IP).

Tensed S

This constraint states that no constituent of a tensed clause (IP) can be moved outside of that clause.

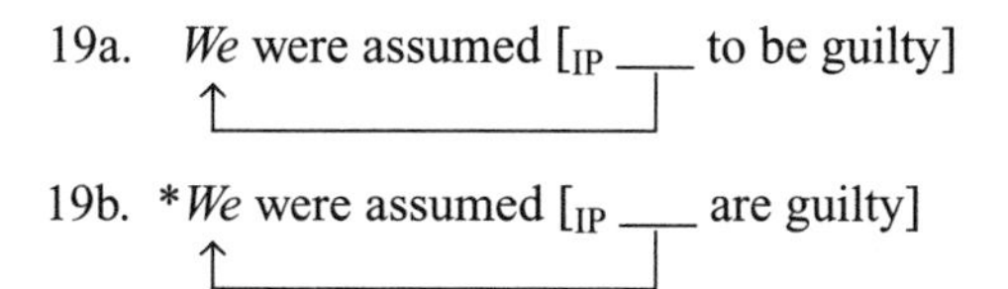

Tensed S allows movement in (19a) because *to be* is not tensed. However, it blocks movement in (19b), because *is* is inflected for tense.

Exercise E

For each of the following transformational movements, state the constraint that is violated.

a.† *[*Burping* is considered [*t* is rude]]

b.† *[[$_{COMP}$ *Of which sewer*] did he crawl out *t*]

c. *[*John* seems [*t* and Mary to be in love]]

d. *[[$_{COMP}$ *which foot in his mouth*] did Joey put *t*]

e. *[[$_{COMP}$ *what*] are you reading [an article [that defends *t*]]]

CASE

So far we have discussed X-bar syntax, which essentially defines the set of permissible underlying structures, and transformations, which essentially create surface structures from underlying structures. Now we will discuss two different constraints on surface structures. One is the **case filter**, which states that all overt NPs must be case marked (i.e., assigned nominative, objective, or possessive case).

Case marking, however, is dependent upon the concept of **government**, which is defined in terms of tree structures. For our purposes, we can simply stipulate the following.

- A preposition governs its object.
- A verb governs its direct object.
- Tense governs its subject.

Accordingly, we have the following **case assignment rules**.

- P assigns objective case to its object.
- A transitive V assigns objective case to its direct object.
- TNS assigns nominative case to its subject.

Consider the following example of case assignment: *She hits me with them.*

- The P *with* assigns objective case to its object *them* (cf. **She hits me with they*).
- The transitive V *hits* assigns objective case to its direct object *me* (cf. **She hits I with them*).
- TNS (carried by the verb *hits*) assigns nominative case to its subject *she* (cf. **Her hits me with them*).

Exercise F

Answer the following questions in terms of the case filter and case assignment rules.

a.† Consider the sentence *John asked me to go*. How is *me* assigned case?

b. Consider the sentence *For you to fail would be a tragedy*. What case is assigned to *you*? How is it assigned?

c.† Consider the sentence **You to fail would be a tragedy*. Why is this sentence ungrammatical?

d. Consider the sentence **I am wondering whether I to go*. Why is this sentence ungrammatical?

e. Consider the sentence **Whom spoke to her?* Why is this sentence ungrammatical?

BINDING

The second constraint on surface structure that we will discuss is binding, which deals with the coreference relations between NPs. All NPs in a surface structure are indexed. An **index** is a numerical subscript on each NP indicating whether it is coreferential (i.e., bound) with another NP or not. For example, consider the following sentences.

20a. Mary_1 said that she_1 couldn't go.
20b. Mary_1 said that she_2 couldn't go.

The indexes in (a) indicate that *she* refers to *Mary*; those in (b) indicate that *she* refers to someone other than *Mary*.

For purposes of binding, there are three types of NPs: **anaphors** (e.g., reflexive pronouns such as *himself*), **pronominals** (e.g., personal pronouns such as *him*), and lexical NPs (e.g., *John, the boy*). Accordingly, there are three binding conditions that a surface structure must meet in order to be grammatical.

- **Anaphor Binding Condition:** anaphors must be bound (i.e., co-indexed) with a "higher" NP within their own clause. (Note: subjects are "higher" than objects in a tree structure.)
- **Pronominal Binding Condition:** pronominals must be free (i.e., not co-indexed with another NP) within their own clause.
- **Lexical Binding Condition:** lexical NPs must be free everywhere (i.e., not co-indexed with any other NP in any clause).

Consider the following examples.

- *John$_1$ said that Bill$_2$ hurt himself$_2$.* The Anaphor Binding Condition explains why *himself* can refer to *Bill* but not *John*. *Himself* is an anaphor and must be bound within its own clause. *Bill* is in the same clause as *himself*, but *John* is in a different clause.
- *John$_1$ said that he$_{1/2}$ got sick.* The Pronominal Binding Condition explains why *he* can refer to either *John* or someone else. *He* is a pronominal and must be free within its own clause. This allows *he* to be bound to an NP in another clause (e.g., *John*) or not bound at all.
- *John$_1$ said that John$_2$ might get sick.* The Lexical Binding Condition explains why the two occurrences of *John* must refer to two different people. *John* is a lexical NP and must be free everywhere. This forces the two *Johns* not to be bound.

Exercise G

Explain why each of the following surface structures is ungrammatical.

a.† *The man$_1$ shaved him$_1$.
b. *He$_1$ shaved the man$_1$.
c. *He$_1$ shaved himself$_2$.
d. *Himself$_1$ shaved him$_1$.
e. *Who$_1$ killed him$_1$?

Minimalism

Our discussion of government and binding theory would not be complete without some mention of what has come to be known as **minimalism**. In 1995, Chomsky published a book entitled *The Minimalist Program*. The emphasis here should be on the word *program*, for what Chomsky has in mind is a "program" for future research rather than a clearly articulated "theory." The term *minimalism* comes from the main goal of the program: to minimize the syntactic paraphernalia necessary to describe sentences. Chomsky's main idea is to get rid of all components of GB theory that are duplicated elsewhere in the grammar. This would include getting rid of X-bar syntax, underlying structure, transformations (i.e., any sort of movement), surface structure, and any sort of indexing.

The obvious question is, why would Chomsky turn around and try to negate most of the theoretical constraints he argued for throughout his career? The answer is that he is driven to pursue simplicity. His goal is to construct the simplest possible rule system for generating the sentences of a language. It must be stressed, however, that the minimalist program has yet to supplant government and binding theory. It is significant that texts on theoretical syntax published as recently as 1997, although they mention minimalism, are nonetheless written from the perspective of GB theory.

Summary

In contrast to standard theory, GB theory adopts what is known as a "modular" approach to grammar, where each module (i.e., component) is extremely simple but interacts with the other modules to account for the complexity of language. The following diagram presents an overview of GB theory, including all of the modules discussed in this chapter.

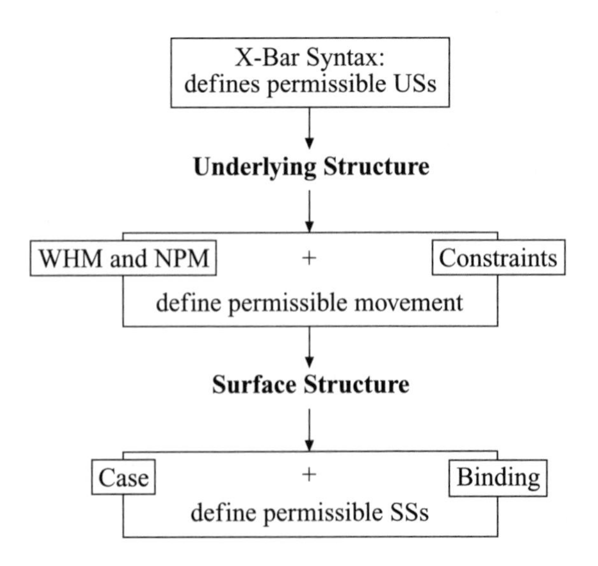

SUPPLEMENTARY EXERCISES

1. Consider the phrase *an English teacher*.

a. This phrase is ambiguous. Give two interpretations of it.

b. What does the phrase *a French English teacher* mean?

c. What does the phrase *an English French teacher* mean?

d. What does the phrase *an English teacher* mean in the sentence *I met an English teacher and a French one*?

e. What does the phrase *an English teacher* mean in the sentence **I met an English teacher and a French one*?

f. Draw two tree diagrams for *an English teacher* that are consistent with the data in (a–e).

2. What kind of NP is *each other* (i.e., anaphor, pronominal, or lexical)? Base your answer on the following data.

A. John told me they hated each other.

B. *John told me each other hated them.

C. *They told me John hated each other.

3. Speakers acquiring English as a second language often make *wanna*-contraction errors such as **Who do you wanna go?* Based on the following examples, determine the circumstances under which *wanna*-contraction is blocked. (Hint: Where does *who* originate in the underlying structure of each sentence?)

A. Who do you *want to* go?

B. *Who do you *wanna* go?

C. Who do you *want to* go with?

D. Who do you *wanna* go with?

4. Speakers acquiring English as a second language often make subject–verb contraction errors such as *Do you know where she's today?* Based on the following examples, determine the circumstances under which subject–verb contraction is blocked.

A.1. Do you know where *she is* today?

A.2. *Do you know where *she's* today?

B.1. You've studied more than *I have.*

B.2. *You've studied more than *I've.*

C.1. You've studied more than *I have* studied.

C.2. You've studied more than *I've* studied.

5. Speakers of English as a second language tend to go through the same stages as native English speakers do in acquiring questions. Both groups tend to acquire *wh*-questions in the following stages.

A. You come from where?
B. Where you come from?
C. Where do you come from?

a. What rule has applied in (B) that has not applied in (A)?
b. What generalization about the auxiliary system and question-formation can be used to account for the difference between (C) and (B)? (Refer back to Chapter 12 if necessary.)

6. Determine what constraint(s) (if any) is violated by each of the following derivations.

a. **Theresa* seems [$_{IP}$ _______ will be upset]

b. **The groceries into the refrigerator* were put _______ by Dave.

c. **Ted* appears [$_{IP}$ _______ and Alice to be a happy couple]

d. **The prisoner* is expected [$_{IP}$ the jury to find [$_{IP}$ _______ to be guilty]

e. **What* do you regret [$_{NP}$ the fact [$_{IP}$ that you said _______]]

7. Consider the following derivation:

What did she say [$_{IP}$ _______ might happen]

This sentence is perfectly acceptable even though it appears to violate a constraint.

a. What constraint does it violate?

b. The fact that this sentence is acceptable can be used to argue that the rule of _________________ is not subject to this constraint.

Part IV

Performance Grammar

In the preceding section on generative grammar, we looked at some of the major tenets of Chomsky's theory, which undoubtedly has sustained the widest interest among theoretical linguists since the 1960s. This is not to say that generative grammar has been universally endorsed or agreed-upon in all its details. Nonetheless, generative theory has become a reference point even for opposing points of view. As one commentator has put it,

> Chomsky has continually been in the forefront of research, setting and revising the agenda of issues of current controversy, while those working in other frameworks have often been put in the position of trying to show that anything he can do they can do better. (Horrocks, pp. 282–283)

This section examines several approaches to English grammar that have developed as alternatives to generative theory.

▲▲▲ CHAPTER 14

Development of Performance Theories

Before examining some of these alternatives to Chomsky's theories, it might be useful to look back at how applied researchers have viewed generative grammar.

EARLY APPEAL OF GENERATIVE GRAMMAR

As it began to gain more widespread acceptance beginning around 1960, the generative approach carried appeal for specialists in areas such as the teaching of English for several reasons.

Emphasis on English

Chomsky's focus on English, especially apparent in *Syntactic Structures* (1957) and *Aspects of the Theory of Syntax* (1965), stood in marked contrast to many works in the earlier structuralist tradition. The underlying assumption behind structuralist approaches was that languages could differ from each other without limit and in unpredictable ways; for example, Bloomfield in *Language* states that "Features which we think ought to be universal may be absent from the very next language that becomes accessible" (p. 20). The structuralist emphasis, because of its roots in anthropological fieldwork, concerned itself largely with compiling inventories of exotic and hitherto uncatalogued languages; it was not believed that generalizations about all languages could be made on the basis of just a few (especially not on the basis of one language, such as English).

Chomsky, in contrast, devoted his first two major works to an in-depth exploration of the properties of English alone. Not only was Chomsky convinced that the syntactic principles underlying English could be extended to other languages, but it was a simple matter of convenience: "The reason that I don't work on other languages [besides English] is that I don't know any very well, it's as simple as that" (1982, p. 82).

Potential for a Performance Model

As you may recall from Chapter 11, Chomsky always intended his grammar to serve as a model of competence (i.e., abstract knowledge about language) rather than performance (i.e., the production and comprehension of language). Nonetheless, Chomsky's generative model was assumed by many applied researchers to mirror the actual steps of language processing itself. For example, consider the following passage from Ross:

> Transformational grammar . . . approaches grammar through the generation, or building, of sentences. This aspect would seem to hold promise for teachers of composition. If students observe how skilled writers construct sentences—that is, what sentence-combining transforms they use, and when they use them—and learn how to handle transform operations, perhaps they can produce sentences more nearly like those of the professionals. (p. 179)

Passages like this one reflect the belief that the abstract organization of generative grammar could be used to model the steps involved in language comprehension (i.e., listening and reading) and production (i.e., speaking and writing). This misconception persisted in spite of Chomsky's repeated warnings against it.

Focus on Syntax

Chomsky's theory has always emphasized syntax rather than smaller units of language. Many structuralists, however, had earlier regarded syntax less as a system in its own right than as a "container" for phonological units (e.g., *cats* consists of four phonemes: /kæts/) and morphological units (e.g., *cats* consists of two morphemes: {cat} + {PLURAL}). For example, the structuralist Bloomfield states that, ideally, linguistics would

> consist of two main investigations: *phonetics,* in which we studied the speech-event without reference to its meaning, investigating only the sound-producing movements of the speaker, the sound waves, and the action of the hearer's ear-drum, and *semantics,* in which we studied the relation of these features to the features of meaning . . . . Actually, however, our knowledge of the world in which we live is so imperfect that we can rarely make accurate statements about the meaning of a speech-form. (p. 74)

In other words, for all practical purposes, Bloomfield conceived of linguistics as the study of the physical aspects of speech and the phonological and morphological units that he thought were directly derivable from it.

In contrast, Chomsky emphasized syntax as an object of investigation in its own right. The importance of this departure is explained by Newmeyer:

> By focusing on syntax, Chomsky was able to lay the groundwork for an explanation of the most distinctive aspect of human language: its creativity. The revolutionary importance of the centrality of syntax cannot be overstated. Phonological and morphological systems are essentially closed and finite; whatever their complexity or intrinsic interest, their study does not lead to an understanding of a speaker's capacity for linguistic novelty, or to an explanation of the infinitude of language. (p. 3)

In other words, at any given point in time, there are a *finite* number of sounds (phonology) and words (morphology), but there are an *infinite* number of sentences (syntax). Thus, Chomsky saw the study of syntax as holding the key to what he called the "creative aspect" of language: the ability of speakers to produce and understand sentences they have never encountered before.

In turn, Chomsky's focus on syntax was more in line with the interests and needs of many applied researchers. In the study of student writing, for example, it can be argued that syntax is a greater source of variety—and "deviance"—in written English than are morphology and phonology. Whereas the latter two domains have relatively limited use for the analysis of expository prose (apart from the study of spelling and vocabulary), syntax is central to concepts such as style. The writing researcher Sharon Crowley states, for example, that "The best hope for the contribution of linguistics to composition has always lain in its potential to enrich students' mastery of style" (1989, p. 487).

DISILLUSIONMENT WITH GENERATIVE GRAMMAR

While Chomsky's early work was greeted by applied researchers with a great deal of excitement, in more recent decades other approaches to English grammar have come to hold equal, if not greater, appeal.

Failure as a Performance Model

One reason that applied researchers have sought alternatives to generative grammar is that Chomsky's model did not provide a replica of real-time language processing. That is, it did not meet the criterion of **psychological reality**: the abstract structures proposed in Standard Theory (e.g., transformations) were not found to correspond directly to the actual strategies used to process language. This should not really be viewed as a failure of the theory since, as we have tried to emphasize, Chomsky never intended generative grammar to be a model of performance.

The strongest evidence against the psychological reality of Standard Theory came from a series of experiments designed to test what has come to be known as the **Derivational Theory of Complexity** (DTC): If transformations are psychologically real, then there should be a correlation between (a) the transformational complexity of a sentence and (b) the degree of difficulty that is involved in decoding that sentence. In other words, derivational complexity should predict processing complexity. For example, a structure requiring, say, five transformations should be decoded faster than one requiring eight transformations.

The DTC was tested fairly extensively in a series of experiments during the 1960s and 1970s; one of the best summaries of this research is found in Fodor, Bever, and Garrett's *The Psychology of Language* (pp. 319 ff.), whose discussion is followed here. It's important, though, to use caution in interpreting the results of these experiments, especially since they sometimes yielded conflicting results.

First, some results that ran counter to the DTC can be explained not by abandoning that theory in its entirety, but rather by viewing derivational complexity as but one factor in perception. Under this view, derivational complexity interacts with other variables and consequently cannot be used as the *sole* predictor of perceptual complexity. For example, Fodor, Bever, and Garrett (p. 327) analyze the following sentences.

1a. *That John left the party quickly* amazed Bill.

1b. *It* amazed Bill *that John left the party quickly*.

Under a Standard Theory analysis, (1a) is derivationally simpler than (1b), which incorporates two transformations that (1a) does not: **extraposition** (rightward movement) of the complement clause *that John left the party quickly*, and ***it*-placement** in subject position. Yet under experimental conditions, (1a) is more difficult to process than (1b). This result runs counter to a theory that uses derivational complexity as the sole measure of perceptual complexity. However, it is consistent with a modified theory that admits other perceptual effects such as the **"heavy NP" condition**: it is easier to process surface structures which place full complement clauses (e.g., *that John left the party quickly*) at the end of the structure, as in (1b), rather than at the beginning, as in (1a).

Second, the DTC was based primarily on the theory outlined in Chomsky's 1957 *Syntactic Structures* model. In other words, the DTC does not hold for early generative theory, but this is not to say that it is invalid for all later versions. Nonetheless, the failure of the DTC created doubt among many applied researchers about the utility of generative grammar in their fields. For example, Shook raises this issue with respect to the relation between grammar instruction and the teaching of writing: "If we admit that modern grammatical models are constructs which work but do not necessarily mirror the mind, we must ask how teaching them will help to bring the unconscious mental processes we do use up to our conscious" (p. 493).

Communication Gap

Applied researchers were not always prepared to deal with a highly technical syntactic theory characterized by abstractness, complexity, and (perhaps above all) constant revision and change. As early as 1968, Wardhaugh warned of the "insuperable problems" that would arise "if any attempt were made to introduce any kind of 'new' grammar into school systems," because, he observed, "many English professors, perhaps even the majority, are unfamiliar with recent developments in linguistics" (p. 303). Likewise, Subbiondo observed that "the TG [transformational grammar] textbooks unfortunately have too often found their way into the teacher's lower desk drawer" and that the teachers rejected the theory largely "due to the simple fact that most teachers have not been adequately prepared to work with TG" (p. 96).

Such remarks suggest the problems inherent in trying to "translate" a technical theory into language that a nonspecialist can understand. For one thing, there is no single, unchanging theory of generative grammar. It is safe to say that even a person thoroughly trained in the 1965 *Aspects* model would find most of the current research on generative grammar incomprehensible. As with any technical subject, a thorough grounding in generative theory requires not only in-depth instruction by a specialist but also constant reading and study in highly specialized journals, if one is to maintain up-to-date knowledge.

Moreover, basic textbooks covering recent developments in generative theory are rare. While dozens of Standard Theory textbooks were published during the 1970s for use in undergraduate English courses, only a few have appeared that summarize more recent developments in generative grammar. And these more recent texts are generally targeted at graduate students in linguistics, rather than at English majors. As a result, while it is relatively easy to find references in the composition literature to Chomsky's earlier major works—most notably *Syntactic Structures* (1957) and *Aspects* (1965)—it is rare to find writing specialists referring to any of his technical works published after 1965. This information lag suggests that those writing specialists familiar with generative grammar are familiar only (at most) with the classic Standard Theory works; and, accordingly, even those interested in keeping abreast of developments in linguistics have found it difficult.

Interest in Discourse

Another major fault that many applied researchers found with generative grammar can, ironically, be viewed as one of its virtues: namely, its emphasis on sentences in isolation. Chomsky's focus on syntax excludes two considerations that have become of increasing concern to writing specialists. First, Chomsky disavowed any intention of explaining the relation of syntactic form to discourse function. For example, while Chomsky provides an account of the structural relationship between active and passive sentences, he does not deal with the distribution of these two structures, or the preference for one structure over the other in a particular discourse context. Second, Chomsky's theory was not designed to account for the effects of either linguistic or extralinguistic context.

Chomsky's apparent lack of concern with form-function relationships, as well as his assertion that judgments about syntax can be based on sentences in isolation, have frequently been brought up as charges against his theory by writing specialists. For example, Crowley states that "Linguistics favors an extremely narrow, noncontextual notion of what it means to be a user of language . . . . until recently, [linguists] have shown little interest in moving beyond the study of the sentence" (p. 499).

In summary, applied researchers were initially attracted to generative grammar because of its focus on syntax, its focus on English, and its implications for the study of language processing. The subsequent decline of generative grammar as a major force in applied fields can be traced to several causes. In particular, research in psycholinguistics failed to confirm the DTC (i.e., that transformations increase processing time); developments in generative grammar have outpaced the rate at which applied researchers have kept pace with this highly specialized theory; and applied researchers have been dissatisfied with the theory's emphasis on sentences isolated from linguistic and extralinguistic contexts.

Exercise A

For each of the following quotations, decide if it would make generative grammar appealing to applied researchers or if it would lead to their disillusionment with generative grammar. In each case, explain why.

a.† "Linguistically based pedagogies necessarily operate as though texts are constructed in a cultural vacuum." (Crowley, p. 499)

b. "Chomsky recognized that an elegant formal theory would have to exclude context." (Faigley, p. 96)

c.† "No research has ever satisfactorily established that the structures that appear in a completed discourse somehow represent the movement of the composer's psyche." (Crowley, p. 497)

d. "Any suggestion that grammar be included in a composition course is likely to fill the teacher with despair, for he believes that if grammar enters his syllabus there will be no room for anything else, given the complexity of modern grammatical description . . . . teachers often feel inadequate to the task of giving a competent account of modern grammar." (Milic, p. 196)

e. "The potential use of this distinction [competence vs. performance] for composition pedagogy began to be realized in the late 1960s, first among sentence combiners, who assumed that competence could be 'triggered' or 'activated' by regular practice in syntactic patterns." (Crowley, p. 494)

f. It is a "questionable assumption that an increase in the length of complexity of sentence patterns somehow represents linguistic growth." (Crowley, pp. 490–91)
g. "As startling as is may sound at first, all students who have acquired English as a native language . . . already possess an immense knowledge of the operations . . . of English, including its syntax. . . . This knowledge, however, is largely unconscious. Students cannot normally explain the operations, or rules, but the knowledge is nonetheless there and waiting to be tapped." (Noguchi, p. 43)

CHOMSKY'S LEGACY

Although generative grammar has not maintained the favor that it once held among many applied researchers, Chomsky's theory has nevertheless left a lasting influence on applied fields in several ways.

Language as a Rule-Governed System

One of Chomsky's major contributions has been to conceive of language as a system of unconscious rules. This notion stands in stark contrast to the earlier structuralist view of language as simply a "habit"—an overlearned response to environmental stimuli. The corollary of Chomsky's view is that errors may be described as *systematic* permutations of the basic rules of the language. Whereas earlier approaches to the study of nonstandard forms had assumed such forms to be "illogical," more recent works have assumed that deviations from standard written English have their own internal logic. Crowley states that

> it may be that linguists' greatest contribution to composition pedagogy was to be this very insistence that teachers look at the sentences their students were composing as instances of language in real use, rather than as samples of their ineptitude with written discourse. . . . Linguists taught teachers to look at the language actually used by their students as a departure for instruction. (pp. 501–502)

Competence versus Performance

Another premise in which generative grammar can be seen to have left its mark is in competence/performance distinction. As explained in Chapter 11, competence is the knowledge of the linguistic rule-system necessary to speak and understand a language. Performance is the implementation of that knowledge in a particular situation. Crowley notes that this distinction provided composition teachers with "a rationale for defending students from the charge that they were ignorant of the grammar of their native language, . . . and of accounting for differences in levels of linguistic performance among students" (p. 494). Translated to pedagogy, the distinction assumes that student writers have the capacity—the latent potential or ability, the competence—to transfer syntactic knowledge into performance. Under this view, one important aspect of learning to write consists of bringing unconscious knowledge to conscious awareness.

Language Universals

As noted in Chapter 4, structuralism (especially as embodied by Bloomfield) tended to focus on the differences among languages. In contrast, although Chomsky's early work focused on English, generative theory has increasingly explored the more abstract similarities that underlie different languages. (For example, operations like *wh*-Movement and NP-Movement are theorized to occur in all languages, not just English.) This quest for language universals coincides with a central goal of generative theory: understanding the innate linguistic knowledge that humans bring to the language-acquisition task at birth, regardless of the particular language to which they are subsequently exposed. The emphasis on language universals has made applied researchers more aware of the common linguistic knowledge shared not just by speakers of different languages but also by speakers of different varieties of the same language (e.g., dialects of English). It has also enhanced the teaching of foreign languages (e.g., English as a second language).

In short, then, while many of the particular theoretical claims of generative grammar have been questioned by applied researchers, Chomsky's more general assumptions about language have influenced their views.

ALTERNATIVES TO GENERATIVE GRAMMAR

In general, alternatives to generative grammar have attempted to investigate language used in context. Unlike the case with "generative" grammar, there is no one widely accepted umbrella term that satisfactorily covers all the phenomena within this area. Thus, for ease of exposition, we will use the term **performance grammar** to refer to this domain.

Contributions to the study of performance grammar have come primarily from three subdisciplines of linguistics: sociolinguistics, psycholinguistics, and discourse analysis. In this section, we will look at some of the landmarks in the development of these subdisciplines; then in Chapters 15 and 16 we will review the key theoretical concepts that have evolved within each one.

Sociolinguistics

This field studies how language is affected by social variables such as ethnicity, gender, socioeconomic class, and geographic region. Sociolinguists also concern themselves with how variables in the social setting, such as the formality or informality of the situation or the relative social status of speaker and listener, affect language. As you can see, sociolinguistics is a wide-ranging field with a number of diverse emphases.

Preeminent among sociolinguists is William Labov, whose most important contribution to the field has perhaps been his insistence on viewing **nonstandard** varieties of English as rule-governed. American dialect studies in the nineteenth and early twentieth centuries tended to focus on the collection of idiosyncratic forms, often associated with regional rather than social variables (e.g., whether speakers from a particular region call a container for carrying water a *bucket* or a *pail*). Labov's research shifted this focus to the discovery of systematic patterns within nonstandard varieties of English.

As an example, consider Labov's comparative analysis of the verb systems in standard English and African American Vernacular English (AAVE). Prior treatments of these systems had frequently assumed the "illogical" or "deficient" nature of the verb system in AAVE (for discussion, see, for example, Labov 1972). What Labov pointed out was the underlying unity between the standard and AAVE systems; AAVE permits deletion of a form of the verb *to be* only in structures where standard English permits contraction:

2a. He is my brother.

2b. He's my brother. (Standard English)

2c. He my brother. (AAVE)

On the other hand, (3b) and (3c) are ungrammatical in the dialects in question:

3a. I don't know who he is.

3b. *I don't know who he's. (ungrammatical in Standard English)

3c. *I don't know who he. (ungrammatical in AAVE)

Thus, the systematic nature of AAVE is clear: this dialect allows *be*-deletion exactly where standard English allows *be*-contraction.

Not surprisingly, much research in sociolinguistics in the United States has focused on the interrelationship of ethnicity and language. This emphasis gained momentum following the civil rights movement of the 1960s and subsequent legislation designed to provide equal educational opportunities to all groups of Americans. As a result, beginning in the 1960s, greater attention was given to the structure of nonstandard dialects such as AAVE.

Psycholinguistics

This field, also known as "the psychology of language," is concerned with the mental *processes* that humans employ in actual language use. Psycholinguistics is concerned with both language production, or **encoding** (i.e., speaking and writing), and language comprehension, or **decoding** (i.e., listening and reading). As such, psycholinguistics explores the relation between competence (abstract knowledge) and performance (the use of such knowledge in language processing). Psycholinguistics is intertwined with disciplines such as **language acquisition** (the study of how humans acquire their native language or a second language), **neurolinguistics** (the study of how language is represented in the brain and of the effect that damage to the brain has on language processing), and **artificial intelligence** (the study of machine understanding of natural language). Like sociolinguistics, psycholinguistics is a wide-ranging field; here we will look at just one example of its methods and subject matter.

One phenomenon that psycholinguists have tried to explain is the relative speed and accuracy with which people comprehend various sentence types. An important finding is the fact humans do not decode sentences simply as a left-to-right string of words; rather, we are sensitive to more abstract syntactic structure. This finding was confirmed in a series of "click" experiments conducted during the 1960s and 1970s by researchers such as Jerry Fodor, Merrill Garrett, and Thomas Bever. In a click experiment, the subject hears a sentence containing short bursts of noise (i.e., clicks). The subject is then asked to report the location of the clicks. For example, the subject might hear a sentence like the following (with clicks interspersed at the locations marked with a "+"):

4a. [That he was happy] + was evident + [from the way he smiled.]

NOMINAL CLAUSE   ADVERBIAL

Two major findings emerged from the click experiments. First, subjects are more likely to report the position of clicks accurately when they occur at major boundaries within the sentence. For example, the location of the clicks in sentence (4a) would be more likely to be reported accurately than those in (4b), which do not occur at major boundaries:

4b. That he was + happy was evident from the + way he smiled.

Second, when presented with sentences like (4b), subjects tend to displace clicks; that is, to perceive them as occurring closer to, or at, major boundary sites. In other words, a subject presented with (4b) would be likely to report the clicks as occurring where they do in (4a).

Results like these clearly indicate that concepts from linguistic theory, such as constituent structure, are not just artifacts of the way that we describe sentences in a theory of grammar. They are also an intrinsic part of the way that we unconsciously process sentences.

Discourse Analysis

This field focuses on the properties of multisentence texts, both written and spoken. The particular text types studied range from conversations to fairy tales to recipes to scientific reports. In general, though, discourse analysts are interested in two primary questions: what principles underlie the structure of various types of discourse, and what strategies do participants use in processing a piece of discourse?

Some research in discourse analysis has grown out of work in psycholinguistics, in particular the relatively new field of artificial intelligence. Researchers in this area, such as Walter Kintsch, Roger Schanck, Teun A. van Dijk, and Terry Winograd, have faced questions not just about the comprehension of individual sentences (a process known as **parsing**), but also about the background knowledge needed to understand more complex pieces of discourse. Other work in discourse analysis has grown out of fields such as literature and philosophy, with their interest in, respectively, literary texts and naturally occurring discourse such as conversations.

Studies of cohesion are characteristic of work in discourse analysis. **Cohesion** describes the relationship, or dependency, between one part of a text and another part: the features that cause different parts of a text to "hang together" into a coherent whole. Seminal works in this area include *Cohesion in English* by M.A.K. Halliday and Ruquaiya Hasan and "Comprehension and the Given-New Contract" by H.H. Clark and S.E. Haviland. Such studies have found that texts are judged as more cohesive when they adhere to the **given-new principle**: that is, when information that has already been mentioned in the discourse (i.e., given information) precedes information that is being mentioned for the first time (i.e., new information). For example, the text in (5a) adheres to the given-new principle.

5a. The matter has been referred to the student conduct board.

The board (GIVEN) will make its decision on Thursday (NEW).

In (5a), *student conduct board* is mentioned in the first sentence, making it the given information in the second sentence. In keeping with the given-new principle, it precedes the new information in the second sentence (*will make its decision on Thursday*). In contrast, compare (5b), in which the given information in the second sentence (*the board*) follows the new information (*a decision will be made on Thursday*).

5b. The matter has been referred to the student conduct board.

A decision will be made on Thursday (NEW) by the board (GIVEN).

This sequence of new-given violates the expected flow of information; hence, (5b) would tend to be judged as less cohesive than (5a).

You may have surmised from this discussion that the boundaries between sociolinguistics, psycholinguistics, and discourse analysis are often fuzzy. Although these fields have discrete labels within linguistics, there is no uniform agreement about the exact lines that separate them. However, certain methodological distinctions are associated with each area; for example, sociolinguistics is typically characterized by fieldwork, psycholinguistics by controlled experimentation, and discourse analysis by detailed analysis of individual texts.

At the same time, however, the phenomena studied within these fields often overlap to a great extent. For example, researchers in both discourse analysis and psycholinguistics have conducted studies on cohesion. In discourse analysis, such studies have concentrated on the texts themselves; while in psycholinguistics, experimental research has attempted to verify the superior comprehensibility of texts that exhibit certain structural properties. Likewise, a psycholinguist might offer a theory of the strategies used to process passive sentences, while a sociolinguist might offer a theory of the social situations in which passive sentences are more likely to be used.

The trait that unifies these apparently disparate approaches is that they are all concerned with language *used in context.* Put another way, they all are concerned with how social, psychological, or discourse forces bear on the production and comprehension of language. It is easy to see why specialists in applied fields such as the study of writing have embraced approaches that study performance with such enthusiasm: they offer an antidote to one of the major problems perceived in generative grammar, namely to that theory's limitation to idealized sentences in isolation. Thus, approaches to grammar that emphasize performance have been viewed by many specialists in applied areas as filling a significant void.

Summary

Although generative grammar held early promise for researchers in applied areas of language study, their later disillusionment led to an increased interest in performance aspects of grammar. This process is summarized in the following table.

Appeal of Generative Grammar

- Emphasized English (as opposed to exotic languages)
- Potential for performance model (i.e., theory of production and comprehension)
- Focused on sentences (as opposed to sounds and words)

Disillusionment with Generative Grammar

- Failure of DTC (i.e., transformations do not necessarily increase processing time)
- Theory not easily accessible to applied researchers
- Applied researchers interested in discourse (as opposed to isolated sentences)

Legacy of Generative Grammar

- Language is a rule-governed system (as opposed to a set of random habits)
- Competence (i.e., knowledge) underlies performance (i.e., behavior)

Performance Grammar

- Sociolinguistics (e.g., *be*-deletion in AAVE): fieldwork
- Psycholinguistics (e.g., "click" experiments): experimentation
- Discourse analysis (e.g., cohesion): text analysis

SUPPLEMENTARY EXERCISES

1. Consider Mina Shaughnessy's description of the student population at the City University of New York, the subject of her landmark study *Errors and Expectations*. First, "Most of them had grown up in one of New York's ethnic or racial enclaves. Many had spoken languages or dialects [other than Standard English] at home" (p. 3). Second, most of them failed to meet "even very modest standards of high-school literacy" (p. 2). Third, Shaughnessy estimates that the typical basic writing student has written an average of 350 words a semester during high school, in contrast to "the 1,000 words a week that a British student is likely to have written in the equivalent of an American high school or even the 350 words a week that an American student in a middle-class high school is likely to have written" (p. 14).

Compare Shaughnessy's CUNY students to Chomsky's "ideal" native speaker:

> Linguistic theory is concerned primarily with the ideal speaker-listener in a completely homogeneous speech-community, who knows its language perfectly and is unaffected by such grammatically irrelevant conditions as memory limitations, distractions, shifts of attention and interest, and errors (random or characteristic) in applying his knowledge of the language in actual performance. (1965, p. 3)

a. What problems would a teacher encounter in trying to apply Chomsky's theories directly in Shaughnessy's classroom?
b. What role would Labov's research play in helping a teacher apply Chomsky's theories?
c. Consider the concept of linguistic competence as defined by Chomsky. Would it be correct to say that a speaker of nonstandard English does not exhibit linguistic competence? Why or why not?

2. For each of the following phenomena, decide if it falls within the domain of sociolinguistics, psycholinguistics, or discourse analysis.

a. One of the following phrases is processed faster than the other.

i. the man that the dog chased
ii. the man the dog chased

b. The following excerpts are from a news account. The reader is able to draw inferences about the speaker from these quotes.

i. "This work be enjoyment and fun for me. I see a lot and talk to a lot of people," says Whigham.
ii. "If you're working and you like your work, you be satisfied, but if you get a job and you're not satisfied, there's no reason to work," he says.
iii. "It's better than stealing. At least you can't get into no trouble like this. If you get out there and you go to stealing, you be downtown," he says.
iv. "Peoples throw away a lot of good stuff," he says. He finds at least 20 full cans of beer a day. "I drinks beer, but I never have to buy any," he said.
v. "I'm just trying to make me a honest living."

c. Consider the following discourse:

The haystack was important. The cloth had ripped. (Clark & Haviland, p. 33)

This discourse is easier to comprehend if you know that it occurs in a passage titled "Sky Diving."

d. One of the following passages is easier to comprehend than the other.

i. Epic poems usually include a long narrative or story. Certain conventions almost always mark this story.
ii. Epic poems usually include a long narrative or story. This story is almost always marked by certain conventions.

e. One of the following phrases is processed faster than the other.

i. John is not unlike his father.
ii. John is like his father.

f. One of the following passages is easier to process than the other.

i. In their seminal work, *Cohesion in English,* Halliday and Hasan argue that cohesion is a nonstructural, semantic relation. Indeed cohesion studies of texts using Halliday and Hasan's scheme have proliferated since its publication. . . . Unfortunately, there has been little substantive addition to the theory of cohesion set forth by Halliday and Hasan fifteen years ago. (Campbell, pp. 221–222)

ii. In their seminal work, *Cohesion in English,* Halliday and Hasan argue that cohesion is a nonstructural, semantic relation. Cohesion studies of texts using Halliday and Hasan's scheme have proliferated since its publication. . . . There has been little substantive addition to the theory of cohesion set forth by Halliday and Hasan fifteen years ago. (Campbell, pp. 221–222)

g. One of the following sentences is harder to process than the other.

i. That I will leave is certain.
ii. It is certain that I will leave.

h. Children go through a stage where they can interpret one of the following sentences correctly but not the other.

i. He came home before he ate lunch.
ii. Before he ate lunch, he came home.

i. One of the following sentences is harder to process than the other.

i. They sold the painting to the little old man sitting in the third row on the left.
ii. They sold the little old man sitting in the third row on the left the painting.

j. Children learn to decode one of the following sentences before the other.

i. John shoved Mary.
ii. Mary was shoved by John.

▲▲▲ CHAPTER 15

Sentence-Level Phenomena in Performance Grammar

In Chapter 14 we looked at some of the fields that have contributed to what we are calling performance grammar. This chapter looks more closely at some of the specific findings from these fields, especially sociolinguistics and psycholinguistics, that deal with the production and comprehension of individual sentences.

SOCIOLINGUISTICS

As we saw in our brief discussion of *be*-deletion in African American Vernacular English in Chapter 14, language use is sensitive to social variables such as ethnicity and class. Here we will look at some features that are characteristic of various nonstandard English dialects. (The following discussion is adapted from Parker and Riley, pp. 164–168.)

Omission of Final -s on Verbs

Consider the sentence *He walk home every day*. We can begin by comparing this sentence to its standard English counterpart, *He walks home every day*. In order to understand why the *-s* morpheme is omitted in some nonstandard dialects, we need to look at the standard English system for the inflection of present tense verbs.

	Singular	**Plural**
1st person	I walk	We walk
2nd person	You walk	You walk
3rd person	He/She walks	They walk

Here we can see immediately that most present tense verbs in standard English have no overt inflection. If we substitute the nonstandard forms (*He/She walk*) for the corresponding standard form, we come out with a perfectly regular system (i.e., no present tense verbs have an overt inflection). This **regularization** of the third-person present tense verb forms extends to all main verbs and auxiliaries in some dialects of English, yielding forms like *He do* for *He does*, *He don't* for *He doesn't*, and *He have* for *He has*.

Invariant Forms of Be

Another nonstandard feature of verbs is the extension of one inflected form of *be* to all forms. Unlike other present tense verbs in English, which have a predominant form (without *-s*) and an exceptional form (with *-s*), *be* has three forms, all of which appear to be exceptional: *am, are*, and *is*. Thus, speakers of some nonstandard dialects regularize all present tense forms of *be* to one single form: for example, *I is, You is, We is*, and *They is*. Note that when this happens *be* is no longer an "irregular" verb (i.e., one with exceptional forms). The point is that nonstandard forms often reflect a highly systematic treatment of English.

Inversion in Questions

In some nonstandard dialects of English, an interrogative such as *What is it?* may be phrased as *What it is?* Let's compare the standard and nonstandard derivations side by side. The difference between them can be explained by assuming that the Question transformation applies in the standard derivation but not in the nonstandard derivation. This situation is summarized here.

	Standard English	**Nonstandard English**
Underlying structure:	it - is - what	it - is - what
Question:	is - it - what	(does not apply)
***Wh*-Movement:**	what - is - it	what - it - is
Surface structure:	*What is it?*	*What it is?*

At this point, it should be clear that the nonstandard derivation omits a step (the Question transformation) that appears in the standard derivation. This should not be interpreted to mean that the nonstandard derivation is "deficient" or "incomplete" in some way. (Note that the nonstandard version is perfectly acceptable as an **indirect question** in standard English: *I wonder what it is.*) Rather, a dialect containing this nonstandard feature is perfectly rule-governed and differs from standard English in a systematic and predictable way.

Exercise A

When a speaker attempts to emulate a style that he or she is not completely familiar with, a phenomenon known as **structural hypercorrection** may occur. This term describes the use of a structure associated with a more formal style in a linguistic environment where it is not typically used. Now consider the following data.

A. To whom should I speak?

B. Whom did you see?

C. Whom is taking you to dinner?

a. Which sentence illustrates structural hypercorrection?
b. What principle has the speaker of these sentences apparently internalized?
c. What principle has the speaker failed to internalize?
d. What forms might result from structural hypercorrection of the following forms?
   i. two children
   ii. Bob Johnson's car
   iii. I want a cookie.

Invariant **Be** *in Questions*

Another nonstandard syntactic feature involves the treatment of main verb *be* in questions such as *Do they be sick?* In standard English, the Question transformation applies to auxiliaries to form an interrogative: *John has seen Mary* becomes *Has John seen Mary?* On the other hand, the Question transformation does not apply to main verbs: *John saw Mary* does not become **Saw John Mary?* Instead, when the declarative structure contains no auxiliary verb, a form of *do* takes the place of the missing auxiliary in the question: *John saw Mary* becomes *Did John see Mary?* Thus, standard English has a general rule for forming questions: the Question transformation applies to auxiliaries but not to main verbs; *do* appears when there is no auxiliary verb.

There is, however, a major exception to this rule in standard English: main verb *be* behaves like an auxiliary rather than a main verb, in that it undergoes the Question transformation. For example, *They are sick* becomes *Are they sick?* Now consider what would happen if main verb *be* behaved like all other main verbs—in other words, if it did not undergo the Question transformation but instead triggered the appearance of *do*. If this were the case, the question form of a nonstandard declarative like *They be sick* would be *Do they be sick?* And, in fact, this is the nonstandard counterpart of standard English *Are they sick?* Here we see another instance where the nonstandard dialect has regularized an exception in standard English, namely the treatment of main verb *be*. The nonstandard dialect treats main verb *be* exactly like all other main verbs.

Exercise B

Consider the following interrogative forms, which are characteristic of British dialects of English.

A. Have you the time?

B. Baa, baa, black sheep, have you any wool?

a. How would these forms appear in modern American English?
b. Does main verb *have* behave more like a main verb or an auxiliary verb in the Question transformation in British English?
c. Does main verb *have* behave more like a main verb or an auxiliary verb in the Question transformation in American English?

Exercise C

Consider the following interchange between a judge and the foreman of a jury.

Judge:	Have you reached a verdict?
Foreman:	We have, Your Honor.
Judge:	What say you?

The judge's second utterance uses an archaic form. How does the grammar needed to describe this archaic form differ from the grammar needed to describe its modern English counterpart?

Negative Fronting

A final example of a socially marked syntactic feature involves moving a negative auxiliary to sentence-initial position when the subject is an indefinite NP (e.g., *everyone, nobody*, and so on). Under this pattern, the standard English sentence *Everybody can't win* would take the form *Can't everybody win* in nonstandard English.

The main point to see from examples like these is that socially marked grammatical variations are highly systematic from a linguistic perspective. They reflect predictable variations of standard English forms and are by no means "illogical" from the standpoint of how language actually works.

Exercise D

The figure below shows the percentage of times that *ain't* was substituted for other verb forms during casual conversation. The results are broken down by both socioeconomic status and gender.

a. Based on this graph, what generalization can be made about the relative use of nonstandard forms among males and females?
b. Among speakers of different socioeconomic status?

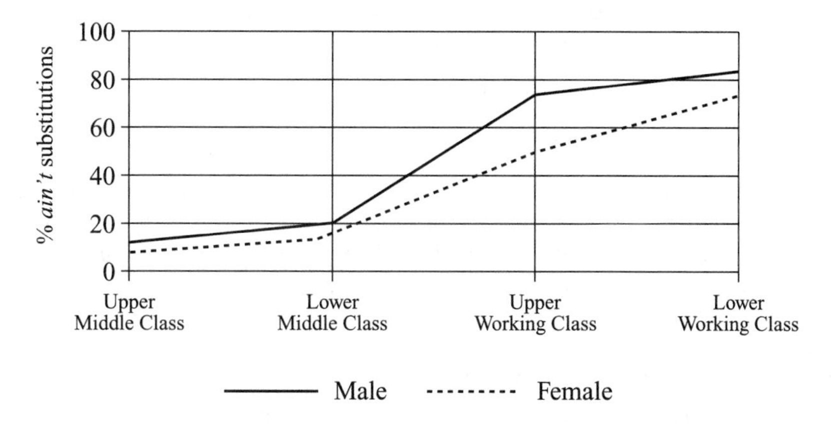

Substitution of *ain't* for other verb forms during casual conversation

PSYCHOLINGUISTICS

Let's move on now to some sentence-level phenomena that have been studied in the realm of psycholinguistics. As we saw in our brief discussion of the "click" experiments in Chapter 14, humans are sensitive to syntactic structure when they decode sentences. Here we will look at how various types of structures appear to affect language comprehension.

Relative Clauses

Consider the following sentences, both of which contain a relative clause (italicized).

1a. The boy *that the woman saw* got sick.

1b. The boy *the woman saw* got sick.

The only difference between the sentences is that the relative pronoun *that* is absent from (1b). Yet subjects are significantly slower and less accurate in processing and paraphrasing sentences like (1b). (Note that if sentence comprehension were merely a matter of processing words, we might expect subjects to be faster at processing (1b), which contains fewer words than (1a).) It appears that the relative pronoun *that* provides an important cue about syntactic structure, signaling that the listener is moving from a main clause to a subordinate clause.

Negative Sentences

Negative sentences (those containing *not* or a contraction of it) take longer to decode than their affirmative counterparts. For example, when asked to judge sentences as true or false, respondents take more time to evaluate negative sentences like (2a) than positive sentences like (2b).

2a. The star is *not above* the circle.

2b. The star is *below* the circle.

Similar processing difficulties are presented by **inherent negatives**. Instead of the negative marker *not*, an inherent negative contains a word whose meaning includes negation. For example, the inherent negative *Three students are absent* is equivalent in meaning to *Three students are not present.*

Exercise E

Consider the following passages from news accounts.

A. **Judge Won't Block Abortion Ruling**

A district court judge Tuesday refused to block his earlier ruling that struck down Minnesota's 16-year-old ban on state funding of Medicaid abortions for low-income women.

B. The group urged Congress "to override President Clinton's veto of the partial-birth abortion ban."

a.† Does the judge referred to in passage (A) support or oppose Medicaid abortions? How many times did you have to read the passage to arrive at your answer?

b. Does the group referred to in passage (B) support or oppose partial-birth abortions? How many times did you have to read the passage to arrive at your answer?

c. Use principles from psycholinguistics to explain why these passages are difficult to process.

d. Revise these passages to make them easier to comprehend.

Passive Sentences

As a rule, passive sentences present more processing difficulties than their active counterparts, although there are some important exceptions to this rule. (As we will see later, the choice of active or passive voice within a discourse often depends on the structure of the surrounding sentences.) For example, (3a) is easier to process than (3b).

3a. The tiger chased the lion. (active)

3b. The lion was chased by the tiger. (passive)

Our general processing strategy seems to be to interpret a noun-verb-noun sequence as agent-action-patient: the **agent** is the entity performing the action, while the **patient** is the entity or thing affected by the action. In other words, we expect the agent to occupy subject position. This pattern typically exists in an active sentence. In a passive sentence, however, the patient occupies subject position. Therefore, when we encounter the structural cues present in passive sentences (i.e., a form of *be* followed by a past participle main verb), we have to revise our general processing strategy, thus slowing down comprehension time.

Interestingly, though, (4a) and (4b) are equivalent in their processing difficulty, even though (4a) is active and (4b) is passive.

4a. The tiger ate the meat.

4b. The meat was eaten by the tiger.

This is because only *the tiger* can be interpreted as the agent in either (4a) or (4b). In this case, our knowledge of the real world (i.e., that tigers can eat meat, but not vice-versa) allows us to interpret (4b) as quickly as (4a).

Clause Order

Clause order also appears to affect the processing of some types of complex sentences. For example, sentences describing temporally ordered events are easier to process if the events are mentioned in the order in which they occurred. This principle predicts that (5a) will be easier to process than (5b).

5a. Go to Window 3 before you fill out your application.

5b. Before you fill out your application, go to Window 3.

Likewise, sentences containing subordinate clauses are easier to process if the subordinate clause follows the main clause. This principle predicts that (6a) will be easier to process than (6b).

6a. These students graduated in four years because they took 15 credits each semester.

6b. Because these students took 15 credits each semester, they graduated in four years.

Interestingly, this principle contradicts the advice given in many writing textbooks. Writing students are often advised to "vary sentence openings" by moving subordinate clauses to sentence-initial position. However, such advice many actually impede reader comprehension.

Heavy NPs

As a final example of sentence-level phenomena, consider the case of heavy NPs. As mentioned in Chapter 14, a heavy NP is either an entire nominal clause (e.g., a *that*-clause) or an NP containing extensive modifiers. Heavy NPs are easier to process if they appear in sentence-final position than if they appear earlier in the sentence. For example, (7b) is easier to process than (7a).

7a. *That she won the election* surprised me.

7b. It surprised me *that she won the election.*

The subject of (7a) is the heavy NP *that she won the election*, a noun clause. In (7b), the noun clause has been moved to sentence-final position, and the subject slot filled by the "dummy" subject *it*.

Likewise, extensively modified NPs are easier to process in sentence-final position. For example, (8b) is easier to process than (8a).

8a. We will mail *all viewers in the Duluth area who send us a self- addressed stamped envelope by December 1st* a program guide.

8b. We will mail a program guide to *all viewers in the Duluth area who send us a self-addressed stamped envelope by December 1st.*

In (8a) the heavy NP (italicized) is followed by the underlying direct object, *a program guide*. In (8b) the heavy NP appears as the last element in the sentence.

Exercise F

Principles of sentence comprehension may interact with, and sometimes contradict, each other. For example, consider the following sentences.

A. The incumbent from the 5th district, who has been campaigning extensively for the past two weeks, won the election.

B. The election was won by the incumbent from the 5th district, who has been campaigning extensively for the past two weeks.

a.† What principle would predict that (A) will be easier to comprehend?
b. What principle would predict that (B) will be easier to comprehend?
c. Which principle do you think should take precedence in this case?

Summary

The main points covered in this chapter are summarized in the following chart.

Performance Grammar: Sentence-Level

Sociolinguistics: Factors that increase social marking

Verbs:
- Omission of *-s* (e.g., *He talk*)
- Invariant *be* (e.g., *We be*)

Questions:
- Absence of inversion (e.g., *Where he is?*)
- *Be* treated as main verb (e.g., *Do they be here?*)

Negatives
- Fronting (e.g., *Don't nobody care*)

Psycholinguistics: Factors that increase processing difficulty

- Omission of relative pronouns (e.g., *the one I saw*)
- Multiple negatives (e.g., *block the ban on...*)
- Passives (e.g., *mistakes were made*)
- Complex sentences
  - Nontemporal ordering (e.g., *I ate after I arrived*)
  - Subordinate clause preceding main clause (e.g., *Because X, Y*)
- Heavy NPs in other than right-most position (e.g., *That she will win is certain*)

SUPPLEMENTARY EXERCISES

1. Some nonstandard forms actually fill gaps or regularize exceptions in the standard English system. Consider the fact that all but one of the following phrases can be contracted in two different ways; the exceptional case has only one contracted form.

A. I am not

B. We are not

C. You are not

D. He/she is not

E. They are not

a. Which phrase has only one contracted form in standard English?
b. By analogy with the other four phrases, how would the "missing" contraction be pronounced?
c. Why do you think the "missing" form is in fact missing from English?

2. Based on Exercise 1, it appears that *ain't* fills a gap in the standard English system by providing an alternative contracted form for the phrase *I am not*. However, the use of *ain't* is not restricted to the first-person subject in nonstandard dialects. Given the following data, in what sense is the nonstandard system more regular than the standard one?

Standard System		**Nonstandard System**	
(no form)	we aren't	I ain't	we ain't
you aren't	you aren't	you ain't	you ain't
he/she/it isn't	they aren't	he/she/it ain't	they ain't

3. Consider the following news item (Budiansky, p. 55).

> When a poll showed that more than one-fifth of Americans thought the Holocaust might never have happened, historians and Jewish groups expressed outrage and concern. A follow-up poll found that people had simply been thrown off by the . . . question.
>
> [Poll 1]: "Does it seem possible or does it seem impossible to you that the Nazi extermination of the Jews never happened?"
>
> | | |
> |---|---|
> | Seems possible | 22.1% |
> | Seems impossible | 65.4% |
>
> [Poll 2]: "Does it seem possible to you that the Nazi extermination of the Jews never happened, or do you feel certain that it happened?"
>
> | | |
> |---|---|
> | Possible it never happened | 1.1% |
> | Feel certain it happened | 91.2% |

Both polls ask for essentially the same information. How might a psycholinguist explain the difference in the results?

4. Consider the following sentence:

> *The horse raced past the barn fell.*

This is a classic example of a "garden-path" sentence—it leads the reader "down the garden path" toward one interpretation, which must be revised once the entire sentence has been processed.

a. How do you think most people interpret the sentence when they begin processing it? (Hint: What is the function of *raced* in this interpretation?)

b. How do you think this interpretation changes by the end of the sentence? (Hint: What is the function of *raced* in this interpretation?)

c. How can you use the following processing strategy to explain your answer to (a): "Interpret a sequence of noun-verb-noun as agent-action-patient"?

d. How could you revise this sentence to make it unambiguous?

5. Many analysts have noted that passive voice tends to occur in a higher proportion in technical and scientific writing than in popular writing. Rodman found four common uses for **agentless passives** (passive structures from which the *by*-phrase containing the agent has been deleted):

> (A) to describe particular experimental procedures

(B) to describe standard experimental procedures

(C) to describe accepted scientific knowledge

(D) to describe natural processes

a. Identify the agentless passives in the following passages. Which use is illustrated by each passage (from Rodman, pp. 168–170)?

   i. The mechanics of isolating vibration are well understood.
   ii. If the pulsar is embedded in a nebula, the electrons are presumably hurled into the nebula and spiral along its own magnetic lines of force, emitting radiation over an enormous range of wavelengths.
   iii. One sample was dissolved prior to thermal treatment. At 30 min. intervals, samples were withdrawn and dissolved in carrier solutions, and the temperature of the bath was increased by approximately 5°C.
   iv. To measure the number of gene copies the cellular DNA is broken into small pieces, the double strands are denatured (separated into single strands) by boiling, and a small amount of the radioactively labeled complementary DNA is added to the mixture under experimental conditions . . . .

b. Why is the agentless passive appropriate for each of these uses? In other words, how can you justify the omission of the agent from these types of passages?

CHAPTER 16

Discourse-Level Phenomena in Performance Grammar

In the preceding chapter we reviewed findings from performance grammar related to sentence-level phenomena. However, much research in performance grammar has also examined the structure of larger units of discourse and the processes that we bring to bear in discourse comprehension. In this section we will look at some of the main findings from this research.

READABILITY

One question of interest in performance grammar is how to measure readability, that is, the speed and comprehension rate with which readers are able to process a text. A number of **readability formulas** have been proposed as a way of calculating readability. Two of the most well-known are the Flesch Index (developed by Rudolph Flesch) and the Gunning Fog Index (developed by Robert Gunning). The **Flesch Index** is calculated as follows.

(1) Start with a 100-word sample.

(2) Count the average number of affixes (prefixes and suffixes) per 100 words.

(3) Subtract the number of personal references (proper names and pronouns) per 100 words.

(4) Divide the number arrived at in step (3) by two.

(5) Add the average number of words per sentence.

The number arrived at in step (5) is measured against the following scale:

0–13	Very easy
13–20	Easy
20–29	Fairly easy

29–36	Standard
36–43	Fairly difficult
43–52	Difficult
52+	Unreadable

The **Fog Index,** which also starts with a sample of 100–125 words, is calculated as follows.

(1) Count the words per sentence. (Each independent clause should be counted as a sentence.)
(2) Divide the total number of words by the total number of sentences (independent clauses) to obtain an average length.
(3) Count the number of long words (3 or more syllables). Omit proper nouns, compounds of short words (e.g., *strawberry*), and words whose third syllable is a suffix like *-ed, -es,* or *-ing* (e.g., *dividing*). Divide the total words in the passage by the number of long words to obtain the percentage of long words.
(4) Add the average sentence length and the percentage of long words and multiply their sum by 0.4. The resulting number corresponds to the grade level needed to read the passage (e.g., a Fog Index of 8 corresponds to eighth grade; 16, to college senior level, and so on).

Exercise A

Calculate the Flesch Index and the Fog Index for the following 100-word passage.

> Singer reviews several strategies that appear to help readers access higher level information such as that contained in schemata and scripts and that help readers identify the **theme** of a text: that is, its main idea. We have already looked at an example of one of these in the "washing clothes" passage: the use of **titles.** Readers also tend to attach thematic status to ideas that are mentioned in the **initial sentences** of a text, especially if there is no title. **Frequently mentioned concepts** also tend to be judged as thematically important. Finally, **grammatical role** appears to signal thematic status.

a. Do the two indexes appear to assign the same level of difficulty to the passage?
b. Do the indexes reflect your subjective judgment of the passage's difficulty? How would you account for any difference? (In other words, what variables are **not** taken into account by the indexes?)

Although sentence length is one item measured in many such formulas, studies have shown that this feature alone does not necessarily account for comprehension. For example, consider the following two sentences (cited in Anderson and Davison, p. 34).

1a. An essential factor in contributory negligence is that it contributes as a proximate cause of the injury.

1b. If the plaintiff was contributorily negligent, he actually helped cause his own injury, through his own negligence.

Each sentence consists of 17 words and would measure roughly the same according to some readability formulas. Yet subjects in an experiment found (1b) significantly easier to recall and paraphrase accurately. In this case it appears that it is not word or sentence length that is critical, but instead the use of the *if . . . then* structure in (1b) and the fact that it puts an abstract definition (i.e., *contributory negligence*) in human terms (i.e., *the plaintiff was contributorily negligent; he actually helped cause his own injury*).

SCHEMATA AND SCRIPTS

A **schema** (plural: **schemata**) is a framework for organizing knowledge about the world. Schema theory proposes that discourse comprehension is enhanced when readers or listeners are able to integrate preexisting knowledge (represented in the schema) with the information in a text. One type of schema is a **script**, a mental representation of the prototypical sequence of events in a familiar situation. For example, it has been hypothesized that a "restaurant script" would be organized according to the following **scene headers**: Entering, Ordering, Eating, and Exiting.

Schemata and scripts provide us with a structured framework for processing the information encountered in a text. As an illustration, consider the following passage discussed by Singer:

> Don decided to have lunch at a restaurant. He took his seat, and ordered his favorite, the tuna sandwich. He straightened his collar while he waited. When the food arrived, Don ate hungrily. When the waiter brought the check, he accidentally spilled coffee on Don. Don was very upset and left without paying. (p. 209)

This passage contains three types of information:

- Presented, Central: Some information in the text makes an explicit reference to scene headers in the script, which are of central importance. For example, *He . . . ordered his favorite* explicitly mentions the scene header Ordering. Likewise, *Don ate hungrily* explicitly mentions the scene header Eating.

- Unpresented, Central: The information that corresponds to the scene header Entering is implied rather than presented. That is, *Don decided to have lunch at a restaurant. He took his seat, and ordered his favorite* implies that he entered the restaurant.
- Presented, Peripheral: Some information is explicitly stated in the text but does not relate to the script at all, namely *He straightened his collar.*

Experiments on the recall of passages such as this one suggest that readers draw upon both the text itself and the script on which it is based. The results of recall tests done after a short term (e.g., 30 minutes after reading) and after a long term (e.g., several days after reading) are quite interesting. First, 29 percent of the Presented Central sentences were recalled in the short-term, and 22 percent were recalled in the long term. Second, the recall of Unpresented Central statements *increased* over time (from 12 percent to 16 percent). Third, the recall of Presented Peripheral sentences *decreased* significantly over time (from 29 percent to 5 percent). These results suggest that, as recall of the text itself erodes, readers rely more and more on their knowledge of the script—they "remember" things that weren't actually in the text and forget things that were.

Singer reviews several strategies that appear to help readers access higher-level information such as that contained in schemata and scripts and that help readers identify the **theme** of a text: that is, its main idea. Readers tend to attach thematic status to ideas that are mentioned in the initial sentences of a text, especially if there is no title. Frequently mentioned concepts also tend to be judged as thematically important. Finally, grammatical role appears to signal thematic status: readers tend to interpret the subject of a sentence as the theme.

COHESION

The theory of cohesion developed by Halliday and Hasan in 1975 attempts to account for how listeners and readers establish relationships between different parts of a text. According to Halliday and Hasan, cohesion can be established by five main properties of the text, which we will review here.

Reference

Reference is achieved through the use of items such as personal and demonstrative pronouns. Reference to a nonlinguistic element is known as **exophora**. For example, suppose that two friends are waiting to order at a fast-food restaurant, and one of them points to a picture of an ice cream cone and remarks, "That looks good. I think I'll have one of those." The words *that* and *those* in this discourse are exophoric reference items, since they refer to nonlinguistic elements (a picture) in the situation. In contrast, reference to another linguistic element in the discourse is known as **endophora**. For example, suppose the following conversation occurs in the car on the way to the fast-food restaurant.

John:	I'm in the mood for a strawberry milkshake.
Mary:	That sounds good.

In this case, *that* derives its meaning from a linguistic element (*a strawberry milkshake*) in the surrounding discourse.

Endophora, in turn, can be further subdivided into **anaphora** and **cataphora**. In the more typical case, **anaphora**, reference is to a preceding element (as in the dialogue about the strawberry milkshake). In **cataphora**, reference is to an element that follows in the discourse. For example, consider the text in (2).

2. These are my goals: to balance the budget, reduce drug use by teenagers, and reduce crime.

In (2), *these* refers forward to the three items listed after the colon.

Substitution

A second, related way to establish cohesion is through substitution, which is achieved through the use of pro-forms such as those discussed in Chapters 5 and 13. The most common nominal substitutes are the pro-forms *one* and *ones*, as in the following example:

3. The morning paper didn't carry a *story about the robbery*, but the evening paper has *one.*

Here *one* substitutes for the N' *story about the robbery*. Pro-VPs include forms of the verb *to do*, as in the following example (where *do* occurs in the inflected form *does*).

4. The public library *hasn't got that journal,* but the university library *does.*

Here *does* substitutes for the VP *hasn't got that journal.*

One difference between reference and substitution is that, while reference can occur exophorically, substitution generally occurs only endophorically. For example, if John and Mary are talking, Mary can point to Ed and say *He looks like he was up late last night.* On the other hand, forms like *one* can substitute only for other linguistic expressions: **One looks like he was up late last night.*

Ellipsis

A third way in which cohesion can be established is through ellipsis, which Halliday and Hasan define as "substitution by zero" (p. 143). In the following example, the elliptical item (*coffee*) is indicated by a blank.

5. I've drunk a lot of *coffee* in my time, but this is the worst _____ I've ever tasted.

Ellipsis can also substitute for a portion of a VP, as in the following case.

6. Evening classes were *canceled* because of the snowstorm. Daytime classes were not _____ , however.

Here the elliptical item is *canceled because of the snowstorm.*

Conjunctions

A fourth way to establish cohesion is through the use of conjunctions. Halliday and Hasan outline four categories of conjunctions, repeated here with some examples.

- **Additive:** *and, furthermore, for instance, likewise*
- **Adversative:** *yet, in fact, however, on the other hand, instead*
- **Causal:** *so, therefore, as a result, because*
- **Temporal:** *then, first . . . second . . . third, finally, in conclusion*

Lexical Cohesion

Fifth, cohesion can be established through the use of lexical cohesion. In this method, the reader is able to establish a link between the meaning of two lexical items (neither of which is a pro-form). **Reiteration** is a general strategy for developing lexical cohesion. The most obvious type of reiteration is **repetition** of an actual lexical item, as in the following passage.

7. More than 1000 school children had to be placed in temporary classrooms. The children are being taught in school cafeterias, gymnasiums, and even locker rooms.

The use of **synonyms** is another method of reiteration. For example, consider this modified version of the preceding passage.

8. More than 1000 school children had to be placed in temporary classrooms. The youngsters are being taught in school cafeterias, gymnasiums, and even locker rooms.

Another type of reiteration is the use of a **general noun** such as *people, woman, boy, thing, matter, place*, and *idea*. The following passages use this strategy.

9. *The athletic director* resigned suddenly last week. Apparently, *the man* was involved in some questionable activities.
10. She doesn't like the way the lawyer is handling *her divorce case.* She's thinking about taking *the matter* to another firm.

11. Some students think that *the main purpose of college is to provide them with vocational training.* I don't agree with *that idea,* though.

A closely related reiteration strategy is the use of a **superordinate** term; that is, a term that names a more general class of some preceding lexical item (although superordinate terms are less generic than general nouns like *thing*). The following passages use this strategy.

12. Would you look at that horse *canter*? He can really *move.*
13. My mother enjoyed *sewing* and *baking.* These *domestic activities* gave her a daily sense of accomplishment.

Lexical cohesion may also be attained through **collocation**. Collocated items are lexical items that regularly co-occur. Examples of collocated items include parts of a series (e.g., *Monday, Tuesday*), parts of a set (e.g., *basement, roof, living room*), and parts related to a whole (e.g., *basement, house*). As Halliday and Hasan point out, though, not all collocative relationships are this systematic. Instead, collocation depends more on the tendency of lexical items "to share the same lexical environment" and "to appear in similar contexts" (p. 286). For example, a passage containing the words *candle, flame,* and *flicker* would exhibit collocational cohesion, as would one mentioning *poetry, literature, reader, writer,* and *style.*

Exercise B

Referring to Halliday and Hasan's five strategies, identify the elements that make the following passage cohesive. (The passage explains how to diagnose and treat a disorder in a horse's sweating mechanism.)

> Your mare may have **anhidrosis**—commonly known as dry coat, puff disease, or simply non-sweating. Common in hot, humid regions such as the Gulf Coast, where it affects as many as one in five horses, it can also strike in less taxing climates. It's a problem for this reason: Horses that can't sweat have no effective way to release the heat building up in their bodies.
>
> Your mare's condition may have come on suddenly: After a week or so of profuse output, her heat production may have shut down abruptly or at least slowed significantly. Or it may have come on gradually: Over the past few months, she may have been sweating less and less—and have tried to cool down by splashing herself with water from her bucket, lying on a moist stall floor, or standing in a pond or stream when turned out. At the same time, her appetite may have decreased, and she may have become increasingly balky about exercise, depressed, and/or easily tired. . . . all signs of possible anhidrosis. (Laird, p. 67)

You should be able to find at least the following:

- Four examples of anaphora
- One example of cataphora
- Two examples of ellipsis
- One example of repetition
- One example of a synonym
- One example of a general noun
- One example of a superordinate term
- Two examples of collocative series

GIVEN AND NEW INFORMATION

Another property of texts that has been shown to increase comprehension is adherence to the given-new principle. (Our discussion of this principle is adapted from Riley et al., pp. 39–40.) The given-new principle assumes that a sentence contains two information units. **Given information** (sometimes called **old information**) is information that the writer assumes is already known to the reader. **New information** is information that the writer assumes is not known to the reader. Experiments have shown that texts are easier to process and remember if they adhere to the following pattern:

- Given information appears in the subject slot (i.e., in a noun phrase at the beginning of the sentence);
- New information appears in the predicate slot (i.e., in the second part of the sentence, containing the verb and its object(s) or complement).

For example, the text in (14a) violates the given-new pattern by presenting information in a sequence of given-new (in the first sentence), new-given (in the second sentence), and new-given (in the third sentence). (Given information is italicized.)

14a. *The Model 101B* is the result of new processing technology. A number of exciting advances are offered by *this product*. A speedier relay time, improved noise reduction, and a Synctron readout mode *are among its new capabilities*.

Now compare the revised version, (14b), which adheres to a sequence of given-new, given-new, given-new.

14b. *The Model 101B* is the result of new processing technology. *This technology* allows us to offer you a number of exciting advances. *The 101B's new capabilities* include a speedier relay time, improved noise reduction, and a Synctron readout mode.

The given-new pattern can be implemented in one of two basic ways: an AB:BC pattern or an AB:AC pattern.

The AB:BC Pattern

The revised example above adheres to an AB:BC pattern, where new information in the predicate of the first sentence becomes given information in the subject of the second sentence, as illustrated below.

15. *The Model 101B* is the result of new processing technology.
    A B

    This technology allows us to offer you a number of exciting advances.
    B C

The AB:AC Pattern

Another way to implement the given-new pattern is to repeat the given information as the subject of each sentence, adding new information in each predicate slot. This pattern is illustrated in the passage below. (Again, given information is italicized.)

16. *The Model 101B* is the result of new processing technology. *This product* offers a number of exciting advances. *It* has a speedier relay time, improved noise reduction, and a Synctron readout mode.

The AB:BC and AB:AC patterns are, of course, not mutually exclusive. They may be used in the same paragraph, as illustrated in the following example.

17. *The Model 101B* is the result of new processing technology. *The 101B* offers a speedier relay time, improved noise reduction, and a Synctron readout mode. *These features* allow you to compile test results quickly and accurately.

In this passage, the first two sentences are linked by the AB:AC pattern. The second and third sentences are linked by the AB:BC pattern.

Note, by the way, that the repetition of information can be acheived in several ways, related to strategies we discussed in the section on cohesion:

- Direct repetition (e.g., . . . *new processing technology. This technology* . . .)
- Use of a synonym (e.g., *The Model 101B . . . . This product* . . .)

- Use of a generic noun (e.g., . . . *speedier relay time, improved noise reduction, and a Synctron readout mode. These features* . . .)
- Use of a pro-form (e.g., *This product offers a numer of exciting advances. It* . . .)

Exercise C

Analyze the given-new patterns used in each of the following passages. (Sentences have been numbered for easy reference.) Do the writers use AB:BC, AB:AC, or a mixture?

a.† [1]This part of the Ramblas isn't nicknamed Rambla del Ocells, or "Street of the Birds," for nothing. [2]There are birds overhead in the trees and birds for sale in cages on the esplanade. [3]They shriek, coo and sing while always keeping a watchful eye on the cats sitting in most of the shop doorways. [4]These outsize felines look you over superciliously as you pass. [5]Maybe they get their chutzpah from the fact that the local dogs (winsomely dressed up in top hats) are used as part of the street circus to help earn money for their owner. (Boylan, p. 130)

b. [1]Agnew was a favorite of GOP audiences across the nation. [2]As he and Nixon in 1972 became the first ticket to be re-elected since Eisenhower and Nixon in 1956, he looked to be a front-runner for the 1976 presidential nomination. [3]But unbeknownst to all but a few, Agnew was under investigation much of the year. [4]His resignation, like Nixon's a year later, discredited for many the traditional morality and respect for the law they had championed. [5]But Agnew seemed unrepentant. [6]After moving to California, he sought a tax deduction for $268,000 in bribes and interest he had had to pay to the state of Maryland. [7]That, like his claim on high office, was denied. (Barone, p. 28)

Exercise D

Revise each passage below so that it adheres to the given-new contract. (From Riley et al., pp. 42–43.)

a. Some fruits contain more oil than others. The amount of oil in a fruit determines the fruit's caloric value. Birds' fruit preferences correlate with this caloric value. In other words, one way that birds choose the foods they eat is through caloric value.

b. I have proposed that a standardized crew cycle be developed and used in the production of future mission time lines. The amount of time and labor currently required to produce a mission time line would be greatly reduced by the use of such a crew cycle.

THEMATIC ROLES

In the late 1960s, Charles Fillmore proposed a treatment of the semantic structure of sentences, in which each NP plays a particular **thematic role** with respect to the action of the verb. (Our discussion of these here is adapted from Campbell et al., pp. 192–193.) Sentence (18) illustrates some of the thematic roles identified by Fillmore.

18. *The clerk* typed *the letter* for *his boss* with *a typewriter.*
    1 2 3 4

According to Fillmore's theory, NP_1 functions as the **agent**, or volitional performer of the action described by the verb. NP_2 functions as the **patient**, or thing affected by the action of the verb. NP_3 functions as the **beneficiary**, or thing which benefits from the action. Finally, NP_4 functions as the **instrument**, or thing which is used to carry out the action.

In English, the normal position for the agent is subject, that for the patient is object, that for the beneficiary is object of the preposition *to* or *for*, and that for the instrument is object of the preposition *with*. At the same time, however, Fillmore's theory recognizes that a given thematic role (e.g., agent, patient, beneficiary, or instrument) can appear in one of a number of syntactic constructions (e.g., subject, object, or object of a preposition). In sentences (19a-19c), for example, the semantic role of instrument appears in three different syntactic positions.

19a. Subject = *A typewriter* was used by the clerk to type the letter for his boss.

19b. Object = The clerk used *a typewriter* to type the letter for his boss.

19c. Object of Preposition = The clerk typed a letter for his boss on *a typewriter*.

Conversely, (20a–20d) illustrate each of the four thematic roles appearing in subject position.

20a. Agent = *The clerk* typed the letter for his boss with a typewriter.

20b. Patient = *The letter* was typed on a typewriter by the clerk for his boss.

20c. Beneficiary = *His boss* had the clerk type the letter on a typewriter.

20d. Instrument = *A typewriter* was used by the clerk to type the letter for his boss.

In short, then, a single thematic role can occupy several syntactic positions, and a single syntactic position can convey several thematic roles.

Exercise E

Identify the thematic role (agent, patient, beneficiary, or instrument) of the italicized NPs in the following passages.

a.† In the 1960s, *Doreen Kimura* developed *a technique* called dichotic listening. *This method* confirms that *most people* process *language* with *the left hemisphere of the brain.*

b. *A graph* should be followed by *commentary* that spells out *the main point of the graph* for *the reader*.

c. *Some standardized tests* are used to measure *academic achievement,* while *others* are used to predict *academic* success.

Exercise F

Campbell et al. propose that a piece of discourse in which the sentences convey the same thematic role (e.g., patient) in the same syntactic position (e.g., subject) will be more unified than one which does not. As an illustration, consider the following passage, which describes four steps of a proposed project. The subject of the sentence describing each stage has been italicized.

> The project will consist of four steps. First, *we* will analyze Belcor's financial statements. Second, *financial ratios* will be compared with the industry norm. Third, *the net tax effects of each alternative* will be evaluated. Fourth, *we* will design an implementation plan for the best alternative.

The four steps described here all have the same agent (i.e., the writers). However, the agent does not consistently occupy one syntactic position.

Prepare two revisions of this passage: one using the agent consistently in subject position, and one using the patient consistently in subject position.

Summary

The points covered in this chapter are summarized in the following chart.

PERFORMANCE GRAMMAR:
Discourse-level factors that affect the comprehension of texts.

Readability:

- Flesch Index (word complexity and sentence length)
- Fog Index (word and sentence length)

Schemata:

- Scripts (i.e., ordering of events)
- Scene headers (i.e., labeling of events)

Cohesion:

- Reference (i.e., can be exophoric—*him*)
- Substitution (must be endophoric—*himself*)
- Ellipsis (i.e., omission—*I'm tired but you're not* ______)
- Conjunctions (e.g., *John and Mary* vs. *John or Mary*)
- Lexical (e.g., repetition)

Given and New Information:

- Given (i.e., that known to reader) appears as subject
- New (i.e., that not known to reader) appears as predicate

Thematic Roles:

- One role (e.g., agent) should appear in same syntactic position (e.g., subject) throughout a discourse

SUPPLEMENTARY EXERCISES

1. Consider the following passage cited by Duin.

> The procedure is actually quite simple. First, you arrange things into different groups. Of course, one pile may be sufficient depending on how much there is to do. If you have to go somewhere else due to lack of facilities, that is the next step; otherwise you are pretty well set. It is important not to overdo things. That is, it is better to do too few things at once than too many. In the short run this may not seem important, but complications can arise. A mistake can be expensive as well. At first the whole

> procedure will seem complicated. Soon, however, it will become just another fact of life. . . . (p. 97)

Subjects in an experiment were asked to read the passage quickly, to put it aside, and to recall as much information as possible. Some subjects, though, were given the title of the passage before they started reading: "Washing Clothes." It was only those subjects who were able to recall a significant amount of information from the passage.

a. How does this finding reinforce the role of schemata in understanding and remembering discourse?
b. Try an informal re-creation of the experiment described above. Have one group of friends read the passage (without a title), put it aside, and try to recall as many details as possible. Then have another group of friends read the passage (with the title), put it aside, and try to recall as many details as possible. Do your findings confirm those of the original experimenters?
c. Propose at least four scene headers for a "washing clothes" script.

2. Kies notes the superiority of passage (A) over passage (B).

A. We have always been a leader in the development of joint venture pipeline systems. This is best exemplified by Colonial Pipeline, the world's largest and most successful pipeline system.

B. We have always been a leader in the development of joint venture pipeline systems. Colonial Pipeline, the world's largest and most successful pipeline system, exemplifies this. (p. 304)

a. Using principles from psycholinguistics, explain why (A) is easier to process than (B).
b. What sentence structure is used in (A) that is not used in (B)?

3. Analyze the given-new patterns used in the following passage. (Sentences have been numbered for easy reference.) Does the writer use AB:BC, AB:AC, or a mixture?

> [1]. . . last fall, a New York City pediatrician charged our reporter $370 for a back-to-school checkup for her 10-year-old daughter. [2]That sum included a $90 fee for the office visit, and separate charges for four lab tests and two vaccinations. [3]If she had been a member of Oxford Health Plan, the doctor would have received $170 for the same bundle of services. [4]If she had been a member of Chubb's HMO, he would have received $285, and if she had been part of Aetna's plan, he would have been paid $173.50. ("Can HMOs Help?" p. 29)

4. Olsen and Johnson point out that simplifying sentence structure does not necessarily make a passage easier to read. For example, a standard readability formula would predict passage (B) to be easier to comprehend that passage (A); however, it is not.

Analyze both passages using the concept of given-new information. How does this help explain the problems that readers had in following passage (B)? (Sentences have been numbered for easy reference.)

A. [1]The night was cloudy, and a drizzling rain, which fell without intermission, added to the obscurity. [2]Steadily, and as noisily as possible, the Spaniards made their way along the main street, which had so lately resounded to the tumult of battle. [3]All was now hushed in silence; they were only reminded of the past by the occasional presence of some solitary corpse, or a dark heap of the slain, which too plainly told where the strife had been hottest. [4]As they passed along the lanes and alleys which opened into the great street, they easily fancied they discerned the shadowy forms of their foe lurking in ambush, ready to spring upon them. (Olsen & Johnson, pp. 229–330)

B. [1]The night was cloudy. [2]A drizzling rain added to the obscurity. [3]It fell without intermission. [4]The Spaniards made their way along the main street. [5]They moved steadily and as noiselessly as possible. [6]The street had so lately resounded to the tumult of battle. [7]All was now hushed in silence. [8]The occasional presence of some solitary corpse reminded them of the past. [9]A dark heap of the slain was another reminder. [10]Plainly, the strife had been hottest there. [11]They passed along the lanes and alleys opening into the great street. [12]They easily fancied the shadowed forms of their foe lurking in ambush. [13]The enemy looked ready to spring upon them. (Olsen & Johnson, p. 230)

5. Revise each passage below so that it adheres to the given-new contract. (From Riley et al., pp. 42–43.)

a. A two-year-old thoroughbred mare was referred for (1) a sesamoid fracture of the right rear leg and (2) upper respiratory problems characterized by a cough and water running out of the mare's nostrils when drinking. The client had first indicated both these problems four months earlier.

b. The use of composite materials in an aircraft reduces the amount of drag on the airplane. The number of seams on the surface of the aircraft is reduced by the use of composites because composites are produced in large panels. The need for rivets is minimized by the use of composites because most composite structures are joined by adhesives.

Glossary

Active sentence One which does not contain a form of *be* followed by a past participle. In an active sentence, the subject is generally the **agent** of the action expressed by the verb (e.g., *My publisher signed the contract*). Cf. **passive sentence**.

Additive conjunction A conjunction that introduces information that elaborates on the first element being conjoined (e.g., *and; for instance*).

Adjectival A word that appears in a position that can be occupied by an adjective (e.g., *the mud hut*). All adjectives are adjectivals, but not all adjectivals are adjectives.

Adjectival clause See **relative clause**.

Adjective The part of speech that modifies a **noun**, e.g., *tall building.* Characterized by comparative (*-er*) and superlative (*-est*) suffixes. *Adjective* is from the Latin word for 'to add to (a noun).'

Adjunct In generative grammar (especially X-bar syntax), the position defined as daughter of X' and sister of X', as follows:

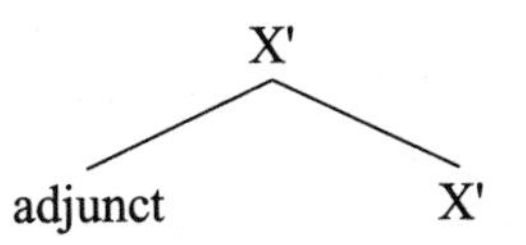

For example, the adjective *tall* functions as an adjunct in the noun phrase *that tall math student*. The term *adjunct* designates a position (like *subject, direct object*, etc.), not a class of words (like *determiner, noun*, etc.).

Adverb The part of speech that modifies a **verb** (e.g., *speak slowly*). Characterized by the *-ly* suffix. *Adverb* is from the Latin phrase for 'related to (a verb).'

Adverbial Any item that fills an adverb position, e.g., *I fell down/off my horse/while jumping*.

Adverbial clause A **subordinate clause** introduced by a **subordinating conjunction**; it modifies the verb of the main clause (e.g., *They failed the test because they didn't study*). Cf. **relative clause**.

Adverbial prepositional phrase A **prepositional phrase** that modifies a verb; e.g., *John shaves in the morning*.

Adverbial verb phrase A **verb phrase** that modifies a verb; e.g., *Some people exercise to avoid stress*.

Adversative conjunction A **conjunction** that introduces information that runs counter to the first element being conjoined (e.g., *however; on the other hand*).

Affix A form that can be attached to the beginning of a word (**prefix**) or end of a word (**suffix**), typically to a noun, verb, adjective, or adverb.

Affix hopping In generative grammar, a transformation that attaches an affix to the following verb form (e.g., *have - en - see* → *have - see+en*).

Agent A **thematic role** describing the NP that performs the action in a sentence; e.g., *John built that table for his parents with his own hands.*

Agentless passive A **passive** structure without a *by*-phrase, e.g., *The contract was signed.*

Analogy Aristotle's theory that language is essentially regular. For example, English nouns typically form their plural by adding *-s*. Cf. **anomaly**.

Anaphor In generative grammar, an NP that *must* have an antecedent in the same clause (e.g., *We were aware of each other*). Cf. **pronominal**.

Anaphora A type of **endophora** in which a pronoun refers to an earlier element in the discourse; e.g., *I've met the new neighbors, but I don't know them well.* **Anaphora** comes from a Greek phrase meaning 'to carry back.' Cf. **cataphora**.

Anaphor binding condition In generative grammar (especially government and binding theory), a principle stating that an **anaphor** must have an antecedent within the same clause; e.g., **John talks to himself.*

Anomaly The Stoics' theory that language is essentially irregular. For example, many English verbs have unpredictable past tense forms: *give/gave, ride/rode, hit/hit*, etc. Cf. **analogy**.

Antecedent An expression (word or phrase) that another expression refers to, e.g., *That man* is the antecedent of *himself* in *That man might hurt himself. Antecedent* is from the Latin phrase 'to go before.'

A-over-A In generative grammar (especially government and binding theory), a constraint stating that a constituent cannot be moved out from under an identical constituent.

Appositive The second of two noun phrases, usually adjacent, that refer to the same entity, e.g., *China, <u>the most populous nation</u>, is not the largest.*

Appositive clause A **noun clause** that functions as an **appositive**; e.g., *I resent the fact <u>that you have a bigger office</u>.*

Article *A(n)* and *the*. They are a type of **determiner** and always modify a noun.

Artificial intelligence The study of machine understanding of natural language.

Aspect The time relation between the utterance of a sentence and the activity or situation reported in the sentence.

Auxiliary *be* A form of *be* that always precedes a **present participle**, e.g., *You <u>are</u> shivering.*

Auxiliary *do* A form of *do* that always precedes an **uninflected** verb form, e.g., *I <u>do</u> remember.*

Auxiliary *have* A form of *have* that always precedes a **past participle**, e.g., *I <u>have</u> fallen.*

Auxiliary verb Any verb other than a main verb. The main verb in a simple sentence is always the rightmost verb, so any other verb is an auxiliary; e.g., *She <u>should have been being</u> watched.*

Behaviorism J. B. Watson's theory that the only legitimate subject matter for psychology is observable and measurable behavior. It specifically excludes the study of the mind.

Beneficiary A **thematic role** describing the NP that benefits from the action in a sentence; e.g., *John built that table for his parents with his own hands.*

Binding In generative grammar (especially government and binding theory), the coreference relation between an NP and its antecedent, indicated by subscripts. An NP and its antecedent are said to be "bound"; e.g., *John*$_1$ *told Mary that he*$_1$ *hurt himself*$_1$.

Case A classification system for nouns and pronouns, according to their grammatical function (e.g., *he* is nominative case; *him* is objective case; and *his* is possessive or genitive case).

Case assignment rules In generative grammar (especially government and binding theory), rules whereby a preposition assigns objective case to its object, a transitive verb assigns objective case to its direct object, and tense assigns nominative case to its subject.

Case filter In generative grammar (especially government and binding theory), a principle stating that every overt NP must be case-marked (i.e., assigned nominative, objective, or possessive case).

Cataphora A type of **endophora** in which a pronoun refers to a later element in the discourse; e.g., *Your choices are these: clean up your room, take out the trash, or mow the lawn.* **Cataphora** comes from a Greek phrase meaning 'to carry downward.' Cf. **anaphora**.

Causal conjunction A **conjunction** that signals a cause-effect relation between the items being conjoined (e.g., *therefore, because*).

Clause A syntactic unit having both a subject and predicate. Clauses are of two types: **independent** (i.e., can stand alone as a sentence) and **dependent** (i.e., cannot stand alone as a sentence).

Cohesion The impression that different parts of a text "hang together" into a related whole.

Co-indexed In generative grammar (especially government and binding theory), the relation between two NP positions that refer to each other. Co-indexing is indicated by identical numerical subscripts. For example, *John* and *himself* are co-indexed in the following structure: [John$_1$ cut himself$_1$].

Collocation The appearance within a discourse of words or phrases that regularly co-occur (e.g., *salt* and *pepper*); can be used to establish **cohesion**.

Common noun Any noun not a **proper noun** (e.g., *actress, city*).

Comparative Adjective form with *-er* suffix (e.g., *shorter*) or *more* (e.g., *more intense*).

Competence According to Chomsky, the unconscious knowledge that underlies a speaker's ability to produce and interpret sentences. Cf. **performance**.

Complement In generative grammar (especially X-bar syntax), the position defined as daughter of X' and sister of X, as follows:

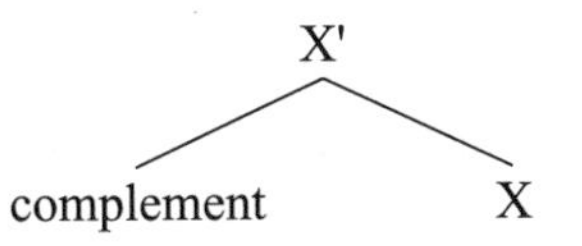

For example, the noun *math* functions as a complement in the noun phrase *that tall math student*. The term complement designates a position (like *subject, direct object*, etc.), not a class of words (like *determiner, noun*, etc.).

Complement In descriptive grammar, an NP, PP, or AP that provides additional information about a subject or object. See **objective complement, subjective complement**.

Complementary distribution The relation between two items that never occur together. For example, the auxiliary verb *do* in English never occurs in a sentence containing another auxiliary (e.g., *will, have*, or *be*). Thus, *do* is in "complementary distribution" with the other auxiliaries.

Complementizer A word (*that, if, whether,* or *for*) that introduces a **noun clause**; e.g., *John asked <u>whether</u> Mary was going.*

Complex sentence A sentence consisting of both a **main clause** and a **subordinate clause**; e.g., *When I opened the door, the cat ran out.*

Conjugation A system for identifying the root of a verb and its range of inflections; e.g., *drive, drives, drove, driven, driving.*

Conjunction The part of speech that connects words, phrases, or clauses; e.g., *or*. *Conjunction* is from the Latin phrase for 'join with.'

Constituent One or more words dominated by a single **node**. For example, *Jane hid the letter from Dan* is ambiguous. *The letter from Dan* can be interpreted as one constituent (i.e., Dan wrote the letter) or two (i.e., Dan doesn't know about the letter).

Constraint In generative grammar (especially government and binding theory), a limitation on where a transformation can move an item. For example, the Tensed S constraint states that NPM cannot move an item out of a clause containing a tensed verb.

Convention Aristotle's theory that words have an arbitrary relationship to what they represent. For example, the word *car* has no relationship to the sound a car makes. Cf. **nature**.

Co-occurrence The frame in which a given part of speech can be used. For example, only a noun can occur between an article (on the left) and a verb phrase (on the right).

Copular or **Copulative verb** A **linking verb**, so-called because it "couples" or "links" the **subject** and the **subjective complement**; e.g., *You look ill.*

Count noun A noun that can be pluralized (e.g., *boy/boys*). Cf. **noncount noun**.

Cycle, the In generative grammar, a constraint stating that transformations must apply to the most deeply embedded clause before applying to a higher clause.

Daughter In generative grammar, a node (i.e., position) in a tree diagram, immediately depending from a higher node. For example, in the following diagram, Y and Z are "daughters" of X:

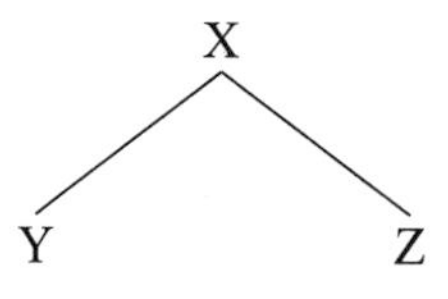

Declension A system for identifying nouns according to person, number, and case. For example, the noun *boy's* is third person, singular number, possessive case.

Decoding Language comprehension (i.e., listening or reading).

Definite A type of **article** consisting of *the*. Cf. **indefinite**.

Demonstrative A type of **determiner** consisting of *this, that, these,* and *those*; a pronoun that "points" to a specific entity or set of entities.

Dependent clause See **subordinate clause**.

Derivation In descriptive grammar, changing the form class of a word by adding an **affix**. For example, *quick* is an adjective; *quickly* is a "derived" adverb. In generative grammar, the "history" of a sentence in terms of the PS grammar and transformations. The derivation of a sentence shows its **underlying structure** and any transformations that have applied, yielding its **surface structure**.

Derivational affixes All prefixes in English and those suffixes that change the form class of the word they're attached to (e.g., *dishonestly*). Cf. **inflectional affixes**.

Derivational Theory of Complexity The assumption that the transformational complexity of a sentence (i.e., the number of steps needed to derive it) should correlate with the degree of difficulty involved in processing it.

Derived form A word created from another part of speech by the addition of an affix; e.g., the verb *criticize* is derived from the noun *critic* by adding the suffix *-ize.*

Derived structure In generative grammar, any structure created by the application of a transformation. It may or may not be a **surface structure**.

Descriptive grammar A set of generalizations that describe the language people *actually* speak rather than prescribing how they should speak it. Also known as **structural grammar**.

Descriptivism The "applied" side of **structuralism**, focussing on questions of usage; especially, the view that usage is relative and varies according to context, social groups, and time. Cf. **prescriptivism**.

Determiner In descriptive grammar, one of the **structure classes**; a class of words that modify nouns but are not adjectives. They include **articles** (e.g., *a*), **demonstratives** (e.g., *this*), **quantifiers** (e.g., *all*), and **possessive pronouns** (e.g., *my*).

Diachronic linguistics The study of a language at two different points in time. *Diachronic* is from the Greek phrase for '(at) two times.' Cf. **synchronic linguistics.**

Direct object The noun phrase following a verb that refers to the thing affected by the action, e.g., *John hit the ball*. The direct object can become the subject in a passive sentence, e.g., *The ball was hit by John.*

Direct question A question taking the form of an **independent clause**: e.g., *What time is it?* Cf. **indirect question**.

Discourse analysis A type of **performance grammar** focusing on multisentence texts, both written and spoken.

Double negative Two words negating a single clause, e.g., *He didn't say nothing*.

Elliptical structure One with a missing element, e.g., *John ate but I didn't [eat]*.

Empty node In generative grammar (especially government and binding theory), a constraint stating that a constituent can be moved only to an empty node (i.e., an unfilled position in a tree structure).

Encoding Language production (i.e., speaking or writing).

Endophora Use of a pronoun to refer to another linguistic element in the text. *Endophora* comes from a Greek phrase meaning 'to carry within.' Cf. **exophora**.

Exophora Use of a pronoun to refer to a nonlinguistic element; e.g., pointing to a sleeping dog and saying *He looks relaxed. Exophora* comes from a Greek phrase meaning 'to carry outward.' Cf. **endophora**.

Expletive *that* Use of *that* as a **complementizer** that introduces a **noun clause**; e.g., *John knows that Mary is going*.

Extraposition Movement of a clause to a more rightward position; e.g., *It bothers me that he smokes* reflects extraposition from *That he smokes bothers me*.

Finite verb A verb inflected for **tense**. Cf. **infinitive**.

Flesch Index A **readability formula** developed by Rudolph Flesch; takes into account affixes, personal references, and words per sentence.

Fog Index A **readability formula** developed by Robert Gunning; takes into account word length, number of independent clauses, and words per sentence.

Form The part of speech or category that a word falls into, regardless of its **function**; generally determined by the inflectional, derivational, and co-occurrence patterns to which the word adheres. For example, *dog* functions adjectivally in the phrase *a dog house*, but is a noun in form.

Form classes In descriptive grammar, words that carry the primary meaning in a sentence: nouns, verbs, adjectives, and adverbs. Cf. **structure classes**.

Fricative A consonant produced by forcing air from the lungs through a constriction in the mouth; e.g., [s] in *sea*. Cf. **stop**.

Fronted Describing a phrase that has been moved into initial position in a **clause**; e.g., *You were following who?/Who were you following?*

Function The role that a part of speech plays within a particular phrase or sentence, regardless of its **form**. For example, *dog* is a noun in form, but it functions as an adjectival in the phrase *the dog house*.

Function classes See **Structure classes.**

Gender A classification system for words (chiefly nouns, pronouns, and their modifiers). In modern English, gender is assigned according to the sex of the entity referred to; e.g., *he* is masculine, *she* is feminine, and *it* is neuter gender.

General noun A generic term such as *people, thing*, or *idea*; can be used to establish **cohesion** by providing a link to a more specific noun (e.g., *I tried to use the lawn mower, but the darned thing wouldn't start*).

Generate As used in generative grammar, it means 'to define formally'; e.g., the rule PP → P - NP "generates" (i.e., is a definition of) prepositional phrase.

Generative grammar A theory of the unconscious knowledge of language that humans possess. Also known as **transformational grammar**.

Gerund clause A **clause** containing a present participle but no tense; e.g., *I insist on your staying for dinner*.

Gerund phrase A verb phrase containing a present participle but no tense; e.g., *I insist on paying for lunch*.

Given information That part of a discourse that the speaker/writer assumes is already known to the addressee. Also known as **old information**. See also **given-new principle**.

Given-new principle A processing strategy that says a text is more cohesive when information that is familiar to the addressee precedes information that is being mentioned for the first time.

Government In generative grammar (especially government and binding theory), a relationship between two nodes in a tree structure, such that a preposition **governs** its object, a verb **governs** its direct object, and tense **governs** its subject.

Government and binding theory The dominant theory in generative grammar today; transformations are simple (i.e., move NP, move WH) and are limited by conditions on movement (i.e., constraints) and co-reference relations (i.e., binding conditions).

Headword The word for which a phrase is named. For example, the headword of an NP is a noun, as in *some mysterious stranger on a train*.

Heavy NP condition A strategy that says sentences are easier to process if noun clauses or heavily modified NPs occur at the end of the sentence rather than at the beginning; e.g., *It surprised Bill that John left the party early* is easier to process than *That John left the party early surprised Bill.*

Helping verb See **auxiliary verb**.

Imperative The **mood** used for commands, characterized by the absence of tense on the verb, e.g., *Be strong.*

Indefinite A type of **article** consisting of *a(n)*. Cf. **definite**.

Indefinite pronoun A pronoun that never has an antecedent; e.g., *everybody, nobody*.

Independent clause See **main clause.**

Indicative The **mood** used for factual descriptions, characterized by third- person singular *-s* on present tense verbs, e.g., *John walks home everyday*.

Indirect object The noun phrase that identifies the recipient or beneficiary of the action expressed by the verb; e.g., *John gave Mary a present*. The indirect object can usually be paraphrased so that it becomes the object of the preposition *to* or *for*; e.g., *John gave a present to Mary*.

Indirect object movement A transformation that moves the indirect object from the right of the direct object to its left and deletes the preposition *to* or *for*; e.g., *He sold a car to his mother* → *He sold his mother a car*.

Indirect question A question taking the form of a **dependent clause**: e.g., *I asked him what time it is*. Cf. **direct question**.

Infinitive One of the five principal parts of the verb in English; the form that follows *to* (e.g., *Try to go*), *do* (e.g., *Don't go*), and modals (e.g., *Who will go?*).

Infinitive clause A **clause** containing an **infinitive** verb form; e.g., *I want you to go home*.

Infinitive phrase A verb phrase consisting of *to* followed by an uninflected verb form (and any objects or complements); e.g., *To know him is to love him*.

Inflection An **affix** that alters the form of a word without changing its part of speech, e.g., the *-s* on *chairs*. *Chair* is a noun, and the plural *chairs* is a noun. English has eight inflections: present, past, present participle, past participle, comparative, superlative, plural, and possessive. Cf. **derivational affix**.

Inherent negative A sentence containing a word whose meaning includes negation (e.g., *Three students are absent*), rather than a form with an overt negative marker (e.g., *not present*). Cf. **negative sentence**.

Instrument A **thematic role** describing the NP used to carry out the action in a sentence; e.g., *John built that table for his parents with his own hands*.

Intensifier Modifier of an adjective or adverb which increases its semantic content (e.g., *very smart*).

Interjection The part of speech that expresses an emotion and is not connected syntactically to the surrounding utterance, e.g., *Wow! Interjection* is from the Latin phrase for 'throw between.'

Interrogative The structure used to ask a *yes/no*-question (e.g., *Can you go?*) or a *wh*-question (e.g., *When can you go?*). Formed by inverting the subject and the first verb.

Interrogative clause A **noun clause** that begins with a *wh*-word; e.g., *I saw what you did*.

Intransitive A verb that does not have a **direct object**; e.g., *John disappeared*. Cf. **transitive**.

Irregular Not conforming to a predictable pattern; e.g., an "irregular" plural in English is formed by changing the vowel in the root (*man/men*). Cf. **regular**.

Irregular verb One that forms its past tense by means other than a dental suffix (i.e., *t/d/ed*), e.g., *sing/sang*. Also known as a **strong verb**.

***It*-placement** Placement of the "dummy" subject *it* in a site from which a clause has undergone **extraposition**; e.g., *It bothers me that he smokes* (from *That he smokes bothers me*).

Kernel In generative grammar, a simple, active, declarative, positive sentence, e.g., *John kissed Mary*. Cf. *John kissed someone who is named Mary, Mary was kissed by John, Did John kiss Mary?,* and *John didn't kiss Mary*.

Language acquisition The process by which humans develop language, especially their first or native language.

Lexical binding condition In generative grammar (especially government and binding theory), a principle stating that a lexical NP (i.e., not an anaphor or a pronoun) cannot have an antecedent; e.g., **Mary talks to Mary*.

Linking verb One that, rather than expressing an action, provides a "link" between the **subject** of a sentence and some characteristic of the subject that is described in the **predicate**; e.g., *This popcorn tastes salty*.

Main clause Any clause that can stand alone as a sentence, e.g., *He is brilliant* (cf. *that he is brilliant; for him to be brilliant; his being brilliant)*. Also known as an **independent clause**.

Main verb The rightmost verb in a simple sentence (e.g., *Dole shouldn't have been running*).

Mass noun See **noncount noun**.

Minimalism Chomsky's most recent extension of generative grammar, "minimizing" the syntactic paraphernalia necessary to describe sentences. For example, minimalism attempts to rid the grammar of any sort of movement rules (i.e., **transformations**).

Modal verb A type of **auxiliary verb** that lacks *-s* with a third person subject in the present tense; e.g., *John can go*.

Modifier Generally any element of a phrase that is not the **head** of that phrase; e.g., *The old man at the bar*.

Mood A classification system for verbs, indicating whether the utterance is a statement (**indicative** mood, e.g., *You left early*), a question (**interrogative**, e.g., *Did you leave early?*), a command (**imperative**, e.g., *Leave early*), or a contingency (**subjunctive**, e.g., *If you leave early . . .*).

Nature Plato's theory that words are essentially imitative of nature. For example, the word *screech* is imitative of the sound a car makes when coming to an abrupt halt. Cf. **convention**.

Negative A transformation that inserts *not* to the right of tense (and the first auxiliary); e.g., *I will go* ⇛ *I will not go*.

Negative sentence A sentence containing a negative marker such as *not* (or a contracted form of it).

Neologism A word that doesn't have any meaning. For example, *brillig* is a neologism in Lewis Carroll's poem "Jabberwocky."

Neurolinguistics The branch of linguistics that studies how language is represented in the brain and the effect that brain damage has on language processing.

New information That part of a discourse that the speaker/writer assumes is not already known to the addressee. See also **given-new principle**.

Node Any non-terminal point in a tree diagram; e.g., the nodes in the following diagram are PP, P, NP, D, and N:

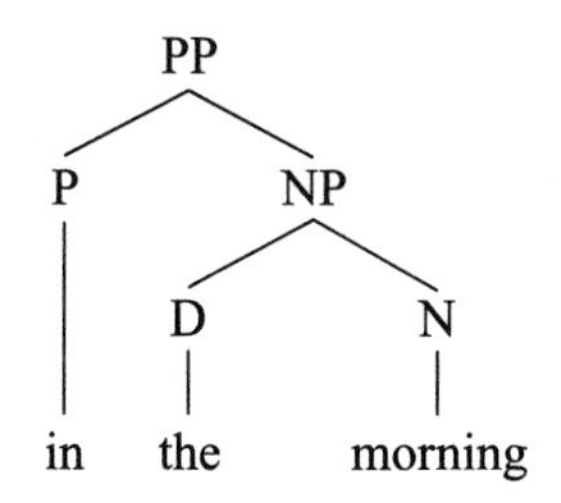

Nominal A word or phrase that serves an NP function (i.e., subject, direct object, indirect object, subjective complement, objective complement, object of a preposition).

Noncount noun A noun that cannot be pluralized (e.g., **furnitures*). Also known as a **mass noun**. Cf. **count noun**.

Nonfinite verb See **infinitive**.

Nonrestrictive relative clause A **relative clause** that does not provide information needed to uniquely identify the noun being modified; instead, it provides optional or additional information (e.g., *My mother, <u>who lives on a farm</u>, can drive a tractor)*. In writing, commas are used around a nonrestrictive relative clause. Cf. **restrictive relative clause**.

Nonspecific A type of NP that does not refer to a particular entity; e.g., *Annie wants to buy <u>a horse</u>, but she hasn't found one yet*. Cf. **specific**.

Nonstandard form One that draws negative attention to itself, e.g., *ain't*. Also known as a **socially marked form**.

Non-terminal node In generative grammar, a point in a tree diagram that dominates something else, e.g., S, NP, AUX, VP, N, TNS, and V in the following diagram.

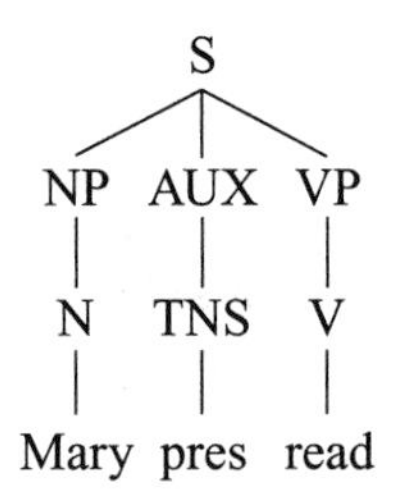

Normative grammar See **prescriptive grammar**.

Noun The part of speech that "names" something; e.g., *boy*. *Noun* is from the Greek word for 'name.' Generally characterized by the ability to take possessive and plural inflections.

Noun clause A **clause** that functions as a **nominal**; e.g., *I saw <u>what you did</u>*.

Noun phrase (NP) A **noun** plus any of its modifiers; e.g., *the man in the moon*.

Noun phrase (NP) movement In generative grammar (especially government and binding theory), a transformation that moves any NP to any empty NP position higher in the structure.

Number A classification system dividing words (especially nouns, pronouns, and verbs) into singular and plural; e.g., *boy* is singular and *boys* is plural.

Objective complement A noun phrase or adjective phrase that follows a **direct object** and adds information about it; e.g., *Mary finds John a bore/offensive.*

Object of a preposition A noun phrase introduced by a preposition, e.g., *at the door*. The object of a preposition normally cannot be separated from its preposition unless the object is a ***wh*-word;** e.g., *Who were you talking to?*

Old information See **given information**.

Paradigm A set of related words having the same root; e.g., *sing, sang, sung, singing.*

Parsing In descriptive grammar, the analysis of a sentence into words, identifying the part of speech to which each belongs, and identifying the function of each; for example, in the sentence *Speak slowly*, *slowly* is an adverb modifying the verb *speak*. In **psycholinguistics**, the unconscious process by which humans analyze and comprehend sentences.

Participle Two of the **principal parts** of a verb. The **present participle** ends in *-ing* and follows a form of *be* in an active sentence (e.g., *is drinking*). The **past participle** follows a form of *have* in an active sentence (e.g., *has drunk*).

Particle A word that looks like a preposition (e.g., *up, out*, etc.) but actually forms part of a verb phrase. Unlike a preposition, a particle can be moved to the right of the NP that follows it (e.g., *I turned in my key/turned my key in*).

Parts of speech The categories into which words can be classified according to their form. In English, for example, words that have a plural form are classified as nouns; those that have a comparative form are classified as adjectives, etc.

Passive A transformation that moves the object to subject position, inserts *be - en* before the main verb, and moves the subject to a *by*-phrase to the right of the verb.

Passive sentence One which contains a form of *be* followed by a **past participle**. The subject of a passive sentence is generally the **patient** of the action expressed by the verb; the **agent**, if present, is expressed in a *by*-phrase following the verb (e.g., *The contract was signed by the writer*). Cf. **active sentence**.

Past participle The form of an English verb typically ending in *-ed* or *-en* and following a form of *have*; e.g., *You have broken your promise*. In an active sentence, the past participle of a verb always follows the auxiliary verb *have*.

Past tense The form of an English verb indicating past time and (typically) ending in *-t/d/ed* when it is the first verb in a simple sentence (e.g., *John smoked*). The first verb form in a simple sentence is always inflected for either past tense (e.g., *John smoked*) or present tense (*John smokes*).

Patient A **thematic role** describing the NP affected by the action in a sentence; e.g., *John built that table for his parents with his own hands*.

Perfect aspect Expressed by the use of auxiliary *have* and a **main verb**; indicates that the activity or situation described in the sentence is completed at some point earlier than the time of utterance (e.g., *We have reached a decision*).

Performance In generative grammar, the actual production and interpretation of sentences by a speaker. Cf. **competence**.

Performance grammar The study of the effect of context and/or real-time limitations on the way speakers process language.

Person A classification system for nouns, distinguishing among the speaker (first person, e.g., *I*), the addressee (second person, e.g., *you*), and the thing spoken of (third person, e.g., *he, she, it*).

Personal pronoun A pronoun with nominative, objective, and possessive forms (e.g., *I/me/my*).

Phrasal verb A verb plus a **particle**, e.g., *Have you taken out the trash?*

Phrase A word or group of words functioning as a unit; e.g., *this man* is an NP, *very old* is an AP, *at home* is a PP, etc. In descriptive grammar, a phrase is distinguished from a **clause** in that a clause has both a subject and a predicate.

Phrase structure (PS) rules In generative grammar, a rule system for describing the constituent structure of phrases; e.g., PP → P - NP states that a prepositional phrase consists of a preposition followed by a noun phrase.

Possessive A type of **determiner** consisting of *my, our, your, its, his, her or, their.*

Post-modifier A modifier of a phrase that follows the **headword**: e.g., *the man talking.*

Post-nominal Any modifier that follows a noun, e.g., *I drink coffee black.*

Predeterminer An item that can occur in an NP before a **determiner;** e.g., *all my children.*

Predicate The verb in a sentence plus any elements, such as an adverbial, direct object or complement, that follow it; e.g., *John met Mary on a flight from New York to Los Angeles.*

Prefix An **affix** attached to the beginning of a word, e.g., *recharge.*

Pre-modifier A modifier of a phrase that precedes the **headword**: e.g., *the man talking.*

Pre-nominal Any modifier that precedes a noun, e.g., *I drink black coffee.*

Preposition The part of speech that never changes form and takes a noun phrase as an object, e.g., *in school, at home,* etc. *Preposition* is from the Latin phrase for 'put before (a noun).'

Prepositional phrase A syntactic unit consisting of a preposition (e.g., *in*) plus a noun phrase (e.g., *the house*).

Preposition stranding Moving a *wh*-word (*who, what,* etc.) to the beginning of a clause and leaving its governing preposition at the end of the clause, e.g., *Where did you come from?*

Prescriptive grammar A prescriptive and proscriptive system of rules that one is expected to follow in speaking and writing the most prestigious variety of a language. Also known as **normative grammar** or **school grammar**.

Prescriptivism The view that usage is fixed and is either "correct" or "incorrect." Cf. **descriptivism**.

Present participle The form of an English verb ending in *-ing* and following a form of *be*; e.g., *You have been winning.*

Present tense The form of an English verb ending in *-s* when it has a third person singular subject (e.g., *John smokes*). The present tense form with other subjects has no *-s* (e.g., *I/You/We/They smoke*). The first verb form in a simple sentence is always inflected for either present tense (*John smokes*) or past tense (*John smoked*).

Principal parts The five forms of an English verb: **infinitive** (e.g., *to go*), **present tense** (e.g., *goes*), **past tense** (e.g., *went*), **present participle** (e.g., *going*), and **past participle** (e.g., *gone*).

Pro-form A word that replaces another part of speech, usually one that occurred earlier. (*Pro-* means 'for.') For example, *They went to Miami, and I went there, too*.

Pro-form substitution A test indicating that a series of words is a **constituent** (i.e., a unit); e.g., *She got promoted and I did, too*.

Progressive aspect Expressed by the use of auxiliary *be* and a **main verb**; indicates an activity or situation in progress (e.g., *We are reaching a decision*).

Pronominal In generative grammar, an NP that *may* have an antecedent in another clause (e.g., *John knew that he would fail*). Cf. **anaphor**.

Pronominal binding condition In generative grammar (especially government and binding theory), a principle stating that a **pronoun** cannot have an antecedent within the same clause; e.g., **Mary talks to her (her = Mary)*.

Pronoun The part of speech that is inflected for gender (e.g., *she*), number (e.g., *they*), or case (e.g., *him*) and can substitute for a noun phrase.

Proper noun The name of a unique, specific entity (e.g., *Elizabeth Taylor, Washington, D.C.*). Cf. **common noun**.

Psycholinguistics The branch of linguistics that studies the mental processes that humans employ in actual language use.

Psychological reality The correspondence between theoretical concepts (e.g., transformations) and the actual psychological strategies that humans use to process language.

Quantifier A type of **determiner** indicating "quantity"; e.g., *each, every, all, some, many*, and numerals.

Question A transformation that moves tense (and the first auxiliary) to the left of the subject; e.g., *He has gone* ⇛ *Has he gone?*

Readability formula A calculation designed to predict the speed and comprehension rate with which readers will process a text.

Reanalysis The process of reconstructing the wrong source for a form. For example, the phrase *that's a whole nother thing* results from the reanalysis of *an+other* as *a+nother*.

Reciprocal pronoun A pronoun that always has an antecedent, but does not end in *-self/selves* (e.g., *John and Mary frightened each other*). Cf. **reflexive pronoun**.

Recoverable item One that is not expressed but that can be reconstructed from the preceding discourse, e.g., *John ate but I didn't [eat]*.

Reed–Kellogg The oldest method of diagramming sentences still widely used in American schools today; it dates from 1877.

Reference A method for achieving **cohesion** through the use of items such as pronouns that link parts of a text with other parts or with things in the real world.

Reflexive pronoun A pronoun that always has an antecedent and has the suffix *-self/selves* (e.g., *John frightened himself*). Cf. **reciprocal pronoun**.

Regular Following a predictable pattern; e.g., the "regular" plural in English is formed by adding an *-s* ending (*boy/boys*). Cf. **irregular**.

Regularization Changing an **irregular** form so that it adheres to a **regular** pattern; e.g., some nonstandard dialects use forms such as *waked* (rather than *woke*), since *waked* adheres to the regular pattern for past tense verbs.

Regular verb One that forms its past tense with a dental suffix (i.e., *t/d/ed*); e.g., *push/pushed*. Also known as a **weak verb**.

Reiteration A strategy for achieving **cohesion** by linking lexical items through the use of **repetition**, **synonyms**, **general nouns**, or **superordinate terms**.

Relative adverb A *wh*-word (i.e., *where, when, why, how*) that serves an adverbial function within a **relative clause** (e.g., *This is the street where I live*).

Relative clause A dependent clause that is "related" to another clause by a **relative**

pronoun (e.g., *That is the man <u>who mugged me</u>*) or a **relative adverb** (e.g., *This is the street <u>where I live</u>*). Also known as an **adjectival clause**.

Relative pronoun A *wh*-word (i.e., *who(m), which, that*) that serves a nominal function within a **relative clause** (e.g., *That is the man <u>who</u> mugged me*).

Repetition A method for achieving **cohesion** by restating exact lexical items; e.g., *Math <u>scores</u> are up, while science <u>scores</u> are down.*

Restrictive relative clause A **relative clause** that supplies information needed to uniquely identify the noun being modified; e.g., *The hand <u>that rocks the cradle</u> rules the world.* In writing, no commas are used around a restrictive relative clause. Cf. **nonrestrictive relative clause**.

Sapir–Whorf Hypothesis The theory that the structure of a person's language influences that person's perception of reality. Named for linguists Edward Sapir and Benjamin Whorf.

Scene headers Names of the typical sequences of events comprising a **script** (e.g., a "movie-going" script might include a scene header such as Buying a Ticket).

Schema (plural: schemata) A psychological framework for organizing pre-existing knowledge about the world. See also **script**.

School grammar See **prescriptive grammar**.

Script A psychological representation of the typical sequence of events in a familiar situation (e.g., a "movie-going" script might include events such as Buying a Ticket, Buying Popcorn, Finding a Seat, etc.). See also **schema** and **scene headers**.

Shorthand notation In generative grammar, a representation of only the terminal nodes of a **tree diagram**. For example, shorthand for

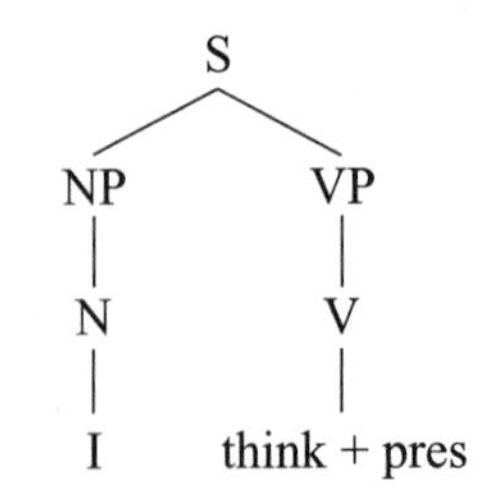

would be *I - think+pres*.

Sister In generative grammar, two **nodes** (i.e., positions) in a tree diagram that immediately branch from the same node. For example, in the following diagram, Y and Z are "sisters" of each other:

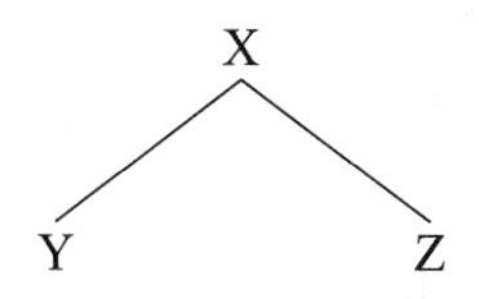

Socially marked form See **nonstandard form**.

Sociolinguistics The branch of linguistics that studies the relationship between language and social variables such as ethnicity, gender, socioeconomic class, and geographic region.

Specific A type of NP that refers to a particular entity: e.g., *Annie wants to buy a horse; it's a very nice Thoroughbred.* Cf. **nonspecific**.

Specified Subject Condition In generative grammar (especially government and binding theory), a constraint on movement stating that a direct object cannot be moved out of a clause containing a subject. For example,

_______ is sure [John to beat *Mary*]
↑_____ X _______________|

Specifier In generative grammar (especially X-bar syntax), the position defined as daughter of XP and sister of X', as follows:

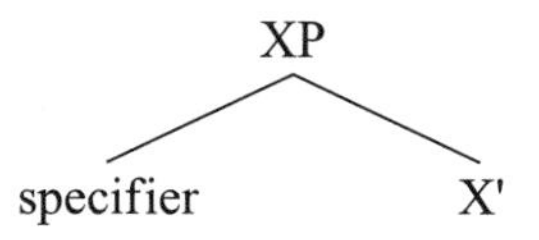

For example, the determiner *that* functions as the specifier of the noun phrase *that tall math student*. The term *specifier* designates a position (like *subject, direct object*, etc.), not a class of words (like *determiner, noun*, etc.).

Standard English A variety of English that does not elicit a negative reaction from educated speakers; characterized by the absence of socially stigmatized forms such as double negatives.

Standard theory An early version of Chomsky's transformational grammar, consisting of a **phrase structure** component describing **kernel** sentences and a set of **transformations** which permute kernel sentences into their various surface forms (e.g., passives, questions, negatives, etc.).

Stop A consonant produced with complete closure at some point in the mouth; e.g., [t] in *tea*. Cf. **fricative**.

Strong verb See **irregular verb**.

Structural grammar See **descriptive grammar**.

Structural hypercorrection Use of a more prestigious form in a linguistic environment where it is not typically used by native speakers of the prestige form; e.g., *Whom is taking you to dinner?*

Structuralism The theoretical foundation of **descriptive grammar**. It's a combination of Saussure's idea that a language can be studied irrespective of its history and Bloomfield's idea that linguistics is a physical science.

Structure classes In descriptive grammar, various classes of words, including pronouns, conjunctions, auxiliary verbs, determiners, and prepositions, that require the presence of a **form class** word. For example, a determiner (*the*) cannot occur without a noun (*men*). Also known as **function class** words.

Subjacency In generative grammar (especially government and binding theory), a constraint stating, in general, that transformations can move an item within a clause or to an adjacent clause.

Subject The NP that agrees with the verb and that undergoes inversion with the verb in question formation.

Subjective complement The phrase following a **linking verb**, e.g., *John appears edgy*.

Subject raising In generative grammar, a transformation that moves the subject of an embedded infinitive clause to subject position in the main clause. For example,

______ is sure [*John* to win]
↑__________|

Subjunctive The **mood** used in hypothetical situations, characterized by the absence of the third-person singular -*s* on present tense verbs (e.g., *I insist*

that John walk home everyday) and by the use of *were* with singular subjects (e.g., *If I were you, I wouldn't do that*).

Subordinate clause Any clause that cannot stand alone as a sentence; e.g., *that she sings, for her to sing, her singing* (cf. *She sings*). Also known as a **dependent clause**.

Subordinating conjunction A **conjunction** that introduces an **adverbial clause;** e.g., *although, because.*

Substitution A method for establishing **cohesion** by using **pro-forms** such as *one* to refer back to earlier linguistic elements; e.g., *My husband caught a cold, and now I have one.*

Suffix An **affix** attached to the end of a word, which modifies its meaning or function. For example, the *-s* on *boys* means 'plural'; the *-ish* on *boyish* means 'in the manner of.'

Superlative Adjective form with *-est* suffix (e.g., *shortest*) or *most* (e.g., *most intense*).

Superordinate A more general term that describes the category to which a more specific item belongs; e.g., *building* is a superordinate of *house*, since a house is a type of building. Can be used to establish cohesion; e.g., *Neurosurgeons are among the most highly trained doctors.*

Suppletion Forms in a **paradigm** having different roots; e.g., *good, better, best.*

Surface structure In generative grammar, that point in the **derivation** of a sentence after all transformations have applied. Cf. **underlying structure**.

Synchronic linguistics The study of a language irrespective of its history or genetic relationship to other languages. *Synchronic* is from the Greek phrase for '(at) one time.' Cf. **diachronic linguistics**.

Synonym A word or phrase with the same meaning as another word or phrase; can be used to establish **cohesion** (e.g., *The investigation has linked donations made to state Democratic parties with additional contributions to the national party*).

Tag question One "tagged" onto the end of a declarative sentence, with subject and auxiliary inverted; e.g., *You have been smoking, haven't you?*

Temporal conjunction A **conjunction** that establishes the order of occurrence of degree of importance among the items being conjoined; e.g., *first, second, third.*

Tense A classification system for verbs, indicating, in general, the time of the action: past tense (e.g., *The tide rose*), present tense (e.g., *The tide rises*), future tense (e.g., *The tide will rise*). English, like all Germanic languages, has only two **inflected** tenses: past and present.

Tensed S In generative grammar (especially government and binding theory), a constraint stating that NP Movement cannot move anything out of a tensed clause.

Thematic role The semantic function of an NP with respect to the verb. Semantic roles include **agent**, **patient**, **beneficiary**, and **instrument**.

Theme The main idea of a text.

Trace In generative grammar (especially government and binding theory), a site from which an item has been moved. For example, in the following diagram, WHM leaves a "trace" when it moves *what* to complementizer:

$_{\text{COMP}}$[what] has he done _t_
↑ WHM |

Trace theory In generative grammar (especially government and binding theory), a principle stating that every moved constituent leaves a **co-indexed** trace (i.e., a marker indicating where it had been).

Transformation In generative grammar, an operation that changes a **kernel** sentence into a nonkernel sentence by inserting, deleting, or moving an item. For example, the Passive transformation changes *John kissed Mary* into *Mary was kissed by John*.

Transformational grammar See **generative grammar**.

Transitive A verb that has a **direct object**; e.g., *John kissed Mary*. Cf. **intransitive**.

Tree diagram In generative grammar, a visual representation of syntactic structure. For example, a tree diagram (i.e., representation of the internal structure) of the phrase *in the morning* would be

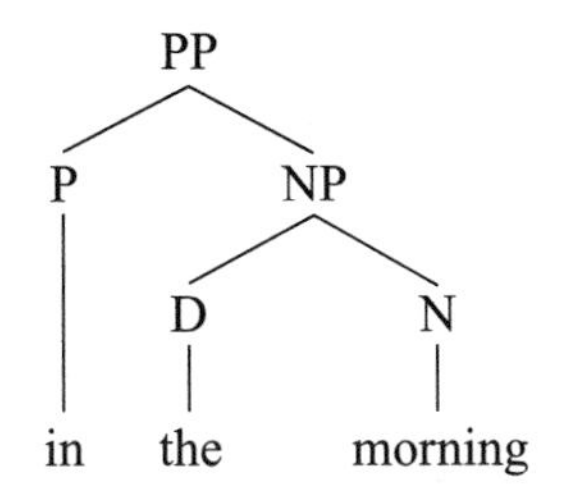

Tree pruning In generative grammar, a convention by which any non-terminal node that dominates nothing else is deleted; e.g.,

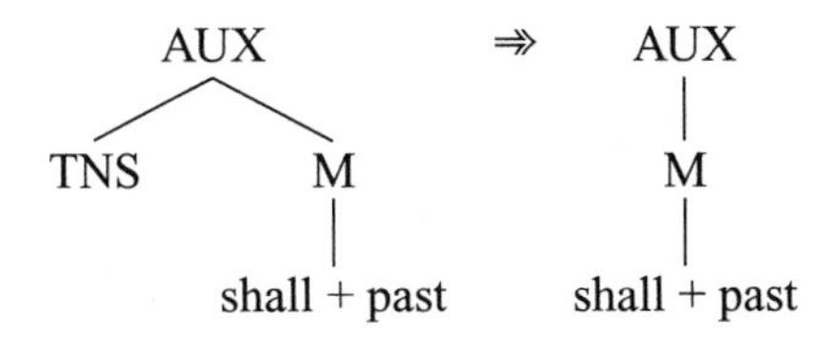

Underlying structure In generative grammar, that point in the **derivation** of a sentence before any transformations have applied; e.g., the underlying structure of *Have you seen him*? would be *You - pres - have - en - see - him*. Cf. **surface structure.**

Uninflected Describing a word that contains no inflection (e.g., *to go* vs. *goes/going/gone*, etc.). The uninflected verb form is also known as the **infinitive** form.

Unit-movement In generative grammar (especially government and binding theory), a constraint stating that only a **constituent** can be moved by a transformation.

Verb The part of speech that designates action or state of being; e.g., *pry. Verb* is from the Latin word for 'word.'

Verb phrase In descriptive grammar, a main verb plus any auxiliary verbs. In generative grammar, a main verb plus any complements or objects.

Vernacular The indigenous language of a country or locality; the everyday language as opposed to the literary language.

Voice A classification system for verbs, indicating, in general, whether the subject of the sentence is the actor (active voice, e.g., *The police shot the sniper*) or the thing acted upon (passive voice, e.g., *The sniper was shot by the police*).

Voiced A speech sound produced with vocal cord vibration; e.g., [v] in *vine*. Cf. **voiceless**.

Voiceless A speech sound produced without a vocal cord vibration; e.g., [f] in *fine*. Cf. voiced.

Weak verb See **regular verb**.

Wh-Movement In generative grammar, a transformation moving any *wh*-phrase to clause-initial position.

Wh-word Any of the following: *who*, *whom*, *whose*, *what*, *where*, *when*, *why*, *which*, *how*.

X-bar syntax In generative grammar (especially government and binding theory), the view that phrases contain intermediate categories (i.e., X'.) larger than lexical categories (i.e., X) and smaller than phrasal categories (i.e., XP). For example, *boy* = N, *tall boy* = N', *a tall boy* = NP.

References

Anderson, R., and Davison, A. (1988). Conceptual and empirical bases of readability formulas. In Alice Davison and Georgia M. Green, eds., *Linguistic complexity and text comprehension: Readability issues reconsidered*, pp. 23–53. Hillsdale, NJ: Lawrence Erlbaum Assoc.

Baron, D. (1989). *Declining grammar*. Urbana, IL: NCTE.

Barone, M. (1996). The rise and fall of Spiro Agnew. *U.S. News & World Report*, Sept. 30, p. 28.

Baugh, A. (1935). *A history of the English language*, New York: Appleton-Century-Crofts.

Bloomfield, L. (1933). *Language*, New York: Holt, Rinehart & Winston.

Boylan, C. (1996). The Ramblas: Heart of Barcelona. *Bon Appetit*, Oct., pp. 128–131.

Brennan, J. F. (1982). *History and systems of psychology*. Englewood Cliffs, NJ: Prentice-Hall.

Budiansky, S. (1995). Consulting the oracle. *U.S. News and World Report*, Dec. 4, pp. 52–58.

Campbell, K. (1991). Structural cohesion in technical texts. *Journal of Technical Writing and Communication*, 21, pp. 221–237.

Campbell, K., Riley, K., and Parker, F. (1990). *You*-perspective: Insights from speech act theory. *Journal of Technical Writing and Communication*, 20, pp. 189–199.

Can HMOs help solve the health-care crisis? *Consumer Reports*, Oct. 1996, pp. 28–33.

Carroll, J. B., ed. (1956). *Language, thought, and reality: Selected writings of Benjamin Lee Whorf*, Cambridge, MA: MIT Press.

Chomsky, N. (1957). *Syntactic structures*. The Hague: Mouton.

Chomsky, N. (1965). *Aspects of the theory of syntax*. Cambridge, MA: MIT Press.

Chomsky, N. (1973). Conditions on transformations. In S. Anderson and P. Kiparsky, eds., *A Festschrift for Morris Halle*. New York: Holt, Rinehart & Winston.

Chomsky, N. (1980). On binding. *Linguistic Inquiry*, 11, pp. 1–46.

Chomsky, N. (1982). *On the generative enterprise*. Cinnaminson, NJ: Foris.

Chomsky, N. (1995). *The minimalist program*. Cambridge, MA: MIT Press.

Clark, H. H., and Clark, E. V. (1977). *Psychology and language: An introduction to psycholinguistics*. New York: Harcourt Brace Jovanovich.

Clark, H. H., and Haviland, S.E. (1977). Comprehension and the given-new contract. In R. Freedle, ed., *Discourse production and comprehension*, Hillsdale, NJ: Lawrence Erlbaum.

Crowley, S. (1989). Linguistics and composition instruction: 1950–1980. *Written Communication*, 6, pp. 480–505.

Duin, A. (1989). Factors that influence how readers learn from text: Guidelines for structuring technical documents. *Technical Communication*, 36, pp. 97–101.

Faigley, L. (1982). Review of *Linguistics, stylistics, and the teaching of composition*, ed. by D. McQuade. *College Composition and Communication*, 33, Feb., pp. 96–98.

Fasold, R. (1984). *The sociolinguistics of society*. New York: Blackwell.

Finegan, E. (1980). *Attitudes toward English*. New York: Teachers College Press.

Fodor, J., Bever, T., and Garrett, M. (1974). *The psychology of language: An introduction to psycholinguistics and generative grammar*. New York: McGraw-Hill.

Francis, W. N. (1958). *The structure of American English*. New York: Ronald Press.

Fries, C. C. (1940). *American English grammar*. New York: D. Appleton-Century.

Hairston, M. (1981). Not all errors are created equal: Nonacademic readers in the professions respond to lapses in usage. *College English*, 43, Dec., pp. 794–806.

Halliday, M. A. K., and Hasan, R. (1976). *Cohesion in English*. London: Longman.

Harris, R., and Taylor, T. (1989). *Landmarks in linguistic thought*. London: Routledge.

Horrocks, G. (1987). *Generative grammar*. London: Longman.

House, H., and Harman, S. (1950). *Descriptive English grammar*, 2nd ed. Englewood Cliffs, NJ: Prentice-Hall.

Kies, D. (1985). Some stylistic features of business and technical writing: The functions of passive voice, nominalization, and agency. *Journal of Technical Writing and Communication*, 15, pp. 299–308.

Krapp, G. (1909). *Modern English: Its growth and present use*. New York: Charles Scribner's Sons.

Labov, W. (1972). *Language in the inner city*. Philadelphia: University of Pennsylvania Press.

Laird, C. (1996). No sweat. *Practical Horseman*, Oct., pp. 66–70, 96.

Larson, C. (1995). Its academic, or is it? *Newsweek*, Nov. 6, p. 31.

Leonard, S. (1932). *Current English usage*. Chicago: Inland Press.

Lowth, R. (1775). *Short introduction to English grammar*. Philadelphia: Aitken.

Marsh, G. (1860). *Lectures on the English language*. New York.

Milic, L. (1986). Composition via stylistics. In D. McQuade, ed., *The territory of language: linguistics, stylistics, and the teaching of composition*. Carbondale: Southern Illinois University Press, pp. 192–203.

Moskowitz, B. A. (1979). The acquisition of language. *Scientific American*, Nov., pp. 82–96.

Müller, M. (1861). *Lectures on the science of language*. London: Longman.

Murray, L. (1816). *An English grammar*, 3rd ed. London: Longman.

Newmeyer, F. (1986). *Linguistic theory in America: The first quarter-century of transformational generative grammar*. New York: Academic Press.

Noguchi, R. (1991). *Grammar and the teaching of writing: Limits and possibilities*. Urbana, IL: NCTE.

Olsen, L., and Johnson, R. (1989). A discourse-based approach to the assessment of readability, *Linguistics and Education*, 1, pp. 207–231.

Parker, F., and Riley, K. (1994). *Linguistics for non-linguists: A primer with exercises*, 2nd ed., Boston: Allyn & Bacon.

Pizzorno, L., ed. (1994). *The complete book of bread machine baking*. Rocklin, CA: Prima.

Priestley, J. (1762). *A course of lectures on the theory of language, and universal grammar*. Warrington.

Quinn, J. (1981). Hopefully, they will shut up. *Newsweek*, Feb. 23, p. 9.

Reed, A., and Kellogg, B. (1886). *Higher lessons in English*. Delmar, NY: Scholars' Facsimiles and Reprints.

Riley, K., Parker, F., Manning, A., and Campbell, K. (1992). *Revising technical and business writing: Principles and applications*, 2nd ed. Superior, WI: Parlay.

Robins, R. H. (1979). *A short history of linguistics*, 2nd ed. London: Longman.

Rodman, L. (1981). The passive in technical and scientific writing. *Journal of Advanced Composition*, 2, pp. 165–172.

Ross, J. (1971). A transformational approach to teaching composition. *College Composition and Communication*, 22, May, pp. 179–184.

de Saussure, F. (1966). *Course in general linguistics*, trans. by W. Baskin. New York: McGraw–Hill.

Shaughnessy, M. (1977). *Errors and expectations: A guide to the teacher of basic writing*. New York: Oxford University Press.

Sherwood, J. (1960). Dr. Kinsey and Professor Fries. *College English*, 21, pp. 275–80.

Shook, R. (1983). Response to Martha Kolln. *College Composition and Communication*, 34, Dec., pp. 491–495.
Simon, J. (1978). Pressure from below. *Esquire*, June 20, pp. 90–91.
Singer, M. (1990). *Psychology of language: An introduction to sentence and discourse processes*. Hillsdale, NJ: Lawrence Erlbaum.
Stubbs, M. (1983). *Discourse analysis*. Chicago: University of Chicago Press.
Subbiondo, J. (1975). Review of *Transformational grammar and the teaching of English*, 2nd ed., by O. Thomas and E. Kintgen, and *The study of social dialects in American English*, by W. Wolfram and R. Fasold. In *College Composition and Communication*, 26, Feb., pp. 96–99.
Traugott, E. (1972). *A history of English syntax*. New York: Holt, Rinehart & Winston.
Warden, D. A. (1976). The influence of context on children's use of identifying expressions and references. *British Journal of Psychology*, 67, pp. 101–112.
Wardhaugh, R. (1968). If grammar, which grammar, and how? *College English*, 29, Jan., pp. 303–309.
Webster, N. (1789). *Dissertations on the English language*. Boston.
Whitney, W. D. (1877). *Essentials of English grammar*. Boston.
Williams, J. M. (1981). The phenomenology of error. *College Composition and Communication*, 32, May, pp. 152–168. Copyright 1981 by the National Council of Teachers of English. Reprinted with permission.

Answers to Selected Exercises

CHAPTER 1. BEFORE THE PRESCRIPTIVE PERIOD

Exercise A, page 10

a. the Greeks, especially Dionysius Thrax

Exercise B, page 12

c. parsing

Exercise D, page 16

c. *moon*
f. *Tamyse* is equivalent to Modern English *Thames* (the river in London); *Zelande* probably refers to Holland (*Sealand*).
h. The *h* is not pronounced, as evidenced by the use of the article *an*.

CHAPTER 2. THE PRESCRIPTIVE PERIOD

Exercise A, page 22

b. Quinn is describing the impulse to refine, i.e., to return to what is perceived as a purer form of English.
d. Larson appears frustrated at the lack of standardization, i.e., adherence to consistent rules of punctuation.

Exercise B, page 23

b. Defoe is referring to new coinages and borrowings.

Exercise E, page 26

a. *have spoke:* in standard Modern English, the past participle *spoken* would be used (instead of the past tense form *spoke*).
b. *begun:* in standard Modern English, the past tense form *began* would be used (instead of the past participle form *begun*).

Exercise G, page 27

a. "significations" refer to meanings; "derivations" refer to etymology (word history) and word formation; "combinations" refer to syntax (sentence structure).

CHAPTER 3. PRESCRIPTIVE RULES

Exercise C, page 36

c. Form (i) is not the interrogative counterpart of *We shall eat*; instead, it's an invitation. Form (ii) is the interrogative counterpart of *We shall eat.*

Exercise F, page 38

a. According to Murray's rule, *she* should be *her* (objective) because the subject of *to be* is *whom* (an objective case pronoun).
b. According to Murray's rule, *who* should be *whom* (objective) because *who* is the complement of *been*; *it* is objective (since it follows the transitive verb *understand*); therefore, *who* should be *whom.*

Exercise J, page pages 42–43

are; flays; washes

Exercise K, page 43

a. *who(m)* or *that* could occur after *man*
b. the preposition *to*, because a preposition requires an object (in this case, the relative pronoun)

Exercise N, page 45

a. . . . *than I (can read)*

CHAPTER 4. THE DESCRIPTIVE PERIOD

Exercise E, page 63

Diachronic, because it describes a change over time.

Exercise F, page 64

English speakers don't make the distinctions because they don't need to make them. Eskimo and Arabic speakers make additional distinctions that are necessitated by their environments.

Exercise G, page 65

Sapir; note the interest in going beyond the more mechanical view of language associated with behaviorism.

Exercise K, page 69

b. *Nominalism* refers to the idea that abstract concepts have no objective reference, but exist only as names. *Rousseauism* refers to the philosophy of Jean Jacques Rousseau (1712–1778), who developed the idea of the "noble savage." Sherwood accuses the "new grammar" of dismissing objective principles and of romanticizing "uneducated" languages.

CHAPTER 5. IDENTIFYING PARTS OF SPEECH

Exercise E, page 77

a. *Walk* is a verb in this sentence. Evidence includes the past tense inflection (*-ed*) and the fact that *walked* co-occurs between the subject (*He*) and the adverbial (*home*).

c. *Walk* is a noun in this sentence. The evidence is that it co-occurs between the article (*a*) and the main verb (*is*).

Exercise F, pages 78–79

b. The antecedent for *did* is *went to the library*; *did* is a pro-VP.

Exercise I, page 82

a. In this sentence, *dog* is indefinite; it could be either nonspecific (like 10a) or specific (like 10b).

Exercise K, page 84

a. Sentence (i) contains a particle; (ii) contains a preposition.

In (i), *down* can be moved to the right of the noun phrase: *John wrote my address <u>down</u>*. In (ii), *down* cannot: **John walked my street <u>down</u>*.

In (ii), the phrase *down my street* can be fronted *(Down my street walked John)* or clefted (*Down my street is where John walked*). In (i), the phrase *down my address* cannot undergo either of these operations: **Down my address wrote John; *It was down my address that John wrote* (cf. *It was my address that John wrote down*).

CHAPTER 6: NOUNS AND PRONOUNS

Exercise B, page 89

a. In this passage, *coffees* refers to 'varieties of coffees,' i.e., different blends.

Exercise F, page 95

In this sentence, *few* appears to function as a true pronoun (rather than a pro-NP).

CHAPTER 7: VERBS AND VERB PHRASES

Exercise B, pages 100–101

a. *was, were*

b. The same pronouns that use *are* in the present tense use *were* in the past tense (*we, you, they*); both *are* and *were* end in *-re*.

Exercise D, page 104

a. *Tim punched Ed.*

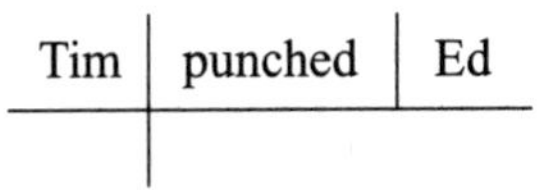

Exercise F, page 105

a. *His parents gave Jeff a new car.*

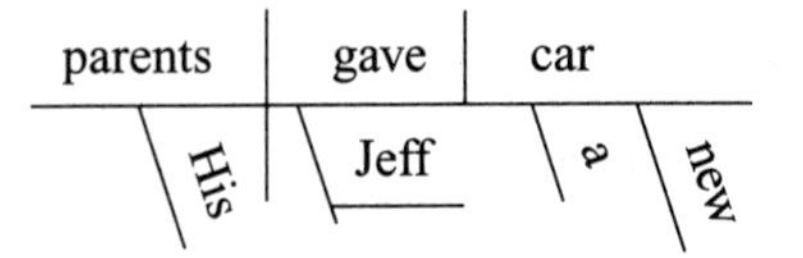

c. *I wrote a short note to her.*

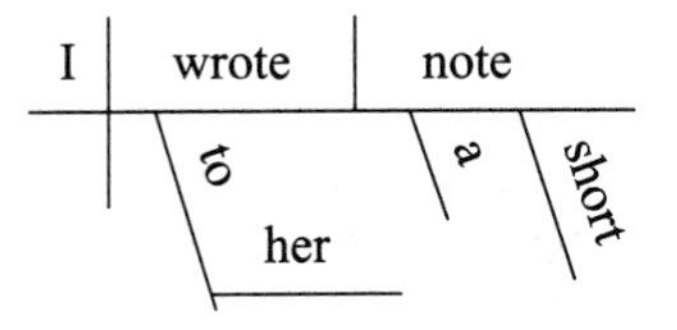

Exercise H, page 106

a. *The committee elected Frieda chair.*

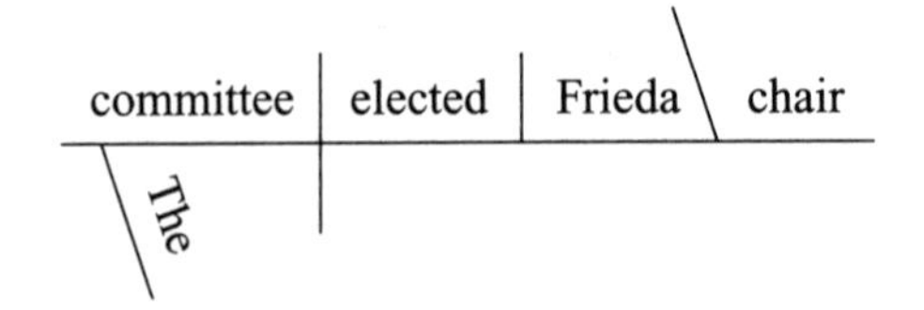

Exercise I, pages 107–108

a. linking

b. transitive

h. intransitive

Exercise J, page 108

a. *She seemed angry.*

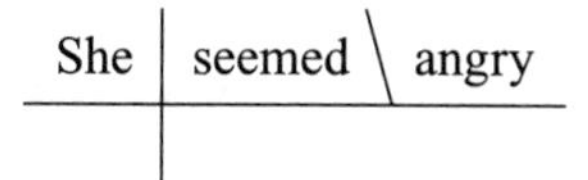

e. *I can't smell anything.*

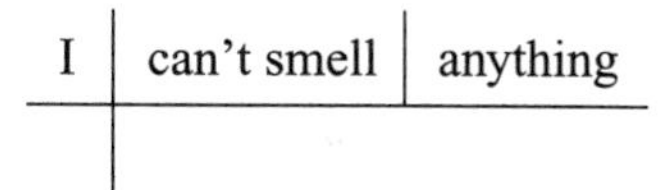

Exercise K, pages 109–110

a. *You weren't on time.* Adjectival (*on time* = *prompt*)

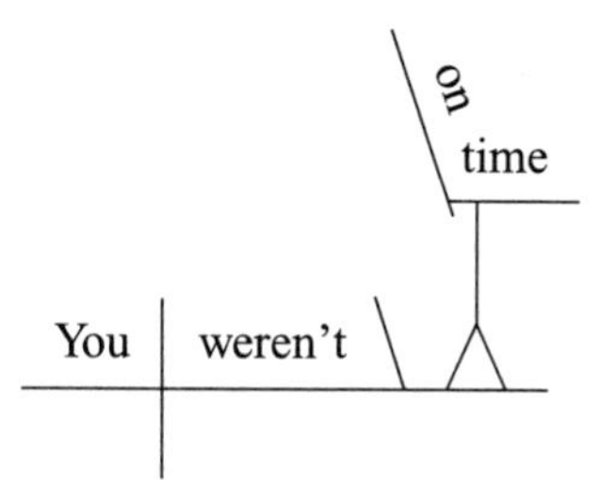

b. *The suitcases are on the train.* Adverbial (*on the train* can be replaced by *there*)

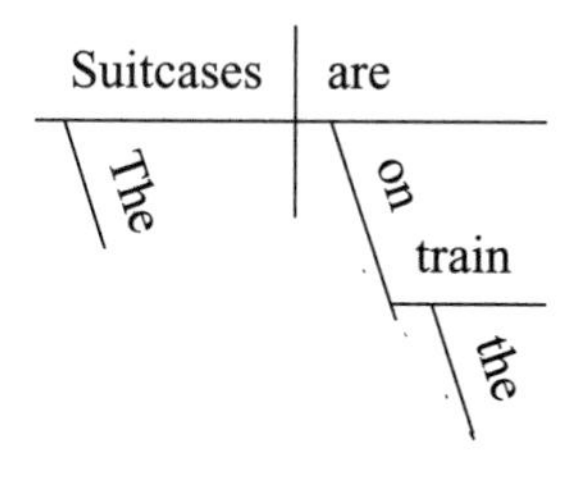

Exercise L, page 111

a. phrasal verb = *bring in;* direct object = *the mail*
The particle can be moved grammatically: *Frank might bring the mail in.*

c. phrasal verb = *settled on;* direct object = *a fair price for the house*
The particle cannot be moved grammatically: **They have settled a fair price for the house on.*

Exercise N, page 113

a. *had* = main verb, past tense
c. *should* = modal verb, past tense
have = auxiliary verb, infinitive (follows a modal)
had = main verb, past participle (follows auxiliary *have*)

Exercise O, page 114

a. *is* = auxiliary verb, present tense
being = main verb, present participle (follows auxiliary *be*)
d. *was* = main verb, past tense

Exercise P, page 116

a. *Yes/no*-question: *Does the committee need a new chair?*
Negative declarative: *The committee does not (doesn't) need a new chair.* Emphatic declarative: *The committee* DOES *need a new chair.*

Exercise Q, page 118

a. *It has been raining for two hours.* (vii) present perfect progressive
c. *Her show is gaining in popularity.* (iv) present progressive

Exercise R, page 120

a. Active. Passive = *A telephone pole was hit by the car.*
b. Passive. Active = *The storm wiped out electricity for three hours.*

CHAPTER 8. MODIFIERS OF NOUNS

Exercise A, page 124

a. *Oedipal:* (i) adjective; (ii) *Oedipus + al*; (iii) noun
b. *edible:* (i) adjective; (ii) *eat + ible*; (iii) verb
f. *toxic:* (i) adjective; (ii) *toxin + ic*; (iii) noun
g. *monstrosity:* (i) *noun*; (ii) *monster + ous + ity*; (iii) *noun*

Exercise B, page 125

a. *A good secretary is an invaluable asset.*

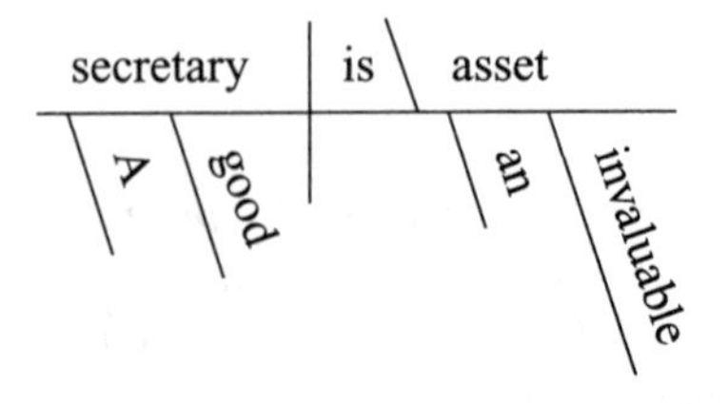

Exercise C, page 127

a. *Our horse trailer has two feed mangers.* *horse* and *feed* are adjectival nouns.

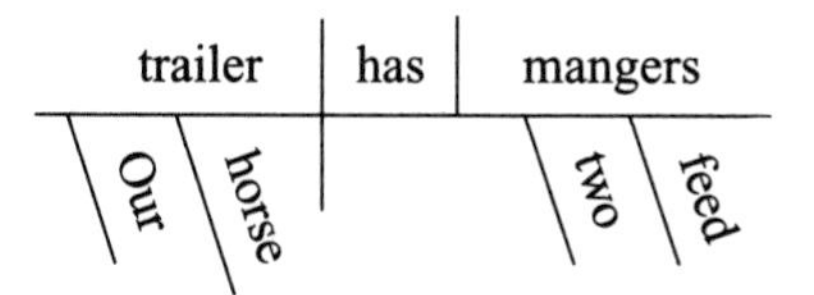

Exercise D, page 128

a. *in the robbery* is adjectival. Evidence is that it moves with the NP *a suspect* when the sentence is made passive: *A suspect in the robbery was arrested by the police.*

Diagram:

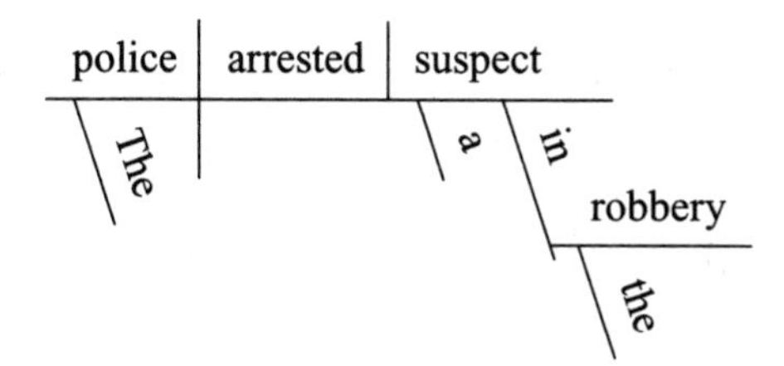

Exercise F, pages 129–130

a. *typed*: *A typed paper is easier to read than a handwritten one.*
d. *written: A written contract is preferable to a verbal agreement.*

Exercise G, page 130

a. *rolling* (modifies *stone*)
c. *to kill* (modifies *license*)
e. *crushed* (modifies *ice*)

Diagrams:

a. *A rolling stone gathers no moss.*

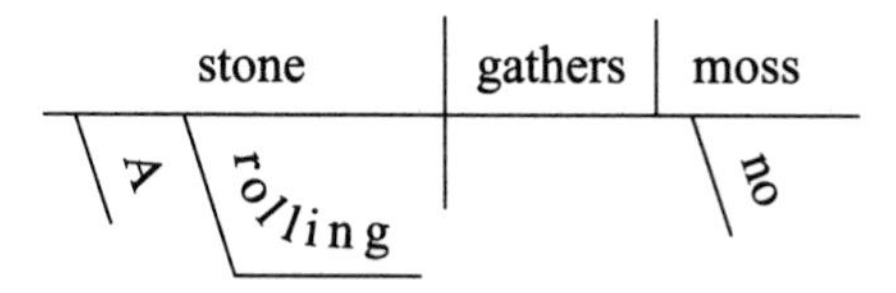

b. *James Bond has a license to kill.*

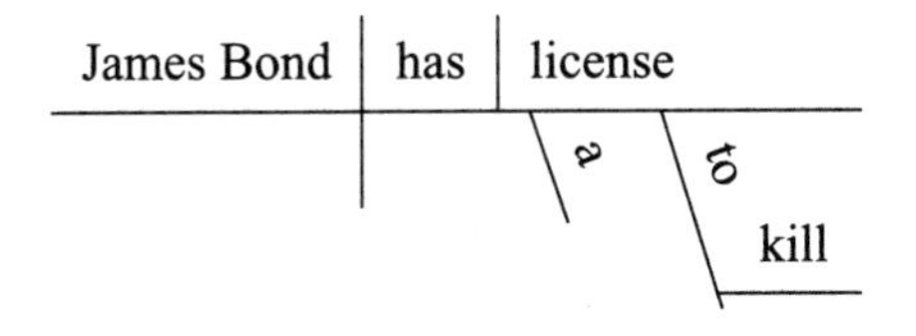

c. *I'd like some crushed ice.*

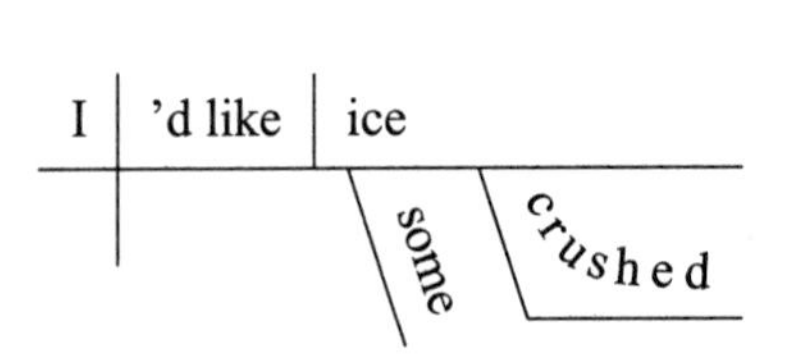

NOTE: To diagram a subject-verb contraction, place the subject and the abbreviated verb form in the subject and verb slots of the diagram, as shown above.

Exercise I, page 132

a. *The latest book (that) he wrote is a best-seller.*
c. *Do you know the person (who) owns this car?*

Exercise J, page 132

a. *that* = direct object of *wrote*
c. *who* = subject of relative clause

Diagrams:

a. *The latest book that he wrote is a best-seller.*

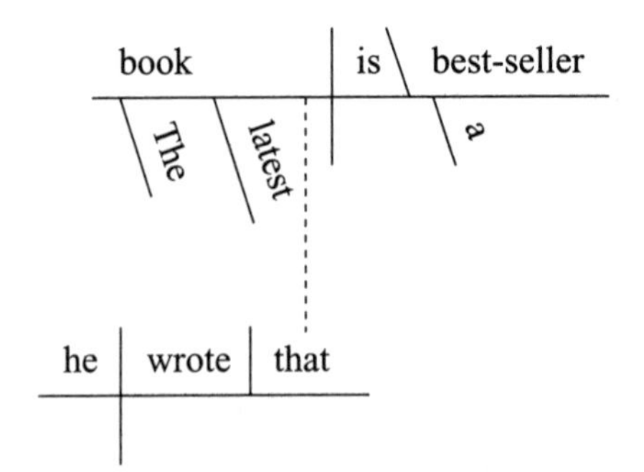

c. *Do you know the person who owns this car?*

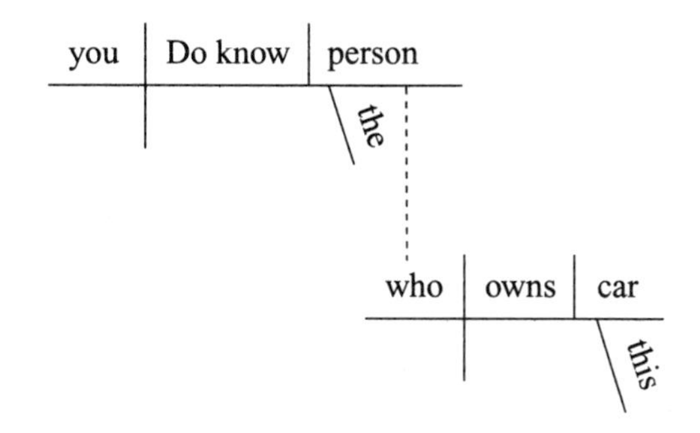

NOTE: To diagram a question, return the question to declarative (statement) form, as shown here.

Exercise L, page 136

a. Restrictive. Nonrestrictive version: *Men, who rely on women to cook for them, often go hungry.* The restrictive version implies that only some men often go hungry, namely those who rely on women to cook for them. The nonrestrictive version implies that all men rely on women to cook for them and, therefore, all men often go hungry.
b. Nonrestrictive. Restrictive version: *The suspect who was arrested by the police on Thursday is a known felon.* The restrictive version implies that there is more than one suspect involved in the crime being discussed; the additional suspect(s) were either arrested on a day other than Thursday or else are still at large.

CHAPTER 9. MODIFIERS OF VERBS

Exercise A, page 140

a. *silly:* adjective
b. *utterly:* adverb (e.g., *I agree with you utterly*) or intensifier (*They are utterly ridiculous*)

Exercise B, page 141

a. *He speaks French very fluently.*

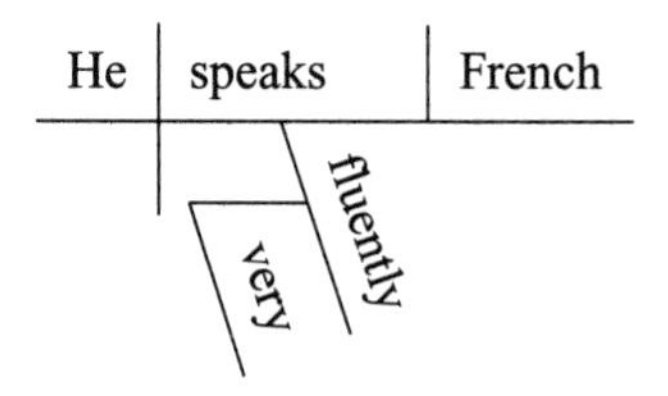

b. *You're always driving too fast.*

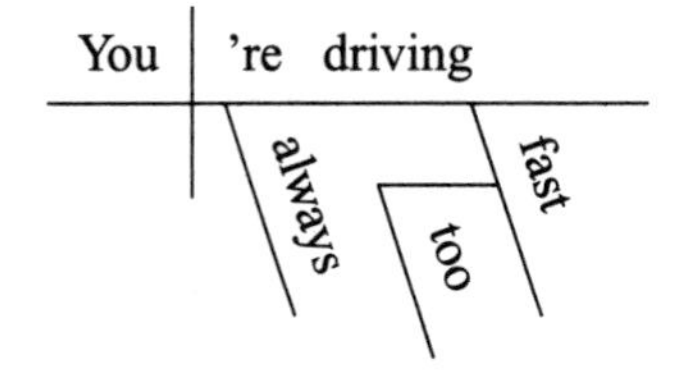

Exercise C, page 141

a. *in a hurry* describes manner.
b. *for three hours* describes time.

Diagrams:

a. *He left in a hurry.*

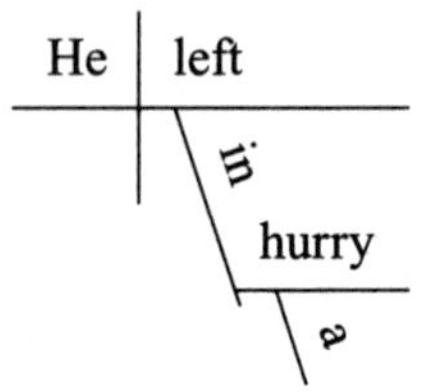

b. *They studied for three hours.*

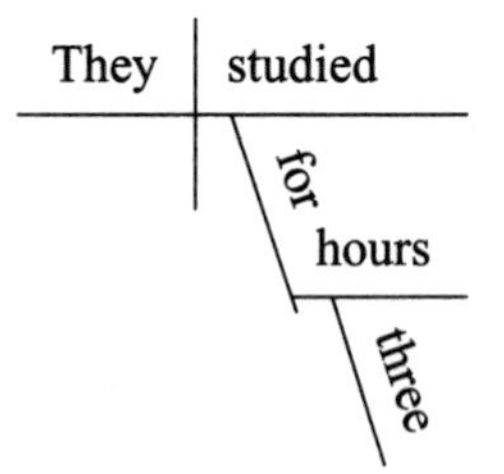

Exercise D, page 142

a. *to the door* = adjectival (modifies *key*)
in her purse = adverbial (modifies *put*)
Evidence from passive: *The key to the door was put in her purse by Marilyn.*

b. *through the woods* = adjectival (modifies *path*)
by the snowstorm = adverbial (modifies *blocked*)
on Tuesday = ambiguous: can be interpreted as either an adjectival (modifying *snowstorm*) or adverbial (modifying *blocked*). Note that two grammatical active versions are possible: *The snowstorm on Tuesday blocked the path through the woods* (adjectival); *The snowstorm blocked the path through the woods on Tuesday* (adverbial).

Diagrams:

a. *Marilyn put the key to the door in her purse.*

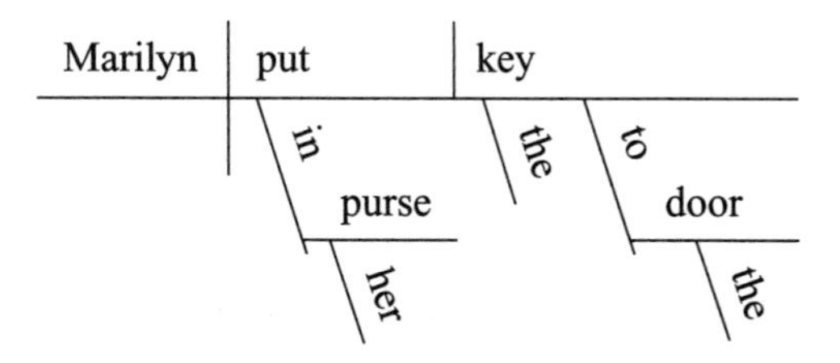

b. *The path through the woods was blocked by the snowstorm on Thursday.* (Note: this requires two diagrams because it is ambiguous.)

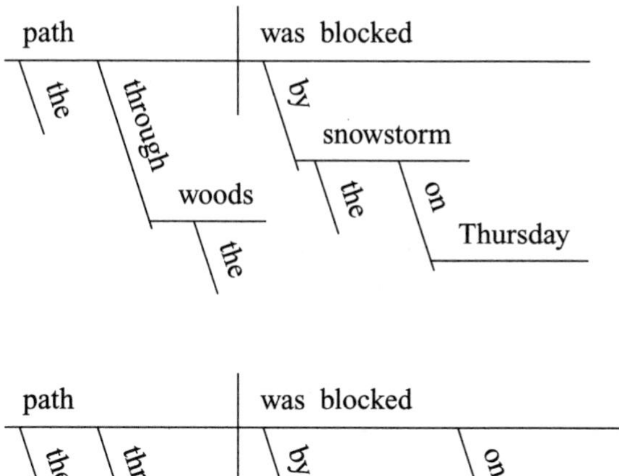

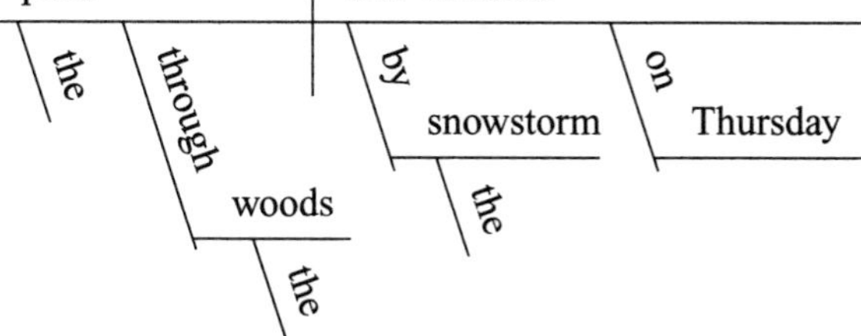

Exercise G, page 144

a. *She was dressed to kill.*
dressed = adjectival (subjective complement)
to kill = adverbial (modifies *dressed*)

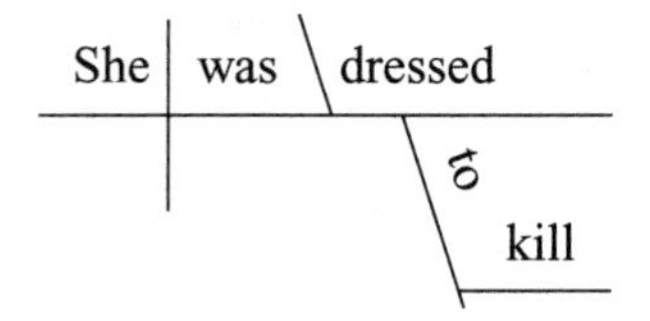

d. *The falling stock market alarmed many investors.*
falling = adjectival (modifies *market*)

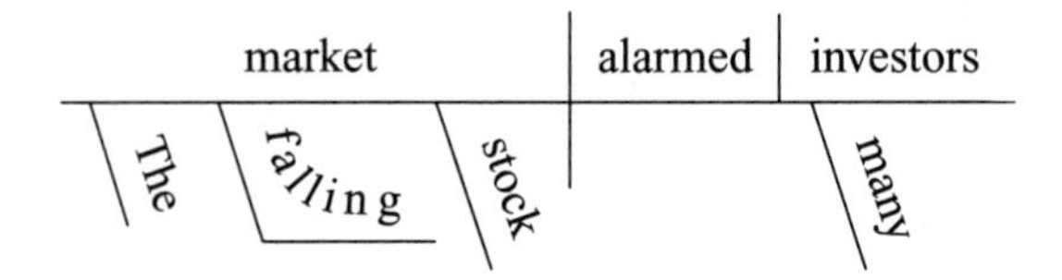

f. *Her son hit a stop sign driving home.*
driving home = adverbial (modifies *hit*)

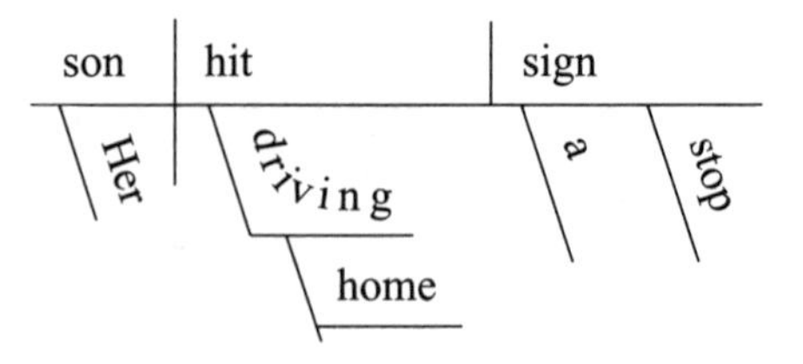

Exercise I, page 147

b. *Although the house has a big yard, it doesn't have enough bedrooms.*

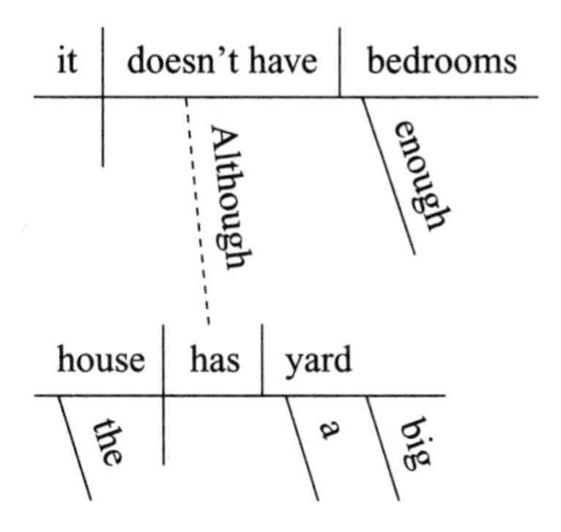

e. *When the Democrats introduced a bill to raise spending, they didn't consider its effects on the domestic economy.*

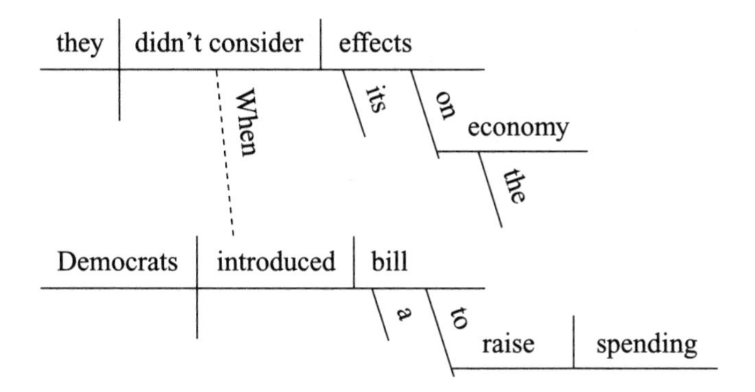

CHAPTER 10. NOMINALS

Exercise C, pages 154–155

a. *where their child goes to school* = subjective complement
c. *where I put my keys* = direct object

Exercise D, page 156

a. *who he bought the present for* = nominal (direct object); *who* = object of the preposition *for*.

c. *who have children* = adjectival (modifies *people*); *who* = subject of *wh*-clause.

Exercise E, page 157

a. *Bermuda is where they are going on their honeymoon.*

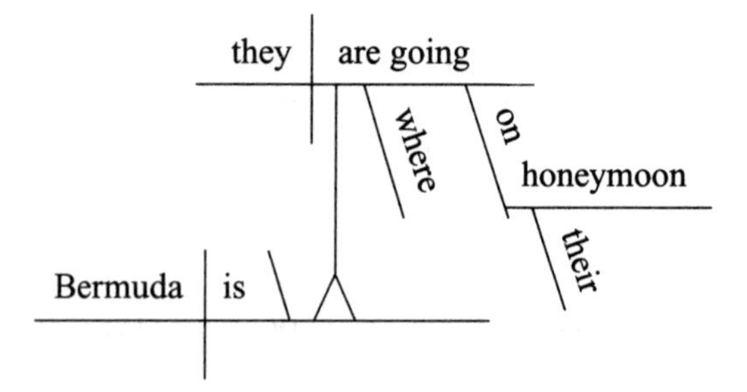

c. *I know the woman who got the job.*

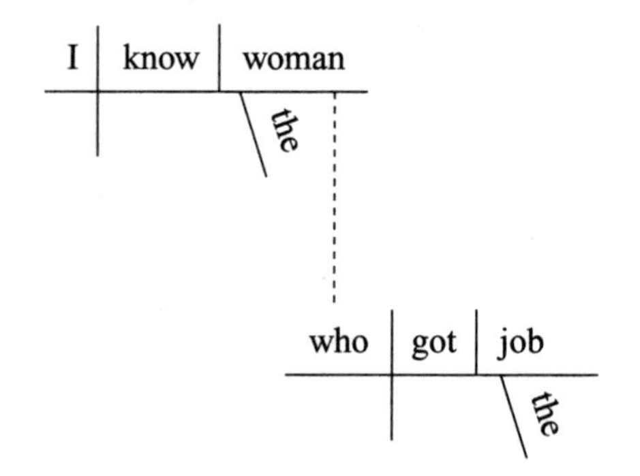

f. *I don't know who the supervisor is.*

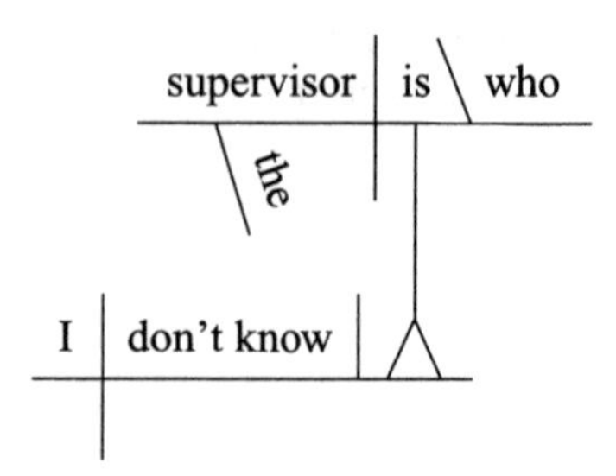

Exercise F, page 158

a. *The best solution might be for them to move.*
infinitive clause = *for them to move;* function = subjective complement.

Diagram:

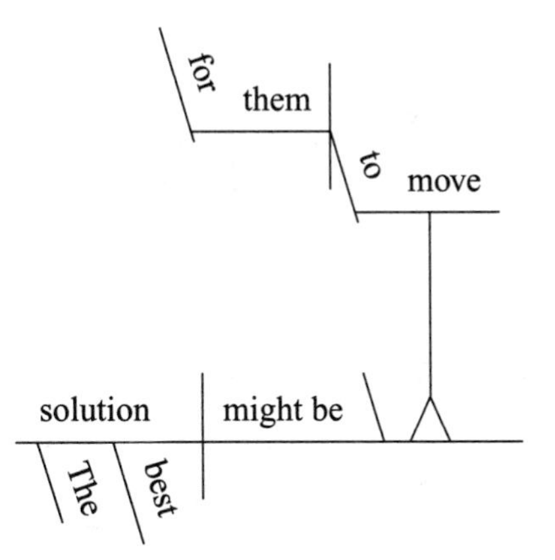

d. *I need you to go to the store for me.*
infinitive clause = *you to go to the store for me*; function = direct object

Diagram:

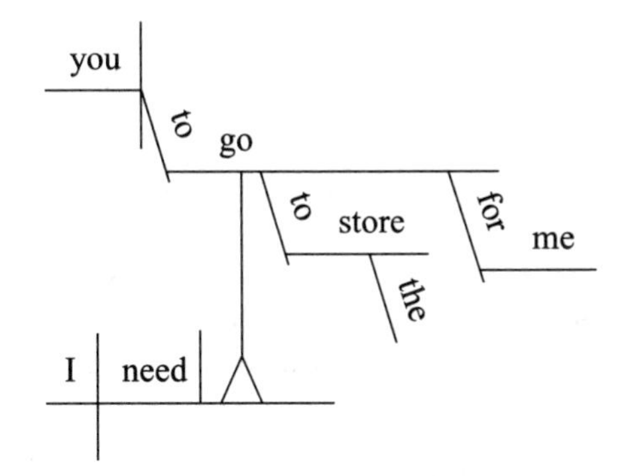

Exercise G, page 159

b. *To err* = subject
e. *to sleep in the living room* = direct object

Exercise I, page 161

a. *Being department head* = subject
c. *reading* = object of the preposition *about*

Exercise J, page 162

a. *We heard about Bill's trying to get a raise.*

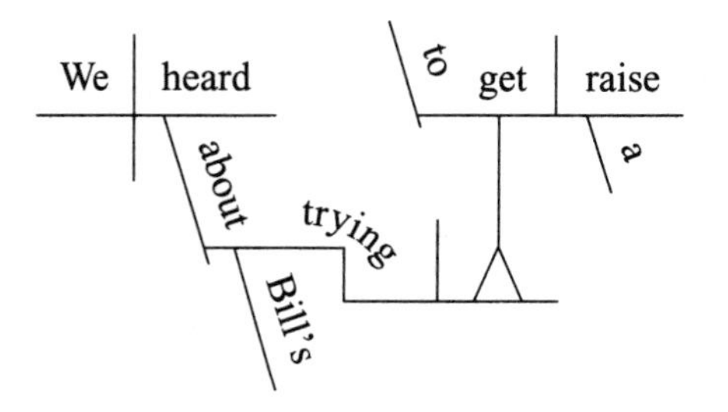

e. *Her favorite pastime is riding horses.*

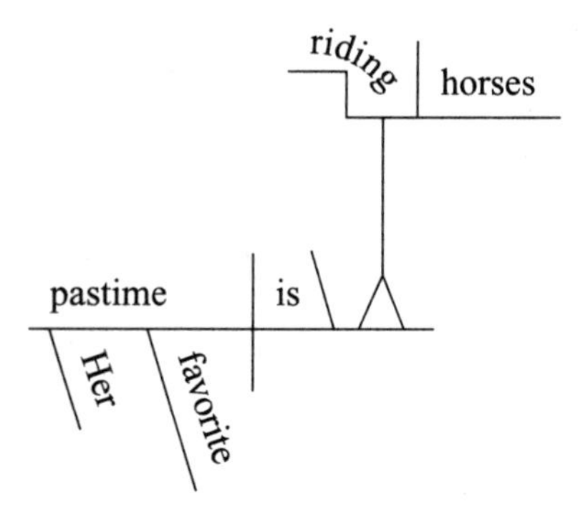

CHAPTER 11. GENERATIVE THEORY

Exercise A, pages 169–170

a. not a kernel (question rather than declarative)
d. not a kernel (negative rather than positive; passive rather than active)

Exercise C, page 174

a. universal (since all languages contain NPs)
b. language-specific (mentions specific English words)
f. universal

CHAPTER 12. STANDARD THEORY

Exercise A, page 181

a. *Several people stumbled.*

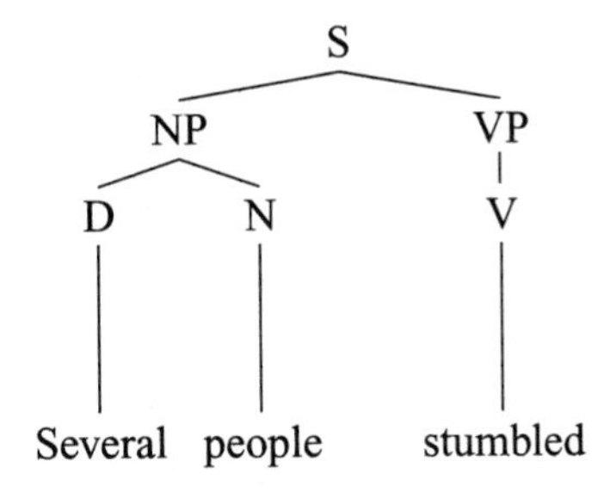

c. *Maxine put the key in the lock.*

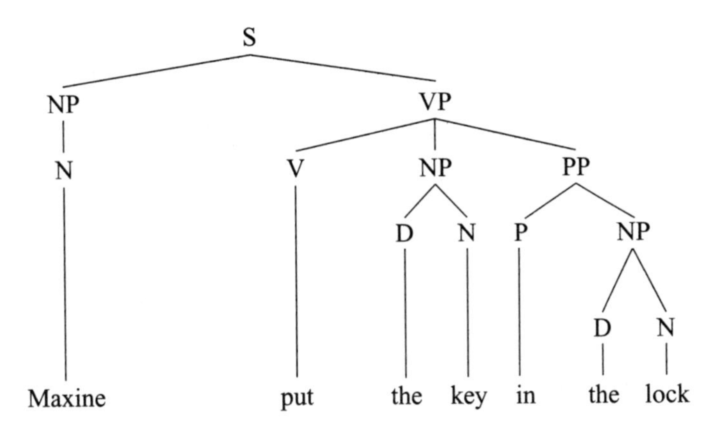

f. *The fish tasted quite salty:* Cannot be generated because the PS rules do not describe *quite*.

i. *Those women are dancers.*

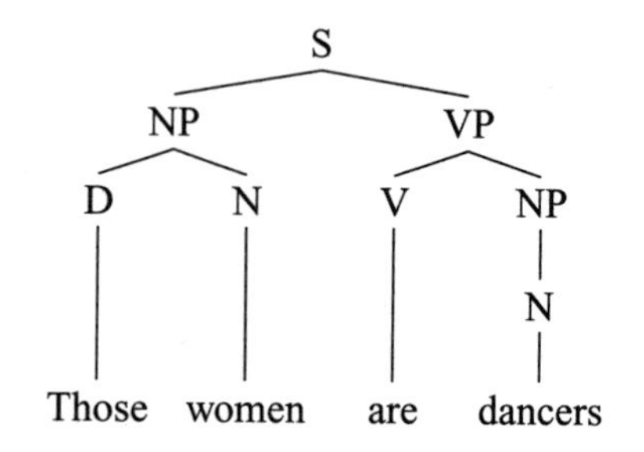

Exercise D, page 187

a. *Pete might be leaving.*
US:

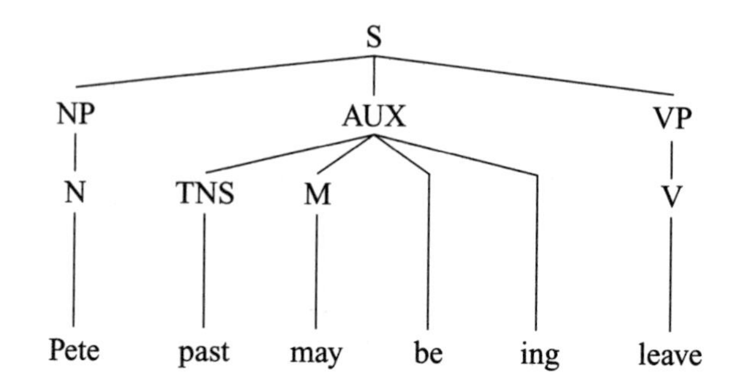

SS via AFFIX HOP:

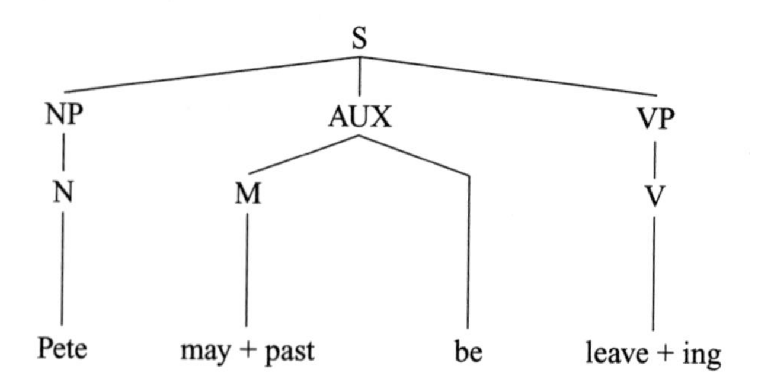

d. *That old guy is being a fool.*
US:

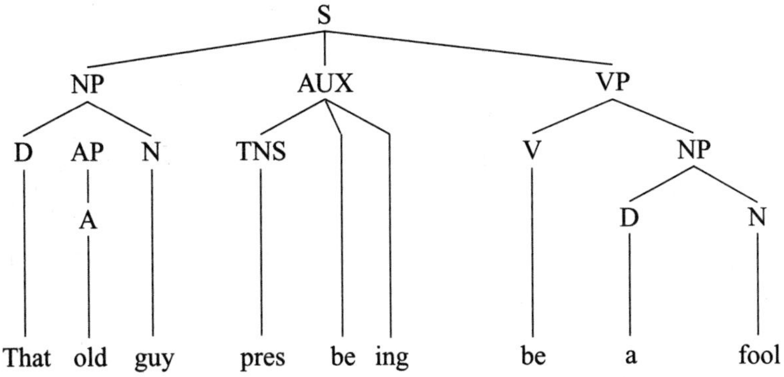

S
NP AUX VP
D AP N TNS V NP
A D N
That old guy pres be ing be a fool

SS via AFFIX HOP:

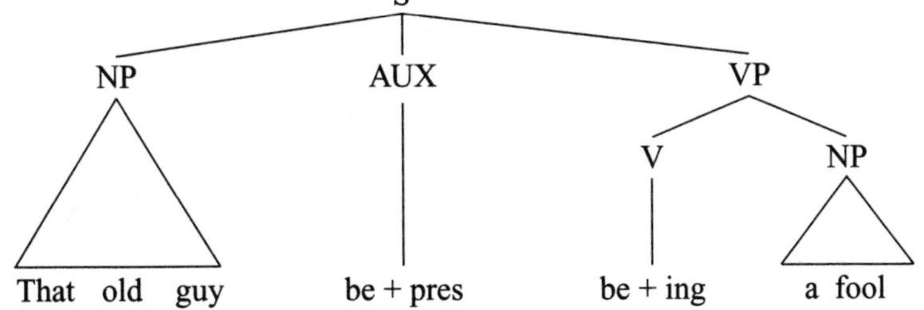

NOTE: A triangle can be used to represent *that old guy* and *a fool* in the second step of the derivation, since the internal of these NPs does not change.

Exercise E, pages 189–190

a. *Mary is sending John an e-mail.*
US:

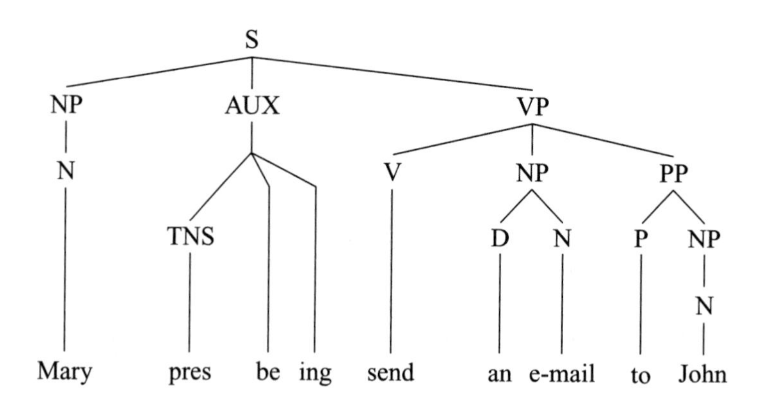

IO MOVEMENT:

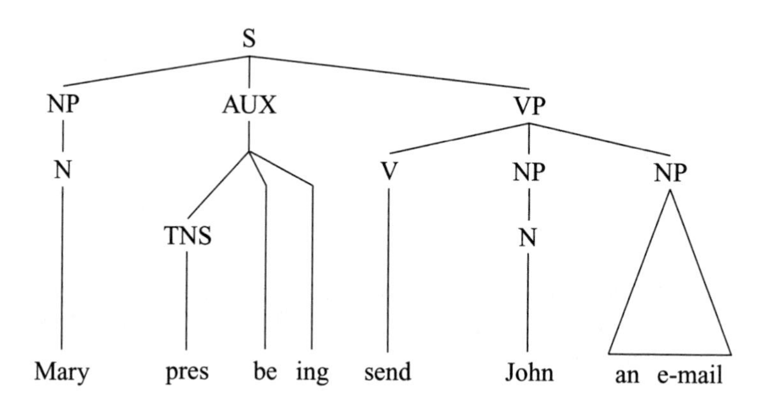

SS via AFFIX HOP:

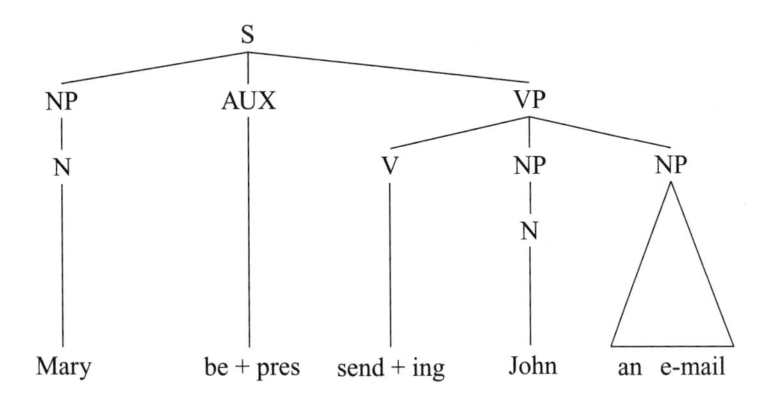

Exercise F, page 192

b. *The tree might have been struck by lightning.*
US: Lightning - past - may - have - en - strike - the tree
PASSIVE: The tree - past - may - have - en - be - en - strike - by lightning
AFFIX HOP: The tree - may+past - have - be+en - strike+en - by lightning

c. *Sidney got a brand new truck*
US: Sidney - past - get - a brand new truck
AFFIX HOP: Sidney - get+past - a brand new truck

Exercise G, page 193

a. *A check was mailed to Mindy by the IRS.*
US: The IRS - past - mail - a check - to Mindy
PASSIVE: A check - past - be - en - mail - to Mindy - by the IRS
AFFIX HOP: A check - be+past - mail+en - to Mindy - by the IRS

Exercise H, page 195

a. *Can you help me?*
US: You - pres - can - help - me
QUESTION: pres - can - you - help - me
AFFIX HOP: can+pres - you - help - me

Exercise I, page 196

a. *You should not have been doing that.*
US: You - past - shall -have - en - be - ing - do - that
NEGATIVE: You - past - shall - not - have - en - be - ing - do - that
AFFIX HOP: You - shall+past - not - have - be+en - do+ing - that

Exercise J, page 198

a. *Can he not read the fine print?*
US: He - pres - can - read - the fine print
NEGATIVE: He - pres - can - not - read - the fine print
QUESTION: pres - can - he - not - read - the fine print
AFFIX HOP: can+pres - he - not -read - the fine print

Exercise K, page 198

a. *Muffy has not been located by the police.*
US: The police - pres - have - en - locate - Muffy
PASSIVE: Muffy - pres - have - en - be - en - locate - by the police
NEGATIVE: Muffy - pres - have - not - en - be - en - locate - by the police
AFFIX HOP: Muffy - have+pres - not - be+en - locate+en - by the police

Exercise L, page 199

a. *Had the children been frightened by the movie?*
US: The movie - past - have - en - frighten - the children
PASSIVE: The children - past - have - en - be - en - frighten - by the movie
QUESTION: past - have - the children - en - be - en - frighten - by the movie
AFFIX HOP: have+past - the children - be+en - frighten+en - by the movie

CHAPTER 13. GOVERNMENT AND BINDING THEORY

Exercise C, page 206

a. *the student with red hair and a beard:* predicted as acceptable, because the coordinated items are both adjuncts.
b. *the student of music and with a beard:* predicted as unacceptable, because *of music* is a complement and *with a beard* is an adjunct.

Exercise E, page 213

a. *[*Burping* is considered [*t* is rude]]

Violates Tensed S constraint.

b. *[[$_{\text{COMP}}$*Of which sewer*] did he crawl out *t*]

Violates A-over-A constraint (*of which sewer* is a PP dominated by another PP, *out of which sewer).*

Exercise F, page 214

a. *me* is assigned objective case by the transitive verb *asked.*

c. There is no element to assign case to *You* within the clause *You to fail* (compare the grammatical structure *For you to fail would be a tragedy;* here *you* is assigned objective case by the preposition *For*).

Exercise G, page 215

a. **The man*$_1$ *shaved him*$_1$. Violates the Pronominal Binding Condition because *him* is bound within its own clause.

CHAPTER 14. DEVELOPMENT OF PERFORMANCE THEORIES

Exercise A, pages 225–226

a. The idea of treating texts as though they exist in a "cultural vacuum" would not appeal to applied researchers because it does not allow them to take into account socioeconomic influences on language.

c. The idea that a writer's thought processes are not represented by grammatical structures would not appeal to applied researchers because it would limit the usefulness of grammatical theory in analyzing the writing process.

CHAPTER 15. SENTENCE-LEVEL PHENOMENA IN PERFORMANCE GRAMMAR

Exercise E, page 240

a. The judge supports Medicaid abortions. It's not unusual for readers to need four or five readings to arrive at this conclusion.

Exercise F, page 242

a. Sentence (A) is active rather than passive.

CHAPTER 16. DISCOURSE-LEVEL PHENOMENA IN PERFORMANCE GRAMMAR

Exercise C, page 255

a. 1–2: AB:BC (B = *birds/birds*)
2–3: BC:BD (B = *birds/They*)
3–4: BD:DE (D = *cats/felines*)
4–5: DE:DF (D = *felines/they*)

Exercise E, page 257

a. *Doreen Kimura*: agent
a technique: patient
This method: agent
most people: agent
language: patient
the left hemisphere of the brain: instrument

Name Index

Subject Index